Sutton Sons

The Culture of Vegetables and Flowers

From Seeds and Roots

Sutton Sons

The Culture of Vegetables and Flowers
From Seeds and Roots

ISBN/EAN: 9783337107598

Printed in Europe, USA, Canada, Australia, Japan

Cover: Foto ©ninafisch / pixelio.de

More available books at **www.hansebooks.com**

THE CULTURE

OF

VEGETABLES AND FLOWERS

From Seeds and Roots.

ALSO

A YEAR'S WORK IN THE VEGETABLE GARDEN,

FLOWERS ALL THE YEAR ROUND,

THE ROTATION AND CHEMISTRY OF CROPS,

THE FORMATION OF LAWNS FROM SEED,

AND

DESCRIPTIONS OF, AND REMEDIES FOR, GARDEN PESTS.

BY

SUTTON AND SONS,

READING.

FIFTH EDITION.

LONDON:
SIMPKIN, MARSHALL, HAMILTON, KENT & CO. LTD.
1892.

All rights reserved.

Preface

TO THE FIFTH EDITION

EIGHTEEN THOUSAND COPIES of this book have been sold. For the present edition, numbering ten thousand, several of the articles have been re-written, some additions made, and the whole text has been carefully revised.

We gladly avail ourselves of this renewed opportunity of tendering grateful acknowledgments to numerous correspondents for kind suggestions.

Sutton & Sons

Reading

Preface

TO THE FIRST EDITION

WE ARE FREQUENTLY ASKED for instructions on the Culture of the several kinds of Vegetables and Flowers. It is impossible to convey this information adequately by correspondence, and the idea of a Volume on the subject naturally suggested itself.

Our aim is to enable an Amateur to produce the finest Vegetables and the most beautiful Flowers in their season. At the same time we hope the skilled Gardener will find in this book hints which may be helpful in the higher branches of his profession.

Sutton & Sons

Reading

Contents

	PAGE
INTRODUCTORY REMARKS	1
THE CULTURE OF VEGETABLES	4
A YEAR'S WORK IN THE VEGETABLE GARDEN	140
THE ROTATION OF CROPS IN THE VEGETABLE GARDEN	187
THE CHEMISTRY OF GARDEN CROPS	192
THE CULTURE OF FLOWERS FROM SEEDS	199
THE CULTURE OF FLOWERING BULBS	277
FLOWERS ALL THE YEAR ROUND	310
THE FORMATION OF LAWNS FROM SEED	365
THE PESTS OF GARDEN PLANTS (*illustrated*)	379
ERADICATION OF GARDEN VERMIN	400
THE FUNGUS PESTS OF GARDEN PLANTS (*illustrated*)	403
THE FUNGUS PESTS OF CERTAIN FLOWERS (*illustrated*)	409
INDEX	415

THE CULTURE OF VEGETABLES

INTRODUCTORY REMARKS

WE are passing through an era of great activity in gardening. Every horticulturist of experience can count up a number of important events that have occurred in his own time, and can see foreshadowings of events of greater importance that appear to be near at hand. And there can be no question that the progress effected in the Vegetable Garden has resulted in a substantial improvement in the quality and variety of its produce.

A comparison of the state of things in any department of the Vegetable Garden with that which prevailed fifty years ago will show that the general growth of knowledge and the improvement of the public taste are most strikingly and pleasingly reflected there. All our esculents, and more especially Melons, Peas, and Potatoes, have undergone very great improvement. As a matter of fact, the past half-century has witnessed as great changes in the Vegetable Garden as it has witnessed in the arts of locomotion, lighting, and sanitation. When Parkinson directed his readers to prepare Melons for eating by mixing with the pulp 'salt and pepper and good store of wine,' he must have been familiar with fruit differing widely from the varieties which are now in favour. Peas have ceased to be 'what they were' because they are so immensely better. While the powers of the plant have been, as it were, concentrated, with the result that it occupies less room and occasions less trouble, its productiveness has been augmented and the quality improved. Formerly it appeared impossible that any Pea of first-class quality should ever be gathered without the aid of a ladder. All the pulse tribe have shared in the advance; and if we compare any dozen or score of the favourite sorts of Peas or Beans to-day with the same number of favourites of half or even a quarter of a century since, we soon discover that the boasted 'advance' is no dream of the enthusiast, but a collective result of the most surprising and gratifying facts. The Potato in its improved forms, which are the effect of systematic selection and hybridisation, has contributed in a wonderful degree to the reformation of the national dietary. Indeed, it may be said that none of the occupants of the Vegetable Garden have refused to be improved by scientific crossing and selecting; and although in some unimportant departments the advances have been small, the aggregate of the changes is enormous.

In considering the general order of work in the Kitchen Garden, the first requirement is that its productive powers shall be taxed to the utmost. There need be no fallowing—no 'resting' of the ground, and if it should so happen that by hard cropping perplexity arises about the disposal of produce, one of three courses can be chosen—to sell, to give, or to dig the stuff in as manure. The last-named course will, in the case of any green crop, pay well, especially in the disposal of the remains of Cabbage, Kale, Turnips, and other such things that have stood through the winter, and occupy ground required for spring seeds. Bury them in trenches, and sow Peas, Beans &c. over them, and in due time full value will be obtained for the buried crops and the labour bestowed upon them. But hard cropping implies abundant manuring and incessant stirring of the soil. To take much off and put little on is like burning the candle at both ends, or expecting the whip to be a sufficient substitute for corn when the horse has extra work to do. Dig deep always, even if the soil be shallow, and then it is advisable to turn the top spit in the usual manner, and break up the subsoil thoroughly with a pickaxe for another twelve or fifteen inches. Where the soil is deep and the staple good, trench a piece every year two spits deep, the autumn being the best time for this work, because of the immense benefit which results from the exposure of newly turned-up soil to rain, snow, frost, and the rest of Nature's great army of fertilising agencies.

Whatever the particular tastes and requirements may be, it is a safe rule always to grow the most popular varieties of every sort of vegetable in quantity, rather than risk the extensive culture of any novelty. At the same time it is well to try novelties in order to ascertain whether better crops can be secured in future seasons. A few famous vegetables that have been grown for generations are as good now as ever they were, and must not be discarded for newer sorts; but if we make a free comparison of all the classes of cultivated vegetables, we shall surely discover that we owe much to the spirit of improvement, and should be but badly off if forced back upon the sorts that were grown by our forefathers. What should we do now, for instance, with no better Potatoes than Scotch Cups, which were formerly considered excellent; or with no better early Pea than the Charlton; or with none but the great solid-hearted Cabbages of olden time, and the common Pumpkin for the best approach to our delicate Vegetable Marrow? Our advice is, give novelties a fair trial, but depend for the main supply of any root or vegetable on the sorts that are well known to be the best in their several classes. We sum up this paragraph with a word of counsel that may be remembered—select the best of everything, and grow everything well. The generous hand will not only be entitled to, but will obtain, the largest harvest.

In regard to practical work there is nothing like system. Crop the ground systematically, as if you expected any day to have to give an account of your procedure to a committee of severe critics. Constantly forecast the next work and the disposition of the ground for the various crops, keeping in mind something like the proportions they should bear to each other. Be particular to have a sufficiency of the flavouring and garnishing herbs always ready and near at hand. These are sometimes wanted suddenly, and it may be no hard matter to gather a tuft of Parsley in the dark in a well-ordered garden, but one's neck may be dislocated in searching for it in the garden of the sloven, though he may have a furlong of the finest Parsley in the world somewhere. Change your crops about from place to place, so as not to grow the same things on the same plots two seasons in succession. This rule, though of great importance, cannot be strictly followed, and may be disregarded to a certain extent where the land is constantly and heavily manured. It is, however, of more importance in connection with the Potato than with aught else, and this valuable esculent should, if possible, be grown on a different plot every year, so that it shall be quite three or four years in travelling round the garden. Lastly, sow everything in drills at the proper distances apart. Broadcasting is a slovenly mode of sowing, and necessitates slovenly cultivation afterwards. When crops are in drills they can be thinned, weeded, and hoed between efficiently—in other words, they can be cultivated. But broadcasting pretty well excludes the cultivator from the land, and can only be commended to the idle man, who will be content with half a crop of poor quality, while perhaps paying rent enough to cover a crop at once the heaviest and the best.

GLOBE ARTICHOKE

(*Cynara Scolymus*)

Globe Artichokes may be treated as annuals, biennials, or perennials, at the discretion of the cultivator. If the seeds are sown in autumn, none will be injured by the winter; and the seedlings that appear in spring will be more vigorous than those from spring-sown seeds. The usual time of sowing, however, is the month of March, and the plants come very quickly after the first kindly shower in April. In a favourable season the yearling plants will flower freely in the autumn, and the few that do not flower will give an early supply in the following year. The simplest routine of cultivation consists in sowing down a plantation annually, and allowing each to stand to the close of the second season: thus keeping two plots going from seeds only, and for every seed-bed making the most liberal preparation. A deep, moist, rich soil is requisite for the production of large fleshy heads, and the plant may be greatly aided by wood ashes and seaweed, for it is partial to saline manures, its home being the sandy sea-shores of Northern Africa.

To form a permanent plantation, prepare the soil by deep digging and liberal manuring, and sow seeds in March, or plant suckers in April. The distance we have found suitable to insure strong plants is four feet each way, but the market growers usually put out suckers in rows four and a half feet asunder, and two feet apart in the rows. In the case of seeds it will be advisable, either to mark the rows by sowing Rape or Turnip thinly, and at once sow or plant between with Lettuce, Dwarf Peas, or Brassicas for planting out; or to wait until the Artichokes appear, and then sow Dwarf Kidney Beans as a stolen crop. But if suckers are planted and a stolen crop is desired, it must be a quick one, such as Brassicas for planting out, or Round Spinach, or saladings.

The suckers should be planted when about nine inches high. Put them in rather deep, tread in firmly, and lay on any rough mulch that may be handy. Should the weather be dry they will require watering, and during hot weather water and liquid manure should be given freely to insure a good supply of large heads. Seedling plants that are started well in a suitable bed take better care of themselves than do plants from suckers, especially in a dry season, their initial vigour causing them to send their roots to a great depth.

To advise on weeding and hoeing to promote a clean and vigorous growth should be needless, because all crops require such attention. But as to the production of large heads, a few words of advice may be useful. It is the practice with some growers to twist a piece of wire round the stem about three inches below the head. This certainly does tend to increase the size, but the same end may be accomplished by other means. In the first place, a rich deep bed and abundant supplies of water will encourage the growth of fine heads. Further aid in the same direction will be derived from the removal of all the lateral heads that appear when they are about as large as an egg. Up to this stage they do not tax the energies of the plants in any great degree; but as the flowers are forming within them, their demands increase rapidly. Their removal, therefore, has an immediate effect on the main heads, and these attain to large dimensions without the aid of wire. The small heads will be valued at many tables for eating raw, as they are eaten in Italy, or cooked as 'artichauts frits,' or 'à la Provençale.' The larger main heads are the best for serving boiled in the usual way. After the heads are used the plants should be cut down.

CHARDS are the blanched summer growth of Globe Artichokes, and are by many preferred to blanched Cardoons. In the early part of July the plants selected for Chards must be cut over about half a foot from the ground. In about a week after this operation they should have a copious watering, which should be repeated weekly, except when heavy rains occur. By the end of September they will have made much growth, and will be ready for blanching. Draw them together and put a band of hay or straw around them, and earth them up and finish the work neatly. The blanching will take fully six weeks, during which time there will be but little growth made—hence the necessity for promoting free growth before earthing up. Any Chards not used before winter sets in may be preserved by lifting and packing in sand in a dry shed.

The Artichoke is hardy on dry soils when the winter is of only average severity. But on moist soils, which are so favourable to the production of fine heads, a severe winter will destroy the plantations unless they have some kind of protection. The usual course of procedure is to cut down the stems and large leaves without touching the smaller central leaves, and to partially earth up the rows with earth taken from between when severe frost appears likely; this protection is strengthened by the addition of light dry litter loosely thrown over. With the return of spring the litter is removed, the earth is dug back, and all the suckers but about three removed, and then a liberal dressing of manure is dug in, care being taken to do as little injury to the plants above and below ground as possible. At the end of five years a plantation will be quite worn out; in somewhat poor soil it will be exhausted in three years.

The cultivation of this elegant vegetable is greatly simplified by sowing a bed annually on soil well prepared as already advised.

JERUSALEM ARTICHOKE

(*Helianthus tuberosus*)

THE JERUSALEM ARTICHOKE is a member of the Sunflower tribe, quite hardy, and productive of wholesome roots that are in favour with many as a delicacy, and by others are regarded as worthless. It is said that wise men learn to eat every good thing the earth produces, and this root is a good thing when properly served; but when cooked in the same way as a Potato it certainly is a very poor vegetable indeed. It is a matter of some interest, however, that in respect of nutritive value it is about equal to the Potato; therefore, in growing it for domestic use, we lose nothing in the way of food, though we are bound to cook it differently.

The Jerusalem Artichoke will grow anywhere, but to insure a fine sample requires a deep friable loam and an open situation. We have grown immense crops on a strong deep clay, but it is not a clay plant because it soon suffers from any excess of moisture. To prepare the ground well for this crop is a matter of importance, for it roots freely and makes an immense top-growth, reaching, when very vigorous, a height of ten or twelve feet. Trench and manure in autumn, and leave the land rough for the winter. Plant in February or March, using whole or cut sets with about three eyes to each, and put them in trenches six inches deep and three feet apart, the sets being one foot apart in the trenches. When the plants appear, hoe the ground between, draw a little fine earth to the stems, and leave the rest to Nature. Take up a portion of the crop in November and store in sand; and as for the rest, dig them when wanted, as recommended in the case of Parsnips. They must be dug with a fork by opening trenches and cleaning out every scrap of the roots, for whatever escapes will grow and become troublesome in the following season.

ASPARAGUS

(*Asparagus officinalis*)

ASPARAGUS is a liliaceous plant of perennial duration. Under favourable conditions it improves with age to such an extent as to justify the best possible cultivation. Plantations that have stood and prospered for twenty or even thirty years are not uncommon, but a fair average term is ten years, after which it is generally advisable to break up a bed, the precaution being first taken to secure a succession bed by sowing seeds on fresh soil well prepared for the purpose. In any and every case the best plantation is obtained by sowing seeds, for the roots do not transplant well. With special care and prompt action, roots may be employed, and these are especially serviceable when time is an object, as, for example, in the formation of a new garden; for seedling plants are slow to make a return as compared with roots, which may be planted almost as safely at two or three years old as at one year. Keeping in view, therefore, that the employment of seed is always to be preferred, unless there are special reasons for resorting to roots, it will be found that the cultivation of Asparagus is a very simple business, although it demands more generous treatment than the usual run of Kitchen Garden crops.

Asparagus will grow in any soil that is well cultivated, but a sandy soil suits it; a deep rich sandy loam being especially suitable. A calcareous soil is by no means unfavourable to Asparagus, as may be seen in the fine quality of the crops grown at Ulm and Augsburg; still, a sand rich in humus is not the less to be desired, as the finest samples of European growth are the produce of the districts around Paris, Brussels, and Berlin. The London Asparagus is for the most part grown near at hand, in deep alluvial soils enriched with abundance of manure, and is greatly prized by epicures for its full flavour and tenderness. Nature gives us the key to every secret that concerns our happiness, and in respect of Asparagus cultivation she is liberal in her teaching. The plant is found growing wild on the sandy coasts of the British Islands—a proof that it loves sand and salt. It is so abundant on the sandy steppes of Southern Russia and Poland as to kill out the grasses, but it takes their place in respect of utility, and the horses and cattle eat it as daily food, and enjoy life and prosper.

The routine cultivation must begin with a thorough preparation of the ground. To be well drained is a matter of the first importance, for stagnant water in the subsoil is fatal to the plant. But a rich loam does not need the extravagant manuring that has been recommended and practised for this purpose. Deep digging and, if the subsoil is good, trenching may be recommended, but an average manuring will suffice, because Asparagus can be effectually aided by annual top dressings, and proper surface culture is of great importance in the subsequent stages. The plantation must be in an open spot, the preparation of the ground should commence in the autumn, and be continued through the winter, a heavy dressing of half-rotten stable dung being put on in the first instance, and trenched in two feet deep. In the course of a month the whole piece should be trenched back. If labour is at command a third trenching may be done with advantage, and the surface may be left ridged up until the time arrives to level it down for seed. It will appear that this routine is of a somewhat costly character, but we are supposing the plantation is to remain for many years, making an abundant return for the first investment. Still we are bound to say that a capital supply for a moderate table may be obtained by preparing a piece of good ground in an open situation in a quite ordinary manner with one deep digging in winter, adding at the time some six inches or so of fat stable dung, and leaving it thus until the time arrives for sowing the seed. Then it will be well to level down and point in half a spade deep a thin coat of rotten dung to make a nice kindly seed-bed.

In any case where a soil known to be unsuitable for Asparagus, as a damp clay or pasty loam, has to be made the best of for the purpose, it will be found an economical practice to remove the top spit, which we suppose to be turf or old cultivated soil, and on the space so cleared prepare a bed of the best mixture possible under the circumstances. Towards this mixture we have the top spit just referred to. Add to this, lime rubbish from destroyed buildings, sand, peat, leaf-mould, surface soil raked from the rear of the shrubberies &c., and the result should be a good compost obtained at an almost nominal cost.

At this juncture several questions of considerable importance arise. And first, whether the crop shall be grown on the flat or in raised beds. Where the soil is sufficiently deep, and the drainage perfect, the flat system answers well. The advantages of raised beds are that they deepen the soil, assist the drainage, promote warmth, and thus aid the growth of an early crop. In fact, raised beds render it possible to grow Asparagus on soils from which this vegetable could not otherwise be obtained. The preparation is the same in either case, and therefore we shall make no further allusion to flat beds, but leave those to adopt them who find their soil and requirements suitable. Now comes the question of distance, on which depends the width of the beds, and we settle the first point by the measure of the plant, and the second by the measure of the man. There are advocates of a square yard or even more being allowed to each root, for which of course some return will be obtained. This must be regarded as a fancy crop, and though monster sticks may occasionally realise, as they have done, 3*l.* or 4*l.* per hundred, there are not many buyers. Even as home produce such sticks are not wanted at every table. An abundant crop of handsome, though not abnormal Asparagus is of far more consequence. After many experiments, we have come to the conclusion that the best mode of insuring a full return of really good sticks, with the least amount of labour, is to lay out the land in three-feet beds, with two-feet alleys between. In some instances no doubt five-feet beds, planted with three rows of roots, one down the middle and another on each side at a distance of eighteen inches, is preferable. For the majority of gardens, however, the three-feet bed is a distinct advantage, were it only for the fact that all excuse for putting a foot on the bed is avoided. On this narrow bed only two rows of plants will be necessary. Put down the line at nine inches from the edge on both sides, and at intervals of fifteen inches in the rows dibble holes three inches deep, dropping two or three seeds in each. This will give a distance between the rows of eighteen inches. In very strong land, heavily manured, the holes may be eighteen inches apart instead of fifteen. April is the right month for sowing.

When the 'grass' from seeds has grown about six inches will be the time for thinning to one plant at every station of fifteen or eighteen inches in the row. Much of the injury reported to follow from close planting has been the result rather of carelessness in thinning. The young plant is such a slender, delicate thing, that, to the thoughtless operator, it seems a folly to thin down certainly to one only. The consequence is that two or three, or perhaps half a dozen, plants are left at each station to 'fight it out,' and these become so intermixed as to appear to be one, though really many, and of course amongst them they produce more shoots than can be fed properly by the limited range of their roots. Severe, or we may say mathematical thinning is a *sine quâ non*, and it requires sharp eyes and careful fingers ; but it must be done if the Asparagus beds are to become, as they should be, the pride of the Kitchen Garden.

The grave question of white *versus* green Asparagus we cannot entertain, except so far as concerns the cultivator only. On the point of taste, therefore, we say nothing ; and in respect of cultivation it is a matter of management merely, whether the sticks be blanched to the very tip, or become green for some few inches therefrom. Blanching is effected in various ways. A mere heaping up of soft soil, such as leaf-mould, will accomplish it. On the Continent many contrivances are resorted to, such as covering the heads with wooden or earthen pipes. In a few districts in France, champagne bottles with the bottoms cut away are employed. But a strong growth being secured, the cultivator will find it an easy matter to regulate the degree of colour according to the requirements of the table he has in view. As a rule, a moderately stout growth, with a fair show of purple colour, is everywhere appreciated, and is the easiest to produce, because the most natural.

There is, however, an interesting point in connection with the production of green Asparagus, and it is, that if wintry weather prevails when the heads are rising (as unfortunately is often the case), the tender green tops may be melted by frost and become worthless, or may be rendered so tough as to place the quality below that of blanched Asparagus, for the blanching is also a protective process, and quickly grown white Asparagus is often more tender and tasty than that which is green, but has been grown slowly. As the season advances and the heads rise rapidly, the green Asparagus acquires its proper flavour and tenderness, and thus practical considerations should more or less influence final decisions on matters of taste. The business of the cultivator is to produce the kind of growth that is required, whether white or green, or of a quality intermediate between the two. This is easily done, making allowance for conditions. When green Asparagus is alone in demand, the cultivator may be advised to have in readiness, as the heads are making their first show, a sufficient supply of some rough and cheap protecting material, such as grass and coarse weeds, cut with a sickle from odd corners of the shrubbery and meadow land, or clean hay and straw litter perfectly free from mildew, but for obvious reasons stable litter should not be used. A very light sprinkling of material over an Asparagus bed that is making a first show of produce, will ward off the morning frosts, and amply compensate for the little trouble in saving many tender green sticks that the frosts would melt to a jelly and render worthless. After May 20 the litter may be removed, if needful; but if appearances are of secondary importance, it may be left to shrink away on the spot.

Asparagus as supplied by market growers is needlessly long in the stem. The bundles have an imposing appearance no doubt, but the useless length adds nothing to the comfort of those at table, and is a wasteful tax on the energy of the plant. For home consumption it will generally suffice if the white portion is three or four inches long, and this determines the depth at which the sticks should be cut. Here it may be useful to remark that deeply buried roots do not thrive so well as those which are nearer the surface, nor do they produce such early crops. The sticks are usually cut by thrusting down a stiff narrow-pointed knife, or specially made saw, close to each shoot, and it is necessary to do this with judgment, or adjacent shoots, which are not sufficiently advanced to reveal their presence by lifting the soil, may be damaged. To avoid this risk of injury by the knife it is possible from some beds to obtain the sticks without the aid of any implement by a twist and pull combined, but the process needs a dexterous hand and is impracticable in tenacious soils. The sticks of a handsome sample will be white four or five inches of their length; the tops close, plump, of a purplish-green colour, and the colour extending two or at most three inches down the stems. Both size and degree of colouring are, however, so entirely questions of taste that no definite rule can be stated. It is more to the purpose to say that, if liberally grown, the plant may be cut from in the third year; and that cutting should cease about the middle of June, or early in July, according to the district. As regards the good of the plant the sooner cutting ceases the better, as the next year's buds have to be formed in the roots by the aid of the leaf growth of this season.

There are two more points of very great importance in respect of the general management. Some crops get on pretty well when neglected and crowded with weeds. But it is not so with Asparagus. The plant appears to have been designed to enjoy life in solitude, being unfit for competition; and if weeds make way in an Asparagus bed, the cultivator will pay a heavy penalty for his neglect of duty. The limitation of the beds to a width of three feet, therefore, is of consequence, because it facilitates weeding without putting a foot on them. The other point arises out of the necessity of affording support to the frail plant in places where it may happen to be exposed to wind. When Asparagus in high summer is rudely shaken, the stems snap off at the base, and the roots lose the service of the whole top-growth in maturing heads for the next season. To prevent this injury is easy enough, but the precautions must be adopted in good time. A free use of light, feathery stakes, such as are employed for the support of Peas, thrust in firmly all over the bed, will insure all needful support when gales are blowing. In the absence of peasticks, stout stakes, placed at suitable distances and connected with lengths of thick tarred twine, will answer equally well. In sheltered gardens the protection of the young growth with litter, and of the mature growth with stakes, need not be resorted to, but in exposed situations they are of primary importance.

The management of Asparagus includes a careful clean-up of the beds in autumn, and a top-dressing in spring. The plants should not be cut down until they change colour, and then all the top-growth may be cleared away, the surface raked clean, and the sides of the beds carefully touched up to make them neat and tidy. It is usual at the same time to dig and manure the alleys, but this practice we object to *in toto*, because it tends directly to the production of lean sticks where fat ones are possible; for the roots run freely in the alleys, and to dig is to destroy them. It is sufficient to make all clean and tidy. In the spring there will be found on the beds a new crop of weeds; these must be cleared off, and then the beds and the alleys should be carefully pricked over with a fork two or three inches deep only, and with great care not to wound any roots. Finally, put on a coat of fat dung about two inches deep, and you may then wait for the first show of heads, when, if needful, litter must be spread to protect the early growth from frost.

In many gardens where there is space for only two or three beds, there will be the very natural desire to secure Asparagus in a shorter time than is possible from seed, and we therefore proceed to indicate the best method of planting roots. Asparagus roots do not take kindly to removal, especially old and established plants. The mere drying of the roots by exposure to the atmosphere is distinctly injurious to them. They will travel from a distance when well packed, but the critical time is between the unpacking and getting them safely into their final home. The obvious lesson is that everything should be made ready for the transfer before the package is opened, and that the actual task of planting should be accomplished in the shortest time possible.

A three-feet bed should be prepared by taking out the soil in such a manner as to leave two ridges for the roots. The space between ridges to be eighteen inches, and the tops of the ridges to be so far below the level of the bed that when the soil is returned, and the bed made to its normal level, the crowns will be about five inches beneath the surface. This may be understood from the following illustration of a section cut across the bed.

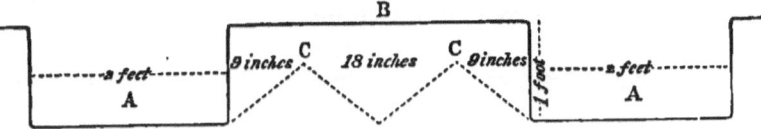

AA represent the alleys between the beds, and B the top of one bed. The dotted lines show the ridges on which the roots are to rest at CC. When the bed is ready, open the package and place the Asparagus on the ridges at fifteen or eighteen inches apart, allowing about half the roots of each plant to fall down on either side of the ridge. As a rule it will be wise to have two pairs of hands engaged in the task. The soil should be filled in expeditiously, and a finishing touch be given to the bed. Very rarely will it be safe to transplant Asparagus until the end of March or beginning of April, for although established roots will pass unharmed through a very severe winter, those that have recently been removed are often killed outright by a lengthened period of cold wet weather, and especially by thawed snow followed by frost.

FORCING is variously practised, and the best possible system, doubtless, is to force in the beds, and thereby train the plants to their work so that they become used to it. The growers that supply Paris with forced Asparagus produce the white sample in the beds, and the green by removal of the roots to frames. Forcing in beds may be accomplished by means of trenches filled with fermenting material, or by hot-water pipes, the beds in either case being covered with frames. Where the demand for forced Asparagus is constant, there can be no doubt the hot-water system is the cheapest as well as the cleanest and surest; for a casual supply forcing in frames answers very well, but it is attended with the disadvantage that when the crop has been secured, the roots are worthless. The practice of forcing may be said to commence with the formation of the seed-bed, for if to be carried on in a systematic and profitable manner, every detail must be provided for in the original arrangements. The width of the beds and of the alleys, and the disposition of the plants, will have to be carefully considered, so as to insure the best results of a costly procedure, and it will be waste of time to begin forcing until the plants have attained their fourth year. The rough method of market growers consists in the employment of hot dung in trenches, and also on the beds, after the frames are put on. The beds are usually four feet wide, the alleys two feet wide and twenty inches deep, and the plants not more than nine inches apart in the row, there being three or four rows of plants in the bed. The frames are put on when forcing commences, but the lights are withheld until the shoots begin to appear. Then the fermenting material is removed from the beds, the lights are put on, and no air is given, mats being added in cold weather, both to keep in the warmth and promote blanching. This method produces a fair market sample, but a much better growth may be obtained by a good hot-water system, as will be understood from a momentary consideration of details. By the employment of fermenting material, the temperature runs up rapidly, sometimes extravagantly, so that it is no uncommon event for the growth to commence at 70° to 80° Fahr. which may produce a handsome sample, but it will be flavourless. The hot-water system allows of perfect control, and the prudent grower will begin at 50°, rise slowly to 60°, and take care not to exceed 65°; the result will be a sample full of flavour, with a finer appearance than the best obtainable by the rougher method.

Forcing in frames is systematically practised in many gardens, and as it exhausts the roots there must be a corresponding production of roots for the purpose. The first requisite is a good lasting hot-bed, covered with about four inches of light soil of any kind, but preferably leaf-mould. The roots are carefully lifted and planted as closely as possible on this bed, and are then covered with fine soil to a depth of six inches. The sashes are then put on and kept close; but a little air may be given as the heads rise, to promote colour and flavour. The heat will generally run to 70°, and that figure should be the maximum allowed. But every experienced grower would prefer to force at 60° or 65°, and to take a little more time for the advantage of a finer sample.

BROAD BEAN

(*Faba vulgaris*)

THE BROAD BEAN is a thrifty plant, as hardy as any in the garden, and very accommodating as to soil. It is quite at home on heavy land, but in common with nearly all the plants of the garden thrives in an especial manner on a deep sandy loam. Considering the usually productive nature of the plant and its comparatively brief occupation of the ground, the common Bean must be regarded as one of our most profitable garden crops. Within recent years changes in fashion have taken place in the cultivation of Beans. It is freely alleged that the Mazagan class are no earlier than the Longpods, and as the latter are admitted to be more productive, no good purpose is served in continuing to grow the former. There is just sufficient truth in the idea to mislead the unwary; but it is not the whole truth, and the good old doctrine of wisdom in many counsellors is illustrated by the fact that Mazagans are still largely grown because of their peculiar suitability for certain purposes. There are no varieties so much valued by those who dry or tin green Beans for soups, as the Mazagans; and as regards quality they are deservedly prized on good tables. But for rough work the Longpods are invaluable; they are nearly but not quite as early as the Mazagans, thoroughly hardy, produce heavy crops, and in appearance and flavour satisfy the world at large, as may be proved by appeal to the markets. For epicures and others who are fastidious in respect of quality, there is the section of Windsor Beans—large, tender, full of flavour, and, when well managed, as green as grass when put upon the table. The cultivation is so simple in its whole routine that we are bound to direct attention first to the varieties, and it will be seen that all have their uses. The least in request is the Dwarf Cluster, but even this is serviceable at times for a crop needing the smallest amount of trouble on newly broken ground, or as a stolen crop where there is space for it awhile, the growth rarely exceeding fourteen inches.

For the first crop of early Beans, Mazagan is the most manageable, and sowings may be made in November of this or of Prolific Longpod on a dry soil in a warm situation, sheltered from the north. The distance must depend upon the sorts, but two feet will answer generally as the distance between the double rows, and the two lines forming the double rows may be four inches apart, and the seed two inches deep. On strong ground a distance of three feet may be allowed between the double rows, but it is not well to give over much space, because the plants protect each other somewhat, and earliness of production is the matter of chief moment. It is good practice to prepare a nice piece of ground sloping to the south, and on this to make a plantation in February of plants carefully lifted from the seed rows, wherever they can be spared as proper thinnings. These should be put in double rows, three feet apart. If transplanted with care they will receive but a slight check, and will give a successional supply very usefully.

A sowing may be made towards the end of January, but for the main crop wait until February or March. A strong soil is suitable, and generally speaking a heavy crop of Beans may be taken from a well-managed clay. But any deep cool soil will answer, and where there is a regular annual demand for Beans, the cultivator may be advised to grow both Longpods and Windsors—the first for earliness and bulk, the second for quality. There are now at command some remarkable varieties of the Longpod class adapted for exhibition, and these are certainly of fair table quality, though inferior to the Windsor. The double rows of maincrop Beans should be fully three feet apart, and the plants should be quite six inches apart in the rows. The preparation of the seed-bed must be of a generous, but need not be of an elaborate, nature. Where grass land and land of questionable quality is broken up and trenched, it will be tolerably safe to crop it with Beans as a first start; and to prepare it for the crop, a good body of fat stable dung should be laid in between the first and second spit, as this will carry the crop through, while insuring to the subsoil that has been brought up a time of seasoning with the least risk of any consequent loss.

There is not much more to be said about growing Beans; the ground must be kept clean, and the hoe will have its work here as elsewhere. The pinching out of the tops as soon as there is a fair show of blossom is a good practice, whether there is fly or no fly, and it is also advisable to root all plants out as fast as they finish their work, for if left they throw up suckers and exhaust the soil to no purpose. The gathering of the crop is often so carelessly performed that the supply is suddenly arrested.

In cases of emergency, Beans may be forwarded in pots in the greenhouse, or on turf sods in frames for planting out, in precisely the same way that Peas for early crops are forwarded. In all such cases care must be taken that the forcing is of the most moderate character, or the crop will be poor and late, instead of being plentiful and early. When pushed on under glass for planting out, the young stock must have as much light and air as possible consistent with safety, and a slow healthy growth will better answer the purpose than a rapid growth producing long legs and pale leaves, because the physique of infancy determines in a great degree that of maturity, not less in plants than in animals.

DWARF BEAN

(*Phaseolus vulgaris*)

AMONGST our summer vegetables Kidney Beans are deservedly in high favour, and are everywhere sown at the earliest moment consistent with reasonable expectations of their safety. This early sowing is altogether laudable, for although it occasionally entails the loss of a plantation, the aggregate result is advantageous, and a very little protection suffices to carry the early plant through the late spring frosts. But those who supply our tables with green delicacies do not sufficiently recognise the importance of late sowings of Kidney Beans. Here, again, a risk must be encountered, but the cost is trifling, and when the summer is prolonged to October the late-sown Beans are highly prized. Even if they produce plentifully through September there is a great point gained, but that cannot be secured from the earliest sowings; it is impossible. After July, or at latest the first week in August, it is useless to sow Beans, but where there is a constant demand for these delicious vegetables, two or three sowings of both Dwarfs and Runners may be made in the course of the month of July, and should have the most sheltered nooks that can be found for them. For the late sowings the earliest sorts should have preference.

Kidney Beans for the main crop require a good though somewhat light soil; but any fairly productive loam will answer the purpose, and the crop will make an ample return for such reasonable digging and dressing as a careful cultivator will not fail to bestow. At the same time it is a matter of some practical importance that the poorest land ever put under tillage will, in an average season, yield serviceable crops of these legumes, and on a rich soil of some depth the Kidney Bean will endure summer drought better than any crop proper to the kitchen garden. Among the numerous varieties in cultivation there need be but little difficulty in making a selection. Earliness of production is of the highest importance up to a certain point; but an early crop being provided for, abundance of production next claims consideration, the heaviest bearers being of course best adapted for main-crop sowing. As regards the sowing and general management, we feel bound to remark that Dwarf Kidney Beans are usually crowded injuriously, even in generally well-managed gardens.

Nothing is gained by this practice; there is loss always when the individual plant is, through deficiency of space, hindered in its full development.

For early crops which are eventually to come to maturity in the open ground, the first sowings may be made in the month of April, either in boxes in a gentle heat, or better still in a frame on a sunny border without artificial heat. The tender growth that is produced by a forcing process is not well adapted for planting out in May; but a plant produced slowly, with plenty of light and air, will be stout and strong, and if put out with care as soon as mild weather occurs in the month of May, will make good progress and yield an early crop. The seed for this purpose should be sown in rather light turfy soil, as the plants may then be lifted without injury to their fleshy roots. A little kindly treatment will be desirable for some time after they are planted, to protect them from sun and frost, as well as to give water, if necessary, although, perhaps, the less watering the better, provided the plants can hold their ground. The plot to which these early sowings are to be transplanted should be light and rich, and lying towards the sun; the lines should be opened by the spade or hoe in preference to using the dibber, and the fine soil from the surface should be carefully closed in upon the roots as fast as they are dropped into their places with their balls of earth unbroken. Rough handling will seriously interfere with the ultimate result, but ordinary care will insure abundant gatherings of first-class produce at a time when there are but few in the market.

Main crops are sown from the last week in April to the middle of June, and for late crops sowings may be made during July, and on to the first week of August. The distance for maincrop rows may be from one and a half to two feet apart, according to the vigour of the variety (such as the productive Canadian Wonder requiring fully two feet), and the distance between the plants may be eight to twelve inches; therefore it is well to drill the seed about four inches apart, and thin out as soon as the rough leaves appear. The ground being in fairly good condition, it will only be necessary to chop over the surface, if at all lumpy, and draw drills to the line with the hoe, which is far better than dibbling, except on very light soil, when dibbling is quite allowable. Generally speaking, if the plot be kept clean, the Beans will take care of themselves; but in droughty weather a heavy watering now and then will be visibly beneficial, for although the plant bears drought well, it is like other good things in requiring something to live upon. In making late sowings, when the ground has become dry and hard, it is advisable to soak the seed in water for five or six hours; the drills may also be watered, and, if possible, the seed should be covered in with rotten dung, spent hops, or some other mulchy stuff to promote and sustain vegetation.

The gathering of the crop should be a matter of discipline. Where it is done carelessly, there will very soon be none to gather, for the swelling of a few seeds in neglected pods will cause the plants to cease bearing. Therefore all the Beans should be gathered when of a proper size, whether they are wanted or not; this is the only way to insure a long-continued supply of good quality both as to colour and tenderness.

The forcing of Dwarf Beans is a simple business, but requires incessant attention, for the difficulty to be constantly kept in view is the liability of the plants to suffer injury from the attacks of the red spider. Pots, boxes, or troughs can be employed, as may be most convenient. But a better plan is to plant them out in a bed in a smallish span-roof house with a service of hot water, and the nearer they are to the glass the better. The bed should be one foot deep, the drills a foot apart, and the plants six inches asunder in the rows. The temperature may, with safety, range from 60° to 80°, commencing, of course, with the lower figure, and rising slowly as the season advances. Air-giving and watering will need careful management, for the most robust growth possible is required, but there must be no chill, and any excess of either moisture or dryness will be immediately injurious. Beginners may be advised not to sow until the turn of the year, or, if forcing for winter supply, not after the first week in October; but experienced practitioners find no difficulty in dealing with sowings made in November and December.

RUNNER BEAN

(*Phaseolus multiflorus*)

RUNNERS are managed in precisely the same way as Dwarf Beans, but need more room, and are never forced. They may, however, be grown in roomy orchard-houses to afford early or late supplies, but the practice is scarcely to be recommended, except in cases where there are special reasons for its adoption. It is seldom profitable to sow Runners before the month of May is fairly in, for they are less hardy than the Dwarfs; but it is of great importance to sow again in

June and July, for late supplies are everywhere valued, and may be insured in plenty, subject only to the caprices of the autumnal weather. The rows of Runners are often injuriously close, and the total crop is thereby diminished. The single rows should be at least five feet apart; and double rows, allowing nine inches between the two rows, should be six or eight feet apart. It will always pay to give support by stakes or trellises, because of the increased production; but Runner Beans make a good return when kept low by tipping, and without any support whatever. When so grown, they should in the height of the season be tipped once or twice a week to keep them within bounds. The preservation of the roots of Runners is sometimes recommended. We can only say it is a ridiculous proceeding, for the utmost care is required to keep the roots through the winter, and they are comparatively worthless in the end. A pint of seed will give a better crop than a thousand roots that have cost great pains for their preservation.

GARDEN BEET

(*Beta vulgaris*)

As a food plant the Beet scarcely obtains the attention it deserves. There is no lack of appreciation of its beauty for purposes of garnishing, or of its flavour as a component of a salad; but other uses to which it is amenable for the comfort and sustenance of man are, in a great degree, neglected. As a simple dish to accompany cold meats the Beet is most acceptable. Dressed with vinegar and white pepper, it is at once appetising, nutritive, and digestible. Served as fritters, it is preferred by many to Mushrooms, as it then resembles them in flavour, and is more easy of digestion. It makes a first-rate pickle, and as an agent in colouring it has its value, because of the perfect wholesomeness of the rich crimson hue it is capable of imparting to any article of food requiring it.

The cultivation of the Beet is of the most simple nature, but a certain amount of care is requisite for the production of a handsome and profitable crop. It will make a fair return to the cultivator in any soil that is properly prepared for it; but to grow it to perfection a light loam is necessary, and this, though rich, should contain no traces of any recent or strong manure. A rank soil, or one to which manure has been added shortly before sowing the seed, will produce ugly roots, some coarse with overgrowth, others forked, and therefore of little value, and others, perhaps, cankered and worthless. The soil should be well prepared by deep digging some time before making up the seed-bed. It is well to grow Beet on plots that have been heavily manured the previous year for Cauliflowers, Celery, or any other crop requiring good cultivation. If the soil from an old Melon or Cucumber bed can be spared, it may be spread over the land and dug in, and the piece should be broken up in good time to become mellow before the seed is sown. Seaweed is a capital manure for Beet, especially if laid at the bottom of the trench in making the ground. A moderate dressing of salt may be added with advantage, as the Beet is a sea-side plant.

The most important crop is that required for salading, for which a deep-coloured Beet of rich flavour, such as Sutton's Red, is to be preferred, and the aim of the cultivator should be to obtain roots of moderate size and of perfect shape and finish. The ground having been trenched two spades deep early in the year, may be made up into four and a half feet beds some time in March, preparatory to sowing the seed. Early sowing is needful for an early crop, but this will be liable to destruction by a late spring frost; the main sowing should never be made until quite the end of April or beginning of May. In the event of a hot dry summer, much of the early sown Beet will run up to flower and be useless. For a neat crop, sow in drills one and a half or two inches deep, and thin out to nine inches apart. Hand weeding will have to follow soon after sowing, and perhaps the hoe may be required to supplement the hand. The thinning should be commenced as early as possible, but it is waste of time to plant the thinnings, and it is equally waste of time to water the crop. In fact, if the ground is well prepared, weeding and thinning comprise the whole remainder of the cultivation.

Some of the smaller and more delicate Beets, of a very dark colour, may be sown in drills a foot or fifteen inches apart and at six inches distance in the drills. We have, indeed, lifted pretty crops of the smaller Beets at four inches, but it is not prudent to crowd the plants, as the result will be thin roots with long necks.

Large Beets are sometimes required, and are usually of a lighter colour and less rich in flavour than the smaller kinds. In growing these a layer of fat manure may be put at the bottom of the trench, as for Salsify and Parsnips on poor land. The ground need not be made up in beds for these, and the seed may be sown broadcast. But we prefer the neater method of beds with alleys and drills, putting the seeds in rows one foot apart and two inches deep. The seed is sometimes dibbled in, but a better plant is obtained by drilling. The greatest care should be taken to keep the crop clean, and to thin to single plants in good time.

A Beet crop may be left in the ground during the winter if aided by a covering of litter during severe frost. But it is safer out of the ground than in it, and the proper time to lift is when a touch of autumn frost has been experienced. Dry earth or sand, in sufficient quantity, should be ready for the storing, and a clamp in a sheltered corner will answer if shed room is scarce. In any case, a dry and cool spot is required, for damp will cause mildew, and warmth will cause growth. In cutting off the tops before storing, take care not to cut too near the crown, or injurious bleeding will follow. On the other hand, the long fang-like roots may be shortened without harm, for the slight bleeding that will occur at that end will not affect more than the half-inch or so next to the cut part. A little experience will teach anyone that Beets must be handled with care, or the goodness will run out of them. Many cooks bake Beet because boiling so often spoils them; but if they are in no way cut or bruised, and are plunged into boiling water and kept boiling for a sufficient length of time—half an hour to two hours, according to size—there will be but trifling difference between boiling and baking.

On stony shallow soils, where it is difficult to grow handsome long Beets, the round variety may be tried with the prospect of a satisfactory result. We have in hot seasons found this useful on a damp clay where fine Beets were rarely obtainable. In rainy seasons, on the other hand, our round Beets have been large and coarse and earthy in flavour, and, as a crop, chiefly useful to replenish the pig trough. From this same unkind clay we have obtained perfect crops of long Beets, by making deep holes with a dibber a foot apart and filling these with sandy stuff from the compost yard and sowing the seed over them. It is a tedious process, but it benefits the land for the next crop, and the Beets pay for it in the first instance.

The Silver Beet is grown for the midrib of the leaf, which is considered by some to be equal to Asparagus. To do justice to this Beet a rank soil and plenty of liquid manure are needed to promote a quick robust growth. The plant is occasionally earthed up, but this is needless, for a good quality may be obtained without it. The leaves should be pulled from the plant, not cut. As these stalks often turn black in cooking, it is advisable to add a few drops of lemon-juice to the water they are boiled in, and, of course, soda should never be used. They should be served up in the same manner as Asparagus. The remainder of the leaf is dressed as Spinach.

BORECOLE, or KALE

(Brassica oleracea acephala)

THE BORECOLES OR KALES are indispensable for the supply of winter vegetables, and their importance is made especially manifest when severe frost has made general havoc in the kitchen garden. Then it is seen that the hardier kinds of Borecoles are proof against any amount of frost that may be expected in these islands, and, while it leaves the plants unharmed, it improves the tops and side sprouts that are required for table purposes.

As regards soil the Borecoles are the least particular of the whole race of Brassicas. They appear to be capable of supplying the table with winter greens even when grown on hard rocky soil, but good loam suits them admirably, and a strong clay well tilled will produce a grand sample. Granting, then, that a good soil is better than a bad one, we urge the sowing of the seed as early as possible for insuring to the plant a long season of growth. But early sowing should be followed by early planting, for it is bad practice to leave the plants crowded in the seed-bed until the summer is far advanced. This, however, is often unavoidable, and it is well to consider in time where the plants are to go, and when, according to averages, the ground will be vacant to receive them. The first sowing may be made early in March, and another in the middle of April. These two sowings will suffice for almost all the purposes that can be imagined. A good seed-bed in an open spot is absolutely necessary. It is usual to draw direct from the seed-bed for planting out as opportunities occur, and this method answers fairly well. But it is better practice to prick out the plants as soon as large enough to prepare them for the final planting, as a stouter and handsomer plant is thereby secured. If it is intended to follow the rough and ready plan, the seed drills should be nine inches apart; but for pricking out six inches will answer, and thus a very small bed will provide a lot of plants. When pricked out, the little plants should be six inches apart each way, and should go to their final quarters as soon as they touch one another. When Borecoles are planted out on the flat in large pieces, a fair distance is two feet apart each way, but some vigorous kinds in good ground will pay for another foot distance, and will yield enormous crops when their time arrives. The planting should be done during showery weather if possible, but these plants have an astonishing degree of vitality, and if put out during drought, a mere spoonful of water to each will suffice to save them, and as the cool weather returns they will grow with vigour. But good cultivation saves a plant from extreme conditions, and it is an excellent practice to dig in green manure when making ground for Kales and the like, as a free summer growth is needful to the formation of a stout productive plant.

We have suggested above that two sowings may be regarded as generally sufficient, but we are bound to take notice of the fact that the late supplies of these vegetables are sometimes disappointing. In a mild winter the Kales reserved for use in spring will be likely to grow when they should stand still, and at the first break of pleasant spring weather they will bolt and become useful to the honey bees, to the injury, perhaps, of the seed growers of the district, and very much to the vexation of the man who expected many a basket of sprouts from them. A May sowing planted out in a cold place may stand until spring is somewhat advanced without bolting, and an August sowing may serve two purposes, the forwardest being useful to cut from in spring, and the backwardest being suitable to plant out for early supplies in the following autumn.

As regards the varieties, they agree pretty nearly in constitution, although they differ much in appearance and in power to resist the excitement of spring weather. But in this section of vegetables there are a few very interesting subjects. The Variegated and Crested Kales are extremely ornamental and eminently useful in large places for decorative purposes. These do not require so rich a soil as the robust Cottager's Kale or Curled Scotch, and they must have the fullest exposure to bring out their peculiarities. It is found that in somewhat dry calcareous soils these plants acquire their highest colour and most elegant proportions. When planted in carriage drives and other places where their colours may be suitably displayed, it is a good plan to cut off their heads soon after the turn of the year, as this promotes the production of side shoots of the most beautiful fresh colours. The Dwarf Green and Dwarf Purple endure an arctic winter uninjured, and both are elegantly crisped. Buckman's Hardy is also excellent for a late supply; and in an average season remains good until quite late in spring. This should be sown with the other Kales in the usual way, but it will be well to make a special sowing in the first week of May, and plant out on a plot which will not have to be disturbed to make way for Potatoes. The crop may be advantageously followed by Celery.

BROCCOLI

(Brassica oleracea botrytis asparagoides)

THE great importance of this crop is indicated by the long list of varieties and the still longer list of synonyms. As a vegetable it needs no praise, and our sole business will be to treat of the cultivation.

Of necessity we begin with generalities. Any good soil will grow Broccoli, but it is a strong-land plant, and a well-tilled clay should yield first-class crops. But there are so many kinds coming into use at various seasons, that the cultivation may be regarded as a somewhat complex subject. We will therefore premise that the best must be made of the soil at command, whatever it may be. The Cornish growers owe their success in great part to their climate, which carries their crops through the winter unhurt; but they grow Broccoli only on rich soil, and keep that in good heart by means of seaweed and other fertilisers. All the details of Broccoli culture require a liberal spirit and careful treatment. But the value of a well-grown crop will justify first-class culture; while, on the other hand, the value of a badly-grown crop will be insufficient to justify the space it covers, to say nothing of the poor labour that has been devoted to it.

Broccoli should always be sown on good seed-beds and be planted out; the seed-beds should be narrow, say three or three and a half feet wide, and the seed should be sown in drills half an inch deep at the utmost—less if possible; and where sparrows haunt the garden it will be well to cover the beds with netting. A quick way of securing all round seeds against small birds is to put a little red lead in a saucer, then lightly sprinkle the seed with water and shake it about in the red lead. Not a bird or mouse will touch seed so treated.

The seed-beds must be tended with scrupulous care to keep down weeds and avert other dangers. It is of great importance to secure a robust plant, short and full of colour, and free from club at the root. Now, cleanliness is in itself a safeguard. It promotes a short sturdy growth, because where there are no weeds or other rubbish the young plant has enough light and air. Early thinning and planting is another important matter. If you are not ready to plant, thin the seed-bed and prick out the seedlings. A first-class crop of Broccoli is worth any amount of trouble, although trouble ought to be an unknown word in the dictionary of a gardener.

As a rule, Broccoli should be planted in fresh ground, and, in mild districts, if the soil is in some degree rank with green manure the crop will be none the worse for it. But rank manure is not needful; a deep, well-dug, sweet loam will produce a healthy growth and neat handsome heads. However, it is proper to remark, that if any rank manure is in the way, or if the ground is poor and wants it, the Broccoli will take to it kindly, and all the rankness will be gone long before they produce their creamy heads. Still it must be clearly understood that the more generous the treatment, the more succulent will be the growth, and in cold climates a succulent condition may endanger the crop when hard weather sets in. With this reservation, we proceed to observe that Broccoli follows well upon Peas, early Potatoes, early Kidney Beans, and Strawberries that are dug in when gathered from for the last time. But it does not follow well upon Cabbage, Turnip, or Cauliflower; if you must plant it to follow any of these, dig deeply, manure heavily, and in planting dust a little freshly slaked lime in the holes. The times of planting will depend on the state of the plants and the proper season of their heading in. But everywhere and always the plants should be got out of the seed-bed into their permanent quarters as soon as possible, for the longer they stay in the seed-bed the more likely are they to become drawn above and clubbed below. As regards distances, too, the soil, the sort, and the season must be considered. For all sorts the distances range from two to two and a half feet; and for most of the medium-sized sorts that have to stand out through the winter for use in spring, a distance of eighteen to twenty-four inches is usually enough, because if they are rather close they protect one another. But with strong sorts in strong soils and kind climates, two feet and a half every way is none too much even for safe wintering. Plant firmly, water if needful, and do not stint it; but, if possible, plant in showery weather, and give no water at all. Watering may save the crop, but the finest pieces of Broccoli are those that are secured without any watering whatever.

It is time now to come to particulars, and we shall begin with the Autumn Broccoli. A few years ago the only Autumn Broccoli known were the so-called Cape varieties, and the White Cape is still worth growing, although other excellent varieties, such as Michaelmas

White, Walcheren, and Veitch's Self-protecting, are now available. To grow Autumn Broccoli profitably, sow in February, March, and April, the early sowings in a frame to insure vigorous growth, and the later sowings in the open ground. Plant out as soon as possible two feet apart each way in fresh land that has been deeply tilled. If the soil is poor, and you cannot make it up to your satisfaction, draw deep drills, fill these with fat manure, and carefully plant by hand, filling in round each root with crumbs from the surface soil. This will give them a good start, and they will take care of themselves afterwards. When they show signs of heading in, run in shallow drills of Prickly Spinach between them, and as this comes up the plants will be drawn, leaving it a fair chance of making a good stolen crop, needing no special preparation whatever. Another sowing may be made in May, but the early sowings, if a little nursed in the first instance, will pay the best, because early Broccoli are scarce, whereas late Broccoli are plentiful.

WINTER BROCCOLI—such as Sutton's Christmas White, Vanguard, Superb Early White, Favourite, Snow's, &c., should not be sown before the end of March and thence to the end of April. As a rule, the April sowing will make the best crop, although much depends on season, soil, and climate. Begin to plant out early, and continue planting until a sufficient breadth of ground is covered. Within reasonable limits it will be found that the time of planting does not much affect the date when the heads turn in, and only in a moderate degree influences the size of them.

SPRING BROCCOLI are capricious, no matter what the world may say. It will happen that sorts planted for cutting in June will turn in during April and May, and the sun rather than the seedsman must often be blamed for their precocity. In average seasons the late sorts are late, but the Broccoli is a sensitive plant, and unseasonable warmth tempts it beyond the bounds of prudence. Sow the spring Broccoli in April and May, the April sowing being the more important. It will not do, however, to follow a strict rule save to this effect, that early and late sowings are the least likely to succeed, while mid-season sowings—say from the middle of April to the middle of May —will, as a rule, make the best crops. Such sorts as Sutton's Pearl, Perfection, Safeguard, and Reading Giant may be sown as early as March and as late as the end of May, and where there is a constant demand for Broccoli in the early months of the year, two or three small sowings will be better than one large sowing.

SUMMER BROCCOLI are useful when Peas are late, and they are

always over in time to make way for the glut of the Pea crop. Late Queen may, in average seasons, be cut in June, if sown about the middle of May in the previous year, and carefully managed. This excellent variety may, as a rule, be relied on, both to withstand a severe winter in an exposed situation and to keep up the supplies of first-class vegetables until the first crop of Cauliflower is ready, and Peas are coming in freely. Generally speaking, smallish heads, neat in shape and pure in colour, are preferred, and they are also the most profitable as a crop and the most acceptable for the table. An open, breezy place should be selected for a plantation of late Broccoli, the land well drained, and not particularly rich with manure. But good land is required, with plenty of light and air to promote a dwarf sturdy growth and late turning in.

Various plans are adopted for the protection of Broccoli during winter. Much is to be said in favour of leaving them to the risk of all events, for certain it is that we get finer crops from undisturbed plants than by any interference with them, provided they escape the assaults of winter frost. But in such a matter we must be guided by the light of experience. In places where Broccoli do not winter well, heeling over may be resorted to. There are several ways of accomplishing this, the one we recommend being managed thus. Open a trench at the north end of a row, and gently push over the plant so that its head may incline to the north, disturbing the roots the least possible. Put a little mould over the stem to settle it, but do not earth it up any more than needful to render it secure. Push over the next, and the next, and so on, finishing off between them neatly and leaving the plants nearly as they were before, save that they now all look northward, and their sloping stems are a little deeper in the earth than they were in the first instance. This should be done during fine weather in November, and if the plants flag a little they should have one good watering at the roots. In the course of about ten days it will be scarcely perceptible that they have been operated on. They may be lifted and replanted with their heads to the north, but this is apt to check them too much. When it is seen that the heads are forming and severe weather is apprehended, some growers take them up with good balls of earth and plant them in a frame, or even pack them neatly in a cellar, and the heads finish fairly well, but not so well as undisturbed plants. It is impossible, however, to cut good heads in winter without some such protective measures. In many gardens glass is employed for protecting winter Broccoli, in which case the plantations are so shaped that the frames will be easily adapted to them without any disturbance of the plants whatever. There must be allowed a good space between the beds to be covered, and the plants must be fifteen to eighteen inches apart, with a view to the protection of the largest number by means of a given stock of frames. Rough frames answer admirably, and there are several cheap protectors manufactured for the purpose, the adoption of which is a question of expense merely, for their efficiency is a settled matter.

Sprouting Broccoli, both white and purple, are invaluable to supply a large bulk of a most acceptable vegetable in winter and early spring, and they would be grown more frequently than at present if their merits were better known. They can be treated in the same way as other hardy winter greens, and should have the most liberal culture possible, for which they will not fail to make an ample return.

BRUSSELS SPROUTS

(*Brassica oleracea bullata gemmifera*)

Brussels Sprouts command respect from prince and peasant as the finest autumnal vegetable we have of the strictly green class, suitable for every table. They are, however, often very poorly grown, because the first principle of success—a long growing season—is not recognised. It is in the power of the cultivator to secure this by sowing seed at the end of February, or early in March, on a bed of light rich soil made in a frame, and from the frame the plants should be pricked out into an open bed of similar light fresh soil as soon as they have made half a dozen leaves. From this bed they should be transferred to their permanent quarters before they crowd one another, the object being at each stage to obtain free growth with a sturdy habit, for mere length of stem is no advantage; it is a disadvantage when the plant is deficient of corresponding substance. This crop is often grown on Potato land, the plants being put out between the rows in the course of the summer. It is better practice, however, to plant Kales or Broccoli in Potato ground, because of the comparative slowness of their growth, and to put the Sprouts on an open plot freely dressed with somewhat fresh manure. If a first-class strain, such as Sutton's Exhibition, is grown, it will not only pay for this little extra care, but will pay also for plenty of room, say two and a half feet apart every way at the least, and one lot, made up of the strongest plants drawn separately, may be in rows three feet apart, and the plants two and a half feet asunder. Those who have heretofore treated Sprouts and Kales on one uniform rough plan will be surprised at the result of the routine we now recommend. The plants will button from the ground line to the top, and the buttons will set so closely that, once taken off, it will be impossible to put them on again. Moderate-sized, spherical, close, grass-green Sprouts are everywhere esteemed, and there is nothing of the class in the season more attractive in the markets.

Another mode of prolonging the season is to sow the seed in the open ground in July or August, the exact time being determined by the locality. In the south, August is early enough; in the north, the middle of July is none too soon. The plants from this sowing should be pricked out wholly or in part, at about six inches apart, for the winter, and be put out to finish their career on a good piece of ground some time in May, the earlier the better. It is desirable to secure strong plants without undue luxuriance, and therefore rich land is not wanted until the final planting, when the best bit of ground should be selected for the crop. If too forward before winter they may suffer from frost, but there is little fear of this if they are not sown too early, or encouraged to make rank growth in the autumn.

The crops treated as above advised will give early supplies of the very finest Sprouts. For successional crops it will be sufficient to sow in the open ground in the latter part of March, or early in April, and plant out in the usual way; in other words, to treat in the commonplace way of the ordinary run of Borecoles. With a good season and in suitable ground there will be an average crop, which will probably hold out far into the winter. It is important to gather the crop in a systematic manner. The Sprouts are perfect when round and close, with not a leaf unfolded. They can be snapped off rapidly, and where the quantity is considerable they should be sorted into sizes. The top Cabbage being left untouched to the last affords protection to the Sprouts; but when these are gone, the top Cabbage has served its purpose, and may be used as a table vegetable if it happens to be worth cooking.

CABBAGE

(*Brassica oleracea capitata*)

THE CABBAGE is a great subject, and competes with the Potato for pre-eminence in the cottage garden, in the market garden, and on the farm, sometimes with such success as to prove the better paying crop of the two. It may be said in a general way that a Cabbage may be grown almost anywhere and anyhow; that it will thrive on any soil, and that the seed may be sown any day in the year. All this is nearly true, and proves that we have a wonderful plant to deal with; but it is too good a friend of man to be treated, even in a book, in an off-hand manner. The Cabbage may be called a lime plant, and a clay plant; but, like almost every other plant that is worth growing, a deep well-tilled loam will suit it better than any other soil under the sun. It has one persistent plague only. Not the Cabbage butterfly; for although that is occasionally a desperate plague, it is not persistent, and may be invisible for years together. Nor is it the aphis, although in a hot dry season that pest is a fell destroyer of the crop. The great plague is club or anbury, for which there is no direct remedy or preventive known. But indirectly the plague may be fought successfully. The crop should be moved about, and wherever Cabbage has been grown, whether in a mere seed-bed or planted out, it should be grown no more until the ground has been well tilled and put to other uses for one year at least, and better if for two or three years. There are happy lands whereon the club has never been seen, and the way to keep these clear is to practise deep digging, liberal manuring, and changing the crops to different ground as much as possible. A mild outbreak of club may generally be met by first removing the warts from the young plants and then dipping them in a puddle made of soot, lime, and clay. But when it appears badly amongst the forward plants, their growth is arrested, the plot becomes offensive, and the only course left is to draw the bad plants, burn them, and give up Cabbage growing on those quarters for several years.

For general purposes Cabbages may be classified as early and late. The early kinds are valuable for their earliness, but are not well adapted for extensive cultivation, and, as compared with midseason and late sorts, may be described as unprofitable. In the scheme of cropping, it may be reckoned that a paying crop of Cabbage will occupy the ground through a whole year; for although this may not be the case exactly, the growing time will be pretty well gone before the ground is clear. After Cabbage, nothing of the brassicaceous genus should be put on the land, and, if possible, the crop to follow should be one requiring less of sulphur and alkalies, for of these the Cabbage is a great consumer, hence the need for abundant manuring in preparation for it. The presence of sulphur explains the offensiveness of the exhalations from Cabbage when in a state of decay.

In many gardens the supply of Cabbage is secured by one sowing of a large late kind annually in July or August. The plants are pricked out from the seed-bed as soon as possible, and are drawn from as wanted from the time that they become suitable to use as Collards, until the latest turn in and go to the house as Cabbage. Then the stumps give a crop of Sprouts, and these are followed by the Collards of the next sowing. But this rough mode of procedure is not to be described as first-class Cabbage culture, and at the best only suggests the immense value of this useful plant. It matters little, however, how many sorts are grown, or how many variations of treatment may prevail, the elements of the business may be quickly disposed of here for all practical purposes.

It will be necessary now to recognise four several sowings, any of which, save the autumnal sowing, may be omitted. We begin with a sowing of the earliest kinds in the month of February. For this, pans or boxes should be used, and the seed should be started in a warm pit or frame. When forward enough, prick out in a bed of light rich soil in a frame, and give plenty of air, and as soon as the plants begin to crowd one another, the season being advanced, plant them out, taking care to lift them tenderly with earth attached to their roots to minimise the check. These will heart quickly and be valued as summer Cabbage. The second sowing is to be made in the last week of March, and to consist of early kinds, and a few of the best type of Coleworts. As these advance to a planting size, they may be put out a few at a time as plots become vacant, and they will be useful in various ways from July to November or later. A third sowing may be made in the first or second week of May of smallish sorts and Coleworts; and these again may be planted out as opportunities occur, both in vacant plots for hearting late in the year, and as stolen crops in odd places to draw as Collards. The second and third sowings need not be pricked out from the seed-bed, but may be taken direct therefrom to the places where they are to finish their course. The fourth sowing is the most important, and the exact time for it must be determined by the locality, for while a strong plant is wanted before winter sets in, a rank growth may be endangered in the event of long-continued and severe frosty weather. The season for sowing spring Cabbage is from the middle of July to the end of August. It is good practice to make two sowings, say, one about July 25, and one about August 15. For these sowings the sorts must be selected as the usual requirements of the cultivator may suggest, and it will be well to include some good Colewort. For the final planting of these there should be well-made ground, following Peas and Beans, or Potatoes, and as much manure should be put on as can be spared, for Cabbage will take all it can get in the way of nourishment. In the planting out, the distances must be regulated with care, with a view to cover the ground closely without crowding the plants that are to remain for hearting. The smaller sorts will do well at a foot apart, but in a strong soil fifteen inches may be allowed between the rows, and a foot between the plants. A profitable mode of cropping where full-hearted Cabbages are wanted in spring is to begin by making two sowings, one of a quick Colewort about July 15, and one of a heavy Cabbage, such as Sutton's Imperial, or Enfield Market, about the end of July or beginning of August. Plant out the Imperials at two feet every way, and then back them with the Coleworts, which are to be planted at a foot apart, in rows alternating with the Imperials, and also between the latter. All the Coleworts are to be drawn as they acquire size and can be got rid of advantageously, and before spring growth commences the very last of them must be cleared off. There will remain a plot of Imperials for hearting, and when the heads of these are taken the stumps will supply another and heavy gathering during the summer. The one autumnal sowing of one sort referred to as practised by many may in this way be improved by making two autumnal sowings and employing two sorts.

All plantings should be done in showery weather if possible, or with a falling barometer promising rain. This cannot always be waited for, and it is a peculiarity of Brassicas, and of Cabbage in particular, that they will endure, after removal, heat and drought for some time with but little harm, and again grow freely after rain. But good cultivation has in view the prevention of any such check, for at the best it is a serious loss of time in the brief growing season. Therefore in droughty weather it will be advisable to draw shallow furrows and water these a day in advance of the planting, and if labour and stuff can be found it will be well to lay in the furrows a sprinkling of short mulchy manure to follow instantly upon the watering; then plant with the dibber, and the work is done. If the mulch cannot be afforded the water must, and to water the furrows in advance is better than watering after the planting, as a few observations will effectually prove. If drought continues, water should be given again and again. The trouble must be counted as nothing compared with the certain loss of time while the plant stands still, to become, perhaps, infested with blue aphis and utterly ruined. As a matter of fact, a little water may be made to go a long way, and every drop judiciously administered will more than repay its cost. The use of the hoe will greatly help the growth, and a little earth may be drawn towards the stems, not to the extent of 'moulding up,' for that is injurious, but to 'firm' the plants in some degree against the gales that are to be expected as the days decline.

Sutton's All Heart is well adapted for gardens where only one sowing of one sort is made annually. It may be used at any age, is quick in maturing, may be planted very close, as it makes but few outside leaves, and in all stages is of excellent table quality. If a second sort for a small garden be required, the best among many good ones, perhaps, is the Early Dwarf York. And when two sorts are grown there should be at least two sowings.

THE RED CABBAGE is grown for pickling and also for stewing, being in demand at many tables as an accompaniment to roasted partridges. The plant requires the best ground that can be provided for it, with double digging and plenty of manure. Two sowings may be made, the first in April for a supply in autumn for cooking, and the second in July for a crop to stand the winter and to supply large heads for pickling.

SAVOY CABBAGE

(*Brassica oleracea bullata*)

THE SAVOY CABBAGE is directly related to Brussels Sprouts, though differing immensely in appearance. It is of great value for the bulk of food it produces, as well as for its quality as a table vegetable during the autumn and winter. In all the essential points the Savoy may be grown in the same way as any other Cabbage, but it is the general practice to sow the seed in spring only, the time being determined by requirements. For an early supply, seed should be sown in February in a frame; and for succession sowings may be made in an open bed in March, April, and May. This vegetable needs a rich, deep soil to produce fine heads, but it will pay better on poor soil than most other kinds of Cabbage, more especially if the smaller sorts are selected. As Savoys do not advantageously supply either Collards or Sprouts, it is advisable to plant in the first instance at the proper distances, say, twelve inches for the small sorts, eighteen for those of medium growth, and twenty to twenty-four where the ground is strong and large heads are required. In private gardens the smaller kinds, such as Tom Thumb and Early Ulm, are much the best, but the market grower must give preference to those that make large, showy heads.

CAPSICUM and CHILI

(*Capsicum annuum, C. baccatum*)

CAPSICUMS AND CHILIS are so interesting and ornamental that it is surprising they are grown in comparatively few gardens. Sometimes there is reason to lament that Cayenne pepper is coloured with deadly drugs, but the remedy is at the hand of many, for Capsicums are of easy culture, and to prepare pepper is by no means a difficult task. All the ornamental Capsicums are adapted for pot culture, as conservatory and table plants, and the simplest course of procedure is to sow the seeds on a hot-bed in February or March, and pot on the young plants as they develop, keeping them on a mild hot-bed, or in a warm house or vinery until the summer is somewhat advanced, when they may be taken to the conservatory. Any light rich soil will answer, and nice plants may be had in pots five to eight inches in diameter, beyond which it is not desirable to go.

The Bird Pepper or Chili is grown as a tender annual, the seed being sown at the end of March on a mild hot-bed, or in a sunny frame ; and the plants carefully nursed until the beginning of June, when they are planted out under a hot wall or fence. They will do very well in a gravel walk if there is a warm wall to help them, but in this case a hole can be made with a trowel for each plant, and a little light rich earth must be provided to insure a good start. In gardens favourably situated, as many are in the south of England, it is sufficient to sow a pinch of seed on an open border in the middle of May, and put a hand glass over it, and the plants from this sowing may be planted in any sunny spot, and will yield an abundant crop of peppers. To prepare these for table use, put a reasonable number into a wire basket, and consign them to a mild oven for about twelve hours. They are not to be cooked but desiccated, and in most cases an ordinary oven, with the door kept open to prevent the heat rising too high, will answer perfectly. Being thus prepared, the next proceeding is to pound them in a mortar with one-fourth their weight of salt, which also should be dried in the oven, and used while hot.

When finely pounded bottle them close, and you will have a perfect sample of Cayenne pepper without any poisonous colouring. One hundred Chilis will make about two ounces of pepper, which will be sufficient in most houses for one year's supply. All the large ornamental Capsicums may be put on strings, and hung up in a dry store-room for use, as required, to flavour soups, make Chili vinegar, Cayenne essence, &c. The last-named condiment is prepared by steeping Capsicums in pure spirits of wine. A few drops of the essence may be used in any soup, or indeed wherever the flavour of Cayenne pepper is required.

CARDOON

(*Cynara Cardunculus*)

THIS plant is nearly related to the Globe Artichoke, and it makes a stately appearance when allowed to flower. Although it is not widely cultivated in this country, it is found in some of our best gardens, and is undoubtedly a wholesome esculent from which a skilful cook will present an excellent dish. The stalks of the inner leaves are stewed, and are also used in soups, as well as for salads, during autumn and winter. The flowers, after being dried, possess the property of coagulating milk, for which purpose they are used in France.

In a retentive soil Cardoons should be grown on the flat, but the plant is a tolerably thirsty subject, and must have sufficient water. Hence on very dry soils it may be necessary to put it in trenches after the manner of Celery, and then it will obtain the full benefit of all the water that may be administered. In any case the soil must be rich and well pulverised if a satisfactory growth is to be obtained.

Towards the end of April rows are marked out three or four feet apart, and groups of seeds sown at intervals of eighteen inches in the rows. The plants are thinned to one at each station, and in due time secured to stakes. Full growth is attained in August, when blanching is commenced by gathering the leaves together, wrapping them round with bands of hay, and earthing up. It requires from eight to ten weeks to accomplish the object fully. The French method is quicker. Seed is sown in pots under glass, and in May the plants are put out three feet apart. When fully grown the Cardoons are firmly secured to stakes by three small straw bands. A covering of straw, three inches thick, is thatched round every plant from bottom to top, and each top is tied and turned over like a nightcap. A little soil is then drawn to the foot, but earthing up is needless. In about a month blanching is completed.

CARROT

(*Daucus Carota*)

THE CARROT is a somewhat fastidious root, for although it is grown in every garden, it is not everywhere produced in the best style possible. The handsome roots of Long Surrey that are seen in the leading markets are the growth of deep sandy soils well tilled. On heavy lumpy land long clean roots cannot be secured by any kind of tillage. But for these unsuitable soils we have Sutton's Gem, the Champion Horn, and Intermediate, which require no great depth of earth; while for deep loams the Long Surrey and Altrincham come in admirably. Turning to the fine art department, the Forcing French Horn Carrot demands attention as an elegant and delicate root that appears on tables where cottagers' Carrots dare not be seen. This variety is well adapted for open ground culture on light warm borders for summer supply, being in demand through the season as a high-class vegetable; but the larger kinds of the Horn section may be allowed to attain their full size, and be stored for use in autumn in advance of the main crop.

Carrots are forced in frames on very gentle hot-beds. They cannot be well grown in houses, and they must be grown slowly to be creditable. It is usual to begin in November, and sow down a bed every three or four weeks until February. In March the first sowings on warm borders in the open garden may be made. A lasting hot-bed is of the first importance, therefore the bulk should be considerable, and the stuff should be robbed of its fire by turning at least three times to insure a regular and moderate heat. In large places leaves are used and answer perfectly, but beds of manure are very manageable, the only precaution needed being to get rid of the first fermentation. Put on the bed about one foot depth of fine, rich soil; if there is any difficulty about this, a depth of eight inches may suffice, but twelve is to be preferred. The bed must be near the glass, and it is a great point gained if a crop can be carried through without once giving water, for watering tends to damage the shape of the roots. Sow broadcast and cover with siftings just deep enough to hide the seed, and shut up. If the heat rises above 70°, give air to keep it down to that figure or to 65°. It will probably decline to 60° by the time the plant appears, but if the bed is a good one it will stand at that figure long enough to make the crop. Thin betimes to two or three inches, give air at every opportunity, let the plant have all the light possible, and cover up in good time when hard weather is expected. Should the heat go down too soon, linings must be used to finish the crop. Radishes and other small things may be grown on the same bed.

The first sowings on warm borders may need the shelter of mats or old lights until the plant has made a good start, but it is not often the plant suffers in any serious degree from spring frosts, as the seed will not germinate until the soil acquires a safe temperature. For all the early crops of Carrot a prepared soil, or a light sandy loam, should be used without any recent manure. For the main crops double digging should be practised, and if the staple is poor a dressing of half-rotten dung may be put in with the bottom spit. But a general manuring as for a surface-rooting crop is not to be thought of, its sure effect being to cause the roots to fork and fang most injuriously. It is good practice to select for Carrots a deep soil that was heavily manured the year before, and to prepare this by double digging without manure in the autumn or winter, so as to have it well pulverised by the time the seed is sown. Then dig it over one spit deep and break the lumps, and make seed-beds four feet wide. Sow in April in drills, mixing the seed with dry earth, the distance between rows to be eight to twelve inches according to the sort; cover the seed with a sprinkling of fine earth, and finish the bed neatly. As soon as possible thin and weed the crop, but do not thin to the full distance in the first instance, as by a little management it will be an easy matter during showery weather to draw delicate young Carrots for the final thinning, and these will admirably succeed the latest of the sowings in frames and warm borders. The Surrey and Altrincham must be in rows a foot asunder, and the plants left to mature at ten inches apart in the rows. Smaller sorts will, of course, require less space.

In July, frame culture of the smaller sorts should commence, but hot-beds may be dispensed with, and lights will not be wanted until there is a crop needing protection, when the lights may be put on, or the frames may be covered with shutters or mats. Thus, in addition to the main crops, a constant succession of young Carrots will be secured for the whole year round, and in every good household they will be appreciated alike for their delicacy and their beauty.

The Carrot crop is soon injured by autumn frost, therefore those grown in frames from late sowings must be protected as already advised, and the main crop should be lifted and stored in dry earth or sand, the tops being removed and the earth rubbed off, but without any attempt to clean them thoroughly, for that should never be done until they are wanted for use.

The wire-worm and the Carrot maggot are persistent enemies of this crop. We have little faith in nostrums and specifics; sound judgment as to the choice of ground, deep digging, and the preparation of the beds in good time, are the preventives of these as of many other garden plagues. It is often observed that main crops sown early in April suffer more than those sown late, and the lesson is plain. It has also been noticed that where the crops have suffered most severely the land was made ready in haste, and the wild birds had no time to purge it of the insects which they daily seek for food.

CAULIFLOWER

(*Brassica oleracea botrytis cauliflora*)

This fine vegetable is managed in much the same way as Broccoli, and it requires similar conditions. But it is less hardy in constitution, more elegant in appearance, more delicate on the table, and needs greater care in cultivation to insure satisfactory results. As regards soil, the Cauliflower will thrive on light land if heavily manured, and a quick growth may be promoted by abundant watering. In Holland, Cauliflowers are grown in sand with water at only the depth of a foot, and the ground is prepared by liberal dressings of cow-manure, which, with the moisture rising from below, promotes a quick growth and a fine quality. In any case, good cultivation is necessary or the crop will be worthless; and whatever the nature of the soil, it must be well broken up and liberally manured.

In gardens where Cauliflowers are in great demand, at least three sowings should be made. The first will be in January or February, in pans or boxes on a gentle hot-bed, or in a frame placed in a sunny sheltered corner, and Sutton's First Crop is best for this sowing. From the pans or boxes the plants should be pricked out early, in a bed prepared in a frame or on a sheltered border made up for the purpose with light rich soil from an old hot-bed. When strong enough, the plants should be finally put out on the best land at command, and have every possible care, the object being to maintain growth from the first without a check, and to keep them clear of weeds and vermin. Occasional hoeing between and heavy watering in dry weather will tend materially to their well-doing. If they begin to turn in during very hot weather, snap one of the inner leaves without breaking it off, and bend it over to protect the head.

The second sowing must be made in April or very early in May. For one main crop the best time to sow is the first week in April, and the seed-bed should be a well-prepared, sheltered border. From this seed-bed the plants should be pricked out once at least, and should be finally planted out in a smallish state, for if they become somewhat large in the seed-bed they will be liable to 'button,' which means that small, worthless heads will be produced as the result of an untimely check. The April sowing will give the least trouble of any, and if the ground is good, the plant from first to last will almost take care of itself, unless the season is very hot and dry, in which case water must be liberally supplied to prevent 'buttoning.'

The third sowing must be made in August or September, and it is essential where Broccoli cannot be depended on. The exact time is a question of climate. In Cornwall and Devon a good plant is secured by sowing in October, while north of the Trent many gardeners find the first week of August to be none too early. This sowing should never be made under glass, but in a sheltered spot on an open border; the soil need not be so rich as for a spring sowing, but a poor soil will not do justice to the crop, and if the ground is dry it should be well watered one day before the seed is sown. When the plants have made some progress, prick them out on a good bed of fresh soil in a sunny spot, and then prepare for their wintering. In the neighbourhood of London, Cauliflowers need more care in wintering than in districts that are colder but have a purer air. Hence it is the practice with many to pot them singly in the 60-size, and store them in frames and cool vineries, and wherever else they can have light and air without heat, and be safe from frost. It must here be remarked, however, that if Cauliflowers are properly managed they will bear a certain amount of frost without material harm, and they may often be found frozen in frames and glasses, and are little the worse for it in the end. Much may be done by the use of hand glasses, the plants being planted out on well-drained ground in clumps for convenience in covering them. Near London they are usually put into their winter quarters by the middle of October, and pot culture in frames has in great part superseded the use of hand-lights. An old Cucumber bed scratched over and dusted with lime makes a good wintering place for Cauliflowers. When all such places are filled, any plants that remain may be planted on an open border near a wall, and they may happen to pass through the winter and prove useful. These border plants will be worth a little attention to help them through, and one of the cleanest ways of shielding them against frost will be to cover with empty pots and put a little dry litter over. But a severe winter will make an end of them, do what you may, and therefore autumn-sown Cauliflowers must be provided with glass in some way to insure their safety, and only the surplus stock should be put out to run the gauntlet.

Those wintered under hand-lights need not be transplanted in the spring. Possibly the plants at the corners may be crippled by frost, in which case they must be removed, and the best plants will remain to finish without disturbance. But all, or the chief part, of those wintered in frames must be planted out as soon as the risk of severe frost is past, and should have good cultivation. The plants in pots may be turned out without hurting a fibre. Those in beds in frames must be lifted with care, and it will be good practice to leave enough in the bed to occupy it fairly, and to remove the lights and allow them to finish there. They will turn in early and make a fine beginning, and thus from one autumn sowing you will obtain two summer plantations.

The Cauliflower has been very materially improved within the past few years, the varieties now in favour being hardier and handsomer than the older kinds, and somewhat quicker in attaining maturity. Hence, where it is convenient to sow so early as January, the autumn sowing may be dispensed with. Sutton's First Crop, sown in January in heat and transplanted early, will produce small heads by the end of May or beginning of June, and sown out of doors in the middle of April will be fit to cut about the middle of July. There is this advantage in quick cultivation, that while we shorten the time and escape all the worry of the wintering, we are safer against buttoning and bolting, which will sometimes occur through the plants becoming too forward under glass, and receiving too great a check when planted out.

To succeed the First Crop sown in January or February there is nothing better than Sutton's Magnum Bonum, which may be sown in February and onwards, first under glass, and the later sowings on a sheltered border. This, when well grown, has every quality of an exhibition Cauliflower, and is first-rate on the table. Favourite,

King of Cauliflowers, Walcheren, and Autumn Mammoth may be sown for succession in April and May, and it is a question if any more are wanted.

The management of the crop has been treated so far as to growth, but we must now say a word about its appropriation. The two points for practical consideration are, how to economise a glut, and how to avoid destruction by frost. Cauliflowers should be cut at daybreak, or as soon after as possible, and should be taken from the ground with the dew upon them. If cut after the dew has evaporated from them, the quality will be some degrees inferior to that of those cut at the dawn of the day. When the heads appear at too rapid a rate for immediate consumption, draw the plants, allowing the earth to remain attached to the roots, and suspend them head downwards in a cool, dark, dry place, and every evening give them a light shower of water from a syringe. The deterioration will be but trifling, and the gain may be considerable, but if left to battle with a burning sun the Cauliflowers will certainly be the worse for it. After being kept in this way for a week, they will still be good, although, like other preserved vegetables, they will not be so good as those freshly cut and in their prime. It often happens that frost occurs before the crop is finished. A similar plan of preserving those that are turning in may be adopted, but it is better to bury them in sand in a shed or under a wall, and, if kept dry, they may remain good for a month or more.

CELERY

(*Apium graveolens*)

CELERY may be regarded as in fair favour with all mankind, and this renders it unnecessary for us to speak in its favour, as in the case of some other vegetables we have felt bound to do. The crop requires the very best of cultivation, but care should be taken not to push the growth too far, for the gigantic Celery shown by members of Celery clubs has, generally speaking, the quality of size only, being tough and tasteless. Nevertheless, the sorts that are held in favour by growers of prize Celery are good in themselves when grown to a moderate size; it is the forcing system alone that deprives them of flavour. Yet another precaution may be needful to prevent a mishap. In a hot summer, Celery will sometimes 'bolt' or run up to flower, in which case it is worthless. This may be the fault of the cultivator more than of the seed or the weather, for a check operates in many cases to hasten the flowering of plants, and it is not unusual for Celery to receive a check through mismanagement. If sown too early it may be impossible to plant out when of suitable size, and the consequent arrest of growth at a most important stage may result in a disposition to flower the first year, instead of waiting for the second. It should be understood, therefore, that early sowing necessitates early planting, and the cultivator should see his way clearly from the first.

The 1st of March is early enough for a first sowing anywhere of a small variety, and this will require a mild hot-bed, or a place in the propagating house. Sow on rich fine soil in boxes, cover lightly and place in a temperature of 60°. As soon as forward enough to prick out, put the plants on a rich bed close to the glass, in a temperature of 60° to 65°, keep liberally moist, and give air, at first with great caution, but increasing as the natural temperature rises until the lights can be removed during the day. The plant may thus be hardened for a first planting on a warm border in a bed consisting of one-half rotten hot-bed manure and one-half of turfy loam. The bed need not be deep, but it must be constantly moist, and old lights should be at hand to give shelter when needful. If well grown in trenches, this first crop will be of the finest quality, and will come in early.

For the general crop a second sowing may be made of the finest Pink and White varieties, also on a mild hot-bed, in the second week of March, and have treatment similar to the first, but once pricking out into the open bed will be sufficient, the forwardest plants being put out first at six inches, and to have shelter if needful; other plantings in the same way to follow until the seed-bed is cleared out. By good management this sowing may be made to serve the purpose of three sowings, the chief point being to prick out the forwardest plants on another mild bed as soon as they are large enough to be lifted out, and to make a succession from the same seed-bed as the plants advance to a suitable size.

The third and last sowing may be made in the second week of April, in an open border, on rich light soil, and should have the shelter of mats or old lights during cold weather. From this, also, there should be two or three prickings out, the first to be transferred to a bit of hard ground, covered with about three inches of rich mulchy stuff, in the warmest spot that can be found, and the last to a similar bed on the coldest spot in the garden. In the final planting the same order should be followed. The result will be a prolonged supply from one sowing, and the first lot will come in early, though sown late, if the plants are kept growing without a check, and receive thoroughly generous culture.

The planting out is an important matter, and each lot will require separate treatment, subordinate to one general and very simple plan. Celery must have rich soil, abundant moisture, and must be blanched to make it fit for table. There are various ways of accomplishing these ends, although they differ but slightly, and the commonest of common sense will guide us in the matter. For the earliest crops the ground must be laid out in trenches, and these must have just as much rich stable manure dug in as can be afforded. To overdo it in this respect seems impossible, for Celery, like the Cauliflower, will make a fine growth in rotten manure alone, without any admixture of loam at all. The trenches should be eighteen inches wide at bottom, ten inches deep, and four feet from centre to centre, and should run north and south. The plants are to be carefully lifted with a trowel, and planted along the centre of the trench six to nine inches apart, and should have water as planted that there may be no check. In a cold soil and a cold season the trenches may be less in depth by two or three inches with advantage. If dry weather ensues, water must be given freely, but there should be no earthing up until the plant has made a full and profitable growth, for the earthing pretty well stops the growth and is but a finishing process, requiring from five to seven weeks to bring the crop to perfection.

The second lot may be put out in the same way, and other plantings may follow at discretion, but this rule must be followed, that as the season advances the trenches must be less deep until the last lot is put out upon the level. This brings us to what may be termed the main crop to be grown on the bed system, which is well adapted for producing a large supply with the least amount of labour, but is quite unsuitable for the early crops.

Celery beds are made four and a half feet wide and ten inches deep, the soil which is taken out being laid up in a slope round the outside of the bed, and the bank thus formed may be planted with any quick crop, such as Kidney Beans. The excavation must be liberally manured, and then the plants are put in across the bed in rows a foot apart, and the plants six inches apart in the rows. Water must be given to each row as planted, and the surface must be several times chopped over with the hoe or a small fork, and watering repeated until the plants have made a start. The bed system is not only economical, but convenient for sheltering in winter, and should have the best attention of gardeners who are expected to supply abundance of Celery throughout the winter and spring, for in such cases a large sample is not required, but quality and continuance are of great importance.

Earthing up is often performed in a rude way, as though the plant were made of wood instead of the most delicate tissue. The first earthing should be done with a trowel, and quite loosely, to allow the heart of the plant room to expand. The result should be a little ring of light earth scarcely pressing the outside leaves, and leaving the whole plant as free as it was before. In the course of ten days the earthing must be carried a stage further by means of the spade. Chop the earth over, and lay it in heaps on each side of the plant. Then gather a plant together with both hands, and liberate one hand, and with it bring the earth to the plant half round the base, and, changing hands, pack up the earth on the other side with the other hand. Be careful not to press the soil very close; also avoid putting any crumbs into the heart of the plant; and do not earth higher than the tops of the leaves next the outside ones. Rather less than that depth is desirable in this second earthing. The centre of the plant should still be free to expand, and for the inmost leaves to rise. In another ten days repeat this process, carrying the earth a stage higher; and in a week from this finish the operation.

The top of the plant must now be closed, and the earth carefully packed so high that only the very tops of the leaves are visible. Finish to a proper slope with the spade, but not in a way to press the plants unduly, the object being simply to obtain a final growth of the innermost leaves in darkness, but otherwise free from restraint.

It is a great point to keep Celery unhurt by frost far on in the winter, and the advantage of growing the late crops on dry light soil, and on the bed system, will be seen in the ease with which it can be preserved. On heavy soil Celery soon suffers from frost, but not so readily on a soil naturally light and dry. Moreover, the bed system is convenient for the adoption of rough means of protection, with whatever materials are at command. In heavy soil fine crops of Celery for autumn use may be grown, but in consequence of the liability of the plant to suffer by winter damp, it is advisable to plant the late crops on the level, and earth up from the adjoining plots in order to keep the roots dry in winter. Another step towards securing a late supply consists in bending the tops on one side at the final earthing, which prevents the trickling of water into the heart of the plant during heavy rain or snow.

The many enemies of Celery, such as slugs, snails, the mole-cricket, and the maggot, are not of much account where good cultivation prevails, but the Celery fly appears to be indifferent to good cultivation, and therefore must be directly dealt with. An occasional careful dusting of the leaves with soot has been found to operate beneficially. It should be done during the month of June on the mornings of days that promise to be sunny. If the soot is put on carelessly it will do more harm than good; a very fine dusting will suffice to render the plant distasteful to the fly. Where the eggs are lodged the leaves will soon appear blistered, and the maggot within must be crushed by pinching the blister between the thumb and finger. Leaves that are much blistered should be removed and burned, but to rob the plants of many of their leaves, or even parts of leaves, will seriously reduce their vigour of growth.

CELERIAC, or TURNIP-ROOTED CELERY, is much prized on the Continent as a cooked table vegetable, and as a salad. In common Celery the stem forms a mere basis to the leaves, but in Celeriac it is developed into a knob weighing from one to five pounds. This is more easily preserved than Celery, and that is one reason of its popularity on the Continent, more especially in Germany, where the winter frost soon makes an end of the more succulent plant that is preferred in this country. Celery cooked in the way of Sea Kale is well known as a delicacy at English tables, and the cooked Celeriac ranks equal in importance with it, though quite a different dish. The stem or axis of the plant is used, and not the stalks. To grow fine Celeriac, a long season is requisite; and therefore it is advisable to sow the seed in a gentle heat early in March, and afterwards prick out and treat as Celery; but after the first stage the treatment is altogether different. For the plantation a light and rich soil is required, and for a small crop it can easily be made so where the staple is heavy, because six inches depth of any sandy soil spread over the common soil will be sufficient. The plants must be put out on the level a foot and a half apart each way, and be planted as shallow as possible. Before planting, trim them carefully to remove lateral shoots that might divide the stems, and after planting water freely. The cultivation will consist in keeping the crop clean, and frequently removing the soil away from the plants, for the more they stand out of the ground the better, provided they are not distressed. They must never want for water, or the roots will not attain to a proper size. The lateral shoots and fibres must be removed to keep the roots intact, but not to such an extent as to arrest progress. When a good growth has been made, and the season is declining, cover the bulbs or stems with a thin coat of fine soil, and in the first week of October lift a portion of the crop and store it in sand, all the leaves being first removed, except those in the centre, which must remain, or the roots may waste their energies in producing another set. The portion of the crop left in the ground will need protection from frost, and this can be accomplished by earthing them over with soil taken from between the rows.

Celeriac is cooked in the same manner as Beet, and requires about the same length of time. The stems, bulbs, or roots (for the knobs, which are true stems, are known by various names) are trimmed and washed, and then put into boiling water without salt or any flavouring, and kept boiling until quite tender; they may then be pared and sliced, and served with white sauce, or left uncut to get cold to be sliced up for salads.

CHICORY

(*Cichorium Intybus*)

A VALUABLE addition to our winter and spring esculents. When stewed and served with melted butter, it bears a slight resemblance to Sea Kale. More frequently, however, it is eaten in the same manner as Celery, with cheese, and it also makes an excellent and most wholesome salad. All the garden varieties have been obtained from the wild plant, and some of the stocks show a decided tendency to revert to the wild condition. It is therefore important to sow a carefully selected strain, or the roots may be worthless for producing heads.

Seed should be sown in April or May, in rows one foot apart, and the plants thinned out to about nine inches in the rows. The soil must be deep and rich, but free from recent manure, except at a depth of twelve inches, when the roots will attain the size of a good Parsnip.

In autumn the roots should be lifted uninjured with the aid of a fork, and only a few at a time, as required. After cutting off the tops just above the crown, they can at once be started into growth, and it is essential that this be made in absolute darkness. French growers plant in a warm bed of the temperature suited to Mushrooms, but this treatment ruins the flavour, and has the effect of making the fibre of the leaves woolly. It is far simpler and better to put the roots into a cellar or shed in which a temperature above the freezing point may be relied on, and from which every ray of light can be excluded. They can be closely packed in deep boxes, with light soil or leaf-mould between. If the soil be fairly moist, watering will not be necessary for a month, and had better not be resorted to until the plants show signs of flagging. Instead of boxes, a couple of long and very wide boards, stood on edge and supported from the outside, make a convenient and effective trough. The packing of the roots with soil can be commenced at one end, and be gradually extended through the entire length, until the part first used is ready for a fresh start. Breaking the leaves is better than cutting, and it may begin about three weeks after the roots are stored. From well-grown specimens, heads may be obtained equal to a compact Cos Lettuce, and by a little management it is easy to maintain a supply from October until the end of May. The quantity of salading to be obtained from a few roots is really astonishing.

CHIVES

(*Allium Schœnoprasum*)

A MILD substitute for the Onion in salads and soups. The plant is a native of Britain, and will grow freely in any ordinary garden soil. Propagation is effected by division of the roots either in spring or autumn. The clumps should be cut regularly in succession whether wanted or not, with the object of maintaining a continuous growth of young and tender shoots. At intervals of four years it will be necessary to lift, divide, and re-plant the roots on fresh ground.

CORN SALAD

(*Valerianella olitoria*)

CORN SALAD OR LAMB'S LETTUCE, so often seen on continental tables, is comparatively unknown in this country. The reason for this is, perhaps, to be found in the fact that, as a raw vegetable, it is not particularly palatable, although when dressed as a salad with oil and the usual condiments, it is altogether delicious, and forms a most refreshing episode in the routine of a good dinner. Corn Salad is a plant of quick growth, and is valued for its early appearance in spring, when elegant salads are much in request. It may be mixed with other vegetables for the purpose, or served alone with a little suitable preparation.

The most important sowings of the seed are made in August and September. Seed may, however, be sown at any time from February to October, but only those who are accustomed to the plant should trouble to secure summer crops, as when Lettuces are plentiful Corn Salad is but rarely required. Any good soil will grow it, but the situation should be dry and open. Sow in drills six inches apart, and thin to six inches in the rows. The crop is taken in the same way as Spinach, either by the removal of separate leaves or cutting over in tufts.

COUVE TRONCHUDA

(*Brassica oleracea costata*)

COUVE TRONCHUDA, or Portugal Cabbage, is a fine vegetable, that should be grown in every garden, including those in which Cabbages generally are not regarded as of great importance. The plant is of noble growth, and requires abundant room in rich ground for the spread of its large leaves, the mid-ribs of which are thick, white, tender, and when cooked in the way of Sea Kale quite superb in quality. When a fair crop of these mid-ribs has been taken there remains the top Cabbage, which is excellent.

Two or three sowings may be made in February, March, and April, and the early ones must be in heat. Transfer to rich soil as early as possible, giving the plants ample room, from two to three feet each way, and aid with plentiful supplies of water in dry weather.

CRESS

(*Lepidium sativum*)

CRESS of any and every kind should be grown in small lots from frequent sowings, and the sorts should be kept separate, and, if possible, on the same border. The soil should be fine and fresh, and there is no occasion for manuring, in fact it is objectionable, but a change of soil must be made occasionally to insure a good growth.

The seed is usually sown too thick, yet thin sowing is not to be recommended. It is important to cut Cress when it is just ready—tender, green, short, and plump. This it will never be if sown too thick, or allowed to stand too long. Instantly upon the plant starting to grow away from salad size it becomes worthless, and should be dug in.

AMERICAN OR LAND CRESS (*Barbarea præcox*) is of excellent quality when grown on a good border, and two or three sowings should be made in the spring and autumn in shady spots.

WATER CRESS (*Nasturtium officinale*) is so highly prized, that many who are out of the reach of ordinary sources of supply would gladly cultivate it were there a reasonable prospect of success. Assertions have been made that it can be grown in any garden without water, but we have never yet seen a sample fit to eat which has been grown without assistance from the water-can. A running stream is not necessary. Make a trench in a shady spot, and well enrich the soil at the bottom of it. In this sow the seed in March, and when the plants are established keep the soil well moistened. The more freely this is done the better will be the result. Other sowings may be made in April, August, and September. We have seen Water Cress successfully cultivated in pots and pans immersed in saucers of water placed in shady positions.

CUCUMBER

(*Cucumis sativus*)

THE CUCUMBER is everywhere valued, and much spirit is shown in its production, even in gardens where few other subjects obtain a fair share of attention. Its exceeding usefulness explains its popularity, and happily the plant is of an accommodating character. In the gardens of the wealthy, Cucumbers are grown at all seasons of the year; in medium-sized gardens, summer Cucumbers are generally deemed sufficient, and there is no difficulty in growing an abundant and continuous supply of the finest quality. The winter cultivation demands suitable appliances and skilful management; but a very small house, with an efficient heating apparatus, will suffice to produce a large and constant supply, and therefore winter Cucumbers need not be regarded as beyond the range of practice of any ordinary well-kept garden.

FRAME CUCUMBERS are the most in demand, and the easiest to grow. The very first point for the cultivator is to determine when to begin, for the rule is to begin too early, and to waste time and opportunity in consequence. We will suppose the Cucumbers are to be grown in a two-light frame, for which will be required four good cart-loads of stable manure. This will require to be put in a heap three weeks before the bed is made up, and the bed will have to last until the season is sufficiently advanced to sustain the heat without any further fermentation. Considering these points, it will be understood that it is a far safer proceeding to begin the first week in April than the first week in March, and unless the way is clearly seen, the later date is certainly preferable, for it reduces to a minimum the conflict with time in the matter of bottom heat. Make up the heap; then, early in March, turn it twice, and at the end of March prepare the bed, firming the stuff with a fork as the work proceeds, but taking care not to tread on the bed. Put on the lights and leave the affair for five or six days, and then lay down a bed of rich loamy soil of a somewhat light and turfy texture, about nine inches deep. It is now optional to sow or plant as may be most convenient. Strong plants in pots, put out at once, will fruit earlier than plants from seeds sown on the bed. But sowing on the bed is good practice for all that, and if this plan is adopted you must sow a few more seeds than the number of plants required, to provide a margin for accidents, and whatever surplus plants you may have will prove useful one way or another, for it is most unusual for Cucumber plants to prove a 'drug in the market.' If it is preferred to begin with plants, the question of providing them must be considered in good time. The seed should be sown at least a month in advance, and should be brought forward on a hot-bed or in a cool part of a stove. Many a successful Cucumber grower has no better means of raising plants than by sowing the seeds in a box or pan of light rich earth, kept in a sunny corner of a common greenhouse, with a slate or tile laid over until the seeds start, and by a little careful management nice thrifty plants are secured in the course of about four weeks. There is very much said in horticultural works on the soil the seeds should be sown in, but we advise the reader not to make too much of that question, for any turfy loam, or even peat, will answer; but a rank soil is certainly unfit, for the object should be to obtain short stout plants of a healthy green colour, not the long-drawn pallid things that are often to be seen on sale, and which by their evident weakness seem destined to illustrate the problems of Cucumber disease.

Having made a beginning with strong plants on a good bed, the two matters of importance are to regulate the temperature and the watering. In the first instance, it will be necessary to shade the plants a little, but as they acquire strength they should have more light and more air than are usually allowed to Cucumbers. A temperature averaging 60° by night and 80° by day will be found safe and profitable, as promoting a healthy growth and lasting fruitfulness. But the rule must be elastic. You may shut up at 90° without harm, and during sunshine the glass may rise to 95° without injury, provided the plants have air and are not dry at the roots. But it is of great moment that the night temperature should be kept near 60°, and not go below it. If you find the night temperature has been above the proper point owing to the heat of the bed, wedge up the lights about half an inch when shutting up, and as the season advances increase this supply of night air, for it keeps the plants in health, provided there is no chill accompanying it. As regards the watering, the important point is to employ soft water of the same temperature as the frame, and therefore a spare can, filled with water, should be always kept in the frame ready for use, and when emptied should be filled again and left for the next watering. Twice a day at least the plants and the sides of the frame should be well wetted with a shower from the syringe. It is better to syringe three times than twice, but this must be in some degree determined by the temperature. The greater the heat, the more freely should air and water be supplied; on the other hand, if the heat runs down, give water with caution, or disaster may follow. In case of emergency the plants will go through a bad time without serious damage if kept almost dry, and then it will be prudent to give but little air. Sometimes the heat of the bed runs out before there is sufficient sun heat to keep the plants growing, but if they can be maintained in health for a week or so, hot weather may set in, and all will come right. But to carry through at such a time demands particular care as to watering and air giving.

As regards stopping and training, we may as well say at once, the less of both the better. Free healthy natural growth will result in an abundant production of fruit, and stopping and training will do but little to promote the end in view. But there is something to be done to secure an even growth, and the exposure of every leaf to light. When the young plant has made three rough leaves, nip out the point to encourage the production of shoots from the base. When the shoots have made four leaves, nip out the points to promote a further growth of side shoots, and after this there must be no more stopping until there is a show of fruit. The growth should be pegged out to cover the bed in the most regular manner possible, and wherever superfluous shoots appear they must be removed. Any crowding will have to be paid for, because crowded shoots are not fruitful. If a great show of fruit appears suddenly, remove a large portion of it, as over-cropping makes a troublesome glut for a short time, and then there is an end of the business; but by keeping the crop down to a reasonable limit, the plants will bear freely to the end of the season. Every fruiting shoot should be stopped at two leaves beyond the fruit, and as the crop progresses there must be occasional pruning out of old shoots to make room for young ones. An error of management likely to occur with a beginner is allowing the bed to become dry below while it is kept quite moist above by means of the syringe. Many cultivators drive a stick into the bed here and there, and from time to time they draw these out and judge by their appearance whether or not the bed needs a heavy watering. To be dry at the root is deadly to the Cucumber plant, and to be in a swamp is not less deadly. It must have abundance of moisture above and below, but stagnation of either air or water will bring disease, ending in a waste of labour.

THE GREENHOUSE CULTIVATION of the Cucumber for a summer crop only is the most profitable and simple as well as the most interesting of all the methods practised. In many gardens the houses that have been filled during the winter with Geraniums and other plants are very poorly furnished during the summer, and present a most unsightly appearance. Now, it is a very easy matter to render them at once profitable and beautiful, for when clothed with green vines bearing handsome Cucumbers, such houses are attractive and pay their way amazingly well. To carry out the routine nicely, the house should be cleared at the end of April, the plants being removed to pits and frames. The beds should, if possible, be made up on slates, laid close over the hot-water pipes, and in making them a mere bushel of soil under each light is enough to begin with. First lay on the slate a large seed-pan bottom upwards, and on that a few flat tiles, and then heap up in a cone about a bushel of nice light turfy loam. Start the fire, and shut up and raise the heat of the empty house to 80° or 90° for one whole day. The next day plant on each hillock a nice short stout Cucumber plant, or sow two seeds. Proceed as advised for frame culture, keeping a temperature of 60° by night and 80° by day, with a rise of 5° to 10° during sunshine. Ply the syringe freely, give air carefully, and use the least amount of shading possible. It will very soon be found that by judicious management in shutting up and air giving, the firing may be dispensed with, and then it remains only to syringe freely and train with care. The plants should not be stopped at all, but be taken up direct to the roof and be trained out on a few wires or tarred string, in the first instance right and left, and afterwards along the rafters to meet at the ridge, and form a rich leafy arcade. The fruits will appear in quantity, and must be thinned to prevent over-cropping. They will mostly be handsome and of the finest quality, their own great leaves shading them sufficiently. As the plants grow, earth must be added to the hillocks until there is a continuous bed, on which a certain number of shoots may be trained where there is sufficient light for them. It is best to begin as advised above, with the aid of fire heat, to start the crop for the sake of gaining time; but if this is not convenient you may begin without fire heat in the last week of May, and the plants will produce fruit until the chill of autumn makes an end of them, and the house is again required for the greenhouse plants.

WINTER CUCUMBERS thrive best in lean-to houses with somewhat steep roofs, as such houses are less liable to chill during cold windy weather, and they catch a maximum of the winter sunshine. In a mild winter, Cucumbers may be grown in any kind of house that can be maintained at a suitable temperature, and the markets are supplied from rough constructions that do duty for many purposes. But when hard times occur, the steep lean-to, with bed along the front, and tank to give equable bottom heat, will prove the most serviceable, as it will neither allow snow to lodge on the glass, nor suffer any serious decline of temperature during the prevalence of sharp frost and keen winds. For late autumn supply any kind of house will suffice, but best of all an airy span. A brick pit will answer every purpose from October to March with good management, and fermenting materials will afford the needful heat. In such cases trenches should be provided for occasional renewal of the bottom heat. But a roomy house and a service of hot water justly stand in favour with experienced cultivators as combining the necessary conditions with convenience of management.

For winter culture, plants are raised from seeds and from cuttings. Seedling plants are the best, because the most vigorous, but they require a little more time than cuttings to arrive at a fruiting state. For pot culture cuttings are best, as we expect only a moderate crop from pot plants, and quickness of production is of great importance.

It is usual to sow the first lot of seeds on the 1st of September, and to sow again on the 1st of October and the 1st of November; after which it is not advisable to sow again until the 1st of February, for the spring crop. If the management is good the first sowing will be in fruit by the time the third batch of seed is sown, say, by the first week of November, and thenceforward throughout the winter there should be no break in the supply.

The management of winter Cucumbers turns upon details chiefly, and will be found in the end to depend rather upon care than skill, for as regards the general principles they are the same as in growing Cucumbers in frames, the task for the cultivator being to carry them out successfully. We will begin by sowing the seed singly in small pots in light turfy loam, or peat with which a fair proportion of sharp sand has been mixed. These pots we place in a heat of $70°$ to $75°$, and for plants to last long we should prefer the lower temperature. As regards the next stage, we may train the plants up rafters, or spread them out on beds, the first being always the better plan where it happens to be convenient. But the prudent cultivator will not be tied to rules, he will cut his coat according to his cloth, and while he has a house of Cucumbers trained to the roof, he will, perhaps, also have a pit filled with plants on beds. To stop severely is bad practice, for we want vigorous growth, but a certain amount of stopping must be done to promote an even growth, and to distribute the fruit fairly both in space and time. There has been too much said about soil, because in many places a suitable turfy loam, or a good fibrous peat, may be obtained, and the accidents that have befallen Cucumber growers have usually been the result of bad management in respect of heat, water, and air, rather than the use of unsuitable soil. But it must not be supposed that we are careless about this matter. Neither a pasty clay, a sour sticky loam, nor a poor sandy or chalky soil will produce fine Cucumbers. On the other hand, rank manure or poor leaf-mould are not favourable materials. There is nothing like mellow loam, which can be enriched and modified at discretion, without going to extremes. This being at command, the rest depends on daily attention and prudent watchfulness, which will be abundantly rewarded, for winter Cucumbers, when well done, are as profitable as any crop grown in our gardens.

RIDGE CUCUMBERS are grown in much the same way as recommended for Vegetable Marrows. They may be put on hillocks or beds, and in either case a foundation of fermenting material is required to insure a crop in the early part of the summer. For a late crop, the natural heat of the soil will be sufficient should the summer prove to be fine, but in a cold season Ridge Cucumbers are disappointing. Of the many methods of growing them, one of the best is to lay out the ground in four-feet beds by taking out the soil to a depth of fifteen inches, and spreading about that depth or more of half-rotted manure, to which may be added any leaves, mouldy hay, and other litter, that may be handy. Cover with a foot depth of good loam, and plant two days afterwards, protecting the plants with hand-lights. The first week in May is as early as will be safe in most places for the planting, and some care will be needed to keep the plants moving fairly until the season is so far advanced as to allow of the removal of the lights. Put them at thirty inches apart down the middle of the bed, and when growing freely, nip out the points *once only*. A crop of Lettuce may be taken from the beds while the plants are advancing.

DANDELION

(*Taraxacum officinale*)

DANDELION has become popular as a salad, its wholesome quality insuring for it general esteem. Nature teaches us the way to grow this plant, for she sows the seed early in the summer, and we find the finest plants on the dry ground, and there are absolutely none to be found in the bogs and swamps. Any gravelly or chalky soil will grow good Dandelion, one fair digging without manure being a sufficient preparation for it. Sow in May or June, and thin to one foot apart every way; keeping the crop scrupulously clean by flat hoeing. Any time in the winter the roots may be lifted and forced in the same way as Sea Kale, or they may be covered with pots in spring to blanch where grown. In any case the spring growth must be made in the dark, for when green the flavour is bitter. Invalids who require this salutary salad may obtain early supplies by planting the roots in boxes in a cellar, and covering with empty boxes turned over them. Only as much water should be given as will keep the roots reasonably moist.

EGG PLANT

(Solanum esculentum, S. melongena ovigerum)

THE EGG PLANT is generally known only as an ornament, but it is a delicious vegetable when sliced and fried in oil, the purple and black fruited kinds being especially serviceable for the table. But the common white, which is best known as an ornamental plant, is fairly good when cooked young, though less rich in flavour than the purple. The cultivation recommended for the ornamental Capsicums will suit the Egg Plants. They are not well adapted for planting out, although in a warm season they will fruit freely under a sunny wall, and will grow in a gravel walk if helped at first with a little good soil round the roots. If required in quantity for the table, the common purple sort might be grown in a frame from plants raised on a hotbed. Generally speaking, a few plants in pots are all that are required where the fruit is not valued as an esculent.

ENDIVE

(Cichorium Endivia)

ENDIVE has advanced in public esteem within the past few years, owing perhaps to a growing taste for wholesome salads, and also, no doubt, to the recurrence of severe winters that have destroyed Lettuces in open quarters. Moreover, the flavour of well-blanched Endive suits most palates that have had experience of salads, and of the salutary properties of the plant we have a hint in its close relation to the Chicory.

The selection of sorts is a question of importance, because the handsome curled varieties that make the best appearance on the table (and might be regarded as ornaments if they were not edible) are the very finest for salads, being tender, and with a fresh nutty flavour. The broad-leaved sorts are not so well adapted for salads as for stews, and they admirably take the place of Lettuces when the latter are not available for soups and ragouts. However, when an emergency occurs, the curled varieties will be found suitable for cooking, and the broad-leaved for salading, and therefore there need be no waste where one sort predominates.

A difficulty common to Endive culture may be got over in the way advised for Celeriac. The plant requires a light, dry, sandy soil; and a portion, at least, of the crop is expected to stand through the winter. Thus on a heavy soil there is a prospect of failure in respect of the late crop, but that is obviated by adopting a made bed—one of smallish dimensions being sufficient to accommodate a large stock of plants. Select an open spot, make a foundation of any hard rubbish that is at hand, and on this put one to two feet of sandy soil. This will form a raised bed of a kind exactly suited to the plant, and will cost but little as compared with its ultimate value. If regularly dressed with manure, and otherwise well managed, the bed will supply Endive in winter and other salads in summer, or it may be cropped with Kidney Beans, which can be removed in August to make way for the usual planting of Endive. Where the soil is naturally light and dry, no such preparation is needed, but Endive does not come to perfection without food, and therefore the soil should be rich and deeply dug.

The seed may be sown as early as March, in a moderate heat, but the latter part of April is early enough for most purposes, and the main sowings are made in June. Later sowings may be made in July and August. But the June sowing is the most important, as by a little careful management it may be made to supply a few early heads and many late ones. Sow in drills an inch deep and six inches apart, and when the plants are an inch high draw the forwardest, and prick them out on a bed of rich light soil in the same way as Celery, and with a little nursing these will make a first plantation. The plants in the seed-bed should be thinned to three inches, and must have water in dry weather. All the thinnings should be pricked out in the first instance to make them strong for planting, but the last lot may go direct to the beds to finish.

The final planting must be on rich, light, dry soil, and water must be given to encourage growth. The distance for the curled varieties is a foot each way, and for the broad-leaved fifteen inches. Sutton's Incomparable may have eighteen inches on strong ground, and it is equally adapted for cooking and salading. In taking the last lot from the seed-bed for planting, a crop should be left to mature without being moved at all; these may be left twelve to fifteen inches apart, and they will give a first and most excellent supply if carefully blanched.

The blanching is an important business, and is variously performed. The customary mode is to tie the leaves together and mould them up to a point, and this answers perfectly, except in wet seasons, when, if the plants stand for some time, the outer leaves begin to rot, and the decay proceeds inwards, to the deterioration or destruction of the plant. A clean and effectual method consists in tying the top of the plant, leaving room for the centre to swell, and then covering with empty pots, which must be pressed down firmly on the earth, and the hole covered with a piece of tile or slate, on which should be laid a piece of turf or a handful of mould. In some gardens coal ashes are used instead of earth to pack round the plants, and they offer the advantage of dryness. But the plants may be blanched without any covering at all, the leaves being first tied over rather tightly at the top, and a week after another tying should be made lower down. The blanching must be carried on in such a way as to insure a succession without a glut at any time, for when sufficiently blanched Endive should be used, or decay will soon set in.

GARLIC

(*Allium sativum*)

THE mode of culture advised for Shallots will suit Garlic also, except that the latter should be planted in February about two inches beneath the surface of the soil, and the bulbs may be grown closer together, about eight or nine inches apart each way.

GOURDS and PUMPKINS

(*Cucurbita*)

THESE may be grown to perfection by precisely the same method as recommended for Ridge Cucumbers; but as they will occupy more space, room must be left for them to extend beyond the limits of the ridge southwards. It is well to put out strong plants from pots and protect them until established, but if these are not obtainable, the seed may be sown where the plants are to stand, and there will in time be plenty of produce, but of course somewhat later in the season than if strong plants had been put out in the first instance. Keep a sharp look-out for slugs, which will flock in from all quarters to feast upon them, but will scarcely touch them after they have been planted a week or so. Any rough fermenting material, such as grass mowings, may be used in making the hills, to give them the aid of a warm bed for a brief space of time, for it is a great gain if they grow freely from the first, and the natural heat will soon be enough for them.

The edible Gourds are useful in all their stages and ages; and if the cultivator has a fancy to grow large, handsome fruits, he can make the business answer by hanging them up for use in winter, when they may be employed in soups in place of Carrots, or in addition to the usual vegetables, and may indeed be cooked in half a dozen different ways. There remains yet one more purpose to which the plants may be applied: supposing you have a great plantation of edible Gourds and Marrows, and would like a peculiarly elegant and delicious dish of Spinach, make a dish by pinching off a sufficiency of the tops of the advancing shoots, and cook them Spinach fashion. If properly done, it is one of the finest vegetables ever eaten. As pinching off the tender tops of the shoots lessens the fruitfulness of the vines, we only recommend this procedure where there is a large plantation.

Gourds may be trained to trellises, fences, and walls. In all such cases, a good bed should be prepared of any light, rich loam, and it will be none the less effective if made on a mound of fermenting material.

HERBS

THE growing of SWEET HERBS from seed may be practised with advantage where the demand for herbs is constant, as it is far easier than raising plants from slips and cuttings, and insures to the cultivator vigorous and true stocks of the several varieties. It is not wise to grow large collections of herbs, for there are not a great number now required for household purposes, and land and time can be more profitably employed. On the other hand, the herbs that retain their ancient popularity are more frequently used than ever they were, for the good reason that people have learned to live well, and the cooks are bound to call upon the gardeners for Mint and Thyme, and Savory and Basil; for Borage, Lavender, Tarragon, and Marjoram. A few of the popular herbs, such as Mint, are never grown from seed, or, at all events, those who venture on the pastime might certainly do better. But a certain number—such, for example, as Basil, Borage, Burnet, Chervil, Dill, Fennel, Marjoram, Marigold, and certain others—are grown from seed, in some cases of necessity, and in others because it is the easiest way of insuring a crop. They nearly all agree in requiring a dry soil and a sunny situation. Mint and Angelica need a moist soil, but the majority of the aromatic herbs make a better growth on a somewhat poor, sandy soil, than in the rich moist borders that prevail in the kitchen garden. Happily they are not very particular, but sunshine they must have for the manufacture of their fragrant essences. Generally speaking, it will be best to sow the seeds in March or April on a fine surface, where the plants are to remain. A border marked off in drills across at one foot apart will answer very well, because as the plants rise they can be thinned out to suit their several habits, and the thinnings of those wanted in quantity may be planted out elsewhere. To thin in good time, to keep clear of weeds, to plant as needs suggest, and to allow every sort sufficient space for development—these are the main points in the management of the Herb Garden.

HORSE-RADISH

(*Cochlearia Armoracia*)

THIS vegetable is highly prized as a condiment to roast beef, but as a rule it is badly grown. The common practice is to consign it to some neglected corner of the garden, where it struggles for existence, and produces sticks which are almost worthless for the table. In the same space a plentiful supply of large handsome sticks may be grown with as little trouble as Carrots or Parsnips. Choose for the crop a piece of good open ground, and in preparing it place a heavy dressing of rotten manure quite at the bottom of each trench. Early in the year select young straight roots from eight to twelve inches long, each having a single crown, and plant them one foot apart each way. By the following autumn these will become large succulent sticks, which will put to shame the ugly striplings grown under starving conditions. The roots may be dug as required; but we do not advocate that method. It is better practice to clear the whole bed at once, and store the produce in sand for use when wanted. This plan should be repeated each year, and a fresh piece of land ought always to be found for the crop.

INDIAN CORN, or MAIZE
(Zea Mays)

MAIZE is a tender plant of great beauty, that may be grown as a table vegetable, a forage plant, or a corn crop, but in the last-named capacity it is rarely profitable in this country owing to the brevity of our summers. As an ornamental plant it is entitled to consideration, and the more so because while adorning the garden with its noble outlines and splendid silken tufts, it will at the same time supply to the table the green cobs that are so much valued when cooked and served in the same manner as Asparagus.

There is a simple rough and ready way of growing Maize, the first step towards which is to prepare a deep rich soil, in a sunny and sheltered situation. Late in April or early in May, dibble, fully five inches deep, the seeds of Maize in rows three feet asunder and one foot apart in the row. When the plants have made some progress, remove every other one, these thinnings to be destroyed or planted at discretion, as young Maize transplants as well as anything. The plantation will almost take care of itself, for the plant is of the most thrifty habit when the weather is warm enough to suit it. But a deluge of water may be given during the hottest weather to great advantage, for in its native country, and indeed wherever it thoroughly thrives, it will be found to depend largely on frequent storms. In good soil, with a vigorous variety, especially in a hot moist season, the rows for the planted-out crop should be four feet apart, and the plants three feet, and then they will pleasantly rustle their leaves together.

KALE (*See* BORECOLE, *page* 23)

KNOL KOHL
(*Brassica oleracea Caulo-rapa*)

KOHL RABI OR KNOL KOHL is thought little of in this country, because we can almost always command tender and tasty Turnips. But on the Continent it is otherwise. There we see Kohl Rabi in every vegetable market, and on many a good table, where it proves a most acceptable vegetable. For all ordinary purposes the green variety is better than the purple. A small crop of this root should be annually grown in every garden, as in case of failure with Turnips it will take their place to tide over an emergency. When served as a vegetable, it has the flavour of a Turnip with a somewhat nutty tendency. The cooks who understand this root boil it with the rind on until tender; the rind is then removed, and the roots are cut into halves or quarters, and served with white sauce.

Kohl Rabi is adapted for heavy soils, on which Turnips are sometimes troublesome. The seed is sown in March or April, and as soon as possible thinned to three inches apart. Further thinnings are planted out in rows a yard apart, and the plants two feet apart in the rows, and they must be planted shallow to encourage the roots to swell above ground. A crop to mature should be left in the seed-bed at any distance, provided the leaves do not overlap. By this mode of management some nice roots of small size may be secured quite early in the season, and they must be drawn directly their leaves meet, to give more and more room to those that are to remain. The hoe must be used here, as also amongst the planted lots, to keep the ground clean and the surface open, but care must be taken not to damage the leaves, or in the least degree to earth up the roots. Any animal that can eat a Turnip will prefer a Knol Kohl, and while it takes the place of the Turnip in feeding cows, it does not affect the flavour of the milk. It is also hardy, and as a rule the roots may stand, to be drawn as wanted, until the spring is far advanced, when they should be cleared off for the benefit of the animals on the home farm, or be dug in as manure.

LEEK

(*Allium Porrum*)

THE LEEK is not appreciated in the southern parts of England as it is in the north, and in Scotland and Wales. It is a fine vegetable where it is well understood, and when stewed in gravy there is nothing of its class that can surpass it in flavour and wholesomeness. One reason of its fame in Scotland and the colder parts of Wales is its exceeding hardiness, for the severest winters do not harm the plant, and it may remain in the open ground until wanted, occasioning no trouble for storage.

There may be three sowings of Leek made in the open ground in February, March, and April, to insure a succession, and also to make good any failures. But for most gardens one sowing about the middle of March will be sufficient, as from this sowing it will be an easy matter to secure an early supply, a main crop and a late crop, for they may be transplanted from the seed-bed at a very early stage, and successive thinnings will make several plantations, and finally, as many may be left in the seed-bed to mature as will form a proper plantation.

The Leek will grow in any soil, and when no thicker than the finger is useful; indeed, in many places where the soil is poor and the climate cold it is rarely seen of a larger size, but is, nevertheless, greatly valued. A rich dry soil suits the plant well, and when liberally grown it attains to a great size, and is very attractive, with its silvery root and brilliant green top. The prudent course of management consists in thinning and planting as opportunities occur, beginning as soon as the plants are six inches high, and putting them in well-prepared ground, which should be thoroughly watered previously, unless already softened by rain. The distance must depend on the nature of the ground and the wants of the cultivator. To grow large Leeks in strong ground, they must be quite a foot apart, but for a crop of small useful roots six inches will suffice. In planting, first shorten the leaves a little (and very little), then drive down the dibber, and put the plant in as deep as the base of the leaves, and close in carefully without pressure. Water liberally, and occasionally stir the ground between, and again cut off the tops of the leaves, and the roots will grow to a large size. If the ground is dangerously damp or pasty, make a bed for the crop with light rich soil, and plant on the level and mould up as the growth advances. On light land, however, it is advisable to grow them in trenches, prepared as for Celery, but the Leeks need not be earthed up. The largest and whitest should not be left to battle with storms, but those left in the seed-bed will take no harm from winter weather, and will be useful when the grandees are eaten up. The finest roots that remain when winter sets in may be taken up in good time and stored in dry sand, and will keep for at least a month. Any that remain over in spring can be turned to account to supply a delicate and comparatively unknown vegetable. As the flower stems rise nip them out, not one should be left. The result of this practice will be the formation on the roots of small roundish white bulbs, which make an excellent dish when stewed in gravy, and may be used for any purpose in cookery for which Onions or Shallots are usually employed. They are called 'Leek Bulbs,' and are obtainable only in early summer.

LETTUCE

(*Lactuca sativa*)

THE LETTUCE is the king of salads, and as a cooked vegetable it has its value; but as it does not compete with the Pea, the Asparagus, or the Cauliflower, we need not make comparisons, but may proceed to the consideration of its uses in the uncooked state. The scientific advisers on diet and health esteem the Lettuce highly for its antiscorbutic properties, and for its especial wholesomeness as a corrective, supplying as it does the blood with vegetable juices that are so needful to accompany flesh foods when cooked vegetables are unattainable. Our summers are usually too brief and too cool to permit us to acquire a true knowledge of the uses of the Lettuce, but in Southern Europe and many parts of the East it acquires the importance of a necessary of life, and those large red Lettuces that are occasionally grown here as curiosities are prized above all others because of their crisp coolness and refreshing flavour under a burning sun.

The numerous varieties may, for practical purposes, be grouped in two classes—Cabbage and Cos Lettuces. They vary greatly in habit and are adapted for different purposes, the first group being invaluable for mixed salads at all seasons, but more especially in winter and early spring; the second group is most serviceable in the summer season, and is adapted for a simple kind of salad, the leaves being more crisp and juicy. A certain number of both classes should be grown in every garden, both for their exceeding usefulness to appetite and health, and their elegance on the table, whether plain or dressed. In the selection of sorts, leading types should be kept in view, as in departing from these types for the mere sake of variety or novelty we are likely to be rewarded for our waywardness by securing bad Lettuces. Some of the varieties produced of late years have no claim to a place in a good list, for their size is a sign of coarseness, and if they afford a great bulk of blanched material, it is too often destitute of flavour, or altogether objectionable. The best types are tender and delicately flavoured, representing centuries of cultivation and selection, and the sub-varieties of these types should retain their leading characteristics, though perhaps they are more hardy and stand longer, and are therefore much to be desired. For the earliest crop we suggest Commodore Nutt, Dwarf Brown Forcing, and Tom Thumb, which produce compact Lettuces of good flavour in a few weeks. These to be followed by Superb White Cos and others of that class. Marvel will make a good succession, with Standwell to come in finally.

The Lettuce requires a light, rich soil, but almost any kind of soil may be so prepared as to insure a fair supply, and in places where fine Cos Lettuces are not readily obtained, it may be possible to grow excellent Cabbage varieties in place of them. A tolerably good garden soil will answer for both classes, and fat stable manure should be liberally used. The best way to prepare ground for the summer crop is to select a piece that has been trenched, and go over it again, laying in a good body of rough green manure, one spade deep, so that the plant will be put on unmanured ground, but will reach the manure at the very period when it is needed, and by which time contact with the earth will have rendered it sweet and mellow. By this mode of procedure the finest growth is secured, and the plants stand well without bolting, as they are saved from the distress consequent on continued dry weather. As regards drought, it must be said that the red-leaved kinds stand remarkably well in a hot summer, and although they do not rank high as table Lettuces in this country, were we to be regularly favoured with roasting summers they would rise in repute and be in great demand. Cabbage Lettuces bear drought fairly well, more especially the diminutive section; but where water is available in a dry, hot season, the Lettuces have as good a claim to a share of it as any crop in the garden. To complete this paragraph, it will be proper to say a few words on the subject of blanching. A first-class strain of White Cos Lettuce will produce tender white hearts without being tied, and, as a rule, therefore, the labour of tying may be saved. The section of which Sutton's Superb White Cos is the type may be said to produce better samples without tying than with this imaginary aid in the finishing. Hence, if tying is practised to please all parties, it need not be done until one or two days before the Lettuces are cut. The market grower must tie his Lettuces, because he cannot sell them unless there is a rope around each to prove that it is a Lettuce. The coarser market kinds certainly are improved by tying, and in this case the operation must be performed when the plants are quite dry, and not more than ten days in advance of the day on which it is intended to pull them. The Bath Cos must be tied always, and when well managed the heart is quite white, with a pretty touch of pink in the centre.

SPRING-SOWN LETTUCES may be forwarded under glass from January to March, from which time sowings may be made successively in the open ground. In any and every case the finest Lettuces are obtained by sowing in the open ground, and leaving the plants to finish in the seed-bed without being transplanted. It will, of course, occur to the practical cultivator that the two systems may be combined, so as to vary the time of turning in, and thus from a single sowing insuring a longer succession than is possible by one system only. We will suppose small sowings made of three or four sorts in January or early in February, and put into a gentle heat to start them. A very little care will keep them going nicely, and of course they must have light and air to any extent commensurate with safety. When about three weeks old, it will be advisable to prick these out into a bed of light rich earth in frames; or if the season is backward, and they need a little more nursing, prick them into large shallow boxes, containing two or three inches of soil, which will be sufficient provided it consists in great part of decayed manure, kept always moist enough for healthy growing. The next step will be to plant them out six inches apart, with a view to draw a certain number as soon as they are large enough to be useful, leaving the remainder at nine to twelve inches, taking care always to thin out in time to prevent any leaves overlapping. Successive sowings made in February and March will be treated in the same way, and will need less nursing. In planting out, it is important to have the plants well hardened, for they are naturally susceptible of wind and sunshine, and if suddenly exposed to either will be likely to perish. And again, when first planted out their delicate leaves will attract all the slugs and snails in the garden, and the discreet way of acting is to regard a plantation of Lettuce as an extensive vermin trap, and thus, knowing where the marauders are, to be ready to catch and kill, or to destroy them by sprinklings of lime, salt, or soot, in all cases being careful to keep these agents at a reasonable distance from the plants.

Sowings in the open ground should be made, not on an ordinary seed-bed, but on a plot well loaded with rich manure at one spit deep, and the seed should be put in drills one foot apart and one inch deep, and from the time the young plants are two inches high they must be drawn freely for 'Cutting Lettuce,' or for planting out elsewhere; this thinning to proceed until a sufficient crop remains to finish off on the ground. The uses of 'Cutting Lettuce' are better known on the Continent than here, as the small tender plants form part of the every-day stock of the itinerant greengrocer, and appear subsequently in the salad bowl with Water Cress and Corn Salad, delicately dressed, with delicious flavourings. In any case a crowded Lettuce crop is an encumbrance to the ground; and one of the evils of the best system, that of sowing where the crop is to finish, is the tendency of the cultivator to be timid in the thinning, which should be done with a bold hand, and in good time.

WINTER LETTUCES are produced and provided for in various ways. In some places Lettuces stand out the winter without covering, and turn in early in the spring. But in other districts Lettuces seldom survive the winter without protection. The summer sowings will afford supplies to a late season of the year, and the crop that remains when frost sets in may be preserved with slight and rough protection. But for profitable production of Winter Lettuces we must have the aid of frames, and care must be taken not to promote a strong growth, for after a term of mild winter weather a sudden and severe frost will probably annihilate those that are in a too thriving condition. In the least likely places, however, it is well to have a small plantation of Winter Lettuces in the open, and to give some rough protection in bad times, as these often prove of great advantage, and even outlive frame crops which have been allowed to get too forward by the aid of warmth and a rich soil. The Hammersmith Cabbage Lettuce, which has no flavour, and the Bath Cos, which is of excellent quality, rank high for their usefulness as hardy Lettuces; but All the Year Round will brave a certain amount of winter weather without harm, if on a dry bottom, and assisted with occasional protection. The best of all the Winter Lettuces, however, is the popular Black-seeded Bath Cos, which is used in almost every good garden, and is rarely injured by frost.

The June sowings may be considered the last of the summer crop. In August we begin for the winter crop, and sow small lots successively until the middle of October, after which it is waste of time and seed to sow any more. The August and September sowings may be made partly on an open border and partly in frames, but the October sowings must be in frames only, for winter may overtake them in the seed-leaf. The seedlings must in all cases be thinned and pricked out as soon as large enough, and should be planted in fine soil, free from recent manure, being carefully handled to avoid needless check. Some should be planted in frames on beds of light soil near the glass at three inches apart, and when these meet they must be thinned for the house as may be necessary; the remainder of the thinnings may be put out on warm borders at six inches, and, if quite convenient, a crop should be left in the seed-bed at six inches. From the frames, the supplies will be ready in time to follow those from late summer sowings, and thus through the winter until the frames are cleared out for the work of the spring. The frame crop must have plenty of air, and be kept as hardy as possible, but with moisture enough to sustain a steady healthy growth. If roughly handled in the planting, or a little starved in respect of moisture, the plants will rise from the centre just when they ought to begin to turn in, and the first few days of warm sunshine will start them in the wrong way. As to those wintered out, there are many ways of protecting them, and when success has crowned the effort there will be a crowded plant. It will be necessary, therefore, to transplant at least half the crop by lifting every other one. This must be done with care, as though they were worth a guinea each. By transplanting early in March to a piece of rich light ground in a warm spot, and doing the work neatly and smartly, the result will be a valuable crop of early Summer Lettuce, while those that remain will help through the spring.

Lettuces do not force well; but as they are so constantly in demand, it is a matter of importance to grow them in every possible way. Nice promising plants from August and September sowings may be selected from the frames, and planted on gentle hot-beds from November to January, and will do well if tenderly lifted. The Commodore Nutt and Dwarf Brown Forcing are the best of the Cabbage varieties for forcing; the Hammersmith is not worth the trouble. The Cos varieties do not differ much as to forcing, none of them being well adapted for the purpose; but the Superb White and Green Cos may be brought to fine condition by taking time enough, so as to make a very moderate warmth suffice. On sunny days the heat should not exceed 75°; but 65° is sufficient, with a night temperature of 45° to 50°.

MAIZE (*See* INDIAN CORN, *page* 62)

MELON

(*Cucumis Melo*)

THE MELON has advanced in public favour considerably of late years, the consequence in part of the spread of knowledge as to the treatment it requires, and in part also owing to the improvement that has been effected in the quality of the fruit. It would shock a modern Melon eater to be advised to cook a Melon, and flavour it with vinegar and salt, as in the early days of English gardening. A good Melon of the present day does not even need the aid of sugar to help it along; the beauty, aroma, and flavour are such that it is not unusual for the epicure to push the luscious Pine aside in order to enjoy this cool, fresh, gratifying fruit that delights without cloying the palate. The newer varieties are remarkable alike for fruitfulness and high quality, and are somewhat hardier than the favourites of years gone by. But we are bound to warn our readers that all the so-called 'hardy' Melons are comparatively worthless if hardy, or comparatively tender if worth a place in the garden. A first-class hardy Melon is at present unknown.

The Melon is grown in much the same way as the Cucumber, but it differs in requiring a firmer soil, a higher temperature, a much stronger light, less water, and more air. It may be said that no man should attempt to grow Melons until he has had some experience in growing Cucumbers. As regards this point, the hard and fast line is useless, but Cucumber-growing is certainly a good practical preparative for the higher walk wherein the Melon is found. But Cucumbers are grown advantageously all the winter through, and Melons are not. The first are eaten green, and the second are eaten ripe; this makes all the difference. Melons that are ripened between October and May are seldom worth the trouble bestowed upon them; therefore we shall say nothing about growing Melons in winter.

THE FRAME CULTURE may advantageously begin about the middle of March by the preparation of a good hot-bed. It is best to use a three-light frame, as the heat will be more constant than with one of smaller size. There should be six loads of stuff laid up for the bed, and the turning should be sufficient to take out the fire, without materially reducing the fermenting power. Begin a fortnight in advance of making up the bed, and be careful at every stage to do things well, as advised for the cultivation of frame Cucumbers. The best soil for Melons is a firm, turfy loam. In a clay district, a certain amount of clay pulverised by frost may be chopped over with turfy loam from an old pasture. If the soil is poor, decayed manure may be added, but the best possible Melons may be grown in a fertile loam without the aid of manures or stimulants of any kind. It is good practice to raise the plants in pots, and have them strong enough to plant out as soon as the newly-made beds have settled down to a steady temperature of about 80°, but below 70° will be unsafe. If plants cannot be prepared in advance, the seed must be sown on the bed, and twice as many should be sown as will be wanted, as a precaution against accidents and to permit of the removal of the weakest.

As regards the bed, it may be made once and for all at the time of planting, a few days being allowed for warming the soil through. But we much prefer to begin with smallish hillocks, or with a thin sharp ridge raised so as almost to touch the lights, and to plant or sow on this ridge, which can be added to from time to time as the plants require more root room. The soil, coming fresh and fresh, sustains a vigorous and healthy root action, which is of the first importance. The high ridge favours the production of stout leaves, and the absorption by the soil of sun-heat, which to the Melon is more than either soil, or water, or air.

The practice of pruning Melons as if they were fodder plants, and might be chopped at for supplies of herbage, is much in vogue, and must be heartily condemned. Melons should never be so crowded as to necessitate cutting out, except in a quite trivial manner. A free and vigorous plant is needed, and it will rarely happen that there is a single leaf anywhere that can be spared. We will propose a practical rule that we have followed in growing Melons for seed—a business of great importance, and on which a large crop of the most perfect fruits is absolutely needful to insure a fair return. The young plants are pinched when there are two rough leaves. The result is two side shoots. These are allowed to produce six or seven leaves, and are then pinched. After this, the plants are permitted to run, and there is no more pinching or pruning until there is a visible crop. Then the fruits that are to remain must be selected, and the shoots be pinched to one eye above each fruit, and only one fruit should remain on a shoot, the others must be removed a few at a time. All overgrowth must be guarded against, for crowded plants will be comparatively worthless. It is not by rudely cutting out that crowding is to be prevented, but by timely pinching out every shoot that is likely to prove superfluous. From first to last there must be a regular plant, and not a shoot should be allowed to grow that is not wanted. Cutting out may produce canker, and crowding results in sterility.

As the Melon is required to ripen its fruits, and the Cucumber is not, the treatment varies in view of this difference. It is not necessary to fertilise the female flowers of the Cucumber, but it is certainly desirable, if not absolutely necessary, to operate on those of the Melon to insure a crop. The early morning, when the leaves are dry and the sun is shining, is the proper time for this task, which is simple enough and well understood. And the necessity for ripening the crop marks another difference of management, for we may allow Cucumber plants to carry many fruits, and to continue producing them until the plants are exhausted. But we must limit the production of Melons to about half a dozen on each plant, and good management requires that these should all ripen at the same time, or nearly so, fully exposed to the sun, and with plenty of ventilation.

The giving of water is an important matter. The plant must never be dry at the root, and must have a light shower twice a day over the leafage, but must never be so moist as is allowable with Cucumbers, and must have dry leaves oftener than wet. It is a golden rule to grow Melons liberally, keeping them sturdy by judicious air-giving, and to give them a little extra watering just as they are coming into flower. Then, as the flowers open, the watering at the root should be discontinued, and the syringe should be used in the evening only at shutting up. If discontinued entirely, red spider will appear, and the crop will be in jeopardy, for that pest can only be kept at a distance by careful management of atmospheric moisture.

Melons in frames do better spread out on the beds than when trained on trellises. When so grown, each fruit must be supported with a flat tile or an inverted flower-plot, and means must be taken, by pegs or otherwise, to prevent it from rolling off, for the twist of stem that ensues may check the fruit or cause it to fall. When the fruits are as large as the top joint of a man's thumb, watering may be resumed, and the syringe may be used twice a day until the fruit begins to change colour, when there must be a return to the dry system, but with care not to carry it to a dangerous extreme.

THE MELON-HOUSE, heated by hot water, is adapted to supply fruit earlier than it is obtainable by frame culture, and is entirely superior to any frame or pit. It appears, however, that in Melon-houses red spider is more often seen than in frames heated by fermenting material; but this point rests on management, and there can be nothing more certain than that a reasonable employment of atmospheric humidity may be made effectual for preventing and removing this pest. For the convenient management of the crop, a lean-to or half-span is to be preferred. The width should not exceed twelve feet, and ten to twelve feet should be the utmost height of the roof.

A service of pipes under the bed will be required; but as we do not attempt to grow Melons in winter, the heating of a Melon-house is a simple affair, and, indeed, very much of the cultivation as the summer advances will be carried on by the aid of sun heat only. The management of the plants in a house differs from the frame management, because a trellis is employed, and the plants are taken up the trellis without stopping until they nearly reach the top, when the points are pinched out to promote the growth of side shoots. In regard to setting the fruit, the same principles prevail as in frame culture, and it is advisable to 'set' the whole crop at once, because if two or three fruits obtain a good start, others that are set later will drop off. As the fruits swell, support must be afforded to prevent any undue strain on the vine, and this should be accomplished by suspending small flat boards of half-inch deal with copper wires, each fruit resting on its board, until the cracking round the stem gives warning that the fruit should be cut and placed in the fruit room for a few days to complete the ripening for the table. In houses of this kind, Melons and Cucumbers are occasionally grown together. But although this may be done, and there are many cultivators expert in the business, the practice cannot be recommended, for ships that sail near the wind will come to grief some day. The moisture and partial shade that suit the Cucumber do not suit the Melon, and it is a poor compromise to make one end of the house shady and moist, and the other end sunny and dry, to establish different conditions with one atmosphere. A glass partition pretty well disposes of the difficulty, for this insures two atmospheres for two different operations.

MUSHROOM

(*Agaricus campestris*)

PERHAPS it would be scarcely accurate to say that the Mushroom is universally esteemed in the mansion and in the cottage; but it certainly has many friends among all classes, few benevolent neutrals, and fewer still who are absolutely hostile to it as an article of food. Those who find, or imagine they find, that this delicacy does not agree with them, might possibly arrive at another conclusion were a different mode of preparation adopted, or were the consumption of it accompanied with a full persuasion that the Mushroom is not merely delicious in flavour, but thoroughly wholesome, rich in flesh-forming constituents, and, for a vegetable, possessed of more than the average proportion of fat-formers and minerals. These facts have been clearly established by chemical analysis, and may dispose of timid misgivings, always supposing the true edible Mushroom, *Agaricus campestris*, to be in question.

Hitherto the artificial production of Mushrooms has never been equal to the demand. Notwithstanding the enormous quantities sent to Covent Garden by the growers around London, many tons are imported from France, although it is generally admitted that they are neither so fine nor so rich in flavour as those produced in this country. If, however, the large centres of population are inadequately supplied, the scarcity of Mushrooms is more keenly felt in the provinces, except perhaps in certain favoured districts, where, after a few warm days in autumn, an abundant crop may be gathered from the neighbouring pastures. Then there is a brave show in the greengrocers' windows for a brief period, followed by entire dearth for weeks and perhaps months. Obviously, therefore, the demand, large as it already is, might be immensely augmented by a commensurate supply. Yet it is not only possible but quite easy to grow Mushrooms for the greater part of the year in very small gardens, even when such gardens are entirely destitute of the appliances generally considered necessary for the higher flights of horticulture. The idea that Mushroom-growing is somewhat of a mystery, forbidden to all but the strictly initiated, has happily been dispelled. If we examine the conditions under which Mushrooms grow freely in pastures, it is surprising how few and simple are the elements of success. The crop generally appears in September, when temperature is genial and fairly equable, with sufficient but not superabundant moisture. The artificial production of Mushrooms in the garden needs only reliable spawn, a sweet, fertile bed, and some means of maintaining a steady temperature under varying atmospheric conditions. When the principles of Mushroom culture are thoroughly mastered, they may be successfully applied in many different ways, and they render the practical work easy and tolerably certain.

Although the Mushroom may be grown from seed, it is seldom done except for strictly scientific purposes. The seeds are, however, largely disseminated by Nature, and, having found a suitable home, they germinate and produce an underground growth which at a hasty glance resembles mildew. It really consists of white gossamer-like films, which increase in number and distinctness as they develop, until they push their way towards the surface, and give rise to the growth above ground of the Mushroom. It follows that if we do not begin the cultivation with seeds or spores, we must resort to the employment of the white films or 'mycelium,' that the growth of the plant may begin in Nature's own way below ground. What is called 'Mushroom Spawn' consists of certain materials from the stable and the field, mixed and prepared in a way to favour the growth of the mycelium of the Mushroom, its appearance being that of an unburnt brick. The preparation of the spawn, though a very simple matter, demands the skill and care of experienced operators ; for if the work is not well done, the spawn will be of poor quality, and will yield a meagre crop, or perhaps fail entirely to produce a single Mushroom. When the spawn is good, it has but to be broken into lumps of a suitable size, and inserted in a bed of earth of the requisite quality, to impregnate the whole body of earth with the necessary white threads. These will take their time to collect from the soil the alkalies and phosphates of which Mushrooms principally consist, and this part of their work being done, the fruits of their labours will be displayed above ground in the elegant and sweet-smelling fungus that few human appetites can resist when it is placed upon the table in the way that it deserves. Experts can readily form an opinion as to whether a cake of Mushroom spawn is or is not in a fit state for planting, and it will be a safe proceeding for the amateur to buy from some House which has a large and constant sale ; otherwise spawn may be purchased which was originally well-made and properly impregnated, but has lost all its vitality through long keeping.

As to soil, it is well known that in a favourable autumn Mushrooms abound in old rich pastures, and those who have command of turves cut from a field of this character have only to stack the sods grass side downwards for a year or two, and they will be in possession of first-class material for Mushroom beds either in the open or under cover. But small gardens, particularly in towns, have no such bank to honour their drafts, and for these it becomes a question of buying a load or two of turfy loam, or of making the soil of the garden answer, perhaps with a preliminary enrichment by artificial manure. In the general interests of the garden, the money for a limited quantity of good loam would probably be well spent, independently of the question of Mushrooms. No great bulk is necessary to cover a moderate-sized Mushroom bed, but the quality of it will certainly have an influence on the number and character of the Mushrooms. As a proof of the exhaustive nature of the fungus, it almost invariably happens that when the soil is used a second time it tends to diminish the size and lower the quality of the crop.

In the management of the manure two essentials must be borne in mind. Not only is nourishment for the plant required, but warmth also. Probably a large proportion of the failures to grow Mushrooms might, if all the facts were known, be traced to some defect in the manure employed, or to some fault in its preparation. It must be rich in the properties which encourage and support the development of Mushrooms, absolutely free from the least objectionable odour, for the plant is most fastidious in its demand for sweetness, although it can dispense with light; and there must remain in the manure when made into a bed a sufficient reserve of fermentation to insure prolonged heat, no matter what the temperature of the atmosphere may be. Of course, the duration of the heat will depend very much on the care with which it is conserved by suitable covering and management. These requirements, formidable as they may seem, can be insured with extreme ease; indeed, the work is apparently far more difficult and complicated on paper than it proves to be in practice.

The manure should come from stables occupied by horses in good health, fed exclusively on hard food. The most suitable store is the floor of a dry shed, or under some protection which will prevent the loss of vital forces. Ammonia, for example, is readily dissipated in the atmosphere or washed away by rain. The manure should neither be allowed to become dust dry, nor to waste its power in premature fermentation. Operations may be commenced with three or four loads. A smaller quantity increases the difficulty of maintaining the requisite temperature when fermentation begins to flag. The first procedure is to make the manure into a high oblong heap well trodden down. If the stuff be somewhat dry, a sprinkling of water over every layer will be necessary. In a few days fermentation will make the heap hot all through, and then it must be taken to pieces and remade, putting all the outside portions into the interior with the object of insuring equal fermentation of the entire bulk. This process will have to be repeated several times at intervals of three or four days until the manure has not only been fermented but sweetened. When ready it will be of a dark colour, soft, damp enough to be cohesive under pressure, but not sufficiently damp to part with any of its moisture, and almost odourless; at all events the odour will not be objectionable, but may be suggestive of Mushrooms. Make a long bed, having a base about four feet wide, and sides sloping to a ridge like the roof of a house, with this difference —the narrow part of the ridge is useless, and the top should, therefore, be rounded off when about a foot across. Some growers prefer a circular bed of six or eight feet diameter at the bottom and tapering towards a point after the shape of a military tent; but here again the point will be worthless, and the bed may terminate abruptly. Either the long bed or the round heap answers admirably. Tread the manure down compactly, and for the sake of appearances endeavour to finish it off in a workmanlike manner. During the first few days there will be a considerable rise in the temperature, which will gradually subside, and when the plunging thermometer shows that it has settled down to a comfortable condition of about 80° the bed must be spawned. Experienced men can determine by the sense of touch when the temperature is right, but the inexperienced should rely entirely on the thermometer. Break the spawn into pieces as large as a turkey's egg, and force them gently a little way into the manure at regular intervals of nine or ten inches all over the bed, closing the manure over and round each piece of spawn. The practice of inserting spawn by means of the dibber is to be strongly condemned, for it leaves smooth, hollow places which arrest the mycelium; and very small pieces of spawn should be avoided because they generally result in small Mushrooms. Immediately the spawning is completed, a thick and even covering of clean straw or litter of some kind should be laid over the bed, secured from wind by canvas, mats, hurdles, or in some other way. Within a week the films of mycelium will begin to extend if the spawn be good. In the contrary case an examination of the pieces will show that they have become darker than when put into the bed, which means that they have perished. Then the question will arise as to whether the bed or the spawn is at fault, and the former must either be spawned again or broken up. Supposing the spawn to show signs of vitality, the time has come for covering the bed with a layer of rather moist soil, pressed lightly but firmly on to the manure with the spade or fork, so that the earth will not slip down. At once restore the covering of litter &c. and wait patiently for about seven or eight weeks for the crop. Meanwhile the plunging thermometer ought to be consulted daily. Until the Mushrooms appear the instrument should not indicate less than 60°, and while in bearing not less than 55°. Experience proves that the most violent alternations of temperature may be combated by regulating the thickness of the covering. Although it may possibly be necessary to resort to eighteen inches of litter or more during hard frost or the prevalence of a cutting east wind, a much thinner covering will suffice in milder weather.

The question will arise as to the period of the year when operations should be commenced. Well, the experts who grow Mushrooms in the open ground for market gather crops almost the year round; but a beginner will do wisely to start under the most favourable natural conditions, and these will be found about midsummer, because the bed will commence bearing before winter creates difficulty as to temperature. A rich firm bed, that has been well managed in the fermentation, will produce firm, handsome Mushrooms. A poor, loose bed will produce only lean, ugly Mushrooms. It is surprising to note the difference in samples as they are presented at exhibitions, and it is perhaps not less surprising that so many should be content with poor samples, when it is a very easy matter indeed, after a little practice, to produce the best. That the spawn has something to do with the final quality is well known, as this, for all practical purposes, may be regarded as the seed of the Mushroom.

It may happen in the first attempt that the temperature of the bed may, through inexperience in the management of it, sink below the point at which Mushrooms can grow, and then we advise the exercise of a little patience. We have known several instances of beds made in autumn producing no crop at the expected time, but which have borne fairly in the following spring or summer. But in the event of the first effort failing outright there is no great loss, for the most costly item—the manure—will still be available for the garden, and an observant man will pretty well understand in what respect he must amend his course of procedure.

Moisture is of great consequence, for a dry Mushroom bed will soon be barren also; but whenever water is given it must be applied tepid from a fine rose, for to slop cold water over a Mushroom bed is about as reasonable a procedure as putting ice into hot soup. Water is best administered in the afternoon of a genial day, and should be sufficient to saturate the bed. Immediately it is done the covering of litter and canvas must be promptly restored to prevent the temperature from being seriously lowered by rapid evaporation. A couple of stakes driven from the crown of the bed to the bottom of it at the time of making up the heap are useful as indicators of moisture, and may occasionally be drawn out and examined.

In gathering the crop, only a small portion of the bed should be uncovered at a time. This should be the rule at all seasons, and the strict observance of it will prevent a mistake in cold weather, for then if the bed is carelessly uncovered and much chilled, the crop will come to a stop, when perhaps it would, if properly handled, be at high tide and full of profit. Another rule should be enforced, to this effect, that every Mushroom must be taken out complete, and if the root does not come with the stem, it must be dug out with a knife. Any trifling with this rule will have to be paid for. The root of a Mushroom, if left in the ground, will produce nothing at all. But it may attract flies, and it certainly will interfere with the movements of the mycelium at that particular spot, and actually prevent the production of any more Mushrooms. The old practitioners were accustomed to leave the root in the ground, and they were content with about one-third of the crop that is now produced on beds that are perhaps not better made than theirs were. But they had a notion about the powers of the root which increased knowledge of the subject has shown to be fallacious.

The facility with which Mushrooms may be raised under simple methods is illustrated by the practice of growing them inside the turf walls of cool pits. In the country turf walls are common, and they offer the advantage of growing Mushrooms in addition to the purpose they usually serve. After determining the size of the pit, and accurately marking it on the ground, cut the turf into narrow strips, say three or four inches wide, and of exactly eighteen inches length. The strips should be closely laid, grass side downwards, across the width of the walls—not longitudinally—except at the corners, where the layers should cross each other. The front and back walls to be rather above the required height, because the turf always settles down a little, and the two ends must gradually rise from front to back. The top layer may be right side up, when it will keep green for a long time. As the work proceeds insert lumps of spawn at intervals in every layer, about three or four inches from the inside edge. A wooden frame will be requisite on the top to carry the glass lights. This structure makes a useful cool pit and a Mushroom bed, from which supplies may sometimes be gathered for years. In the summer it will be necessary to keep the walls moist by means of the syringe, or they will cease bearing.

But Mushrooms may be grown almost anywhere, even in a cellar, or on the wall of a warm stable, provided only that the mode of procedure is in a reasonable degree adapted to the requirements of the fungus. Ordinary pits and frames are also serviceable, and many gardeners obtain good crops in autumn by the simple process of inserting a few lumps of spawn in a Cucumber or Melon bed while the plants are still in bearing. Between spawning and cropping a period of six or eight weeks usually elapses, so that if the plan just mentioned be adopted, the spawn should be introduced in the height of summer, both to insure it a warm bed and to allow time for the crop to mature before the season runs out. Sheds and outhouses not only afford shelter and space for beds on the floor, but the walls may be fitted with shelves on which Mushrooms may be grown as plentifully as anywhere. In all cases the shelves should be two feet apart vertically, and each shelf should have a ledge nine inches deep. The walls of a house may be quickly and cheaply fitted with wood-work for the purpose, but brick is so much better than wood that whenever it is possible to employ brick it should have the preference. As regards the ledges, they should be of stout planking in any case, and should not be fixed because of the necessity for clearing the shelves and renewing the soil periodically. The details of cultivation are the same within doors as without, but the roof gives valuable protection, and helps to maintain the beds at a suitable temperature.

A proper Mushroom house for production during winter should be heated with hot water, and have an opaque roof. There is nothing so good for the crop as a roof of thatch, but there are many objections to it, and usually slate is employed. A double roof will pay for its extra cost by promoting an equable temperature. A few side lights fitted with shutters will be necessary, as there should be a good light for working purposes, but the crop does not need light, and a more steady temperature can be maintained in a dark house than in a light one. The most convenient dimensions for a Mushroom house are: length, twenty-five feet; width, twelve feet; height at sides, six feet, to allow of a bed on the floor, and a shelf four feet above it; the ridge rising sufficiently for head room, and to shoot off water. There will be room for a central path of four feet, and a bed of four feet on each side. An earth or tile floor and a slate or stone shelf will, with one four-inch flow and return pipe, complete the arrangements. The less wood and the less concrete the better; there is nothing like cheap porous red tiles for the floor and stone for the shelves, with loose planks on edge to keep up the soil, a few uprights being sufficient to hold them in their places.

Temperatures at every point are of great importance. The bed should be near 80° when the spawn is inserted. The air temperature requisite to the rising crop is 60° to 65°, which is the usual temperature of the season when Mushrooms appear in the meadows.

While the bed is bearing, a temperature of 55° will suffice, but at any point below this minimum production will be slow and may come to a stop. When giving water, take care that it is at a temperature rather above than below that of the bed.

MUSTARD

(*Sinapis alba, and S. nigra*)

MUSTARD is much valued as a pungent salad, and for mixing in the bowl it may take the place of Water Cress when the latter is not at command. Mustard is often sown with Cress, but it is bad practice, for the two plants do not grow at the same pace, and there is nothing gained by mixing them. The proper sort for salading is the common White Mustard, but Brown Mustard may be used for the purpose. Rape is employed for market work, but should be shunned in the garden. As the crop is cut in the seed-leaf, it is necessary to sow often, but the frequency must be regulated by the demand. Supplies may be kept up through the winter by sowing in shallow boxes, which can be put into vineries, forcing pits, and other odd places. Boxes answer admirably, as they can be put on the pipes if needful, and they favour the complete cutting of a crop without remainders, and that is of importance in the case of a vegetable that runs out of use so quickly and is so easily produced. From Lady Day to Michaelmas, Mustard may be sown on the open border with other saladings, but as the summer advances a shady place must be found for it.

ONION

(*Allium Cepa*)

THE ONION has the good fortune to be generally appreciated and well grown almost everywhere. It is an ancient root, and has warmed the hearts of many heroes, but its best claim to respect is that it enhances the flavour and digestibility of many important articles of food that would fail to nourish us without its aid, while to others it adds a zest that contributes alike to enjoyment and health. Although there are but few difficulties to be encountered in the cultivation of the Onion, there is a marked difference between a well-grown crop and one under poor management. There is moreover, what may be termed a fine art department in Onion culture, one result being special exhibitions, in which bulbs of great beauty and weight are brought forward in competition for the amusement and edification of the sight-seeing public. Thus when the first principles have been mastered, there may be, for the earnest cultivator of this useful root, many more things to be learned, and that may be worth learning, alike for their interest and utility.

The Onion can be grown on any kind of soil, but poor land must be assisted by liberal manuring. A soil that will not produce large Onions may produce small ones, and the smallest are acceptable when no others are to be had. But for handsome bulbs and a heavy crop we require a deep rich loam of a somewhat light texture, although an adhesive loam, or even a clay, may be improved for the purpose; while on a sandy soil excellent results may be obtained by good management, more especially in a wet season. In any case the soil must be well prepared by deep digging, breaking the lumps, and laying up in ridges to be acted on by the weather, and if needful its texture should be amended, as far as possible, at the same time. A coat of clay may be spread over a piece of sand, to be thoroughly incorporated with it, and, on the other hand, where the staple is clay, sand may be added advantageously. All such corrective measures yield an adequate return if prudently carried out, because Onions may be grown from year to year on the same ground; and thus in places where the soil is decidedly unsuitable a plot may be specially prepared for Onions, and if the first crop does not fully pay the cost, those that follow will do so. But the plant is not fastidious, and it is easy work almost anywhere to grow useful Onions. The first step in preparing land is to make it loose and fine throughout, and as much as possible to do this some time before the seed is sown. For sowing in spring, the beds should be prepared in the rough before winter, and when the time comes for levelling down and finishing, the top crust will be found well pulverised, and in a kindly state to receive the seed. Stagnant moisture is deadly to Onions, therefore swampy ground is most unfit; but a sufficient degree of dryness for a summer crop may often be secured by trenching, and leaving rather deep alleys between the beds to carry off surface water during heavy rains.

As almost any soil will suit the Onion, so also will almost any kind of manure, provided simply that it be not rank or offensive. This strongly flavoured plant likes good but sweet living, and it is sheer folly to load the ground for it with coarse and stimulating manures.

Yet it is often done, and the result is a stiff-necked generation of bulbs that refuse to ripen, or there may be complete failure of the crop through disease or plethora. But any fertiliser that is at hand, whether from the pigstye, or the sweepings of poultry yards or pigeon lofts, may be turned to account by the simple process of first making it into a compost with fresh soil, and then digging it in some time in advance of the season for sowing, and in reasonable but not excessive quantity. All such aids to plant growth as guano, charcoal, and well-rotted farmyard manure, may be used advantageously for the Onion crop; but there are two fertilisers of especial value, and costing least of any, that are universally employed by large growers, both to help the growth and prevent maggot and canker. These are soot and salt, which are sown together when the ground is finally prepared for the seed, and in quantity only sufficient to colour the ground. They exercise a magical influence, and those who make money by growing Onions take care to employ them as a necessary part of their business routine.

SPRING-SOWN ONIONS require to be put on rich, mellow ground, the top spit of which is of a somewhat fine texture, and at the time of sowing almost dry. Having been well dug and manured in good time, the top spit only should be dug over when it is finally made ready for the seed. The work must be done with care, and the beds should be marked off in breadths of four feet, with one-foot alleys between. Lumps must be broken with the spade, and the surface should be worked to a regular but very slight convex. A skilful workman will make it as even as if cast in a mould without once touching either rake or hoe. Light soil should be trodden over to consolidate it, and may then be just touched with the rake to improve the surface, when it is ready for the seed. Onions are sown in March and April at distances varying from six to twelve inches, according to the character of the sort and the size of bulbs required. The drills must be drawn across the bed, at right angles to the alleys, for when drawn the other way it is difficult to keep the ground properly weeded. Make the drills very shallow for ripe keeping Onions, but they may be two inches deep for thick-necked Onions that are to be used as Leeks, and the growth of the neck may be promoted as the plants grow by earthing them up. But for keeping Onions, the seed should be only just covered with fine earth taken from the alleys and thrown over, after which the drills must be lightly trodden, the surface again touched over with the rake, and if the soil is dry and works nicely, the business may be finished by gently patting the bed all over with the back of the spade. If the ground is damp or heavy, this final touch may be omitted, as the Onion makes a weak grass that cannot well push through earth that is caked over it. But speaking generally, an Onion bed newly sown should be like a long pie, and as smooth as if finished with a rolling-pin. To the beginner this will appear a protracted and complicated story, but the expert will attest that Onions require and will abundantly pay for special management, and if we do not begin well in the business we shall surely not end well.

As soon as possible after the crop is visible, the ground between should be delicately chopped over with the hoe to check the weeds that will then be rising. And immediately the rows are defined, a first thinning should be made with a two-inch hoe, care being taken to leave a good plant on the ground. The next thinning will produce young Onions for saladings, and this kind of thinning may be continued by removing plants equally all over the bed to insure an even crop, the final distance for bulbing being from three to six inches. The hoe must be kept at work between, for if weeds are allowed to make way, the crop will be seriously injured. When Onions are doing well, they lift themselves up and *sit* on the earth, needing light and air upon their bulbs to the very axis whence the roots diverge. If weeds spread amongst them the bulbs are robbed of air and light, and their keeping properties are impaired. But in the use of the hoe care must be taken not to loosen the ground or to draw any earth towards the bulbs. When all the thinning has been done, and the weeds are kept down, it will perhaps be observed that in places there are clusters of bulbs fighting for a place and rising out of the ground together as though enjoying the conflict. Now with almost any other kind of plant this crowding would bode mischief, but with Onions it is not so. Bulbs that grow in crowds and rise out of the ground will never be so large as those that have plenty of room, but they will be of excellent quality, and will keep better than any that have had ample space for high development. It is a pity to touch these accidental clusters, for the removal of a portion will perhaps loosen the ground, and so spoil the character of those that are left, for fine Onions are rarely produced in loose ground, and hence the necessity for care in the use of the hoe. Watering is not often needed, and we may go so far as to say that, in a general way, it is objectionable. But a long drought on light land may put the crop in jeopardy, unless watering is resorted to, in which case weak manure water will be beneficial. Still, watering must be discontinued in good time, or it will prevent the ripening of the bulbs, and if a sign is wanted the growth will afford it, for from the time the bulbs have attained to a reasonable size the water will do more harm than good.

The harvesting of the crop requires as much care as the growing of it. If all goes well, the bulbs will ripen naturally, and being drawn and dried on the ground for a few days with their roots looking southward, may be gathered up and topped and tailed and bunched as may be most convenient. But there may be a little hesitation of the plant in respect of finishing its growth, the result, perhaps, of cool moist weather, when dry hot weather would be better. In this case the growth may be checked by passing a rod (as the handle of a rake, for example) over the bed to bend down the tops. After this the tops will turn yellow, and the necks will shrink, and advantage must be taken of fine weather to draw the Onions and lay them out to dry. A gravel path or a dry shed fully open to the sun will ripen them more completely than the bed they have been grown on; but where large pieces of Onions are grown they must be ripened where they grew, and experience teaches when they may be drawn with safety.

As to keeping Onions, any dry, cool, airy place will answer. But if a difficulty arises there is an easy way out of it, for Onions may be hung in bunches on an open wall under the shelter of the eaves of any building, and thus the outsides of barns and stables and cottages may be converted into Onion stores, leaving the inside free for things that are less able to take care of themselves. During severe frost they must be taken down and piled up anywhere in a safe place, but may be put on their hooks again when the weather softens, for a slight frost will not harm them in the least, and the wall will keep them comparatively warm and dry. When the best part of the crop has been bunched or roped, the remainder may be thrown into a heap in a cool dry shed, and a few mats may be put over them, and in this way they will keep without sprouting for at least three months. But damp will start them into growth, and the only way to save them then is to top and tail them again, and store as dry as possible in smallish parcels.

To GROW LARGE ONIONS the same principles must be observed as already set forth, but the cultivator must give the plant more space and more time. One mode of enlarging the time is to sow seeds of the large-growing kinds in autumn and transplant them in spring to beds of rich soil, prepared as described for the sowing of spring seeds. The rows should be fifteen inches apart, and the bulbs nine inches in the row. The work should be done by drawing deep drills, into which is thrown a compost of earth and pigeons' droppings, or some equally strong, but suitably prepared, fertiliser. A little earth is then drawn back into the drill, and the roots are placed and moulded up with the hands, the ground being afterwards carefully trodden to firm them in and make a proper finish. Another and less desirable but often successful mode of procedure, is to sow the seed on poor ground about the middle of May, so as to secure a crop of small ripe bulbs the same season. These are harvested with care and put in small parcels in nets, which are suspended in a light, airy loft or seed-room, and are planted out in spring in the same way as advised for autumn-sown crops. It is the nature of the Onion to run up to seed in its second season, and a few of these May sowings will do so when planted out. But the bulk of them will make a second growth and swell to a large size, not having had time the previous year (through being sown late) to mature within them the germs of the fructifying process.

AUTUMN-SOWN ONIONS, intended for an ordinary useful crop, are to be sown in the same way as advised for spring sowing. The time of sowing is important, as they should be forward enough before winter to be useful, but not so forward as to be in danger of injury from severe frost. The Tripoli Onions are the most profitable for drawing during winter and spring, as they soon acquire size and make a good show, but on well-drained ground all the sorts are hardy, and such as the Improved Reading and the White Spanish section, which are so much prized as household and market Onions, may be sown in autumn as safely as any others. It may be well in most places to sow a small piece of White Italian in the latter part of July, and to make a large sowing of the best keeping sorts about the middle of August—say, for the far north the first of the month, and for the far south the very last day. In places where spring-sown Onions do not ripen in good time in consequence of cold wet weather, autumn sowing may prove advantageous, as the ripening will take place when the summer is at its best, and the crop may be taken off before the season breaks down.

PICKLING ONIONS may be obtained by sowing any of the white or straw-coloured varieties that are grown for keeping, but the large sorts, such as Tripoli, Strasburg, &c., are quite unfit; the best are the Queen and Paris Silver-skin, as they are very white when pickled, and are moderately mild in flavour. A piece of poor dry ground should be selected, and this should be made fine on the surface. Sow in the month of April thickly, but evenly, cover lightly, and roll or tread to give a firm seed-bed, and make a good finish. Be careful to keep down weeds, and do not thin the crop at all. If sown very shallow the bulbs will be round; if sown an inch deep they will be oval or pear-shaped.

The Potato or Underground Onion is not much grown in this country, in consequence of occasional losses of the crop in severe winters. In the south of England the rule as to growing it is to plant on the shortest day, and take up on the longest. It requires a rich, deep soil, and to be planted in rows twelve inches apart, the bulbs nine inches apart in the row. Some cultivators earth them up like Potatoes, but we prefer to let the bulbs rise into the light, even by the removal of the earth, so as to form a basin around each, taking care, of course, not to lay bare the roots in so doing. When the planted bulbs have put forth a good head of leaves, they form clusters of bulbs around them, and the best growth is made in the full daylight, the bulbs sitting on and not in the soil.

The Onion Grub (*Anthomyia ceparum*) is often very troublesome to the crop, especially in its early stages, and its presence may be known by the grass becoming yellow and falling on the ground. It will then be found that the white portion, which should become the bulb, has been pierced to the centre by a fleshy, shining maggot, a quarter of an inch in length, this being the larva of an ashy-coloured, ill-looking, two-winged fly. Where this plague has acquired such a hold as to be a serious nuisance, care should be taken to clear out all the old store of Onions instantly upon a sufficiency of young Onions becoming available in spring, and to burn them without hesitation. If left to become garden waste in the usual way, these old Onions will do much to perpetuate and augment the plague. A regular use of salt and soot will be found an effectual preventive, and the dusting of the ground with charcoal during the summer is also calculated to be useful, as the flies will lay their eggs on the charcoal, instead of the plant, and the larvæ will perish as soon as they come forth, instead of prospering as they would do if located on the plant. It is a singular fact, but a fact it is, that transplanted Onions are rarely touched with grub, this pest appearing to require a spring-sown crop for its well-doing. We do not profess to explain the matter, for we must stop somewhere, and may well do so with this practical suggestion of a mode of evading the only plague the Onion grower ever need fear.

PARSLEY

(*Carum Petroselinum*)

PARSLEY will teach those who have eyes exactly how it should be grown. There will appear here, there, and elsewhere in a garden, stray or rogue Parsley plants. No matter how regularly the hoeing and weeding may be done, a stray Parsley plant will appear all alone, perhaps in the midst of Lettuces, or Cauliflowers, or Onions. When these rogues escape destruction they become magnificent plants, and the gardener sometimes leaves them to enjoy the conditions they have selected, and in which they evidently prosper. It scarcely matters what kind of ground these rogue Parsleys are found in, they are always richly curled and sumptuous specimens, proving that isolation suits the plant; it likes to spread with free air and light around it, and when the opportunity occurs, it will show what a Parsley can be, and should be, whether wanted for use or ornament, or to remain in its own chosen nook as a magnificent vagabond. The lesson for the cultivator is that Parsley should have plenty of room from the very first, and this lesson, we feel bound to say, cannot be too often enforced upon young gardeners, for they are apt to sow Parsley far more thickly than is wise, and to be injuriously slow and timid in thinning the crop when the plants are actually crowding one another out of existence.

Parsley, like many other good things, will grow almost anywhere and anyhow, but to make a handsome crop a deep, rich, moist soil is required. It attains to fine quality on a well-tilled clay, but the kindly loam that suits almost everything suits this plant perfectly, and every good garden should show a handsome sample, for beauty is the first required qualification. To keep the house fairly well supplied, sowings should be made in February, May, and July, but with a little management continuous supplies may be obtained from one annual sowing in April, as from this two or three plantings may be made that will spread the growth over two seasons, or at least a sufficient length of time to prevent a gap between the old and the new crops. When the plant pushes for seed it becomes useless, and had best be got rid of; but by planting at various times in various places, a sufficiency may be expected to go through a second season without bolting, after which it will be necessary to root them out and consign them to the rubbish heap. Parsley is often grown as an edging, but it is only in large gardens where this can be done advantageously, and then a very handsome edging is secured. In small gardens it is best to sow on a bed in lines one foot apart, and thin out first to three inches and finally to six inches, the best of the thinnings being planted a foot apart, to last over as proposed above. When Parsley has stood some time it becomes coarse, but the young growth may be renewed by cutting over ; this operation being also useful to defer the flowering, which is surely hastened by leaving the plants alone. For the winter supply a late plantation made in a sheltered spot will usually suffice, for the plant is very hardy, but it may be expedient sometimes to put old frames over a piece worth keeping, or to protect during hard weather with dry litter. In gathering, care should be taken to pick separately the young leaves that are nearly full grown, and to take only one or two from each plant. It costs no more time to fill a basket by taking a leaf or two here and there from a whole row than to strip two or three plants, and the difference in the end will be considerable as regards the total produce and quality of the crop.

PARSNIP

(*Pastinaca sativa*)

THE PARSNIP is one of the most profitable roots the earth produces. Probably its sweet flavour imposes a limit on its usefulness, but bad cooking doubtless has much to answer for, the people in our great towns being, in too many instances, quite ignorant of the proper mode of cooking this nourishing root. When cut in strips and slightly boiled and served up almost crisp, it is a poor thing for human food ; but when cooked whole in such a way as to appear on the table like a mass of marrow, it is at once a digestible dainty and a substantial food that the people might consume more largely than they do, to their advantage.

The Parsnip requires only one special condition for its welfare, and that is a piece of ground prepared for it by honest digging. Rich ground it does not need, but the crop will certainly be the finer from a deep fertile sandy loam than from a poor soil of any kind. But the one great point is to trench the ground in autumn and lay it up rough for the winter. Then at the very first opportunity in February or March, it can be levelled down and the seed sown, and the job got out of hand before the rush of spring work comes on. A fine seed-bed should be prepared either in one large piece or in four-feet strips, as may best suit other arrangements. Sow in shallow drills eighteen inches apart, dropping the seeds from the hand in twos and threes at a distance of six inches apart; cover lightly, and touch over with the hoe or rake to make a neat finish. As soon as the plants are visible, ply the hoe to keep down weeds and thin the crop slightly to prevent crowding anywhere. The thinning should be carried on from time to time until the plants are a foot apart; or if the ground is strong and large roots are required, they may be allowed fifteen inches. It may be well to lift a few roots in November, this being done with a strong two-tined fork, a few spits of earth being removed first at one end or corner of the piece to facilitate removal without breaking the roots: these may be put aside for immediate use, but the general bulk of the crop should remain in the ground to be dug as wanted, for the Parsnip keeps better in the ground than out of it, and in the event of severe frost a coat of rough litter will suffice to prevent injury. Whatever remains over in the month of February should be lifted and trimmed up and stored in the coolest place that can be found, a coat of earth or sand being sufficient to protect them from the injurious action of the atmosphere.

GARDEN PEA

(*Pisum sativum*)

THE GARDEN PEA is of such great importance that it is common to estimate the work of the garden by the general character of this crop. As an article of food, it is the most nutritious of all vegetables; and because it is rich in phosphates and alkalies, it makes a heavy demand upon the soil, and constitutes what is termed an exhausting crop. In poor land it makes a poor return; it cannot live on nothing, as is almost the case with Buckwheat and a few other crops; and because of the brief space of time that elapses between the sowing of the seed and the gathering of the produce, the land should be well prepared for it, that the roots may ramify freely, and quickly collect the food the plant requires.

The soil for Peas should be rich, deep, and friable, and should contain a notable proportion of calcareous matter. Old gardens should be refreshed with a dressing of lime occasionally, or of lime rubbish from destroyed buildings, to compensate for the consumption of calcareous matters by the various crops. For early Peas, a warm dry sandy soil is to be preferred; for late crops, and especially for robust and productive varieties, a strong loam or a well-tilled clay answers admirably, and it is wise to select plots that were in the previous year occupied with Celery and other crops for which the land was freely manured and much 'knocked about.' Heavy manuring is not needed for the earliest crops, unless the soil is very poor, but for the late crops it will always pay to trench the ground, and put a good body of rotten manure at the depth of the first spit, for the roots to run in about the time when the pods are swelling. In all cases it is advisable not to enrich in any special manner the top crust for Peas. When the young plant finds abundant nutriment near at hand, it does not root freely, and is actually in danger of being poisoned; but when the plant is fairly formed, and has entered upon the fruiting stage, the roots may ramify in rich soil to advantage. Hence the desirability of growing Peas in ground that was heavily manured and frequently stirred in the previous year, and of putting a coat of rotten manure between the two spits in trenching. As regards the last-named operation, it should be remarked that as Peas require a somewhat fine tilth, the top spit should be kept on the top where it is likely the second spit will prove lumpy, pasty, or otherwise unkind. In this case, bastard trenching will be sufficient; but when the second spit may be brought up with safety, it should be done for the sake of a fresh soil and a deep friable bed.

Early Peas are produced in a variety of ways. The simplest consists in sowing one or more of the quick-growing varieties in November, December, and January, on sloping sheltered borders expressly prepared for the purpose, and provided with reed hurdles to screen the plants from cutting winds. Where the assaults of mice are to be apprehended, it is an excellent plan to soak the seed in paraffin oil for twenty minutes, and then, having sown in drills only one inch deep, heap over the drill three inches of fine sand. If this cannot be done, sow in drills fully two inches deep, for shallow sowing will not promote earliness, but it is likely to promote weakness of the plant. It is not usual to grow any other crop with first early Peas, but the rows must be far enough apart to prevent them from shading one another, and, if possible, let them run north and south, that they may have an equable enjoyment of the sunshine. As soon as the plant is fairly out of the ground, dust it with soot carefully, so as just to spoil the flavour of the tender leaves without choking them.

When they have made a growth of about three inches, put short brushwood to support and shelter them, deferring the taller sticks until they are required. Then fork the ground between, taking care not to go too near to the plant. But the sticks must be provided in good time, lest the plant should be distressed, for not only do the sticks give needful support, but they afford much shelter, as is the case with the small brushwood supplied in the first instance.

Thus far, as to growing early Peas on the flat. A variation of the plan consists in laying the earth up in ridges, east and west, two feet high at the top of each ridge, and sloping at an angle of 45°, the seed being sown on the sides of the ridges mid-way up the slope. This plan places the entire crop in the position of two plantations, one facing due south, and the other due north. If all goes well the south crop will be very early, and the north crop will immediately succeed it. In the event of trying winter weather, one plantation may be destroyed, and the other may survive; and as regards the survivor, the chances are in favour of the north crop, because of the protection that snow may afford it; but on this point nothing definite can be said. It is just a question when entering upon a precarious business, whether there shall be one or two strings to the bow.

Another simple but effectual mode of growing early Peas is to sow close under a warm wall. But in doing this, care must be taken that some other crop for which the wall is primarily provided is not injured, for this would be 'robbing Peter to pay Paul,' with a considerable loss, perhaps, in the end to the luckless negotiator. But on this recommendation we can establish a proposal of some practical importance. A wall three or four feet high answers as well to protect early Peas as one eight or ten feet high, and wood is almost as effectual as brick or stone. Consequently a small plot could be provided with dwarf walls for early Peas in many places where rough material and cheap labour are available for the purpose, and a few other early crops, such as Lettuce, and afterwards Kidney Beans, might share the advantage and help to pay the cost.

We now come to the modes of growing early Peas by the aid of glass. The surest and simplest method is to provide a sufficiency of grass turf cut from a short clean pasture or common. There is in this case a risk of wireworm and black bot; but if the turf is provided in good time and is laid up in the yard ready for use, it will be searched by the small birds and pretty well cleansed of the insect larvæ that may have lurked in it when first removed. Lay the turves out in a frame, grass side downwards, and water them with water in which a very small quantity of salt has been dissolved, for this will cause the remaining bots and slugs to wriggle out, and by means of a little patient labour they can be gathered and destroyed. Sow the seed rather thickly in lines along the centre of each strip of turf, and cover with fine earth. By keeping the frame close, a more regular sprouting of the seed will be insured; but as soon as the plants rise, air must be given, and this part of the business must be regulated according to the weather. All now depends on the cultivator, for having a very large command of conditions, it may be said that he is removed somewhat from the sport of the elements, which makes wreck of many of our endeavours. In this view, then, there are three points to be kept in mind. In the first place, a short stout slow-growing plant is wanted, for a tall lean fast-growing plant will at the end of the story refuse to furnish the dish of Peas aimed at. Give air and water judiciously, and protect from vermin and all other enemies. A little dry lime or soot may be dusted over the plants occasionally, but not to choke or even colour the leaves. All going well, plant out in the month of March or April, on ground prepared for the purpose, and laying the plant-bearing turves in strips, without any disturbance whatever of the roots. Then earth them up with fine stuff from between the rows, and put sticks to support and shelter them.

A more troublesome, but often a safer method, is to raise the plants in pots. We object to the plan that prevails in some gardens of sowing round the sides of large pots, and then opening out the ball to make the Peas meet in line. That many practise this plan with success is true, and we leave the masters of the business to their own devices. But those who are not masters of the business may be advised to sow in what are called 54-sized pots, but at the utmost 48-size (5-inch) is, in our opinion, the largest allowable. The details of management need not detain us. The object of the cultivator should be to obtain a sturdy plant, and there should be no 'pushing,' unless the desire be to illustrate the proverb 'the more haste the less speed'— a proverb that a prudent post-boy can illustrate if you give him a long journey on short time with weak steeds. He will check the speed at first, even if the slowness chafes the traveller. But he will probably reach the destination in proper time, instead of breaking down half-way as he might have done by urging his weak team too early in the race. Plant out from the pots into the rows by the aid of a trowel, at one foot apart, without breaking the balls, and earth up tenderly, and put stakes at once, and the work is almost finished. All that remains is to visit them daily, and as soon as they show flower nip out the tops.

Main crops require plenty of room, and that is really the chief point in growing them. We will suppose the ground to be well prepared as already advised; the next matter of importance is the distance between the rows. The market gardener is usually under some kind of compulsion to sow Peas in solid pieces, just far enough apart for fair growth, and to leave them to sprawl instead of being staked, because of the cost of the proceeding. But the garden that supplies a household is not subject to the severe conditions of the case cited, and Peas may be said to go to the dinner table at retail and not at wholesale price. Moreover, high quality is of importance, and here the domestic as distinguished from the commercial gardener has an immense advantage, for well-grown 'Garden Peas' surpass in beauty and flavour the best market samples procurable, no matter how or where. To produce these fine Peas there must be plenty of space allowed between the rows, and it will be found good practice to grow Peas and early Potatoes on the same plot, and to put short sticks to the Peas as soon as they are forward enough to afford shelter to the Potatoes, for by this management the first top growth of the Potatoes may be saved from the late May frosts, and the Peas will give double the crop of a crowded plantation. As regards the time of sowing, seasons and climates must be considered. But we may offer advice of general value by saying that there is nothing gained by sowing main-crop Peas so early as to subject the plant to a conflict with frost. It should be understood that the finest sorts of Peas are somewhat tender in constitution, and the wrinkled sorts are more tender than the round. Hence, in any case, the wrinkled seeds should be sown rather more thickly than the round, to allow for losses; but robust-habited Peas should never be sown so thickly as the early sorts, for every plant needs room to branch and spread, and gather sunshine by means of its leaves for the ultimate manufacture of superb Green Peas. The months of March, April, May, and June are the times for sowing main crops of Peas. After June early sorts may be sown again, and will require more than ordinary care to insure profitable results. Late sowings should be kept as cool as possible by screening them from the sun, for the young plant cannot endure the full force of the summer sun.

On the first appearance of the plant, a slight dusting of lime or soot will be of advantage to render it distasteful to slugs and sparrows, but this is more needful for the early than the later crops. When main-crop Peas have grown two or three inches, they are pretty safe against the small marauders. It is of importance to stake them early and to stake them well, the size and strength of the sticks being, as a matter of course, proportioned to the habit of the variety. Before putting sticks, earth the rows up carefully, both to give support, and to comfort the base of the plant in the event of hot dry weather setting in. And here we must remark on the immense advantage we derive from the labours of the hybridisers who, in recent years, have secured for us varieties of Peas characterised by a dwarf, strong growth, great productiveness, and high quality. We advise the use of sticks, for at a reasonable cost they will more than pay their way. But the newer dwarf kinds do very well, and yield abundantly, if allowed to grow without any support whatever, as the seed grower and market gardener usually leave them. A little extra care is required in gathering the crop from Peas that are not staked, and we think it proper to say that some young gardeners are apt to handle the haulm roughly, the result being the destruction of many plants in their prime. The tall sorts may with advantage be tipped when they first show flowers, and if after this they make free growth they may be again tipped, to concentrate the energies of the plant on the formation of fine pods. But a free leaf growth is of the first importance, therefore frequent tipping is not to be thought of, and the plant must have abundant light and air to maintain the leaf growth in its fullest vigour.

In the event of prolonged dry weather, measures must be taken to supply water in good time and in liberal quantity. The advantage of deep digging and manuring between the two spits will now be discovered, for Peas thus circumstanced will pass through the trial, even if not aided with water, although much better with it; whereas similar sorts, in poor shallow ground, will soon become hopelessly mildewed, and not even water will save them. In giving water, it will be well to open a shallow trench about a foot distant from the rows on the shady side, and in this pour the water so as to fill the trench; by this method water and labour will be best economised, and the plant will have the full benefit of the operation.

The enemies of Peas are fewer in number than might be expected in the case of so nutritive a plant. Against the weevil (*Bruchus*), the moth (*Plusia*), and the fly (*Phytomyza*), we are comparatively powerless, and perhaps the safest course is to occasionally dust the plants with lime or soot, in which case care must be taken to do the work neatly, or the leaf growth will be checked to the injury of the crop. Light dustings will suffice to render the plant unpalatable without interfering with its health, but a heavy careless hand will do more harm than all the insects by loading the leafage with obnoxious matter. The one great enemy of the Pea crop is our old loquacious neighbour, the sparrow, whose depredations begin with the appearance of the plant, and are renewed from the moment when the pods contain something worth having. Other small birds haunt the ground, but the sparrow is the leader of the gang. Ordinary frighteners used in the ordinary way are of little use; the best are lines, to which at intervals white feathers, or strips of white paper, or pieces of bright tin are attached. We have found the surest way to guard the crop against feathered plunderers is to have work in hand on the plot, so as to keep up a constant bustle, and this shows the advantage of putting the rows at such a distance as will allow the formation of Celery trenches between them. We want a crop to come off, and another to be put on while the Peas are in bearing; and early Potatoes, to be followed by Celery, may be suggested as a rotation suitable in many instances. Even then the birds will have a good time of it in the morning, unless the workmen are on the ground early. However, on this delicate point, the 'early bird' that carries a spade will have an advantage, because the sparrow is really a late riser, and does not begin business until other birds have had breakfast, and have finished at least one musical performance.

POTATO

(*Solanum tuberosum*)

The Potato has been designated the 'King of the Kitchen Garden,' and perhaps we should so regard it. Of its importance it would be idle to speak; but we may be permitted to remark that in our opinion the Potato is destined to a far higher position, not only in our daily dietary, but in the useful and decorative arts, as well as in various manufactures, than it has attained to as yet. The exceedingly simple manner in which gum may be prepared from Potato starch, the cheap rate at which a good substitute for arrowroot may be produced, and the ready manufacture from the Potato, after the starch is removed from it, of substantial imitations of horn and ivory, suggest that in this root there is more wealth hidden than has hitherto been dreamt of in our philosophy. As a farm and garden crop its value may at any moment be influenced by such considerations, and it should be added that the dietetic value of the Potato appears to be always advancing. As a food it is properly associated with animal products of some kind or other, being in itself deficient of flesh-forming constituents; but when in this proper association it appears capable of superseding all other vegetable foods, bread alone excepted. We are not about to recommend our readers to abstain from Asparagus, and Peas, and Spinach, and regard Potatoes as a sufficient substitute for such delicacies; but it is well to remember that while this useful root is, by virtue of its starchy compounds, an important article of food, it has a direct tendency to promote health and that freshness of complexion that appears to prevail most amongst well-fed people who customarily use Potatoes. So universal and emphatic are the testimonies of commanders of ships, and more especially of those who are exposed to privations in the Arctic regions, to its power of preventing and of curing scurvy, that it is not unlikely that preserved Potatoes will, as a prophylactic, supplement lemon and lime-juice, with the advantage of affording nourishment to the seaman, which these aids do not.

EARLY POTATOES are produced in various ways, and by very simple appliances. The Potato will not bear the slightest touch of frost. It is a sub-tropical plant, and will endure considerable heat if at the same time it can enjoy light, air, and sufficient moisture. In some respects it may be likened to the Lettuce, for if crowded or overheated, or subjected to sudden checks, it bolts—in other words, it produces plenty of top and no bottom, just as Lettuces similarly treated produce flowering stems and no hearts. We will here propose a very simple and practical procedure for obtaining a nice crop of Potatoes in the month of June, without any forcing or troublesome arrangements whatever. This system fairly mastered, endless modifications will be easily effected as circumstances and judgment may suggest.

We begin by selecting an early variety of the best quality, such as Sutton's Ashleaf. Some time towards the end of January the sets are packed closely in shallow boxes, one layer deep only, and these are placed in full daylight safe from frost, but are not subjected to heat in any way. It may be well to sprinkle them slightly with water now and then, but a little of this goes a long way, and it is not absolutely necessary. Having made a beginning by starting the sets into growth in full daylight, we proceed to prepare the ground. This must be light, warm, dry, and rather rich without being rank. If there is a length of wall at command, and we are perplexed to find some nice stuff for the early Potatoes, we will go to the potting shed and seize all the sandy soil that has been turned out of pots, and having mixed with it as much as can be spared of leaf-mould and quite rotten manure, we proceed to lay the mixture in a ridge at the foot of the wall, and thus we prepare for the earliest crop without the aid of frames. As walls do not anywhere run in such lengths as to provide for all the early Potatoes that are wanted, we select a plot of ground lying warm and dry to the sun, and having spread over it a liberal allowance of decayed manure, and any light fertilising stuff, such as the red and black residue from the burning of hedge clippings, turf and weeds, we dig this in. The ground being ready, it is lined out in neat ridges two feet apart, running north and south. These ridges must be shallow, rising not more than six inches above the general level. On every fourth ridge sow early Peas that are not likely to grow more than two and a half to three feet in height. This being done in February, the land is ready for Potatoes in the first week of March. Plant on the fine stuff laid up next the wall in the first instance, and then on the ridges, where there is room for three rows of Potatoes between every two rows of Peas. In the process of planting, it will be advisable to rub off all the weak eyes and thin out those on the crown, two or three strong eyes being quite sufficient. This can easily be accomplished as the sets are laid into their places in a shallow drill opened on the top of the ridge. The sets may be put a foot apart, and have four inches of fine soil over them. Prick the ground over with a fork between the rows, leaving it quite rough, but regular and workmanlike. The Peas will soon appear, and will require attention. Draw a little fine earth to them, and stake them carefully with small brushwood. If snails and slugs appear, give dustings of lime or soot, and as soon as possible supply stakes of sufficient height and strength to carry the crop. By the time the Potatoes begin to show their shaws the Peas will constitute an effectual shelter for them against east winds, and it will be found that the morning frosts that are often so injurious to Potatoes in the month of May will scarcely touch a crop that has the advantage of this kind of protection. But to that alone we must not trust. One serious freezing that blackens the shaws will delay and diminish the Potato crop. Therefore, when the green tops first appear, cover them to the depth of an inch with fine earth from between the rows, and repeat this until they are six inches deep, always allowing the leaves to see the light, except when a sharp frost occurs, when it will be advisable to cover them with a few inches of light dry litter in just the same way that we cover a bed of Radishes. There are many methods of protecting Potatoes. A plank on edge on the east side of a row will suffice to tide through an ordinary white frost. A few stout pegs on which mats or reed hurdles can be laid will answer admirably, but care must be taken that the plant is not pressed upon, and that the covering is removed as soon as the danger is over.

Those grown under the wall will be ready first, and those in the bed will follow. Very serviceable crops may be secured by planting in the spaces between the trees of a fruit wall, without any harm to the trees whatever. Those grown on the south face of a good wall will be of excellent quality, and three weeks in advance of the earliest crops in the open quarters. But east and west walls may be made to contribute, and even north walls are useful, if planted a week later and a little deeper. In all cases the sets should be put close to the wall to enjoy the warmth, and dryness, and shelter it affords. When the crop is lifted, the soil specially laid up for it may be taken away, or scattered over the border. But the bulk will be so slight that it will not matter much what becomes of it. However, in a new place with a clay soil it may be prudent to remove it, and keep it ready as an aid in seed sowing, for there are times and places where a little fine stuff is worth a great deal to give a crop of some kind a proper start.

The employment of frames in the cultivation of early Potatoes must be regarded as a profitable proceeding, as we thereby secure to the plant the protection it needs in its early stages; and by removing the lights when the season is sufficiently advanced, we commence the summer with a strong plant ready to form tubers, instead of one but just emerging from the ground. A rough contrivance answers if fairly weather-proof, and where old lights are available, or even frames and mats, a little well-directed labour will accomplish the rest. A suitable measurement for a frame is a width of six feet and a length proportionate to the produce required. It may be two feet high at the back, and fifteen inches in front, and must face the south as nearly as possible. Whatever the soil may be, it will be advisable not to plant in it, but to wheel in some light turfy or sandy soil, or a mixture prepared for the purpose, and this must form a bed at least nine inches deep. This may appear a great task, but it will not perplex the earnest cultivator, and it will bring its reward when the crop is lifted. However, it scarcely needs to be said that Potatoes planted in the open ground may have frames put over them, to help them along in the early stages, and it would pay well in any garden to have portable frames for the purpose, as these could be used to assist Cucumbers and Marrows when the Potatoes no longer needed them, and to protect Celery and other crops during hard winter weather.

THE MAIN CROP, as the source of supply for fully nine months out of twelve, deserves every proper attention. And this brings us to the consideration of a few important matters. Potatoes are grown with advantage on so many diverse soils, and in such unlikely climates, that the plant appears, on a first casual consideration, to be altogether indifferent to conditions. It is an immense advantage that it has this universal character, for even in Iceland, where the brief cold summer barely affords grass for the stunted cattle, the people occasionally secure useful crops of Potatoes. But the truth must be told that for the profitable cultivation of this crop certain conditions are absolutely essential. Amongst these an open situation and a well-drained soil are perhaps the most important. To this might be added favourable weather, because a bad season frustrates every hope and labour. But on this point the less said the better, seeing that we must take the weather as it comes, knowing that good cultivation will in a great degree mitigate the effects of unfavourable atmospheric conditions. Having an open situation and a well-drained soil, it is much to be preferred that the soil be of a deep, friable, loamy nature ; in other words, a good medium soil, suitable for deep tillage, but neither a decided clay, chalk, nor sand. A fertile sandy loam, lying well as regards sunshine and drainage, may generally be considered a first-rate Potato soil, and none can say it is not so until experience has supplied the proof. The comparative indifference of the Potato to conditions is seen in the fact that excellent crops are grown on thin soils overlying chalk and limestone. So again, grand crops are often taken from poor sandy soils, and from newly broken bog and moss, as well as from clay lands that have had some amount of tillage to form a friable top crust. But when all is said and done, we shall always prefer, in the first instance, a deep mellow loam, and all the better if it contains a reasonable proportion of sand and calcareous matters, as good loams generally do. The Potato is too important a crop to be lightly dealt with in respect of the conditions that are most favourable for its production, and therefore we advise those who propose to speculate largely to look for loamy lands, and failing to find them to give preference to calcareous and sandy soils rather than to clays or retentive soils of any kind.

There prevails much prejudice against manuring land for Potatoes, and where the land is strong enough to make a paying crop, it may be prudent to do without manure, and to give a good dressing for the next crop to restore the land to a reasonable condition. But it is the practice of many of the most successful market growers in the country to manure for this crop, and in some instances the manure—long, and but half-rotted—is laid in the trenches at the time of planting, and the sets are laid on the manure, and closed in with the earth from the sides; the work being done with mechanical accuracy, so as to consume the least amount of time possible, but leaving the field in an orderly state. Generally speaking, land intended for Potatoes should be deeply dug, and, if needful, manured in the autumn. About twenty to thirty cartloads of half-rotten manure per acre may be dug or ploughed in to as great a depth as possible, consistent with the nature of the subsoil, and the appliances at command. In breaking up pasture with the spade, bastard trenching will generally prove advantageous. The land is lined off in two-feet breadths, and the top spit of the first piece is removed to the last piece, which will often be close at hand by the rule of working a certain distance down and back again. The under spit will then be well broken up, and the manure thrown in, and the top spit of the next piece will be turned in turf downwards, making a sandwich of the manure. If this is done in autumn, there will be a mellow top crust produced by the spring, and the best way to plant will be in trenches unless the land is very light, in which case the dibber may be used.

As light lands are often profitably devoted to Potato culture, and more especially to the production of first-class early Potatoes for the markets, a few words on their management may be useful here. If on the light land you have a choice of aspects, by all means select the plots that slope to the south-west; the dangerous aspects are north and east. The land should be ploughed up in autumn and left rough, but it is not economical to manure light lands in autumn. At the time of planting, the furrows should be cut with a plough fitted with a double mould-board, and the manure spread evenly along them previous to laying in the sets. A good dressing per acre will consist of fifteen loads of farmyard manure, and four cwt. of artificials, consisting of one and a half cwt. of guano, two of superphosphate of lime, and half a cwt. of muriate of potash. When the sets are laid, cover them by splitting the ridges with the plough. If planted early in March, the crop should come off in time for Turnips, for which the land will be in good heart, and they should be sown as quickly as possible after the clearing of the Potatoes.

Amongst the many subjects that open out before us at this point are the selection and preparation of the sets. Why are smallish tubers chosen in one case and planted whole, and why, in another case, are large tubers chosen and divided before planting, to make two or more sets of each? Because there is a principle on which sound practice rests, and it is this : the number of shoots starting from any one growing point must be limited, for if they become crowded the crop will be less than the land is capable of producing ! Keeping this principle in view, we proceed to remark, in the first place, that carefully selected seed of moderate size may be planted as it comes from the store without any preparation whatever, and with a fair prospect of a profitable result. But certain varieties produce few tubers of seed size, and when large they must be divided in such a manner as to insure at least two eyes in each set. As a matter of fact, profitable crops are grown in the most simple way ; the seed is neither sprouted nor disbudded, and with a well-made soil and a favourable season, the return is ample, and all claims are satisfied. Potato-growing entails much labour, therefore it is important to distinguish between tasks that are necessary and those that are optional.

But where the time and strength can be found for first-class cultivation, it should have the preference over the rough and ready methods that are satisfactory on a large scale. Exhibitions of Potatoes are for the most part sustained by persons who can find the time to do things with extra care, and they have their reward in their crops as well as in their prizes, for what may be styled Exhibition culture consists simply in growing the main crop in the best possible way, and preferring many sorts where in any other case a few would suffice. Here, then, on the best plan, we begin with sets most carefully selected, to insure true typical form and colour, and these are, some six weeks or so before planting time, put in shallow boxes, or baskets one layer deep, to sprout in full daylight, but quite safe from frost. In the first instance, a number of sprouts appear, and a large proportion are rubbed off. The object of the cultivator is to secure one or two stout, short shoots of a green or purple colour, the long white threads that are often produced in the store being regarded as useless. When large sets are employed, they are allowed to make three or four stout shoots, and at the time of planting—not before—these sets are cut so as to leave to each large piece only one or two good sprouts or sprits. As for the smaller sets that are not to be divided, it is the rule to cut a small piece off each of these at the time of planting to facilitate the decay of the tuber when it has accomplished its work, for having nourished the first growth the sooner it disappears the better. Thus, with a little extra trouble, we have got ready for planting, and the main reasons for taking this extra trouble are doubtless fully apparent. According to a good old rule, we want the best seed possible, and the best soil possible, these two items forming the first chapter. By sprouting the seed we gain time, which is equivalent to a lengthening of the season. By limiting the growth we prevent crowding above ground, for where the shoots are crowded the tubers will not be crowded, a few strong shaws with all their leaves exposed to the air and light being capable of better work than a large number contending for air and light that are insufficient for them all. And finally, by cutting the sets, whether to divide them, or simply to hasten their decay, we insure that they will not be in the way when the crop is dug; for when planted without being cut they become useless, ugly things, and once planted we never want to see them again.

The distance at which the sets are planted is of such importance, that a crop too much crowded will be positively worthless. But we must crowd the ground as much as we dare, for if we only waste a minute space of ground in each breadth, or in the spaces between the sets, the total crop will be many bushels short of the possible quantity. The guiding principle must be to allow to every separate plant ample room to spread, and absorb the air and sunshine, in accordance with the character of the sort and the condition of the soil. A considerable proportion of the losses from disease may be traced to overcrowding in the first instance, the tangled haulm being rendered weak through want of air, and then becoming loaded with water, and in contact with wet ground, the disease has made havoc where, had the management been founded on sound principles, there might have been a vigorous, healthy growth. It will be seen that if a doubt arises, and a mistake seems likely, care should be taken to insure that the mistake is on the right side. In other words, it is safer to allow too much than too little space, and it must be confessed the exhibition growers allow a very large space. As much as five feet from row to row is often allowed for the strong-growing varieties, and four feet for the medium varieties, and even then, with the land so well prepared as it is, the shaws meet across the rows, and enormous crops are lifted. For a very comprehensive rule, it may be said that the distance between the rows may vary from fifteen inches for the early sorts of dwarf growth, to forty inches for the vigorous-growing late sorts. Between these measurements we find a rule for medium growers, for which, on good ground, a distance of twenty-six to thirty-six inches is usually allowed. The distance between the sets must in like manner be determined by the growth, and will range from six inches for crops to be dug early, to sixteen or twenty inches for the robust kinds. The medium main-crop Potatoes will generally do well at twelve inches apart, and pay better than at nine inches. Much, however, depends on the season, for when great space is allowed, and the season proves warm and showery, there will be more large tubers than the grower will care for ; whereas, if planted somewhat closer, the crop would be of smaller size and more uniform. As to the depth, that is determined after planting. A good average for the final depth is six inches, but another inch may be allowed on light soil.

The next point that claims attention is the time of planting. There has been much debate as to the advisability of planting in autumn, and a great deal might be said about it here. But we cannot afford space to treat of speculative matters, and we need only say that there is almost complete concurrence among practical men in favour of spring planting, the months of February, March, and April being the most suitable, and the month of March the best of any. Good crops have been dug by us from plantings made on Midsummer Day, but such late planting is not to be thought of, unless there are some special reasons to justify it. Still, it is always well, in practical matters, to know the limits of possibility; and to put the case very broadly, we may say that Potato planting may be carried on as weather permits from the shortest day to the longest, but for profitable work and average seasons, and the climates in which the Potato usually prospers, the best time for planting is the month of March.

The planting being accomplished, the cultivation will begin. It is too much the practice to regard the summer cultivation as a matter of secondary importance. It must be admitted that every stage in the cultivation of the Potato is costly, and the labour bill certainly does run up. From one point of view that is a great argument in favour of the Potato as a farm crop, for it makes labour at times when it can be spared from other work, and beyond doubt, up to a certain point, the money expended comes back with interest. As soon as the shaws appear, the ground should be ploughed or dug between, and if there is any fear of frost the shaws should be lightly moulded over. As the growth advances, it must be earthed up, and care must be taken not to earth up too much, for, taking six inches as the best average depth, it may be said that the crop will be diminished in proportion to the increase of this depth. It is an urgent reason for early work between the rows that a prosperous crop will soon put a stop to it. The moment it becomes likely that the shaws will be bruised by traffic between the rows they must be left to finish their course in their own way. The formation of tubers below will be—accidents excepted—in the ratio of the healthy growth above ground. To damage the green growth is to damage the root growth, just as you might insure the wreck of a ship by cutting a particular rope, or the failure of a horse by depriving him of food. The Potato may be said to be manufactured out of sunshine and alkaline salts. The green leaves constitute the machinery of the manufacture, for which the solar light from above, and the potash, phosphate of lime, phosphate of magnesia, and phosphoric acid from below are the raw materials.

In the course of cultivating the Potato crop it will probably be noticed that an occasional strange blotch is conspicuous. There will be seen here or there a head of green shaws of a different colour or growth to the rest. When this occurs there are 'rogues' to be dealt with, and there are two ways of dealing with them. The severe and proper way is to dig them out and consign them to the rubbish heap as soon as they discover themselves by their false faces. But a compromise is possible, and in small gardens may be accomplished with advantage. Mark every rogue with a stake, and dig all these first, and take care that they are eaten. The remaining stock will be pure, and to insure this result is really worth some trouble. Those who have been in the habit of saving their own seed will thoroughly appreciate the advice thus offered; for when the stock shows no disposition to revert to long-lost character, it cannot be supposed that with but a limited space at disposal, both for growing and storing Potatoes, a certain admixture will not sometimes occur. Hence the importance of depending on seed procured from those who, having every facility for the purpose, can and do offer stocks of all the best varieties entirely true to name and free from rogues.

In common with all other crops, the Potato needs as often as possible a fresh soil, and a renewal of seed from some distant source. The need for a change of soil is made apparent by an analysis of the root, which contains large proportions of potash, phosphorus, and sulphur, with smaller proportions of magnesia and lime, without which the plant cannot prosper. A succession of heavy crops of Potatoes on the same land may be said to take from the soil all its available potash and phosphates, and this crop will not, like some others, take soda instead of potash when the last-named alkali runs short. Here then is a chemical reason for change of soil. Another reason is found in the history of the species of fungi that prey on the Potato when its growth is checked by heavy rains and a low temperature. These leave their spores in the soil, like wolves hiding in ambush, to destroy the next crop. They are powerless to attack any other crop; therefore a suitable rotation gives them time to die out and leave the land clean as regards the *peronospora* and other parasites that destroy our Potato crops. As for occasional change of seed, that rests on an old experience, and should scarcely need enforcing. One word may be said here by way of explanation, and it is this: the seed house which aims to put a good article in the market adopts measures altogether different to those followed by the majority of persons who have not been trained to the business. It is a common experience to find that those who save their own seed from year to year have as a result a constantly declining strain, so that every year the growth is weaker, less true, and less profitable. It is so all through, but is especially the case with Potatoes. We do not say that all who save their own seed act unwisely, for some are most expert in the business. But we do say that seed saving is not learned in a day, and many who think they save shillings when they save seeds, actually lose pounds by burdening themselves with a bad article. The art of roguing is but one part of the seed-saving process. There is the proper storing, and the selecting and sorting processes, to which eyes and hands must be trained, and there must be no scruple about the sacrifice of false, ugly, immature or diseased samples. The point we have in view is to advise the Potato grower to be sure of his seed, and when a doubt arises as to the purity and healthiness of the sample at command, it may be remembered that the seed merchant practises methods of purgation that produce the best seed possible, while by growing his seed in many different parts of England, and on very diverse soils, he can furnish stocks which make an admirable change of seed for any description of land.

In certain districts of the north, it is not unusual to obtain two crops of Potatoes in one season from the same plot of land. The return is so profitable that it is surprising a similar proceeding is not adopted in the south, where the conditions of success appear to be still more favourable. To insure the highest possible return, it is absolutely necessary that the sets should be carefully sprouted in advance of the planting time. This is easily managed by placing the tubers in shallow wooden trays or baskets fully exposed to light and air, but heat must be avoided, or the sets will be forced injuriously. The result is a growth of short stout shoots, that are ready at once to make a healthy start. The land is previously opened in wide ridges, and when planting time arrives the furrows are heavily dressed with manure. The sets are laid upon the manure at proper distances, and the ridges are split so as to make a new ridge above them. For the first crop some reliable early Potato is chosen, and while it is growing the trays are filled again with a main-crop or late variety for sprouting. The early crop is fit to lift in from eight to eleven weeks, and can be placed in the market when prices rule high. The ground is at once opened again into ridges and furrows by the double mould-board plough, care being taken that the ridges are in exactly the same positions that they occupied over the first crop. The furrows are then dressed with manure, upon which the sets are placed, and the ridges are split to cover them as before. In about a week the shaws begin to be visible, and the usual routine is followed. Thus the second crop is practically grown on fresh soil, and the produce is ready in ample time for the late season trade. This practice necessitates very liberal dressings of manure, but it is a thoroughly paying procedure, and the land is finally left in capital condition for carrying a crop of Cabbage.

The disease will always claim mention in a paper on the Potato. We intend to dismiss the subject in a few words. In entering into Potato culture, whether upon a large or small scale, we must do the same as in entering upon any other undertaking. We count the cost and consider the risks, and hope for a profit. The aid which scientific men have rendered towards the suppression of disease is at present limited to the knowledge they have acquired as to the history and character of the Potato fungus. This will no doubt ultimately result in practical benefit. But up to the present time the murrain has to be fought with the plough, spade, draining tool, and above all with a wise selection of sorts. Now it is an acknowledged fact that many—indeed we might say almost all—Potatoes that have been cultivated for a number of years appear to have lost their vigour, and are liable to succumb to the disease; but several kinds that have recently been raised from seed possess a constitution which almost completely defies the *peronospora*. These kinds belong, however, chiefly to the main-crop or late-growing class, and thus we reach the conclusion that, although we cannot stamp out the disease, because it is developed by meteorological conditions over which we have no control, yet the foe which cannot be annihilated may be evaded. This is partly accomplished by sound cultivation as already remarked on, but the good work may be continued by raising and maintaining in the fullest vigour those varieties that do not readily succumb to influences that have so often devastated the Potato crop. Since the introduction of Sutton's Magnum Bonum Potato there is a disposition to believe in ' Disease-proof Potatoes.' There is no such thing absolutely, and perhaps there never will be, any more than there is a disease-proof wheat, or rye, or dog, or horse, or man. But varieties of Potatoes differ in their relative liability to attack, and it has been one of our aims to secure from amongst thousands of carefully selected seedlings varieties combining the highest cropping and table qualities with the least liability to disease, in seasons when the conditions favour the spread of the fungus. Scientific men have not yet explained why the varieties differ in this respect, but practical men have discovered that initial vigour of growth is the main defence against the plague. It is sufficient here to say that as the growing of a good variety costs no more than the growing of a poor variety, the cultivator should bestow his care on the very best that he can obtain, for a little extra cost for seed in the first instance is as nothing to the multiplied chances of success a good variety carries with it. To sum up this subject, then, we say that disease may be avoided in the early crops by cultivating sorts which may be lifted before the plague generally appears; and on soils which will not produce an early crop, only such varieties should be grown as have been proved to be practically free from its attacks. For these let there be a dry, warm bed, sufficient food, the fullest exposure to the life-giving powers of light and conditions favourable to early ripening, and having secured these we have made ourselves in a great degree safe against disease.

PUMPKIN (*See* GOURD, *page* 59)

RADISH

(Raphanus sativus)

THE RADISH is often badly grown through being sown too thickly on lumpy ground, in places not favourable to quick vegetation. Radishes grown slowly become tough, pungent, and worthless. On the other hand, those which are grown quickly on rich, mellow ground are elegant in appearance, delicate in flavour, and as digestible as any salad in common use. It should be understood that earliness is of the very first importance; large Radishes are never wanted; but the ground should be good, and well broken up, to insure a quick growth and a handsome sample.

For the earliest crops it is advisable to make a semi-hot-bed, by removing a portion of the surface soil, and laying down about two feet depth of half-rotten stable manure, on which spread four inches of fine earth, and then cover with old frames. Sow the seed thinly, and put on the lights. When the plants appear, give air at every opportunity to keep the growth dwarf and stout, and cover with mats during frost, always taking care to uncover as often as possible to give light, for if the tops are drawn the bottoms will be worthless. Where the plants are crowded thin them, allowing every plant just room enough to spread out its top without overlapping its neighbour. Sowings made in this way in December, January, and February will supply an abundance of beautiful Radishes in early spring, when they are greatly valued. The second crop (which in many gardens will be the first) may be sown on warm dry borders in February. Within a few days after sowing, collect a quantity of dry litter, and lay it up ready for use in a shed. It happens often that we have warm, bright weather in February, and the Radishes start quickly and make good progress, and then may come a severe frost, when the litter must be spread as lightly as possible, three or four inches thick. These open-ground sowings will bear cold well, but they should not be allowed to get frozen, and therefore semi-hot-beds may be employed. If the consumption of time and materials appears excessive for such a purpose, it should be remembered that this is a capital way of preparing for the next crop, whatever it may be, and is a particularly good method of preparing for Peas that are to be sown in the month of April, by which time the earliest sown Radishes will be off the ground.

Successive sowings should be made in the coolest place that can be found for them, and the usual practice of four-feet beds will answer very well. In many gardens sufficient supplies of Radishes are obtained by sowing in the alleys between seed-beds, but care must be taken that this plan does not interfere with the proper work of hoeing, weeding, thinning, &c. When seed is sown on light soils a moderate firming with the back of the spade may be desirable, but generally speaking it is sufficient to cover the seed lightly and so leave it. To thin the crop early is, however, of great importance, no matter how wasteful the process may seem, for wherever the plants are crowded they will make large useless tops, and small useless roots, and prove altogether unprofitable. For the earliest sowings we have choice of many sorts, long, round, and oval; but the long Radishes are not well adapted for late sowing, whereas the round and oval sorts stand pretty well in hot weather if on good ground in a cool situation with the help of a slight amount of shade. As the year advances we return to the practice recommended for the earliest crops. The sowings made in October and November must be on dry borders sloping to the south, and must be protected from frost by means of light litter. It is not a difficult task even in a small garden to keep up supplies of Radishes throughout the year; but there are large-growing kinds that are much prized by some, who use them in winter in the preparation of salads. The Black Spanish Radish is sown in July and August, in drills nine inches apart, and thinned to six inches in the rows. In November or December the roots are lifted and stored in sand for use. The flesh in the centre is tough and strong-flavoured, but next the rind it is mild and tender, and usually this is the part that is sliced for a winter salad.

RHUBARB

(*Rheum hybridum*)

RHUBARB is so much valued that we need not recommend it. There are some remarkably fine sorts in cultivation. Reading Ruby stands alone for its deep colour and excellent flavour. Dancer's Early Scarlet and Royal Albert are also good, and, being precocious and hardy, are well adapted for garden culture, as but little labour is needed to insure plenty of sticks of high quality very early in the year. For main crop and late use, Linnæus and Victoria produce abundant supplies of fine flavour.

Although an accommodating plant, Rhubarb requires for profitable production a rich deep soil, well worked, and heavily manured with rotten manure, and a situation remote from trees, but in some degree sheltered. It will be observed that the markets are supplied from sheltered alluvial soils, that have been much cultivated, and kept in high condition by abundant manuring. On the other hand, the coarser kinds will make a free and early growth on a damp clay, if sheltered from the east winds that so often damage early spring vegetation. The shortest way to establish a plantation is to purchase selected roots of first-class named varieties, and plant them in one long row, three to four feet apart, or in a bed or compartment four feet apart each way. A few of the more delicate kinds will do very well at two and a half feet each way, but for large-growing sorts this would be injuriously close. Plant with the top bud two inches deep, tread in moderately firm, then lightly prick the ground over, and so leave it. Rhubarb may be planted at any time in spring or autumn, but the spring is better of the two. In any case where a special cultivation is determined on, it will be found that bone manure has a wonderful effect on the growth of Rhubarb.

It is not sufficient to say that the plantation must be kept free from weeds, for we are bound to advise that the plant should be allowed to make one whole season's growth before a single stalk is pulled. And we must again advise that the pulling in the second season, and every season thereafter, to the very end of the chapter, whenever that may be, should be moderate and careful, for every leaf removed weakens the plant, and it must be allowed to recover and regain its strength to prepare for the work of the next season. Some people know not when to leave off pulling at Rhubarb, but they have to leave off when there is none to pull; and it is a pity this should happen, because after the delicate and elegant supplies of early spring are past, Rhubarb is but a poor thing, and to ruin a plantation to get stalks for wine is a great folly. For wine-making a special plantation should be made, from which not one stick should be taken for table use. The summer stalks will then be of a suitable character.

Rhubarb is easily forced in any place where there is a moderate warmth, and it is only needful to pack the roots in boxes with moss or any light soil, or even rough litter—for the roots will push into any moist material and find sufficient food. If fully exposed to the light, forced Rhubarb has a full colour; but the quality is better, and the colour quite sufficient, if it is forced in the dark; hence when put under the stage in a greenhouse, or any other place where there is a fair share of daylight, it is well to put an empty box or barrel over to promote a certain degree of blanching.

When raised from seed some interesting varieties may be secured, and as a matter of fact several valuable and distinct varieties have been raised within the past few years. The seed should be sown in spring in any light soil, and the young plants should have frame culture until strong enough to plant out. If a great number are grown, they should all be kept in pots until the end of the season, and then the common-looking and unpromising plants should be destroyed, and the others reserved for planting out the next spring.

SALSIFY

(*Tragopogon porrifolius*)

SALSIFY may be sown from March to May, but two sowings will in most cases be sufficient. Drill the seed fifteen inches apart and one inch deep. Thin from time to time until the plants stand at nine to ten, or in an extreme case twelve inches. In ordinary soils nine inches will be sufficient. Hoe frequently between, but do not use a fork or spade anywhere near the crop, for the loosening of the ground will cause the roots to branch.

A deep sandy soil with a coat of manure put in the bottom of the trench will produce fine roots of Salsify. But there should be no recent manure within fifteen inches of the surface, or the roots will be forked and ugly. In a soil that produces handsome roots naturally, the preparation may consist in a good digging only, but generally speaking the more liberal routine will give a better result.

In November lift a portion of the crop and store in sand, and lift further supplies as required. A portion may be left to supply Chards in spring. These are the flowering shoots which rise green and tender, and must be cut when not more than five or six inches long. They are dressed and served in the same way as Asparagus.

Salsify is a root of high quality, the growing of which is generally considered a test of a gardener's skill. Perhaps the after-dressing and serving of Salsify may be a test of the skill of the cook, but upon that point we will not insist. It is a less troublesome root than Scorzonera, and superior to it in beauty and flavour—in fact, it is often dressed and served as 'Vegetable Oyster,' having somewhat the flavour of the favourite bivalve.

Salsify roots require to be prepared for use by scraping them, and then steeping in water containing a little lemon juice or vinegar. They are boiled until tender, and served with white sauce. To prepare them as the 'Vegetable Oyster,' the roots are first boiled and allowed to get cold, then cut in slices and quickly fried in butter to a light golden brown, being dusted with salt and white pepper while cooking. A small quantity of Parsley may be fried with them, but it is not necessary.

SAVOY (*See page* 34)

SCORZONERA

(*Scorzonera hispanica*)

SCORZONERA is not much grown in this country, but as it is prized on the Continent, it might be introduced to many English tables with advantage. The main point in the cultivation is to obtain large clean roots, for the carelessly grown samples will be small, forked, and fibrous. Trench a piece of ground and mix a good dressing of half-rotten manure with the bottom spit, taking care there is none in the top spit. Make a nice seed-bed, and sow in the month of March, in shallow drills fifteen inches apart, and as the plants advance thin them until they stand a foot apart in the drill. Keep the crop clean, and it will be fit for use in September. Lift as wanted in the same manner as Parsnips.

To cook the roots they must be first scraped and thrown into water in which there are a few drops of lemon juice. Let them remain half an hour, then boil in salted water in the same way as Carrots until quite tender, and serve with white sauce. If left to get cold, and then sliced and fried in butter, they make a good side dish.

SEA KALE

(*Crambe maritima*)

SEA KALE is by many considered superior to Asparagus, but it is so different in flavour and general character that we think there is no more room for a comparison than there is between a Broccoli and a Cabbage. Only one comparison, in our opinion, can be made with advantage, and it is that of the two Sea Kale is the more easy to cultivate, and the more decidedly profitable if regarded solely as an article of food. This comparison, therefore, has a practical bearing, and we would say that in forming a new garden, and in cases where it may not be possible to grow both these esculents advantageously, Sea Kale should have attention first, as a thing that will require but a small investment, and that will surely pay its way, not only with quick returns but with large profits, to the general advantage of the household.

Sea Kale requires strong ground, fully exposed to the sun, and enriched with any good manure that may be handy, our old friend that is born of the well-provendered stable being undoubtedly the best of all. The most satisfactory way to begin is with well-grown roots, as they make a return at once with the least imaginable trouble. Let the ground be well dug two spits deep, and put a coat of manure between; or if it is a good substantial loam, plant without manure, and the results will be excellent. As the thriving plant covers a considerable space, and there must be a certain amount of traffic on the ground to manage it, there should be one row in the centre of a four-feet bed, with a broad alley on one side; or better still, mark out a ten-feet space, with a three-feet alley on each side, and in this space plant three rows two and a half feet apart, and the roots two feet apart. The planting may be done at any time after the leaves have fallen, late in autumn, and during winter and early spring. On warm, dry ground, winter planting answers perfectly, and enables the gardener to get rid of the job, for there is always enough to do in the spring months. But on damp ground and in exposed situations, the best time to plant is the month of March. Put down the line, and open a trench one foot deep, and plant the roots with their crowns two inches below the surface, filling in and treading firmly as each trench is planted. The precaution may be taken to pare off all the pointed prominent buds on each crown, as this will prevent the rise of flower stems; but if this is neglected, the cultivator must take care to cut out all the flowering shoots that appear, for the production of flowers will prove detrimental to the crop of Sea Kale in the following season. Our custom, when a plantation has been thus made, is to grow another crop with it the first season. The ground between the rows is marked out in narrow strips, and lightly forked over, and if a coat of rotten manure can be spared it is pricked in, and a neat seed-bed is made of every strip, eighteen to twenty-four inches wide. On this we sow Onions, Lettuces, and other light crops; and as the

Sea Kale advances we take care to remove whatever would interfere with their expansion, for the stolen crop should not stand in the way of that intended for permanent occupation. A crop of early Cauliflower, small Cabbage, or even Potatoes, may be taken, in which case there will be room for only one row alternately with each row of Kale, and perhaps one row also in the alleys.

The growth of the Kale should be promoted by all legitimate means, and in high summer it will take water, liquid manure, and mulchings of rich stuff, to almost any extent, with advantage. The irrigation that suits the Kale will probably also suit the stolen crop, but irrigation is not good for Onions or Potatoes; where these crops are grown care must be given to bestow the fluid on the Sea Kale only.

As the leaves decay in the autumn, they should be removed, and the ground kept thoroughly clean. When finally cleaned up, let it be forked over, but with care not to put the tool too near the plants, and if manure is plentiful lay down a coat for a finish, or fork it in at the general clear up. There should now commence a systematic saving of clean leaves. Mere vegetable rubbish is not to be thought of. Proceed to cover the ground with leaves in heaps or ridges sufficient to make a coat finally of about one foot deep, or say nine inches at the very least. If there is any store of rough planking on the premises, let the planks be laid on the ridges of leaves on whichever side the prevailing wind may be. This will prevent the leaves being blown away, and the planks will be handy for the next stage in the business.

At the turn of the year put the planks on edge by driving posts down in any rough way that will hold them firmly for a brief season, and then spread the leaves equally. If there are not sufficient to cover the bed the requisite thickness, put up a good heap over each crown, and sprinkle a little earth to keep the heap together. But a better mode of procedure is to have a sufficiency of Sea Kale pots with movable covers, or in place of these large flower pots, or old boxes. Put these over the crowns, and then heap the leaves over and around, and the preliminaries are completed. A very early growth will be the result, and the quality will be finer than that of forced Sea Kale. You have but to uncover occasionally to see how the crop goes on, remembering that perfect darkness is needed to blanch it completely, and to produce a plump and delicate sample. Cut close over, taking a small portion of the woody part of the crown, and when all the growth of a crown is taken, remove the pot or box, but leave a thin coat of leaves on the cut crown to protect it, as at the time of cutting Sea Kale keen east winds are prevalent, and it is unfair to the plants to expose them suddenly. When the crop has been taken, remove the leaves and the planks, and dig in between the rows a good coat of fat manure. The growth will be too strong now for a stolen crop, and will so continue for many years. After the crop has been secured, each crown will throw out a number of buds or shoots. These should all be removed except two or three of the strongest, which will form the crowns for cutting in the following year. At the same time take away any small blanched shoots that may have been left because they were too small or insignificant for table use. This proceeding will prevent the production of flower stems, which is injurious to the plant. There never need be any fear of diminishing the crop by the process, because plenty of buds around the crowns, that do not show themselves in the first instance, will come forward in due time.

It is so easy to force Sea Kale that the cultivator may safely be left to his own devices. But it will be well perhaps to say that perfect darkness is requisite, and the temperature should not exceed 60° at any time, this being the maximum figure. A rise above 60° will produce a lean or wiry sample. It is sufficient to begin with a temperature of 45°, and to rise no higher than 55°, to insure a really creditable growth. The market growers are not very particular as to temperature, but then they do not eat the crop, or know much of it after it has left their hands. With the gardener in a domestic establishment the case is different; and we venture to advise the young men—to whom book advice is often valuable as entailing no obligations —that Sea Kale slowly forced may be nearly as good as that grown under pots in the open without any heat at all; better than such it cannot be. Any pits or odd places may be made use of for this crop, no matter what the general business in such places may be, provided only that the heat is not too great. Pack the roots in mould or leaves, or even half-rotten manure, and shut them up to exclude light, and the crop will be ready in five or six weeks, unless you commence very early, in which case seven weeks at least must be allowed from the time of planting to that of the first cutting. Roots that have been lifted for forcing should be thrown away when the crop has been secured, but roots forced in the open ground suffer so little by the process that they may be forced every year through half a lifetime ere it becomes necessary to renew the plantation, provided, of course, that the work is well done. The outdoor forcing is accomplished in the way described for growing the crop, with the aid of leaves only, but with certain differences. In the first place care must be taken to let the plants feel the cold, but at the same time to prevent the ground becoming frozen. A touch of frost will render them more ready to grow when the cultivator brings his persuasions to bear by heaping hot manure over the pots, and covering the bed with a thick coat of the same. This is all that can be done, but it is sufficient. In cases where leaves and other such materials are not available, good Sea Kale may be grown by simply raising over each crown a heap of sand or sifted coal ashes, provided some clean material be interposed to keep the sand or ashes from actual contact with the plant. When this heap begins to crack at the top it will be worth while to examine it at the bottom, when there will be found a fine head of blanched Sea Kale, and the mound will have served its purpose.

To grow Sea Kale from seed is a simple matter enough, but there is a loss of a year as compared with growing it from roots. The ground should be rich and well worked, and the seed should be sown in March or April in drills one foot asunder, if for planting out, or in patches two and a half feet apart, if to remain. It is believed by many that Sea Kale should stand where sown, and we admit that analogies are in favour of the proposal. But we see every year such grand produce from transplanted roots that we have not the courage to insist on a course of procedure that we believe to be theoretically correct. The fact is, the root is tough and enduring, and suffers but little by moderate exposure to the atmosphere if handled in a reasonable manner. But to return to the seeds: they sprout quickly, and, soon after, the plants make rapid progress. Let them have liberal culture, keep them scrupulously clean, and thin them in good time to at least two feet apart. If quite convenient, give them a light sprinkling of salt occasionally in the summer: they will enjoy it, and the leaves will not be injured in the least.

SHALLOT

(*Allium ascalonicum*)

THE old-fashioned mode of culture is to plant on the shortest, and dig the crop on the longest, day; but that is only applicable to the milder parts of the country. As a rule, spring is the best time for planting, and it should be done as early as the ground can be got into working order—certainly not later than the middle of April. The soil should be in a friable condition, and it must be trodden firmly, after the manner usual for an Onion bed. Merely press the bulbs into the soil sufficiently to keep them in position, and put them in rows one foot apart, and nine inches apart in the rows. They should not be earthed up, but, on the contrary, when approaching maturity, the soil should be drawn away so as to expose the bulbs, for this facilitates the ripening process.

When large bulbs are required for exhibition or other purposes, the cloves—as the divisions of each root are called—should be planted separately : but for general use moderate-sized bulbs, planted whole, will produce a heavier crop.

To store the roots for any length of time, it will be necessary to have them well ripened, and this point demands consideration. If dry weather could be insured for harvesting the crop, it might be allowed to finish in the ground ; but as this cannot be relied on, it is a wise precaution to lift the crop on some suitable opportunity before it is quite ready, and allow the ripening to be completed in a protected airy place.

SORREL

(*Rumex scutatus*)

THE large-leaved or French Sorrel is rapidly winning appreciation for its wholesome qualities and distinct flavour. It is not only served as a separate dish, but mingled with Spinach, and also as an ingredient in soups, sauces, and salads. Leaves of the finest quality are always obtainable from plants a year old, and when the crop has been gathered the ground may with advantage be utilised for some other purpose. Light soil in fairly good heart suits the plant. The seed should be sown in shallow drills six or eight inches apart, and the seedlings must be thinned early, leaving three or four inches between them in the rows. To keep the bed free from weeds is the only attention necessary, unless an occasional watering becomes imperative. In September the entire crop may be transferred to fresh ground, allowing eighteen inches between the plants, or part may be drawn and the remainder left at that distance. In the following spring, the flower stems will begin to rise, and if these are allowed to develop they reduce the size of the leaves, and seriously impair their quality, hence the heads should be pinched out as fast as they are presented.

SPINACH

(Spinacia oleracea)

SPINACH plays an important part in the economy of the dinner table. There are unfortunate beings who cannot eat it, for they describe it as bitter, sooty, and nauseous. Probably an equal number of persons regard it as a most princely vegetable. The rest of mankind proclaim it a wholesome, savoury, and acceptable esculent. It will grow anywhere and anyhow. Therefore we have not to commence this article with serious proposals; but some little management is needed to keep up a constant supply, not simply of Spinach but of fine Spinach with large, dark green leaves, that when properly cooked will be found, like the best Potatoes, to have butter in them already, as the result of good cultivation.

To produce first-class Spinach we need a well-tilled rich loam, but a capital sample may be grown on clay that has been some time in cultivation. The early sowings of Round or Summer Spinach should be in a sheltered situation, but not directly shaded. Sow in drills one foot apart, and one inch deep, beginning in January, although the first sowing may fail, and continue to sow about every fortnight until the middle of May. The earliest sowings should be on dry ground, but the later sowings will do well on damp ground with a little shade from the midday sun. It is important to thin the crop early, as it should not be in the least drawn. This is the only essential point in securing a fine growth, for if the plant cannot spread from the beginning it will never become luxuriant, and will soon run up to seed. Thin at first to six inches, and if large enough for use, send the thinnings into the house. Thin finally and before the leaves overlap to twelve inches. Every plant will cover the space, and it will suffice to take the largest leaves, two or three only from each plant, and thus a basket may be filled in a few minutes with really fine Spinach.

As the heat of the summer increases, the Spinach crop will be inclined to bolt. The starved plant will bolt first; the plant in rich moist soil, with plenty of room to spread, will be more leisurely about it, and will give time for the production of a succession crop to take its place. The sowings from May to August should be small and numerous, and on rich moist land, to be aided, if needful, with water. In many gardens there is a sufficient variety of vegetables after the middle of June to render it unnecessary to keep up the supplies of Spinach, and it is best to dispense with it if possible during July and August.

The sowing of Winter Spinach should commence in July, and be continued until the end of September, subject to the capabilities of the place. In gardens near towns, where the land is at all heavy, it is generally useless to sow after August, as the autumnal fogs are likely to destroy a plant that is only just out of the seed-leaf. But in favoured localities, with a warm soil and a soft air, the seed may be sown up to the very end of the year with but little risk of loss. The winter crops are sometimes sown broadcast, but drilling is to be preferred, and the rows must be fully fifteen inches apart. Thin at first to three inches, and afterwards to six inches, and leave them at this distance, for Winter Spinach may be a little crowded with advantage, because the weather and the black bot will now and then remove a plant. Should ground vermin be found worth serious attention, the best way to proceed will be to scratch shallow furrows very near the plants, taking care not to injure them. This may be done with the hoe, but if time can be spared it will be better to do it with a short pointed stick, having at hand, as the work progresses, a vessel into which to throw the grubs as they come to light when the earth is disturbed. Where small birds are in sufficient numbers, they will observe the disturbance of the earth, and diligently search for the grubs at hours when the cultivator is no longer on the search himself.

The July sowings will be useful in the autumn and throughout the winter, as the weather may determine; the later sowings will be useful in spring. Leaves only should be taken when the plant is large enough to supply them, and previous to this plants should be drawn only where they can be spared to make room for the remainder. But upon the symptoms of bolting being visible in the spring, cut the plants over at the collar, and at once prepare the ground for another crop.

NEW ZEALAND SPINACH. (*Tetragonia expansa.*) Gardeners are only too well acquainted with the difficulty of maintaining an unbroken supply of true Spinach during the burning summer months. But the weather which makes it almost impossible to produce a satisfactory crop of *Spinacia oleracea* brings New Zealand Spinach to perfection. And the latter is prized by some persons because it lacks the peculiar bitterness of the former. The plant is rather tender, and therefore to obtain an early supply the seed must be raised in heat. It may be sown in pots or pans at the end of March or beginning of April. The seedlings must be transferred to small pots immediately they are large enough, and be gradually hardened in preparation for removal to the open ground towards the end of May. They should be put into light soil in a sunny position, and be allowed three or four feet apart each way. It is not unusual to grow them on a heap of used potting soil, where they can ramble without restraint. The growth is rapid, and there must be no stint of water in dry weather. In five or six weeks the first lot of tender shoots will be ready for pinching off. Those who do not care to incur trouble under glass may sow in the open in the early part of May, and thin the plants to the distance named.

PERPETUAL SPINACH, OR SPINACH BEET. (*Beta Cicla.*) This is a true Beet, although it has only an ordinary tap-root. It is, however, a valuable plant for producing a continuous supply of leaves which make an excellent Spinach at a period of the year when the ordinary Summer Spinach is past its prime. For beet-roots a rich soil is objectionable, because it results in coarseness ; but as roots are not a consideration in this case, and an abundant growth of leaves is wanted, there should be liberal treatment. Sow in March and April, and again at the end of July or beginning of August, in rows one foot apart, and thin the plants to a distance of six or eight inches in the rows. When the leaves are ready for gathering, they must be removed, whether wanted or not, to insure continued growth.

STRAWBERRY

(*Fragaria*)

PROBABLY the first thought will be that the Strawberry is a fruit, and that the consideration of its treatment is out of place in a series of articles on the culture of vegetables. The answer is that the plant forms an essential feature in every good kitchen garden, and the general routine of work has to be arranged with due regard to this crop, so that we make no apology for alluding to it here.

The Strawberry is the most certain of all our hardy fruits, and is much valued both for eating fresh as a summer luxury and as a preserve for winter use. Although it deserves the best of cultivation, its needs are few, for under the poorest system of management it is often extremely fruitful, and not unseldom the most profitable crop in the garden. We have choice of seeds, divisions, and runners in making a plantation of strawberries. The universal way is the best way, and it consists in planting rooted runners of named sorts in an open sunny spot in well-prepared ground any time during spring or autumn, when fresh and good runners are obtainable; but late planting is undesirable, for when the plants have not time to establish themselves before winter sets in many are lost. If, therefore, the planting cannot be accomplished at the latest by the beginning of October, it is better to defer the task until the spring. Plants put in at the latter time should have the flower stems removed, and will then yield a heavy crop in the succeeding season.

The best soil for the plant is a rich, moist, sandy loam, but a heavy soil will answer perfectly if it is well prepared. The ground should be trenched and heavily enriched with rotten manure placed between the top and bottom spit, where the plants will reach it when they are most in need. In a new soil that is rather stiff, it will be advisable, when the trenching has been completed, to put down the line and cut shallow trenches, which should be filled with any rather fine kindly stuff that may be at hand, such as old hot-bed soil, leaf-mould, or a mixture of material turned out of pots, with some good decayed manure. In this the young plants will root freely and quickly without becoming gross, for we want a certain degree of vigour; but an excessive leaf growth may result in losses during winter, and a small crop of fruit the following year. Well-cultivated soils need no such special preparation, but in any case a good digging and a liberal manuring are absolutely necessary. And here it may be well to state that after the plants have obtained a firm hold of the soil, it matters not how hard the ground becomes. The practice of some growers in running a plough lightly between the rows either for a mulch, or to give the plants the full benefit of rain, does not in the least degree upset this conclusion, for this only creates a loose and friable surface, and the operation is so managed that the soil near the roots remains undisturbed. It may be accepted as a secret of successful Strawberry culture that the bed should be firm and compact, and, in forcing, this principle is so far recognised that the soil is positively rammed into the pots.

If Strawberry plants come to hand somewhat dry, unpack them quickly, and spread them in small lots in a cool shady place, and sprinkle lightly with water to refresh them. A deluge of water is not needed, and in fact will do harm, but enough to moisten them will put them in a condition to begin growing as soon as they are properly located. The distances in planting will have to be determined by the relative vigour of the varieties and the nature of the ground. As a rule the rows should be two feet apart, and the plants eighteen inches in the rows, but some varieties require fully two and a half feet between the rows. It is good practice to leave a three-feet space between every two rows for necessary traffic. A modification of the plan consists in planting a foot apart each way; and immediately the first crop of fruit is off, every alternate row is removed, and then every alternate plant in each row is also taken out. This places the remainder at two feet every way. The ground is then dug between and a heavy coat of manure put on.

The general management comprises keeping down weeds, supplying water abundantly in dry weather, especially when the berries are swelling, and removing runners as fast as they appear, for to allow them to get ahead is most injurious, and any serious neglect of the matter is likely to ruin the plantation. The Strawberry plant makes no proper return on a dry lumpy soil. Large plantations that cannot be watered must be aided in the height of the season by covering the ground with any light material which will prevent evaporation. As to obtaining runners, that is an easy matter enough, but there is a good way and a bad way. To allow them to spread and root promiscuously is the bad way; it injures the plants, makes the bed disorderly, and does not produce good runners. At the time when runners begin to push, dig and manure the surrounding spaces, and allow a certain number of runners to come out from each side of the rows. As they approach maturity and are disposed to make roots, lay tiles or stones upon the runners near to the young plants to favour the process, but a neater way will be to peg them down. Or they may be fixed by short pegs in small pots, filled with light rich earth and plunged conveniently for the purpose.

To keep the crop clean many plans are adopted, and the plant probably takes its name from the old custom of covering the ground with straw for the purpose. The cultivator must be left to his own devices, because of the difficulty in many places of obtaining suitable material. But we must warn the beginner in Strawberry culture against grass mowings as more or less objectionable. They sometimes answer perfectly, and at other times they encourage slugs and snails to spoil the crop, and if partially rotted by wet weather communicate to the fruit a bad flavour. There is a very simple means of feeding the crop and making a clean bed for the fruit. It consists in putting on a good coat of long, strong manure in February, and in doing this it is no great harm if the plants are in some degree covered. They will soon push up and show themselves, and by the time the fruit appears the straw will be washed clean, and the crop being thus aided will be a great one, weather permitting. As regards cutting off the leaves, we advise the removal of old large leaves as soon as the crop is gathered. But this should be done with a knife; to use a scythe amongst Strawberries is to ruin the plantation. The object of removing old leaves is to admit light and air to the young leaves, for on the free growth of these the formation of good crowns for the next year's use depends. By encouraging the young leaves to grow, root action is promoted, and the embryo buds are formed that will, in the next summer, develop into Strawberries.

Some gardeners recommend the removal of the Strawberry plantation every three years. It is a better plan to make a small plantation annually, and at the same time destroy an old plantation that has served its turn. But we are bound to say that Strawberry plantations, well made and well kept, will often last and prove profitable for six or even more years. But this will never be the case where there is a stint of manure or water, or where the runners are allowed to run in their own way to make a Strawberry mat and a jam of the wrong sort. The Strawberry fancier does not wish to keep a plantation any great length of time, and he must plant annually to taste the new sorts. This to many people is one of the chief delights of the garden, and it certainly has its attractions.

Strawberries are forced in large quantities in good gardens; and even in small places much pleasure is derived from a few plants nicely fruited under glass in the spring of the year. The earliest runners should be very firmly potted, and grown liberally, until the growing season is over. Runners from forced plants are generally preferred because of their earliness. A substantial soil is required, and the pots must be well drained. Success depends on beginning early and forcing slowly, the plants to be as near the glass as possible, and to be very carefully managed that they are not injured by sudden bursts of sunshine when somewhat dry at the roots. To guard against this, it is good practice to put a few inches of half-rotten manure on the shelf and let them root through, in which case the labour of watering will be somewhat lessened, but must be carefully attended to for all that. It is no uncommon thing for a beginner in this business to lose the whole stock of thriving plants through a little neglect of the watering. The highest temperature allowable up to the fruiting stage is 45° to 50° in the first instance, afterwards 50° to 60°. When there is a fair crop of berries formed the remaining flowers must be removed, for to overload the plants will ruin them, and the temperature may be raised to 65° or 70°. As the colouring proceeds the minimum may be 65° and the maximum 80°. Beyond this entails great risk, and so high a temperature is allowable only when the sun shines and the plants are kept well supplied with water. During the colouring process the water supply must be reduced, but not to such an extent as to cause the leaves to flag, for it should be observed that if the leaves of Strawberries once droop through deficiency of moisture at the root, it is more than probable that they will never rise again.

To grow Strawberries from seed is an interesting business, and should be systematically practised to insure a supply of the delicate Alpine varieties. The seed may be sown as soon as gathered, or may be kept until spring. Being remarkably hardy, it is an easy matter to raise plants in an open bed of light rich soil, by sowing the seeds in shallow drills six inches apart. From this bed they should be transplanted to the places they are to remain in for fruiting, the soil being rather lighter and finer than for the larger kinds of Strawberries. But it is better practice to sow the seed in pans filled with a light rich compost, consisting of turfy loam, leaf-mould, and rotten hot-bed manure, and assist germination with a gentle heat. From these pans the plants should be pricked out in a bed of light soil in a frame, or on a nearly exhausted hot-bed, whence they should be taken to the open ground to remain for fruiting. From spring-sown seeds thus treated a moderate crop may be obtained in the autumn, and a full crop the following year, after which the plants should be destroyed, a succession being kept up by sowing annually. By slowly growing from spring-sown seeds and potting in autumn, it is not a difficult matter to have Alpines in fruit under glass at Christmas.

SUNFLOWER

(*Helianthus annuus*)

THE SUNFLOWER may be spoken of as a plant that is for ever promising to perform wonders, but abandoning the task when it is about half completed. It may become a farm crop, but it seems to wait for a man of genius to discover its capabilities. It is possible that we have fibre in the stem, fodder in the leaves, as well as poultry food in the seeds, and the latter may also be made to yield a valuable oil, suitable for culinary purposes. Only one capability has been actually demonstrated, and that is the value of the seeds in fattening poultry. The best way to use the heads is to hang them up, so that the birds can pick the seeds out without otherwise touching them. As regards cultivation, sow in pans in April, and put on a gentle hot-bed, or shut up close in a sunny frame. The plants will soon appear. Give them light and air, and plant out when they are two or three inches high. But Sunflowers can be grown without any kind of artificial aid. A simple and effectual method is to make the spot intended for them very rich, and dibble the seed an inch deep on the first day of May.

TOMATO

(*Lycopersicum esculentum*)

THE taste for Tomatoes, like certain engagements, often begins with a little antipathy, but it is soon acquired and not infrequently develops into passionate love for the fruit both cooked and in its natural condition. Within memory of those who would feel insulted were they called middle-aged, the consumption of Tomatoes in this country was limited to a select circle of epicures. In the United States the fruit has long been recognised as a necessary article of food, and as a matter of fact our transatlantic cousins have taught us the value of its refreshing, appetising, and corrective qualities. Still the advance in public favour has been accelerated by the improved quality, enhanced beauty, and increased variety, effected by several of our own talented specialists in horticulture.

The Tomato is a tender, but not a tropical plant, and it requires a moderately high temperature, free access of air, and above all a full flood of solar light to bring it to perfection. The necessary heat is easily managed in any garden equipped with ordinary forcing appliances; so also is a current of air in properly constructed buildings; but the deficiency of light during the darker months renders it almost impossible to ripen fruit in mid-winter; otherwise no trouble would be experienced in sending Tomatoes to table every day throughout the year. Our long nights and murky atmosphere afford the growers of sunnier lands an opportunity of consigning vast quantities to this country, under the serious disadvantage, however, of being compelled to cut the fruit prematurely. Hence the ripening is completed during the voyage instead of on the plant, to the detriment of colour and flavour, and with the additional objection of rendering the skin disagreeably tough. Imported Tomatoes are indeed only tolerable to an educated palate when English-grown fruit cannot be obtained. This remark does not apply to the fruit obtained from the Channel Islands, where Tomatoes are skilfully grown, carefully packed, and so expeditiously conveyed to the London market that there need be no appreciable deterioration in quality.

In a private garden the object to be aimed at is a daily supply, commensurate with household requirements, commencing on the earliest possible date in spring, and extending far into autumnal days, without interval or waste from beginning to end. And it will be obvious that the methods which are adapted for securing this desirable object can be indefinitely extended to meet a great public demand.

Almost every imaginable glass structure can be employed for growing Tomatoes, from the small suburban greenhouse to the vast span-roof, hundreds of feet in length, devoted to their culture in Guernsey and Jersey. And it is not essential that the crop should be grown alone. Potatoes, French Beans, Strawberries and Vines may be forced in the same building, provided there be no obstruction to light and air, nor any interference with the conditions which experience has proved to be imperative for sustaining the plants in vigorous health. For very early gathering there must be a service of hot-water pipes, but as the spring advances it is easy to ripen fruit in cool houses, and later on plants in borders will in ordinary seasons yield an abundant return without artificial protection of any kind.

Tomatoes can be propagated from cuttings, and for a winter crop this method offers the advantages of quickness and certainty of setting. The disadvantage is that the plants are less robust in constitution than seedlings, and this is a serious addition to the difficulties of winter culture. We therefore leave the system of propagation by cuttings to those who need no advice from us. Seed may be sown at almost any time of the year, but the most important months are September, December, February, and March. In gardens favourably situated in the south of England and furnished with the most perfect appliances, seed is sown in all these months and in others also; but in smaller gardens sowings are restricted to February and March. Whenever a start is made sow thinly in pans or boxes, and do not allow the seedlings to remain in them for an unnecessary day. Immediately two or at most four leaves are formed either prick off into other pans or boxes, or transfer singly to thumb pots, and as a rule the pots will be found preferable. The soil for these pans or pots should be stored in the greenhouse a few days in advance of the transfer, so that the compost may acquire the proper temperature and save the plants from an untimely check. In small houses place the plants near the glass that they may remain short in the joint, but on cold nights they must be taken down to avoid injury from fluctuations of temperature. In large houses, where the light is well diffused, there is no need to incur this trouble, for the seedlings will do equally well on the ground level. In due time shift into 48-size pots, from which they can go straight to borders or into a larger size if they are to be fruited in pots. About fourteen weeks will be required to prepare the plants for borders in the winter season, but a shorter period will suffice in spring and summer. Plants from a September sowing will not mature fruit in much less than six months, while a March sowing will yield a return in four months or less. Much depends on the character of the season, and more on skill and attention. Those who sow in the middle of February should sow again a fortnight later for succession crops, and finally in the early part of March for plants to be hardened preparatory to their being put into the open ground at the end of May or beginning of June.

In the first instance, there need be no anxiety about soil. Any fairly good sandy loam will answer for the seed-pans, and if too stiff it may be freely mixed with sharp sand or the sifted sweepings from roads and gravel walks. A fibrous loam, cut from a rich pasture, and laid up in a heap for twelve months, will, with an addition of grit, make an ideal soil for pots or borders. As the plants advance, leaf-mould or thoroughly decayed manure in moderate quantity should be supplied; but, instead of incorporating it with the loam in the usual way, it will be found advantageous to place the manure immediately above the crocks, and the roots will find it at the right time. But the quantity of manure must not be overdone, especially in the earlier stages of growth, because excessive luxuriance neither promotes fruitfulness nor conduces to early ripening. After the fruit has set, a mulch of decayed manure will aid the plants in finishing a heavy crop, brilliant in colour and superb in flavour. Manure which is only partially fermented will not do at all. The ammonia it liberates exerts so deadly a power that we have seen thousands of plants scorched in a few hours, as with the blast of a furnace.

In its demand for potash the Tomato closely resembles the Potato, and of the two the former is the more exacting. So quickly does this crop exhaust the soil, that in small houses it is usual to take out the earth to a depth of fifteen or eighteen inches every second or third year, and replace it with virgin loam. On a small scale this is rather a serious matter, and for an extensive range of houses with limited resources the exchange of soil becomes an impossibility. Some of the Guernsey growers meet the difficulty by constructing vast houses upon flanged wheels, resting on iron rails to facilitate removal to fresh ground. Others grow the Tomatoes alternately in the bed and in pots, but this is only a partial remedy. Constant dressings of manure result in the formation of humus, which, as it becomes sour, has to be sweetened by the solvent influence of lime. Even this treatment will only extend the fertility of the soil for a limited number of years. Sooner or later the crop ceases to make a return for the labour and expense lavished upon it. The most enduring method is that which is based on chemical knowledge of the constituents of the soil, and the relation which the plant bears to it. One of the most successful growers for the London market almost entirely avoids the use of stable manure, and he is able, by applications of nitrate of potash, crushed dissolved bones, and the occasional use of lime, to grow splendid crops in the same houses year after year.

Another method of dealing with the soil under glass deserves mention. There may be a difficulty in securing sufficient loam of a suitable character for the entire border. In such a case break the existing surface, whatever the nature of it may be, and upon this make a ridge of sandy loam about eighteen inches or two feet wide, and deep enough to cover the balls of earth when the plants are turned out of the pots. As the roots show on the surface, more soil must be added, and finally they can be fed with a mulch or with liquid manure. It is important that the liquid should be weak, and then it may be alternated with pure water, either for borders or pots.

All the conditions which answer for border work are applicable to pots, and a limited number of plants brought forward in succession will supply the requirements of a small household from early spring until near Christmas. The pot system is conducive to free setting and to early ripening, and for these reasons it is worth attention. The plants should be kept short in the joint by frequent shifts until the twelve-inch pot is reached, and this size will accommodate two cordons or one plant having two branches, each of which will require a separate stake for its support. Plunging the pots can be adopted to save labour in watering.

No advantage is to be gained by attempting to force Tomatoes in a higher temperature than is consistent with healthy progress, although in winter there is great temptation in the direction of overheating. Full time for development in moderate heat will bring stout joints, and impart a vigorous constitution that materially aids the plants in resisting the insidious attacks of disease. The waning autumn and dull winter days are the most troublesome periods of management, and it is remarkable that of two days equal in duration and apparently in other conditions, the autumnal appears to be less favourable than the spring day. The difficulty of carrying plants through the winter deters many gardeners from commencing operations until February is well advanced. But if, on the one hand, a high temperature is injurious, a low temperature must be avoided; although for a time it may not appear to be harmful. A temperature of 60° or 65° suits the seed-pans, and after transfer to pots and the roots have become established, the thermometer should not register less than 55° during the night. It may rise 10° by means of fire heat in the daytime, and during bursts of sunshine another 10° or 15° will be quite safe, always assuming that the roots are not dry, and that the plants have free ventilation.

The judicious administration of water forms an important feature in the culture of the Tomato. The plant is too succulent to endure drought with impunity, and it is mere folly to toy with the water-can. Saturate down to the roots, and then leave the plants alone until more water is wanted. No hard and fast rule can be stated as to frequency. It depends on the condition of the soil, the period of the year, and the age of the plants. Borders and soil for pots should be made sufficiently moist in advance, so that watering will not be necessary immediately after the plants are transferred. The prevalent opinion that excessive watering generates disease is not confirmed by our experience. Of course the watering should not be excessive for many reasons, but the diseases which are often attributed to over-watering are the result of atmospheric mismanagement.

Authorities are not agreed as to whether branched plants or simple cordons yield the better results. In our judgment the single stem deserves preference, and it is now more extensively grown than any other form, although plants having two branches are almost equally popular. Certainly the cordon can be managed with extreme ease; it is admittedly the earliest producer, and there is a general consensus of opinion that the fruit it produces is unsurpassed in size and quality. The doubtful point is quantity, but even here the difference, if any, is too trifling to be worth the consideration of private growers. Cordons are formed by removing the laterals as fast as they appear, and when the fruit has set, or the requisite height is attained, the top is also pinched out.

The space allowed for each plant varies greatly, especially among growers for market. Under glass every branched Tomato should be allowed at least three feet each way, and in the open ground four feet between rows facilitates the work. For cordons we advocate a distance between the rows of three feet, and a space of two feet in the row is not too much. The stems require support of some kind, and, although more expensive, stakes are preferable to string; but of course the stems may be secured to wires whenever it is convenient to run the plants immediately under the glass.

Another point upon which authorities differ is the extent to which Tomatoes should be denuded of their foliage. Some growers condemn the procedure entirely; others reduce their plants to skeletons. Both extremes are objectionable, for when all the leaves are permitted to remain there is delay or partial failure in colouring the fruit, and the almost entire removal of foliage checks the root action injuriously. In practice it answers well to wait until the fruit has set, then by pinching out the leading point of each leaf, commencing at the bottom, ripening and colouring are promoted, and the health of the plant remains unimpaired.

In dull weather, and especially in short days, a difficulty is sometimes experienced in setting the fruit, particularly the first bunch. After fruit has begun to swell on one bunch, the remainder set with comparative ease. A rather higher temperature than usual combined with free movement of the atmosphere is generally sufficient to insure fertilisation, especially with the ribbed varieties. But some of the handsome smooth kinds are a little shy, and they can be assisted by a very simple expedient. If necessary water the plants early in the afternoon, and close the house rather before the usual time. The warm atmosphere will develop plenty of pollen, and a gentle shaking of the flower bunches with a slight touch from a hazel twig will liberate visible clouds, which will effectually set the fruit. Another method is to lift a flat label or paper-knife against the flowers. The label becomes covered with pollen, and by gently touching each flower with a slight upward pressure a great number can be fertilised in a few minutes. A soft brush passed over the flowers daily has the same effect. Plants in the open ground need no such attention if they are in good health and the season is at all genial. In almost every bunch of flowers one will be found that is fasciated or confused, and it should be pinched out to prevent the formation of large and ugly fruit. The remainder of the bunch will be the finer for its absence.

As a near relation of the Potato, the Tomato is equally susceptible to unfavourable atmospheric influences; but the former is grown in the open, subject to caprices of the seasons, while the latter is chiefly cultivated under glass with the aid of fire heat, and this affords a practical mastery of the situation. Under such conditions the presence of disease should be regarded as convincing evidence of mismanagement. The deadliest foe of the Tomato is the fungus which attacks the leaves, and of all fragile forms of parasitic vegetation this is surely the most delicately sensitive. A passing breath, or the rapid movement of the hand over the surface, and the fungus is dispersed, filling the atmosphere with countless spores. Another disease begins with a dark spot in the fruit, which rapidly spreads from one plant to another. Both diseases are generated by conditions which to a large extent are avoidable in houses properly heated and possessing facilities for free ventilation. In a stagnant humid atmosphere disease may be evolved within twenty-four hours, and this fact conveys a lesson which cannot be misunderstood. Still foggy nights present the greatest difficulty; but however dull and motionless the atmosphere may be without, the air within the house must be kept in circulation. If necessary increase the fire heat to maintain temperature, open the top-lights, and admit air freely against the hot pipes, so that it may be warmed on its entrance. One of the best means of effecting this both in Tomato houses and Vineries is to insert tubes in the wall just above the ground level, of such a length as to project the air directly on the pipes. As a rule this treatment alone will maintain the plants in health; but as prevention is better than cure, the atmosphere may be impregnated with the fine powder of *Sulfosteatite coprique* disseminated by means of common bellows; and this powder should be promptly used in the event of disease appearing.

The sudden drooping of plants, known as 'sleeping,' arises from exhaustion of the soil. A mulch or a soaking of water will sometimes partially revive these plants, but it seldom answers to retain them. Deficiency in the soil of nitrogen and potash is the secret, and the remedy is entirely in the grower's hands.

For the open ground it is important to choose a variety that ripens early. The plants should be vigorous, and they must be carefully hardened before they are put out. The end of May is usually the right time, but Tomatoes will not endure a keen east wind or nipping frost. During the prevalence of unfavourable weather it is advisable to wait a week or more rather than risk the destruction of the plants. When the temperature appears to be fairly reliable, put them into holes a foot deep and eighteen inches across, filled with light soil not too rich. For a few nights until the roots take hold slight protection should be at hand to assure safety; Sea-Kale pots answer admirably and are easily placed in position. In addition to beds all sorts of places are suitable for Tomatoes, such as under warm palings or walls, on sloping banks and in sheltered nooks, where they will thrive and yield valuable fruit. Thus in cottage gardens a supply of this delicacy may be insured for part of the year equal in quality to fruit which is grown in the glass houses of the wealthy.

TURNIP

(*Brassica Rapa*)

THE TURNIP is not a difficult garden crop, indeed the simplest management will produce an ample supply, and any fairly good ground will suffice for it. But whatever is worth doing is worth doing well, and a gardener may be pardoned for taking an especial pride in producing a sufficiency of handsome and tender Turnips. The great point is to insure a succession through a long season, or say, the whole year round, for Turnips are always in request, and at certain periods of the year delicate young roots are greatly valued for the table.

The finest Turnips are grown in deep, sandy loam, kept in a high state of cultivation. Useful Turnips may be grown on any soil, but a handsome sample of the finest quality cannot be produced on heavy clay or a thin limestone soil. In common with other fast-growing plants of the cruciferous order, Turnips must have lime in some form, and it will occasionally be necessary in many gardens to give a dressing of it in addition to the ordinary manure. Superphosphate, bone and old plaster or mortar from destroyed buildings, are all valuable in preparing the soil for this crop.

It is advisable to sow Turnips in drills on a fine tilth, and it is an advantage to have a sufficiency of some stimulating manure near the surface to hurry the growth of the young plant, for the danger of fly belongs to the seed-leaf stage. Generally speaking, the Turnip fly does but little harm in gardens; but where it is much feared, the seed should be sown in prepared drills to encourage a quick growth. Draw the drills twelve to fifteen inches apart, three inches deep, and about the same width, and almost fill them with rotten manure, or with a mixture of earth and guano, or wood ashes; cover this with a little fine soil to prevent injury to the seed; then sow, and lightly conceal the seed with earth as a finish. If the ground is sufficiently moist, growth will commence almost immediately, and the plant will come up strong, and very quickly put forth rough leaves. In the general management more depends on timely and judicious thinning than upon any other point. If Turnips are not well thinned, so that each plant can spread its green head unimpeded by the leaves of a neighbour, a good growth cannot be expected; and thinning by the hoe should be commenced as soon as the rough leaves appear. The operation must be repeated until the plants are at a suitable distance, and then comes the process of singling, which should be done by hand. It will be found that in many cases two or three little plants stand together looking like one. There must be only one left at each station, and that should be the shortest. The distances may vary from four to ten inches, according to the vigour of the variety and the kind of Turnips required. An easy and profitable plan is to allow a certain number of bulbs to swell to supply young Turnips, and, by drawing these, leave room for the remainder of the crop to attain its proper size for storing.

To obtain a succession of Turnips is a matter of considerable importance, and should have constant attention in every good garden. An early crop of small bulbs may be grown, by sowing in January on a very gentle hot-bed as prescribed for early Radishes, and it may be well to add here, that in an emergency, white Turnip Radishes may be made to take the place of Turnips, both to flavour soups and to appear as a dish in the usual way. Fast-growing Turnips may be sown on an open sheltered border in February, to be carefully watched and protected when unkind weather prevails. In March, April, and May, sowings should be made consistently with the probable wants of the household, but the May sowings should comprise two or three sorts in the event of hot dry weather spoiling some of them. The principal sowings for autumn and winter use are made in June and July, and it will often pay to sow as late as August 15, but when the month is out it is likely to prove a waste of time to sow Turnips any more until the turn of the year.

The Turnip likes a light soil, but does not well endure the occasional dryness to which light soils are subject. This fact accounts for many failures of the crop in a hot dry season, for sunshine suits the Turnip, but it must have moisture or suffer deterioration in some way. If, therefore, the soil becomes dry, and there is no prospect of rain to put things in order, the Turnips should have water, not simply to moisten the surface, but to go to the roots, for frequent watering is not good for the crop, as it tends to spoil the beauty of the bulbs, and promotes a rank leaf-growth which is not wanted. An occasional heavy watering in dry weather will also do much towards the repression of the many enemies that beset this useful root—the jumpers, the grubs, the weevils, and the rest of the crew will be routed out of their snug hiding-places in the dusty soil when the watering takes place, and the death of many will follow. But so long as the soil is fairly moist at the depth the roots are ranging, there is no need for watering, and the time it would consume may be utilised for other work.

On the approach of winter a certain portion of the Turnip crop should be lifted and stored. In doing this the tops must be cut off, not too close, but just leaving a slight green neck, and the roots should be rather shortened than removed; at all events, to cut the roots off close is bad practice, as when so treated the bulbs do not keep well. Any rough storage answers for Turnips, the object being to keep them plump by excluding the atmosphere, and at the same time render them safe against frost. The portion of the crop left in the ground may be lifted as wanted in the same way as Parsnips, but this should be done systematically, so that the ground which is cleared may be dug over and ridged up before winter. Those that remain will be in a piece, and will give a good crop of spring greens, after which they may be made use of as manure by putting them at the bottom of a trench.

Some of the foes that war against the Turnip crop are alluded to at greater length later on. Happily the gardener has many friends that are insufficiently known to the farmer, not the least important being the starlings, song birds, and occasionally (but not often) the sparrows. Where the cultivation is good and small birds abound, the Turnip crop is pretty safe, and the general routine of culture sketched above will certainly promote, if it does not absolutely secure, its safety. The worst foes of the Turnip in the field are the fly and the caterpillar; but in the garden, and more especially the old garden, the anbury, or 'fingers and toes,' is the most to be feared. When this happens, the cultivator may rest satisfied that the soil is in fault, and this may be owing to a bad routine of cropping. Wherever anbury appears, whether on Cabbages or Turnips or any other cruciferous plant, there should be worked out a complete change in the order of cropping, taking care not to put any brassicaceous plants on the plots where the disease has occurred for two or three seasons, and allowing at least one whole year to pass without growing any of the cruciferous order upon them. In the meantime, for other crops the land should be well trenched and limed, and generously cultivated. The result will be profitable crops of other kinds of vegetables, and a refreshing of the soil that will enable it to carry brassicaceous plants again, with but little risk of the recurrence of anbury. Good cultivation is the only panacea known against the plagues that assail our crops. This does not surely secure them, for the elements are capricious and beyond our control; but where good cultivation prevails the failures are few, and even unfavourable seasons do not utterly obliterate the results of our labours.

VEGETABLE MARROW

(*Cucurbita Pepo ovifera*)

THE VEGETABLE MARROW does not, in a general way, obtain the right kind of attention in gardens. It is much valued as a summer vegetable; and it is very generally grown, but too often the aim of the cultivator is to obtain large Marrows, that at the very best are coarse and troublesome to the cook, and are always wanting in substance and flavour, instead of smallish Marrows, which are easily dressed, elegant on the table, and combine with a substantial and somewhat glutinous pulp a most delicious flavour. Two fears beset the average gardener: he is afraid to grow small sorts, and he is afraid to cut them when quite young. When he can overcome these fears he will appreciate the smaller Marrows that have of late years been secured by patient labour in cross-breeding, for while they are of the highest quality, they are also early and productive, far surpassing all the larger Marrows in quickness and usefulness. The market grower we do not pretend to advise, for he must grow what he can sell; and if the smaller Marrows are insufficiently appreciated in gardens, we cannot hope to see them on sale in shops. The big watery Marrows will doubtless keep their place in commerce, notwithstanding the improvements that have been effected by certain persons who may be described as epicures in gardening.

The Vegetable Marrow will grow in any good soil, and though a very tender plant is so accommodating in its nature that if the seed is sown on a piece of newly dug clay land in the latter part of May, or early in June, the plants will thrive and produce a heavy crop the same season. We put this as an extreme case, but we do not recommend such a rough-and-ready mode of growing this valuable esculent. The fact is, it pays better to grow it well than to grow it ill; and in a country where land and labour are costly, and the summer very uncertain, it is best to take such a thing in hand scientifically, and provide for it as many favourable conditions as possible. Three conditions we will here insist upon : a moderate bottom heat from fermenting material ; a kindly, loamy soil, quite mellow, in which the roots can run freely ; and a sufficiency of water, for this is a thirsty plant, and the more vigorous the growth the more satisfactory will be the result.

Frame culture is of some importance, because early Marrows are highly valued, indeed almost overvalued, at good tables. For this business we require the neat-growing, small-fruited kinds, which yield a great crop in a small compass. The best place for an early crop of Marrows is a brick pit, with hot-water pipes for top heat, and a bed of fermenting materials for bottom heat. It is no difficult matter to obtain a supply in a house with Cucumbers, but it is better to grow the Marrows apart, as they require less heat and less moisture than Cucumbers. In making up the bed, it is well to employ leaves largely, say to the extent of one-half, the remainder being stable manure that has been twice turned. Such a bed will give a mild heat for a great length of time, and the plants can be put out upon it within three days of its being made up. When grown in a common frame, the arrangements are much the same as advised for the frame cultivation of the Cucumber, the chief points of difference being that Marrows should have less heat and more air. The temperature for Marrows under cover may range from 55° the minimum, to 80° the maximum ; the safe medium being about 65° when the weather is cold and dull ; running to 80° when strong sunshine prevails, and the plants are growing freely with plenty of air. As for the general management, we require a bed nine inches deep, of good fibrous loam, regular supplies of water of the same temperature as the pits, so that the bed is always reasonably moist, and every evening a slight syringing over the leaves and the walls before shutting up. The training out is a very simple matter. Let them run in their own way until they have made shoots eighteen inches long, then nip out the points. After this there must be no more stopping, but occasionally the laterals must be suppressed to prevent crowding. Give air freely at every opportunity, and be careful not to administer too much water, or the mistake will be paid for by a deficiency of fruit.

To grow Marrows in the open air, the best course of procedure is to remove a portion of the top soil, to form a shallow trench four feet wide. Into this, carry one foot to eighteen inches depth of half-rotten manure, or a mixture of equal parts of manure and leaves, and cover with the soil that was taken out. This will produce a very gentle hot-bed that will last until the natural ground heat is sufficient to keep the plants in vigorous health. The middle of May is quite early enough to make up the bed, and in the course of two or three days the plants may be put out, and covered with hand-lights or small frames, which on the following day should be tilted at bottom to admit a little air, and if strong sunshine occurs, a Rhubarb leaf may be laid over to subdue the glare upon the young plants. We will suppose these plants to have been raised in a Cucumber frame from seed sown in April. If you cannot secure plants, sow seeds in patches of two or three on the bed, and cover with large flower-pots wrong way up, and with a piece of tile to stop the hole. This plan hastens germination, and the pots may be used as protectors if glass frames are not at command, being taken off during the day and put on at night, the hole being left open to give a little air. During bad weather, the pots should remain all day over the plants, but as soon as possible must be again taken off to keep the growth short, and green, and vigorous. The plants should be put singly down the centre of the bed, three feet apart, and as a matter of course the seeds should be sown at the same distance, and each clump of two or three should be reduced to one when the plants are somewhat forward. It is advisable not to be in a hurry to thin the plants, for the slugs will probably compel some modification of arrangements, so that sometimes it will be necessary to lift a clump, and divide the plants, to fill up gaps where the slugs have made a clearance. An occasional inspection in the after part of the day, and again in the early morning, will be the best course to keep down the slugs, as they may then be caught and disposed of; but a dusting of soot around each clump will do much to protect the plants against silent marauders. As for after management, there is no occasion whatever for any stopping or training, but now and then a stout peg may be placed to keep some strong vine in order. But the necessity for moisture must not be overlooked, for if the ground becomes dry the plants will suffer; but with moisture enough they will continue growing and bearing until the frost destroys them. The Marrows should be cut when quite young, for not only are they more useful on the table when small and tender, but the plants will bear five times as many as when a few are permitted to attain their full size. The explanation of the case is very simple. The production of the young fruits does not in any appreciable degree exhaust the plants; but when the fruits are allowed to develop, the production of a succession is pretty well brought to a stop. And as seedy Marrows are objectionable for the table, it is clearly an injustice to the plants to allow fruits to become seedy when it is intended to cut them for household purposes. Marrows are sometimes grown in abundance, and of the finest quality, on a different plan from that generally adopted. About a foot depth of earth is thrown out in a long line four feet wide. Into the shallow four-feet trench one or two feet depth of good rotten manure is placed, and the earth taken out is returned upon it. The plants are put in immediately, and protected with hand-glasses, frames, or even baskets if the weather is unkind, but they are expected to 'rough it' if the weather is favourable. Sheets of oiled paper, raised by a small flower-pot in the centre, and with stones laid on the corners to prevent their being blown away, make a capital temporary protection for the young plants. They may be allowed to grow from under the papers and harden themselves. In due time collect the papers and store for use in the following year. The bed becomes moderately warm immediately, and the warmth lasts long enough for the plants to root freely and start into vigorous growth. Thenceforward nothing is done; the plants grow as they like, and produce an extravagant quantity of fruit. The most delicately flavoured Marrows, as a rule, are the smallest, and these should be cooked whole, and be carefully pressed before serving, and be served whole if possible, or at most only cut into halves, and of course there is no occasion to remove the seeds.

A YEAR'S WORK
IN
THE VEGETABLE GARDEN

INTRODUCTORY REMARKS

THE following monthly notes are not intended to supersede the detailed instructions on the several kinds of Vegetables which appear in the preceding pages. The present object is to call attention to the work that must be done, and the work that must be prepared for, as the changes of the seasons require and the state of the weather may permit; yet some amount of detail is included, for to offer reminders simply would be to exclude the great mass of amateurs and the less experienced of practical gardeners from participation in the advantages of these monthly notes, and restrict their use to a few practical men who are masters of every detail of the business of gardening. The routine under each month is generally in harmony with that already recommended, but certain variations of practice are suggested which may prove of service in some districts and under particular circumstances.

A work on gardening demands of the reader the exercise of judgment. If blindly followed it may prove as often wrong as right; for it is not in the power of the authors to influence the weather in favour of their directions, or to insure to those who may follow their guidance a single one amongst the many conditions requisite to success. Although the times named for certain operations are the best in the average, peculiarities of climate and of season will require some modifications which each one must discover for himself; and after the seed of any vegetable has been sown it is not always needful to give subsequent reminders of successional sowings. These naturally follow in accordance with the requirements of each particular garden. With such allowances duly made, these notes will, it is hoped, prove thoroughly practical, and tend materially to aid the cultivator in obtaining from the vegetable garden an abundance of everything in its season, and of a quality, too, of which he need not be ashamed.

JANUARY

WE are now at the mercy of the weather, and must shape our course accordingly. During heavy rains keep off the ground, but prepare to go on it the moment it is fit to bear your weight without poaching. Make ready for the busy spring. Survey the stock of pea-sticks, haul out all the rubbish from the yard, and make a 'smother' of waste prunings and heaps of twitch and other stuff for which you have no decided use. If properly done, the result will be a black ash of the most fertilising nature, such as a mere fire will not produce. During hard frost wheel out manure and lay it in heaps ready to be spread and dug in where seed-beds are to be made. If the weather is open and dry, trench spare plots and make ready well-manured plots for sowing Peas and Beans. So far as may be convenient, all *preparatory* work should be pushed on with vigour, and every effort should be made to lay up as much land in the rough as possible; for the more it is frozen through, the greater will be its fertility, and the more beautiful, as well as more abundant, the crops.

It is a matter of the most ordinary prudence to be prepared to resist the shock of a severe frost; and yet, when this event occurs, many suffer loss because they are not prepared for it. Good brick walls and substantial roofs are needed for the safe keeping of fruits and the more valuable kinds of roots; but when rough methods are resorted to, such as clamping and pitting, there should be a large body of stuff employed, for a severe frost will find its way through any thin covering, no matter what the material may be. As there is not much to do now out of doors, it is a good time to look over the notes which were made concerning various crops in the past season, and to attend to the seed list.

SEED SOWING should be practised with exceeding caution; but great things may be done now where there are warm, sheltered, dry borders, and suitable appliances for screening and forwarding early crops. Under these favourable conditions we advise the sowing of small breadths of a few choice subjects towards the end of the month;

and, this being done, every care should be taken to nurse the seedlings through the trying times that are before them. Such things as tender young Radishes, Onions, small Salads, Spinach, Cabbage, and Horn Carrots never come in too early; the trouble often is that they are seen in the market while as yet they are invisible in the garden. Hedges of Hornbeam, Laurel, or Holly, to break the force of the wind, are valuable for sheltering early borders, and walls are great aids to earliness by the warmth they reflect and the dryness they promote.

The soil for these early crops should be light and rich, and the position extra well drained, to prevent the slightest accumulation of water during heavy rains. Supposing you have such a border, sow upon it, as early as weather will permit, any of the smaller sorts of Cabbage Lettuce, Silver-skin Onion, Long Scarlet Radish, Round Spinach, Cabbage, and French Horn Carrot. All these crops may be grown in frames with greater safety, and in many exposed places the warm border is almost an impossibility. Reed hurdles and loose dry litter should be always ready when early cropping is in hand; and old lights, and even old doors, and any and every kind of screen may be made use of at times to protect the early seed-beds from snow, severe frost, and the dry blast of an east wind.

FORCING is one of the fine arts in the English garden. It is an art easily acquired up to a certain point, but beyond that point full of difficulty. Every step in this business is a conflict with Nature, and in such a conflict man is never the stronger party. A golden rule is to be found in the proverb, 'The more haste, the less speed.' Whatever the source of heat, it should be moderate at first and should be augmented slowly. The earlier the forced articles are required the more careful should be the preparation for them, and the more moderate the temperature in the first instance. But there must be command of a constant as well as sufficient temperature, for any check occurring when a forced crop has made some progress will be fatal to success. The beginner should acquire experience with Rhubarb and Sea Kale, then with Asparagus and Mushrooms and Kidney Beans, and so on to 'higher heights' of this branch of practical gardening.

ARTICHOKES, GLOBE, must be protected with litter, for they are not quite hardy.

ASPARAGUS beds should be heavily manured, but the beds should not be dug. Be content to lay the manure on, and the rains will wash the goodness down to the roots in due time. In gardens near the coast, seaweed is the best of manure for Asparagus, and the use of salt can then be dispensed with.

BEANS may be sown in frames, and towards the end of the month in the open quarters. Most of the Longpod section are nearly as early as the smaller sorts, and far more profitable. But the smaller sorts are prized for a certain elegance on the table, and they occupy but little space to give a very fair return. Sow on ground deeply dug and well manured.

CABBAGE may be planted out at any time when weather permits, provided you have or can obtain the plants; and it is well to keep vacant plots going with a few breadths of Cabbage at every season of the year, for we never know when they may be acceptable, even in the height of summer, if there has been a hard run upon other vegetables, or some important crop has failed outright.

CAULIFLOWER may be sown in a gentle hot-bed or in a pan in the greenhouse, or even in a frame, to make a start for planting out in March or April.

CRESS to be enjoyed must be produced from a constant succession of small but frequent sowings. All the sorts are good but different in flavour, and they should be used only while the shoots are young and tender. Sow at intervals of a few days in pans, as in the case of Mustard, until it is possible to cultivate in the open air, and then give a shady position during summer on a mellow and rather moist soil.

CUCUMBERS are never ready too soon to meet the demand in early spring. They are grown in houses more or less adapted to their requirements, and also in frames over hot-beds. At this time of year, however, frames are somewhat troublesome to manage, and in trying weather they are a little hazardous, although later in the season there is no difficulty whatever with them. For the present, therefore, we shall confine our remarks to house culture. Almost any greenhouse may be made to answer, but the work can be carried on most successfully and with the greatest economy in houses which are expressly constructed for Cucumbers. For winter work a lean-to, facing south, possesses special advantages. But for general utility, if we had to erect a building on a well-drained soil, it should be dwarf, sunk three feet in the ground, with brick walls up to the eaves, and lighted only from the roof. Such a structure is less influenced by atmospheric changes than a building wholly above ground. The size, of course, is optional; and quite a small house will supply an ordinary family with Cucumbers. But a small house is not economical either in fuel or in labour. A building thirty feet long, by twelve feet wide, six feet high at the sides, and eight and a half feet high at the ridge, will not only grow Cucumbers and Melons, but will also be of immense service for many other plants. A division across the middle by a wall rising four feet, surmounted with a glass screen fitted to the roof, and finished with a door partially of glass, will greatly augment its usefulness. There should be an alley down the centre four or five feet wide, bounded by walls reaching four feet above the floor. These walls should be nine inches thick for two feet six inches of their height, but for the upper parts the brickwork should only be four and a half inches thick. Thus a ledge will be left on the inner side of each wall. The main walls should also have ledges corresponding in height, upon which slates can be laid to carry the soil. There should be a space of about an inch between each slate to insure drainage, and by putting tiles or an inverted turf over every opening, the soil cannot be washed away. The hot-water pipes will be in chambers immediately beneath the plants. To these chambers access must be obtained by openings, fitted with sliding doors, in the alley walls. The heat can then be admitted direct into the house whenever it may be desirable. Ventilation should be provided for under the ridge at each end, as well as in the roof. In such a house it is easy to grow Cucumbers all the year round, except, perhaps, in the dead of winter, when the short dark days render the task difficult, no matter how perfect the appliances may be. The division in the centre will be found valuable at all times, and especially when one set of plants is failing; for another set can be brought into bearing exactly when wanted. But whatever the structure may be, the mode of culture will be substantially the same in any case. As to soil, then. A compost made of mellow turfy loam and leaf-mould in equal parts will be effective and sweet. In the absence of leaf-mould, use two parts of loam and one of thoroughly decayed manure, with a few pieces of charcoal added. Sweetness is not absolutely necessary for success, but nevertheless we like to have it, so that a visit to the Cucumber house may be a source of pleasure. This it cannot be if rank manure has been used. Raise the seed, singly in small 60-pots, and sow enough, for however good the seed, some is almost sure to fail at this critical period. Give the plants one shift into the 48-size, to keep them going until they are ready for putting into the beds. Cucumbers grow with great rapidity, and should never know a check, least of all by starvation. Upon the slates make as many heaps of soil as are required, and in the centre of each heap put one plant. As the roots extend, add more soil until the heaps meet, and finally become level with the top of the brickwork. This treatment will supply food as the roots develop and help to maintain the plants in bearing for a long period. Stout wires running parallel with the length of the house, a foot below the glass, will carry the vines. Temperature should never fall below 60° at night; but as the season advances, if the thermometer registers 90° on sunny days no harm will be done, provided the roots are not dry, and the air be kept properly moist by plying the syringe. On dull days one good sprinkling over the foliage will suffice, and it should be done in the morning. In warm sunny weather, however, two or three syringings will be beneficial; but the work must not be done so late as to risk the foliage being wet when night comes on. There will be occasions when it may be advisable to avoid touching the leaves with water, if there is no probability of their drying before nightfall. In such a case, the moisture can be kept up by freely sprinkling the floor and walls. Cucumbers cannot thrive if they are dry at the roots, but although there should be no stint of water, it must be given with judgment; and it is of the utmost importance that the drainage should be effectual, for stagnant water is even more injurious than a dry soil. A few sticks placed in various parts of the bed, and reaching down to the slates, will serve as indicators. Draw and inspect them occasionally, and a pretty correct idea of the condition of the soil will be obtained. The water should be of the same temperature as the house, for if applied cold the plants will sustain a serious check. In the event of the bed falling somewhat below the proper temperature, the water may with advantage be a few degrees higher than usual.

HORSE-RADISH should be planted early, to insure fine roots for next Christmas beef.

LETTUCES will soon be in demand, and the early hearts will be particularly precious. Sow a few sorts in pans, in frames, or on gentle hot-beds, to be ready for planting out by-and-by.

MELON.—Although the Melon is a fruit, its culture naturally forms part of the routine of a vegetable garden. Up to a certain point it may be grown in the same house with Cucumbers; but after that point is reached, the two plants need widely different treatment. Cucumbers are cut when young, and must be grown in a warm and humid atmosphere from beginning to end. Melons need warmth, and at the commencement moisture also; but the fruit has to be ripened, and after it is set dry treatment becomes essential for the

L

production of a rich flavour with plenty of aroma. In large gardens, three crops of Melons are usually grown in the same house in one season. A light soil is advisable at the beginning of the year, but a heavier compost may be employed with advantage as the season advances. For the first sowing select an early variety, such as Hero of Lockinge, and put the seed in separate pots at the beginning of this month. Re-pot the plants once, and they will be ready for the beds by the first week of February. Melons from this sowing should be fit for table in May, and that is quite as early as they can be produced with any sugar in them. Until the fruits begin to swell, the treatment advised for Cucumbers will suit Melons also. Afterwards the watering will need careful management. It would be an advantage if the fruit could be finished off without a drop of water from the time they are about two inches in diameter, but the hot pipes render it almost impossible. Still, water must not be given more frequently than is actually necessary to keep the plants going, and when it is applied let there be a thorough soaking. At the same time ventilation will demand constant attention, and provided the temperature can be maintained, it is scarcely possible to give air too freely. In the early stage of growth, and in mild weather, if the thermometer registers 65° at 9 P.M., the cultivator may sleep peacefully so far as Melons are concerned. As the season advances, the temperature may be increased to 70° by night, and 75° to 90° by day. With reference to stopping, it may be sufficient to say that it is a waste of energy to allow the plant to make a large quantity of vine, which has afterwards to be cut away. By judiciously pinching out the shoots, the plant can be equally spread over the allotted space. The flowers must be fertilised, and in this respect the treatment differs from that advised for Cucumbers. The practice has the advantage of allowing the fruits to be evenly distributed over the vine, and from four to six, according to the size of the variety, will be enough for each plant to ripen.

MUSTARD.—Those who care for salads will need a supply of this article almost all through the year, and to secure a succession it will be necessary to sow at regular intervals. It is a good plan to keep a few boxes in use for the purpose in a plant-house or pit, sowing one or two at a time as required to insure a succession, and taking care not to sow wastefully. It may be grown out of doors all the summer, on a shady border, but nothing beats boxes or large pans under glass. Mustard and Cress should never be sown in the same row or the same pan but separately, because they do not grow at the same pace, and the former may be fit for use a week or so before the latter. Do not be content to use Rape, or any other substitute, but sow the genuine article.

PEAS may be sown in open quarters, and the driest and warmest places must be selected. It is next to impossible to grow them too well; for if the haulm runs up higher than usual, the produce will be the finer. Remember, too, that if you dig deep trenches and put in a lot of manure for Peas, the ground is so far prepared for Broccoli, Celery, and late Cauliflowers to follow, for the early-sown Peas will be off the ground in time for another paying crop. As everybody wants an early dish of Peas, sow Ringleader, Earliest Blue, American Wonder, or Emerald Gem, in pots, or on strips of turf laid grass-side downwards, in boxes having movable bottoms that can be withdrawn by a dexterous hand when the transfer is made from frames to the open ground. Troughs for Peas can be made in almost no time out of waste wood that may be found in the yard, or a few lengths of old zinc spouting blocked up at the ends will answer admirably. In the absence of such aids, common flower-pots answer pretty well. The seed should have the shelter of a frame or pit, but should have the least possible stimulus from artificial heat, except in cases where there is all the skill at command to promote very early production.

POTATOES are prized when they come in early, and may be forwarded on beds of leaves and exhausted hot-beds by covering with light rich soil, and employing old frames for protection, with litter handy in case of frost. For this early work take the earliest sorts of Kidneys and Rounds, because the heavy main-cropping varieties are not quick enough.

RADISHES are more or less in demand for the greater part of the year. The early crops are, however, especially valued, and there need not be the least difficulty in producing a supply. A half-spent hot-bed, or, indeed, any position that affords shelter and warmth, will answer admirably for raising this crop, until it may be trusted to a suitable position in the open.

SEA KALE may be covered with pots or a good depth of litter, or a combination of pots and litter. This should be done early, as at the first move of vegetation this delicious vegetable will come into use, and will generally be of finer quality than if forced. It happens, however, to be the easiest of all things to force, and so, wherever it is cared for, it may be had in plenty from Christmas (or earlier) until May. As it must be thoroughly blanched, covering is needful in all cases.

SPINACH may be sown in open quarters. If the frost destroys the plant, sow again. Some risk must be encountered for an early dish of this highly-prized vegetable. The autumn-sown Spinach must be kept clear of weeds, and in gathering (if it happens to be fit to supply a gathering) pick off the leaves separately with a little care.

TOMATOES have ceased to be a luxury for the few, and have become a necessity among all classes of the community. Concurrently with its increase in popularity, the fruit has been developed into many beautiful forms, differing in flavour and in the time of ripening. Of the immense value of the Tomato as an article of diet we need say nothing, but we may confidently affirm that its merits for decorative purposes have not as yet been fully recognised. We have seen long racemes of bright vermilion fruit employed with striking effect in epergnes, and there is a natural fitness in using them for decorating the dinner table. All the Tomatoes can be grown and ripened under glass in almost any fashion which may suit the cultivator's convenience. Pits, frames, vineries, and Peach houses will all bring the fruit to perfection, either in pots or planted out. Magnificent crops are also grown in the manner usual with Cucumbers, but in a lower temperature; and those who have an early Cucumber house at liberty later in the year may turn it to good account for Tomatoes. The soil for them should be prepared and laid up in the autumn. It must not be too rich, or there will be much foliage and little fruit, and the flowering will also be late. A compost of leaf-mould and loam with an addition of sand will suit Tomatoes admirably; but raw manure should be regarded as poison. Sow thinly in well-drained pots firmly filled with soil. Barely cover the seed with fine earth, and place the pots in a temperature of 60° or 65°. When large enough to handle, transfer the seedlings to small pots, and, if necessary, shade them for a few days. Keep them near the glass until the roots are established, and allow them to suffer no check from first to last.

FEBRUARY

THE work of this month is to be carried on as weather permits, but with greater activity and more confidence, for the winter is, we hope, pretty well gone. Earnest digging, liberal manuring, and scrupulous cleansing are the tasks that stand forward in the work of the month as of pre-eminent importance. Many weeds, groundsel especially, will now be coming into flower, and if allowed to seed will make enormous work to keep them down. It is well, however, to remember—what few people do remember, because the fact has not been pressed upon their attention—that weeds of all kinds, so long as they are not in flower, are really useful as manure when dug into the soil. Therefore, a weedy patch is not of necessity going to ruin; but if the weeds are not stopped in time they spread by their seeds and mar the order and decency of the garden. Dig them in, and their decay will nourish the next crop. If you practise early sowing and aim at the earliest possible produce of everything, you must be always ready to protect by means of litter, spruce branches, mats, and such like, as circumstances require. Let not the weather surprise you; the vigilant gardener is always armed for any emergency. Read the notes for January before proceeding further; and in respect of what remains undone, spare the necessity of reminders here.

FRAME GROUND should be kept scrupulously clean and orderly. Many things will require liberal watering now, but water must not be carelessly given, because damp is hurtful during frosty weather. Take care that the plants are not crowding and starving, or they will come to no good.

BEANS may be sown both for early and main crops now, and with but little risk of damage by spring frosts. The driest and warmest situation should be selected for the early sorts, and the strongest land for the late ones. If any were sown in frames last month, take care to harden them cautiously preparatory to planting out; for if caught by a sharp frost, every plant will perish.

BROCCOLI.—Sow Walcheren on a warm sheltered border, and a pinch in a frame. With such an important crop at this time of year, you ought to have at least two strings to your bow.

CABBAGE may be sown in pans or boxes placed in a frame, to be planted out in due time for summer use. Where plantations stand rather thick, draw as fast as possible from amongst them every alternate plant, to allow the remainder ample space for hearting. It is well to remember that the smallest and loosest hearts of immature Cabbages make a more delicate dish than the most complete white hearts ever known. For our own eating give us a small Cabbage, green all through; but when grown for market, there must be bulk and substance. Cabbages are wanted at all times and seasons to mend and patch, and to make stolen crops, and take the place of anything that fails past recovery.

CAPSICUM AND CHILI should be sown now or in March on a hot-bed, and be potted on until the plants are fit to be placed in the greenhouse or conservatory.

CAULIFLOWER.—Another sowing should be made under glass to supply a succession of plants.

CORN SALAD thrives well in any soil not particularly heavy, the best being sandy or a fertile loam. Sow in drills six inches apart; keep the hoe well at work, and when ready thin the plants out to six inches apart. They should be eaten young.

COUVE TRONCHUDA produces two distinct dishes. The top forms a Cabbage of the most delicate flavour and colour, and furnishes the best possible dish of greens in autumn; and the mid-ribs of the largest leaves may be cooked in the manner of Sea Kale, and will be found excellent. Though tender, this delicious vegetable may be secured for use in summer and autumn and far on into the winter, by successive sowings in February, March, and April; the first sowings to be assisted with heat. The plants should be put out as early as possible on rich soil at from two to three feet each way; they must have plenty of water in a dry summer. The season of Portugal Cabbage may be prolonged by taking up what plants are left before severe frost occurs, and heeling them into a bank of dry earth in a shed or outhouse.

GARLIC to be planted in rows nine inches apart, and two inches deep in rich mellow soil.

LETTUCE.—Sow again on warm border and in frames. Plant out in mild weather any that are fit from frames and hot-beds, first making sure that they are well hardened.

MUSTARD.—It is easy work with a frame to have Mustard at any time; and many small sowings are better than large ones, which only result in waste to-day and want to-morrow.

PARSLEY to be sown in the latter part of the month; it will soon be wanted in quantity.

PARSNIP should be sown as early as possible, on the deepest and best ground as regards texture; but it need not be on the richest, for if the roots can push down they will get what they want from the subsoil, and therefore it is of great importance to put this crop on ground that was dug twice in the autumn.

PEA.—Sow early sorts in quantity now, in accordance with probable requirements; but there will be a loss rather than a gain of time if they are sown on pasty ground or during bad weather We have now many grand sorts that are of moderate growth, and therefore occasion the least imaginable trouble in their management; but a few of the tallest are still in favour, because of their late bearing and high quality. However, there is time yet for sowing mid-season and late Peas; but the sooner some of the first earlies are in the better. It is customary to sow many rows in a plot rather close together, but it is better practice to put them so far apart as to admit of two or three rows of early Potatoes between every two rows of Peas. This insures abundance of light and air to the Peas, and the latter are of great value to protect the Potatoes from May frosts that often kill down the rising shaws. A warm, dry, fertile soil is needed for first early Peas. Those already up and in a bad plight should be dug in and the rows sown again. It is worthy of note that if Peas are thoroughly pinched and starved by hard weather, they rarely prove a success: so, if they go wrong, sacrifice them without hesitation and begin again. Where early rows are doing well take care of them, and put sticks to them at once, as the sticks afford considerable protection, and they may be rendered additionally protective by strewing on the windward side small hedge clippings and other such light dry stuff.

POTATO.—A small quantity for early use should be planted when the ground is dry and the weather soft. If planted when frost or cold winds prevail, sets may become somewhat shrivelled before they are covered, and every care should be taken to maintain the initial vigour of the plant. The first early sorts will necessarily have the chief attention now, and warm sheltered spots should be selected for them. Any fairly good soil will produce a passable crop of Potatoes; but to secure a first-class sample of any early sort, the ground should be made up with the aid of turfy soil and charrings of hedge clippings and other light, warm, nourishing material. Strong manures are not to be desired, but a mellow, kindly, fertile soil is really necessary, and it will always pay well to take extra pains in its preparation, because all the light rubbish that accumulates in yards and outhouses can be turned to account with only a moderate amount of labour, and the result of careful appropriation of such rubbish will be thoroughly satisfactory. Burn all the chips and sticks and other stubborn stuff, and lay the mixture in the trenches when planting, so that the roots may find it at their first start. Potato disease usually breaks out in autumn, and therefore early planting is a safe precaution, for it insures early ripening of the crop, which is consequently harvested before the time when disease generally appears.

RADISHES, to be mild, tender, and handsome, must be grown

rapidly. If checked they become hot, tough, and worthless. Much may be done to forward a crop by means of dry litter and mats to protect from frost, removing the protection in favourable weather to give the crop the fullest possible benefit of air and sunshine. Old worn-out frames that will scarcely hold together will pay their first cost over again with the aid of a little skill in growing Radishes. In all cases, the long Radishes are the best to sow early; the Turnip and Oval-shaped varieties are generally most prized for late sowing.

RHUBARB should be taken up and divided and planted again in rich moist soil, every separate piece to have only one good eye. Do not gather this season from the new plantation, but always have a piece one year old to supply the kitchen. This method will insure sticks to be proud of, not only for size, but for colour and flavour. The small high-coloured sorts are the best for home use.

SAVOYS are valued by some when small, and by others they are prized for size as much as for their excellent flavour when well frosted. Large Savoys must have a long season of growth; therefore sow as soon as possible, either in a frame, or on a rich, mellow seed-bed, and be ready to prick them out before they become crowded.

SEA KALE.—The plantations reserved for latest supplies should not be covered until they begin to push naturally, and then the coverings must be put on to cause the sticks to rise white and tender. Open-ground Sea Kale may be uncovered as soon as cut, but a little litter should be left about to give protection, and help the young shoots to rise because the blanching and cutting of the sticks is a severe tax on the plant, and it now has to begin life afresh, and prepare for the work of the next season.

SHALLOT.—It is not generally known that when well grown the clumps are bigger than a man's fist, and each separate bulb thicker than a walnut. To grow them well they must have time; so plant early, on rich ground, in rows one foot apart and the bulbs six or nine inches asunder. Press them into the earth deep enough to hold them firmly, but they are not to be quite buried.

SPINACH.—Sow the Round-seeded plentifully; if you overdo it, the extra crop can be dug in as manure, and in that way will pay.

TOMATO.—In many gardens the first sowing is made about the 20th of this month, and if treated fairly the plants will come into bearing in about four months. Use good porous soil for the seed-pans. Sow very thinly in a temperature of 60° or 65°, and get the plants into thumb pots while they are quite small.

TURNIP of a small white kind, such as Snowball, may be sown on warm borders, but it is too early yet for large breadths in open quarters.

MARCH

THIS is the great season for garden work, and the gardener must be up with the lark and go to bed with the robin, which is the latest of birds to bid farewell to a sunny day. The first care should be to make good all arrears, especially in the preparation of seed-beds, and the cleaning of plots that are in any way disorderly. Where early-sown crops have evidently failed, sow again without complaining; seed costs but little, and a good plant is the earnest of a good crop; a bad plant will probably never pay the rent of the ground it occupies. Keen east winds commit vast havoc, but a little protection provided in time will do wonders to ward off their effects, and the sunny days that are now so welcome, and that we are pretty sure to have, will afford opportunity for giving air to plants in frames, for clearing away litter, and for the regular routine work of the season.

Almost every kind of seed sown in the vegetable garden may be sown in the month of March. Make successional sowings of whatever it may be advisable to put under cover or on heat, and then proceed with open-ground sowings as weather and circumstances permit. The weather is the master of out-door work, and it is sheer waste of time to fight against it. It is better to wait to the end of the month, or even far into the next, before sowing a seed than to sow on pasty ground. But it matters not how dry the ground may be; and if the wind blows keenly, that should only be an inducement to brisk action, for seeds well sown have everything in their favour if they are not too early for the district. Very important indeed it is now to secure a

HOT-BED.—To make one is easy enough, but it is of no use to half make it, for half-acres in this department do not bear good corn. In the first place, secure a great bulk of manure, and if it is long and green, turn it two or three times, taking care that it is always moderately moist, but never actually wet. If the stuff is too dry, sprinkle with water at every turn, and let it steam away to take the rankest fire out of it. Then make it up where required in a square heap, allowing it to settle in its own way without treading or beating. Put on a foot-depth of light rich soil after the frames are in their places, and wait a few days to sow the seed in case of a great heat rising. When the heat is steady and comfortable, sow seeds in pots and pans, as needful, the quantity required of each separate crop, and stand them on bricks above the bed, and the heat will then be none too much for them. In the course of a few days finish the work by putting in a body of earth. Do not attempt to hurry the growth of anything overmuch, for undue haste will produce a weak plant; rather give air and light in plenty, but with care to prevent injurious check, and the plants will be short and healthy from the first.

ARTICHOKES, GLOBE, to be cleared of protecting material as soon as weather permits, and fresh plantations made ready for suckers to be put in next month. A new plantation may also be prepared for by sowing seeds; in fact, a sowing ought to be made every year. Where early produce is required, the plants should be protected during winter to supply suckers in the spring; but, if late supplies suffice, the sowing of a few rows every year will reduce the labour, and render the production of Globe Artichokes a very simple affair.

ARTICHOKES, JERUSALEM, may be planted now advantageously. Use whole sets if convenient, or plant cut sets with about three eyes in each. Strong, deep soil produces the best crop, and large roots are always preferred by the cook because of the inevitable waste in preparing this vegetable. The Jerusalem Artichoke is certainly not properly appreciated, and one reason is that it is often carelessly grown in any out-of-the-way starving corner, whereas it needs a sunny, open spot, and a strong deep soil, and plenty of room. To hide an ugly fence during summer there is no more useful plant grown.

ASPARAGUS.—Little attention is required as yet, except to remove every weed as soon as it can be seen. If the beds are dry, and there are no indications of coming rain, one good soaking of water or weak sewage will be very beneficial. Mark out and make beds for sowing seed next month.

BEAN.—Plant out those raised in frames, and earth up those that are forward enough of early sowings. Sow for main crops and late supplies. In late districts a few of the earliest sorts may be sown to come in before the Windsor section.

BEET.—Sow a little for an early supply, in well-dug mellow soil.

BROCCOLI for autumn use to be sown early; and at the end of the month sow again in quantity for winter supplies. Plant out in mild weather from frames as soon as the plants are fit and well hardened.

BRUSSELS SPROUTS.—For an early gathering of large buttons a

sowing should be made now, on the warm border. This fine vegetable requires a long period of growth to attain perfection, and those who sow late rarely see such buttons as the plant is capable of producing. The plants should have the best seed-bed that can be found for them.

CABBAGE of two or three kinds should be sown now to supply plants for filling up as crops are taken off, and also to patch and mend where failures happen. Where the owner of a garden has opportunities of helping his poorer neighbours, one of the best methods is to supply them with Cabbage and Winter Greens for planting in their garden plots. In many instances they cannot well get up a stock of their own, and are too likely to begin with bad seed—very much to their after-discouragement in gardening, and to the detriment of their domestic comfort in respect of the wholesome food the garden should supply. We have seen much good accomplished at the most trifling cost by the annual sowing of a few breadths of useful Brassicas, to supply railway men and factory operatives with plants of a far better kind than they could either raise or purchase in their own way. The rankest manure may be employed in preparing ground for Cabbage; this will allow of the use of the well-rotted manure for seed-beds, and other purposes for which it will be required.

CARROT.—Sow Early Horn at the first opportunity, but wait for signs of settled spring weather to sow the main crops of large sorts, and then put them on deeply dug ground without manure.

CAULIFLOWER.—Plant out as weather permits from hand-lights and frames, choosing the best ground you have. In preparing a plot for Cauliflower, use plenty of manure; and if it is only half-rotten, it will be better than if old and mellow.

CELERIAC.—So far as seed sowing is concerned, Celeriac may be treated in the same way as Celery.

CELERY.—For the earliest supply, say in September, sow on the first of the month a pinch of seed of one or more of the smaller pink or white sorts on a mild hot-bed, or in an early vinery. As soon as the plants are large enough to handle, prick them out three inches apart on a nice mellow bed of rich soil on a half-spent hot-bed; give them plenty of light, with free ventilation as weather allows, and constant supplies of water. About the middle of the month, sow again and prick out as before; but if no hot-bed is available, a well-prepared bed in a frame in a sunny position will answer; or, if the season is somewhat advanced, a bed of rotten manure, two or three inches deep, on a piece of hard ground, will suffice, if the plants are kept regularly watered. From this bed they will lift with nice roots for planting out, scarcely feeling the removal at all.

CHIVES to be divided and re-planted on a spot which has not previously been occupied with the crop.

CUCUMBER.—The vines should now be in a flourishing condition, but it is necessary to look forward to the day when they will fall into the sere and yellow leaf. More seed sown singly in pots will provide a succession of plants. Re-pot them once or twice if necessary, and when large enough turn them out between the first lot. As the old plants fail, the new-comers will supply their places. Some growers take down the vines, and strike them at a distance from the original roots. A more common practice is to take cuttings from plants which have proved extra good. These have the advantage of being very fruitful, and the disadvantage of being less robust than plants raised from seed. Setting the bloom, as it is called, is not only useless, but is a mischievous procedure. It results in the enlargement of one end of the fruit, and ruins its appearance. If seed be the object, of course the process is justifiable; but for the table a 'bottle nose' cannot be regarded as an ornament. Besides, the ripening of seed in a single fruit will materially diminish the usefulness of the plant, and perhaps entirely end its career. Stopping the vine is a necessity, but it should not be done too soon. In the early stage of growth, it reduces the vigour of the plant and retards its fruiting; but when the fruit is visible, stopping aids its development, and at the same time tends to regulate and equalise the growth.

Frame culture of Cucumbers is usually begun in March. There are men who can produce fruit from hot-beds all the year round, but it is a difficult task, and as a rule ought not to be expected. At this time of year, however, success is fairly within reach of ordinary skill. In quite the early part of the month put seed singly into pots, and keep them in a warm moist place. The plants will then be ready for frames at the end of the month. The most important business is the preparation of the bed, and in this, as in all else, there is a right and a wrong way of doing the work. Accurately set out the space on which it is to be made. If there is plenty of manure, make the bed large enough to project eighteen inches beyond the lights all round. But if manure is scarce, cut the margin closer, and trust to a hot lining when the heat begins to flag. Commence with the outside of the bed, employing the long stuff in its construction; and keep this part of the work a little in advance of the centre until the full height is reached. A bed made in this way will not fall to pieces, and the heat will be durable in proportion to its size and thickness. Where fallen leaves are abundant, they should be used for the middle of the bed, and they will give a more lasting heat than short manure. When the bed has settled down to a steady temperature, add six or nine inches of mellow loam over the entire surface, upon which place the frames. To insure drainage, it is an excellent plan to place common flake hurdles on the top of the heap before adding the soil. These do not in the least interfere with the free running of the roots. It is usual to have two plants under each light, but where the management is good, one is quite enough. The subsequent work consists of shading and sheltering, to prevent any serious check from trying weather, and in giving just water enough and no more. The fermenting material should sustain the temperature of the frame, even during frosty nights, and mats will screen off strong sunshine as well as cold winds. The plants will need stopping earlier than those grown in houses, and as there are no hot pipes to dissipate the moisture, rather less water will be necessary both in the soil and from the syringe. But the water employed should always be of the same temperature as the bed. This is easily managed by keeping a full can standing with the plants. In large frames, where there is a good body of manure, and the loam is mellow and turfy, pieces of Mushroom spawn can be inserted all over the bed. The Mushrooms may appear while the bed is in full bearing; but if they do not, they will come when the plants are cleared out, and pay well to keep the lights in use another month or so.

GARLIC may still be planted, but no time is to be lost.

HERBS of many kinds may be sown or divided, and it will be well to look over the Herb quarter and see how things stand for the supplies that will be required, for presently there may be such an excess of work that this department may be injuriously neglected.

HORSE-RADISH to be planted if not done already.

KOHL RABI or KNOL KOHL to be sown in small quantity at the end of the month. If cooked while young they take the place of Turnips on the table, and are useful in case the early Turnips fail in a hot, dry season.

LEEK.—Sow the main crop in very rich, well-prepared soil, and rather thickly, as they will have to be planted out. With a little management this sowing will yield a succession of Leeks.

LETTUCE.—Plant out and sow again in quantity. All the kinds may be sown now, but make sure of enough of the Cos, Commodore

Nutt, and other summer sorts. In hot, dry soils, where Lettuces usually run to seed early, try some of the red-leaved kinds, for though less delicate than the green and white, they will be useful in the event of a scorching summer. Lettuces require a deep free soil with plenty of manure.

MELON.—Raise a few seeds singly in pots, in readiness for putting under frames on hot-beds next month. Re-pot the plants, and repeat the process if the beds are not ready, for Melons must not be starved, especially in the early stage of growth. Some growers make up the beds in March, and sow upon them when the heat becomes steady, but the practice is somewhat precarious. In a cold, late spring the heat may not last a sufficient time to carry the plants safely into warm weather. Hence it is more reliable to raise them now in a warm house, and make the bed at the beginning of April.

ONION.—Sow the main crop in drills nine inches apart, and tread or beat the ground firm. This crop requires a rich soil in a thoroughly clean and mellow condition, and it makes a capital finish to the seed-bed to give it a good coat of charred rubbish or smother ash before sowing the seed.

PARSNIP.—Sow main crop in shallow drills eighteen inches apart in good soil deeply dug. The seed should be lightly covered, and fresh seed is indispensable. The Student is the very best Parsnip known.

PEA.—Sow now the finest sorts obtainable of tall-growing Marrows, and the large-podded dwarf kinds of the second early class. Take care to put them on the best seed-bed that can be made, and allow sufficient room between the taller sorts for a few rows of Cabbage, Broccoli, or Potatoes. A crowded quarter of Peas is never properly productive; for they smother each other, and the shaded parts of the haulm produce next to nothing.

POTATOES for main crops should now be got in, and the planting be finished by the end of the month or beginning of April.

SCORZONERA to be treated much the same as Salsify. See note on the latter under April.

SEA KALE to be sown in well-prepared beds; or plantations may be made by cuttings of the smaller roots of the thickness of a lead pencil, and about four inches in length. Plant them top end uppermost, and deep enough to be just covered.

SORREL is greatly valued in many households, and the finest quality can easily be grown from seed. Sow in shallow drills drawn on light soil, six or eight inches apart, and when quite small thin to a distance of three or four inches between the plants. No gathering from the crop must be expected in the year of sowing, and it is scarcely necessary to add, that weeds must not be permitted to smother the plantation.

SPINACH.—Sow in plenty. The Perpetual or Spinach Beet is one of the most useful vegetables known, as it endures heat and cold with impunity, and when common Spinach is running to seed the Perpetual variety remains green and succulent, and fit to supply the table all the summer long.

SPINACH, NEW ZEALAND, is another excellent vegetable in high summer when the Round-seeded variety is worthless. It is rather a tender plant, and for an early supply the seed must be sown in moderate heat, either in this month or in April. Get the seedlings into small pots when large enough, and gradually harden them before planting in the open about the end of May.

STRAWBERRIES.—Spring is undoubtedly preferable to autumn planting, and results in a finer crop of fruit in the following year. Just as growth is commencing is the most favourable time, and this, of course, depends on the character of the season. The Alpine varieties are annually raised from spring-sown seeds in pans, or in drills on a rich border.

TOMATO.—In ordinary seasons and in the southern counties there is no difficulty in producing handsome Tomatoes in the open border; but to ripen the fruit with certainty it is imperative that an early variety be chosen. With the rise of latitude, however, the crop becomes increasingly precarious, until in the north it is impossible to finish Tomatoes without the aid of glass. For plants which are to ripen fruit in the open, a sowing should be made early in the month, in the manner advised under January. Plants which are ready should be transferred to small thumb-pots. Put them in so that the first leaves touch the rim of the pot, and place them in a close frame or warm part of the greenhouse for a few days until the roots take hold. To save them from becoming leggy, give each plant ample space, and avoid a forcing temperature. A shelf in a greenhouse is a good position, and plants in a single row upon it will grow stout and short-jointed. Thrips and aphis are extremely partial to Tomatoes. Frequent sprinklings in bright weather will help to keep down the former, and will at the same time benefit the plants. Both pests can be destroyed by fumigating with tobacco, and when the remedy is to be applied water should be withheld on that day. A moderate amount of smoke in the evening, and another application in the morning, will be more destructive to the vermin, and less injurious to the plants, than one strong dose. The usual syringing must follow. Plants for the open ground must not be starved while in pots; they will need potting on until the 4½-inch size is reached, and it is important that they should never be dry at the roots. Shading will only be necessary during fierce sunshine; in early morning and late in the afternoon they will be better without it.

TURNIP to be sown in quantity towards the end of the month.

WATER CRESS.—It is quite a mistake to suppose that a running stream is necessary for growing this plant, and it is equally a mistake to suppose that the proper flavour can be secured without the constant use of water. Sow in a trench, water regularly and copiously, and mild and tender Water Cress will reward the labour.

WINTER GREENS of all kinds to be sown in plenty and in considerable variety, for in the event of a severe winter some kinds will prove hardier than others.

APRIL

VEGETATION is now in full activity, the temperature increases rapidly, frosts are less frequent, and showers and sunshine alternate in their mutual endeavours to clothe the earth with verdure and flowers. The gardener is bound to be vigilant now to assist Nature in her endeavours to benefit him; he must promote the growth of his crops by all the means in his power; by plying the hoe to keep down weeds and open the soil to sunshine and showers; by thinning and regulating his plantations, that air and light may have free access to the plants left to attain maturity; by continuing to shelter as may be needed; and by administering water during dry weather, that vegetation may benefit to the utmost by the happy accession of increasing sunlight.

ARTICHOKE, GLOBE.—Suckers to be put in the plantations prepared for them last month, in rows four or four and a half feet apart, and the plants two feet apart in the rows.

ASPARAGUS beds should be again dressed and made quite clean. If new beds are required, there must be no time lost either to sow seed or get in plants. Our advice to those who require only one small plantation is to form it by planting strong roots, but those who intend to grow Asparagus largely may sow down a bed every year, until they have enough, and then leave well alone; for a bed properly made will last ten years at the very least, if taken care of. It has been clearly demonstrated that this elegant and much-esteemed vegetable may be grown to perfection in any garden with little more expense than attends other crops, provided only that a reasonable amount of skill is brought to bear upon the undertaking. A deep, rich, sandy loam suits it, but we have seen most thriving beds in the garden of an experimental horticulturist who had for a basis of his work an untamed clay, that became a swamp during a wet winter. In making these beds he purchased builders' rubbish at a trifling outlay, and having sorted out the 'hard stuff' for road making, mixed the small stuff with turf, hedge and ditch parings, and whatever old hot-bed soil could be spared, and made his beds upon and above the clay, and laid narrow walks and cheap tiles between them. Finer 'grass' than these beds supplied has not been seen in the market ; and the grower declared that the cost was scarcely more than making a seed-bed for Cabbages. Where the staple is sandy or a light loam, Asparagus may be reckoned on to thrive if reasonably well prepared for. A good body of manure should be dug in, and a mellow seed-bed should be secured. This being done, care must be taken to sow thinly, and, in due time, to thin severely, for a crowded plant will never supply fat sticks. Beds may be made by planting roots instead of seeds, but the roots must be fresh or they will not prosper. The advantage of using plants is that 'grass' may be cut so much earlier than when produced from seed.

AUBERGINES—the fruits of Egg-plants—play a more important part in the cookery of the French and Italians than with us. It is well, however, to bear in mind that, apart from their value as ornamental plants, they make a delicious dish when properly cooked. Seed may be raised in heat, but when summer comes the plants thrive in rich soil at the foot of a wall facing south.

The white and purple varieties are grown both for ornament and for cooking. Sow now in heat, and in June the plants should be ready for transferring to rich soil in a sheltered spot, allowing each one a space of two feet.

BEANS, KIDNEY, may be sown towards the end of the month, but not in quantity, because of the risk of destruction by frost. Very much may be done, however, to expedite the supply of this valuable vegetable, a very little protection being sufficient to carry the young plants through a bad time in the event of late frosts and storms. In proportion to the means at command, sowings made early will live or die, as determined by the weather. But sowings made at the end of the month will probably prosper. These esculents are of the greatest

M

value, for they neither require a rich soil nor a good season. In years of excessive drought, that have put Cauliflowers, Broccoli, and many other summer vegetables *hors de combat*, the Kidney Beans of all sorts braved the weather and bore abundantly.

BEET.—At quite the end of the month sow in drills, a foot or fifteen inches apart, on deep, well-dug ground, without manure. Large Beets are not desired for the kitchen, but rather small, deeply coloured, handsome roots are always valued, and these can only be grown in soil that has been stirred to a good depth, and is quite free of recent manuring.

BROCCOLI.—Make another sowing of several sorts, giving preference as yet to the early ones. In particularly late districts, and perhaps pretty generally in the north, the late Broccoli should be sown now, but in the midlands and the south there is time to spare for sowing them as yet. Be particular to have a good seed-bed, that the plants may grow well from the first; if the early growth be starved, the plants become the victims of club and other ruinous maladies.

BRUSSELS SPROUTS.—There must be no delay in sowing for the main crop. Rich soil and plenty of room are essential.

CABBAGE.—Sow the larger kinds for autumn use, and one or two rows of the smaller kinds for planting in odd places as early crops are cleared off. Pigs and poultry will always dispose of surplus Cabbage advantageously, so there can be no serious objection to keeping up a constant succession. Plant out from seed-beds as fast as the plants become strong enough, for stifling and starving tend to club, mildew, and blindness. In respect of club in general, it may be observed that in land deeply dug, abundantly manured, and with a constant change of crops from plot to plot, club is scarcely known, and therefore it may be regarded as a defect of some sort in the movements of the cultivator. Where Red Cabbage is in demand for use with game in autumn, seed should be sown now.

CARDOONS to be sown on land heavily manured in rows four feet apart, the seeds in clumps of three each, eighteen inches apart. They are sometimes sown in trenches, but we do not approve of that system, for they do not require moisture to the extent of Celery, and the blanching can be effectually accomplished without it. Our advice is, therefore, plant on the level, except the ground be particularly dry and hot, and then trenches will be of great service to promote a free growth, for Cardoons should be large and fat to have their proper flavour.

CARROT.—Sow the main crops.

CAULIFLOWERS to be planted out at every opportunity, warm showery weather being most favourable. If cold weather should follow, a large proportion of the plants will be destroyed unless protected, and there is no cheaper protection than empty flower-pots, which may be left on all day as well as all night in extreme cases when a killing east wind is blowing. Sow now and prick the plants out early to save buttoning, and they will make a quick return.

CELERY.—Sow in a warm corner of the open ground on a bed consisting in great part of rotten manure. It will happen in a good season that this outdoor sowing will prove the best after all, as it will have no check from first to last, and will be in just the right state for planting out when the ground is ready for it after Peas and other early crops. If Celery suffers at any time a serious check, it is apt to make hollow stems and lack every good quality except size, which is, after all, but a poor quality if the sticks are hollow and watery. Prick out the plants from seed-pans on a bed of rotten manure, on a hard bottom, in frames or in sheltered nooks, and look after them with extra care for a week or two. Good Celery cannot be grown by the haphazard gardener.

CHICORY.—This wholesome esculent is used in a variety of ways, and is very much prized in some households. The blanched heads make an acceptable accompaniment to cheese, are valuable for salading, and may be stewed and served with melted butter in the same manner as Sea Kale. To grow large clean roots a deep rich soil is required. If manure must be added, use that which is well decayed, and bury it at least twelve inches, for near the surface it will produce fanged roots. Prepare the seed-bed as for Parsnips, sow in drills twelve inches apart, and thin the plants to nine inches in the rows. In October the roots will be ready for lifting, preparatory to being packed in dark quarters for blanching.

ENDIVE.—Sow a small quantity in moderate heat for the first supply, in drills six inches apart, and when an inch high prick out on to a bed of rich light soil.

HERBS.—Chervil, Fennel, Hyssop, and other flavouring and medicinal Herbs, may be sown now better than at any other time, as they will start at once into full growth, and need little other after-care than thinning and weeding. Rich soil is not required, but the position must be dry and sunny.

LEEK to be sown again if the former sowing is insufficient or has failed.

LETTUCE to be sown for succession, the quick-growing, tenderhearted kinds being the best to sow now. Plant out from frames and seed-pans. A few forward plants may be tied, but as a rule tying is less desirable than most people suppose. Certainly, after tying, the hearts soon rot if not quickly eaten, and as fine Lettuces as can be desired may now be grown without tying, the close-hearting sorts being very much improved in that respect.

MELON.—Sow again for a second crop in houses, and grow the plants in pots until they reach a foot high. The early crop will then be ripe, and the house can be cleared and syringed for a fresh start. From this sowing fruit should be ready about the beginning of July. The frame culture advised for Cucumbers will be right for Melons, until the fruit attain the size of a small orange. Then a thorough soaking must be given, and under proper management no more water should be necessary. A dry atmosphere and free ventilation are essential to bring the fruit to perfection. Stopping must be commenced early by pinching out the leader, and only one eye should be allowed beyond the fruit which are to remain. Six will be enough for one plant to carry, and they should be nearly of a size, for if one fruit obtains a strong lead, it will be impossible to ripen the others. The remainder should be gradually removed while young. The worst foe of the Melon is red spider, and it is difficult to apply a remedy without doing mischief. Water will destroy it, but this may have disastrous results on the fruit. The best preventive is stout well-grown plants. Weakly specimens appear to invite attack, and are incapable of struggling against it. Still under the best management it is sometimes difficult to finish off Melons without having red spider to assist in the operation. Melon plants are occasionally lost through decay at the collar. The best means of preventing it is to lay small pieces of charcoal in a circle round the stem.

ONION to be sown for winter use, if not already done, or if any mishap has befallen former sowings. This task must be disposed of early, for Onions should have good hold of the ground before hot weather comes.

ONIONS FOR PICKLING should be grown thickly on poor ground made firm. The plants are not to be thinned, but may be allowed to stand as thick as pebbles on the sea-shore. The starving system produces abundance of small handsome bulbs that ripen early, which are the very things wanted for pickling. The Queen and Paris Silver-skin are adapted for the purpose.

PARSLEY to be sown in plenty for summer and autumn supply;

thin as soon as up, to give each plant plenty of room; and in thinning, take out those plants which are least curled.

PEAS to be sown again for succession, the finest second earliest being the best to sow now.

SALSIFY.—This delicious root, which is sometimes designated the 'Vegetable Oyster,' requires a piece of ground deeply trenched, with a thick layer of manure at the bottom of the trench, and not a particle of manure in the body of soil above it. The roots strike down into the manure, and acquire a good size with great regularity, and the quality is fine. If carelessly grown, they become forked and fibrous, and are much wasted in the cooking, besides being of inferior flavour. Sow in rows fifteen inches apart, any time from the end of March to the beginning of May. Two sowings will generally suffice.

SORREL.—As the flower stems rise from the previous year's plants they must be cut out, or the leaves will come small and be of indifferent quality. Yearling plants are always the most productive, and it is therefore advisable to destroy each crop after it has served its purpose.

SPINACH.—Sow the Prickly-seeded, which does not run so soon as the Round. If a plantation of Spinach Beet has not yet been secured, sow at once, as there is ample time yet for a free growth and a valuable plant.

TURNIP to be sown for succession, and the plantations advancing to be freely hoed between and severely thinned.

VEGETABLE MARROW.—An early sowing to be made in pots, in readiness for planting out immediately weather admits of it. Three plants in a pot are enough, and they must not be weakened by excessive heat.

WINTER GREENS.—A sowing of Borecole should be made, and if a supply is required in spring, it will be well to sow again in the first week of May.

MAY

HIGH-PRESSURE times continue, for the heat increases daily, and the season of production is already shortened by two months. The most pressing business is to repair all losses, for even now, if affairs have gone wrong, it is possible to get up a stock of Winter Greens, and to sow all the sorts of seeds that should have been sown in March and April, with a reasonable chance of profitable results.

It must not be expected, however, that the most brisk and skilful can overtake those who have been doing well from the first dawn of spring, and who have not omitted to sow a single seed at the proper time from the day when seed-sowing became requisite. The heat of the earth is now sufficient to start many seeds into growth that are customarily sown in heat a month or two earlier; and, therefore, those who cannot make hot-beds may grow many choice things if they will be content to have them a week or two later than their more fortunate neighbours. In sowing seeds of the more tender subjects, such as Capsicums, Marrows, and Cucumbers, it will be better to lose a few days, in order to make sure of the result desired, rather than to be in undue haste and have the seed destroyed by heavy rains, or the young plants nipped off by frost. Do not, therefore, sow any of these seeds in the open ground until the weather is somewhat settled and sunny, for if they meet with any serious check they will scarcely recover during the whole of the season.

ASPARAGUS in seed-beds to be thinned as soon as possible, so that wherever two or three plants rise together, the number should be reduced to one. But there is time yet for seedlings to appear. The bearing beds are more attractive, for they show their toothsome tops, and to fill a basket with them while the grass is wet with dew is a task for an artist as much as for a market woman who never heard of æsthetics. The cutting must be done in a systematic manner, and if practicable always by the same person. It is better to cut all the shoots as fast as they acquire a proper size, and sort them for use according to quality, rather than to pick and choose the fat shoots and throw the whole plantation into disorder. Green-topped Asparagus is in favour in this country; but those who prefer it blanched have simply to earth it up sufficiently, and cut below the surface, taking care to avoid injuring the young shoots which have not pushed through. It is not for us to decide on any matter of individual taste, but we will give a word of practical advice that may be of value to many. It is not the custom to protect Asparagus in open beds; but it should be, for the keen frosts that often occur when the sticks are rising destroy a large number. This may be prevented by covering with any kind of light, dry litter, which will not in the least interfere with that full greening of the tops which English people generally prefer, because the light and air will reach the plant; but the edge of the frost will be blunted by the litter. If there is nothing at hand for this purpose, let a man go round with the sickle, and cut a lot of long grass from the rough parts of the shrubbery, and put a light handful over every crown in the bed. The sticks will rise with the litter upon them like night-caps, and will be plump and green and unhurt by frost.

BEANS may be sown for a late crop, but on hot soils they are not likely to pay. It is customary to top Beans when in flower, and the practice has its advantages. In case the black fly takes possession, topping is a necessity, for the insect can only subsist on the youngest leaves at the top of the plant, and the process pretty well clears them away.

BEANS, KIDNEY, of all kinds to be sown in quantity. Where appearances are important, sow a mixture of several sorts of Runners, and train them to form a bower. Dwarf Kidney Beans are but seldom allowed as much space as they require, and the rows, therefore, should be thinned early, for crowded plants never bear so well as those that enjoy light and air on all sides. In continental cookery a good dish is made of the beans shelled out when about half ripe. These being served in rich gravy are at once savoury and wholesome. The best kinds to grow for this purpose are the White-seeded Runners, which, in many places, may be worth growing for use as dry haricots. In this case, of course, the pods should be allowed to ripen, but if intended to be cooked for a summer dish, they should be gathered when the Beans are full grown, but not yet ripe.

BEET.—The main crop should be sown in the early part of the month. Thin and weed the early sown, and if the ground has been suitably prepared it will be needless to give water to this crop. As Beet is not wanted large, it is not advisable to sow any great breadth until the beginning of May, or it is liable to become coarse.

BROCCOLI to be sown for succession. Plant out from frames and forward seed-beds at every opportunity. About the middle of the month sow for cutting in May and June of next year.

BRUSSELS SPROUTS.—For the sake of a few fine buttons in the first dripping days of autumn, when Peas and Runners and Marrows are gone, put out as soon as possible some of the forwardest plants you have, giving them a rich soil and sunny position.

CABBAGE.—Plant out from seed-beds at every opportunity, choosing if possible the advent of showery weather. Sow the smaller sorts and Coleworts, especially in favoured districts where there is usually no check to vegetation until the turn of the year.

CAPSICUM may be sown out of doors about the middle of the

month, and nice green pods for picking may be secured in the autumn.

CARROT.—Thin the main crops early, and sow a few rows of Champion Horn or Intermediate, for use in a small state during late summer, when they make an elegant and delicate dish.

CAULIFLOWERS must have water in dry weather; they are the most hungry and thirsty plants in the garden, but pay well for good living. Plant out from frames as fast as ready, for they do no good to stand crowded and starving.

CELERY trenches must be prepared in time, though, strange to say, this task is generally deferred until the plants have really become weak through overcrowding. In a small garden it is never advisable to have Celery very forward, for the simple reason that trenches cannot be made for it until Peas come off and other early crops are over. To insure fine Celery, the cultivator must be in advance of events rather than lag behind them. Plenty of manure must be used; it is scarcely possible, in fact, to employ too much, and liberality is not waste, because the ground will be in capital condition for the next crop. There are many modes of planting Celery, but the simplest is to make the trenches four feet apart, and a foot and a half wide, and put the plants six to nine inches apart, according to the sorts. This work must be done neatly, with an artistic finish. In planting take off suckers, and if any of the leaves are blistered, pinch the blisters, and finish by dusting the plantation with soot. As Celery loves moisture, give water freely in dry weather.

CUCUMBERS of excellent quality may be grown on ridges or hills, should the season be favourable. Supposing the cultivator to have the means of obtaining plenty of manure, ridges, which are to run east and west, are preferable to hills. The soil should be thrown out three feet wide and two feet deep, and be laid upon the north side. Then put three feet of hot manure in the trench, and cover with the soil that was taken out, so as to form an easy slope to the south, and with a steep slope on the north side carefully finished to prevent its crumbling down before the season ends. The plants should be put out on the slope as soon as possible after the ridges are made ready, and it would be well to cover them with hand-lights until they have made a free growth, and the weather has become quite summery. It is a good plan to grow one or two rows of Runner Beans a short distance from the ridge on the north side to give shelter, and in case of bad weather after the plants are in bearing, pea-sticks or dry litter laid about them lightly will afford protection, but stable manure must not be used. In case manure is not abundant, make a few small hills in a sheltered, sunny spot, with whatever you can find in the way of turf, rotten manure, or leaf-mould, taking care that nothing injurious to vegetation is mixed with it. Put several inches of a mixture of good loam and rotten manure on the hills, and plant and protect as in the case of ridges. If plants are not obtainable, sow seeds; there will still be a chance of Cucumbers during July, August, and September; for if they thrive at all, they are pretty brisk in their movements. Three observations remain to be made on this subject. In the first place, what are known as 'Ridge' Cucumbers only should be grown in the open air; the large sorts grown in houses are unfit. In the second place, the plants should only be pinched once, and there is no occasion for the niggling business which gardeners call 'setting the bloom'; provide for their roots a good bed, and then let them grow as they please. In the third place, as encouragement, we feel bound to say that, as Cucumbers are grown to be eaten as well as to be looked at, those from ridges are less handsome than house Cucumbers, but are quite equal to them in flavour. Save, therefore, that he cannot command fruit fit for exhibition, the cottager may at least obtain fruit fit to eat, and in this respect rival his wealthy neighbour who would not eat a 'field Cucumber' for all the world.

DANDELION somewhat resembles the Endive, and is one of the earliest and most wholesome additions to the salad-bowl. Sow now, and again in June, in drills one foot asunder, and thin out the plants to one foot apart in the rows. These will be ready for use in the following winter and spring.

GOURDS AND PUMPKINS.—An early show of fruit necessitates raising seeds under glass for planting on prepared beds, and the plants must be protected by means of lights or any other arrangement that can be improvised as a defence against late frosts. Of course the seeds can be sown upon the actual bed, but it is a loss of time. The rapidity with which the plants grow is a sufficient indication that generous feeding and copious supplies of water in dry weather are imperative.

INDIAN CORN is grown in this country as an ornament to our gardens, and also for the green cobs which are used as a vegetable. Sow early in the month on rich light soil, and in a hot season, especially when accompanied by moisture, there will be rapid growth. The cobs to be gathered for cooking when of full size, but while quite green.

LETTUCE.—Sow for succession where the plants are to remain, and plant out at every opportunity. Extra care must be taken now to shade and water after planting, to insure a quick growth and prevent the plants running to seed. The larger Cabbage Lettuces will prove useful if sown now.

MELON.—It is not too late to grow Melons in frames, provided a start can be made with strong plants.

PEA.—Sow second early dwarf sorts, and if there is any prospect of a break in the supply, sow also a few rows of the earliest. It is a good plan now to prepare trenches as for Celery, but less deep, and sow Peas in them, as the trenches can be quickly filled with water in case of dry weather, and the vigorous growth insured will be proof against mildew.

SAVOY sown now will produce small useful hearts for winter use. By many these small hearts will be preferred to large ones as more delicate, and therefore a sowing of Tom Thumb may be advised.

SPINACH, NEW ZEALAND, can be sown in the open ground in the early part of this month, and should be thinned to about a yard apart. The growth somewhat resembles that of the Ice Plant. The tender young tops are pinched off for cooking, and they make an elegant Spinach, which has no bitter flavour, and therefore can be eaten by many persons who object to the sooty flavour of ordinary Spinach.

TOMATO.—By the third week in May the plants for the open border should be hardened. In a cold pit or frame they may be gradually exposed until the lights can be left off altogether, even at night. A thick layer of ashes at the bottom of the frame will insure drainage and keep off vermin. If the plants are allowed plenty of space, and are well managed, they will possess dark healthy foliage, needing no support from sticks until they are in final quarters. Do not put them out before the end of the month or the beginning of June, and choose a quiet day for the work. If possible, give them a sunny spot under the shelter of a wall having a southern or western aspect. On a stiff soil it is advisable to plant on ridges, and not too deeply; for deep planting encourages strong growth, and strong growth defers the production of fruit. Tomatoes are sometimes grown in beds, and then it is necessary to give them abundant room. For branched plants three feet between the plants in the rows, and the rows four feet apart, will afford space for trying and watering. Each plant should have the support of a stout stake firmly fixed in the soil, and rising four feet above it; and once a week at least the tying should be attended to. As to stopping, the centre stem should be allowed to grow until the early flowers have set. It is from these early flowers that out-door Tomatoes can be successfully ripened, and the removal of the main shoot delays their production. But after fifteen or twenty fruits are visible, the top of the leading stem may be shortened to the length of the stake. The fruiting branches should also be kept short beyond the fruit, and large leaves must be shortened to allow free access of sunshine. Should the single stem system be adopted, three feet between the rows and two feet between plants in the rows will suffice. On a light soil and in dry weather, weak liquid manure may, with advantage, be alternated with pure water, but this practice must not be carried far enough to make the plants gross, or ripening will be delayed. Fruit intended for exhibition must be selected with judgment, and with this end in view four to six specimens of any large variety will be sufficient for one plant to bring to perfection.

TURNIP to be sown for succession. It is well now to keep to the small white early sorts.

VEGETABLE MARROW.—In cottage gardens luxuriant vines may every year be seen trailing over the sides of heaps of decayed turf or manure. All forward vegetables are prized, and Marrows are no exception to the rule. An early supply from the open ground is most readily insured by raising strong plants in pots and putting them on rich warm beds as early as the season and district will permit. Late frosts must be guarded against by some kind of protection, and slugs must be deterred from eating up the plants.

JUNE

IN a considerable measure the crops will now take care of themselves, and we may consider the chief anxieties and activities of the season over. Our notes, therefore, will now be more brief. We do not counsel the cultivator to 'rest and be thankful.' It is better for him to work, but he must be thankful all the same if he would be happy in his healthy and entertaining employment. Watering and weeding are the principal labours of this month, and both must be pursued with diligence. Where systematic irrigation with sewage can be carried on, the most wonderful results may be expected; but ordinary watering, where every drop has to be dipped and carried, is often injurious rather than beneficial, for the simple reason that it is only half done.

In such cases we should advise the cultivator to abstain from giving water as long as possible, and then to give it in abundance, watering only a small plot every day in order to saturate the ground, and taking a week or more to go over a piece which would be done in a day by mere surface dribblings.

ASPARAGUS should be in full supply, and may be cut until the middle or end of the month. When cutting should cease depends on the district. In the South of England the 14th is about the proper time to make the last cut; north of the Trent, the 20th may be soon enough; and further north, cutting may be continued until July. The point to be borne in mind is that the plant must be allowed time to grow freely without any further check, in order to store up the material to make tender shoots next year. It is a good plan to insert stakes in Asparagus beds such as are used for Peas, to give support to the green growth against gales of wind; for when the stems are snapped by storms, as they often are, the roots lose their aid, and are weakened for their future work. Manure water will do great things for Asparagus now, and a dressing of salt may be given with advantage.

BEANS may yet be sown, but as they are not much in request in the latter part of the season, a small sowing will probably suffice.

BEANS, KIDNEY, may be sown about the middle of the month, to supply tender pods when those from the early sowings are past. A late crop of Runners will pay well almost anywhere, for they bear until the frost cuts them down, and that may not happen until far into November.

BROCCOLI.—Take advantage of showers to continue planting out.

CABBAGE.—Towards the end of the month sow a good breadth of small Cabbages and Coleworts. They will be immensely valuable to plant out as the summer crops are cleared away.

CAPSICUMS may be planted out in a sunny sheltered spot.

CAULIFLOWERS that are planted out now from seed-beds must have plentiful supplies of water, and be shaded during mid-day for a week. It is customary to snap one of the inner leaves over the heads to protect them.

CELERY to be planted out without loss of time, in showery weather if possible; but if the weather is hot and dry, shade and give water. The work must be well done, hence it is advisable to lift no more plants than can be quickly planted, watered in and shaded, for exposure tends to exhaustion, and Celery ought never to suffer a check in even the slightest degree. When planted, dust lightly with soot or wood ashes. Pea-sticks laid across the trenches will give shade enough with very little trouble.

CUCUMBERS FOR PICKLING may be sown on ridges.

ENDIVE is not generally wanted while good Lettuces abound, but it takes the place of Lettuce in autumn and winter, when the more delicate vegetable is scarce. Sow in drills an inch deep and six inches apart. Thin the plants, and transfer the thinnings to rich light soil. They must be liberally grown on well-manured land with the aid of water in dry weather.

LETTUCE to be sown and planted at every opportunity. A few rows of large Cos varieties should be sown in trenches prepared as for Celery, there to be thinned and allowed to stand. They will form fine hearts, and be valued at a time when Lettuces are scarce.

MELON.—For a final crop in houses sow as previously directed, and grow the plants on in pots, until the house can be cleared of the former set for their reception. The growth should be pushed forward to insure ripe fruit before the end of September. In the event of dull weather at the finish, there will be all the greater need of abundant but judicious ventilation, and of a warm dry atmosphere at night. Before they become heavy every fruit should have the support of a thin piece of board suspended by wire at both ends.

MUSHROOMS may be prepared for now that the demands of the gardener on the stable are diminishing. The first step towards success is to accumulate a good long heap of horse-droppings with the least possible amount of litter. Let this ferment moderately, and turn it two or three times, always making a long heap of it, which keeps down the fermentation. When the fire is somewhat taken out of it, make up the bed with a mixture of about four parts of the fermented manure, and one part of turfy loam well incorporated. Beat the stuff together with the flat of the spade as the work proceeds, fashioning the bed in the form of a ridge about three feet wide at the base, and of any length that may be convenient. Give the work a neat finish, or the Mushrooms will certainly not repay you. Put in rather large lumps of spawn when the bed is nicely warm, cover with a thin layer of fine soil, and protect with mats or clean straw. This is a quick and easy way of growing Mushrooms, and by commencing now, the season is all before one. Nine times in ten, people begin preparations for Mushroom growing about a month too late, for the spawn runs during the hot weather, and the crop rises when the weather moderates, and the cool autumnal rains occur.

ONIONS to be sown for salading. Forward beds of large sorts to be thinned in good time. The best Onions for keeping are those of moderate size, perfectly ripened: therefore the thinning should not be too severe.

PEAS may still be sown. The second early sorts will pay well if the season is favourable, but the first earlies will be more sure, as one or two showers will carry them through to maturity.

TURNIPS may be sown in variety and in quantity after Midsummer Day. Sow on well-prepared ground, and put a sprinkle of artificial manure in the drills with the seed. By hastening the early growth of the plant the fly is kept in check.

JULY

JULY is like January in one respect for gardeners, for everything depends upon the weather. It may be hot, with frequent heavy rains, and vegetation in the most luxuriant growth; or the earth may be iron and the heavens brass, with scarcely a green blade to be seen. The light flying showers that usually occur in July do not render watering unnecessary; in fact, a heavy soaking of a crop after a moderate rainfall is a valuable aid to its growth, for it requires a long-continued heavy down-pour to penetrate to the roots.

GARDEN RUBBISH is apt to accumulate in odd corners and become dangerously offensive. The stumps of Cabbages and Cauliflowers soon give off the most obnoxious odours, and a whole parish may be annoyed by the want of thought in one particular garden. The short and easy way with all soft decaying rubbish is to put it at the bottom of the trench in preparing land for planting. There it ceases to be a nuisance and becomes a valuable manure.

BEAN, KIDNEY.—A few Dwarfs and Runners may be useful, but it is not advisable to sow largely, as they may be cut off by frost just as they are beginning to bear.

BROCCOLI to be planted out as before; many of the plants left over from former plantings will now be stout and strong, and make useful successions.

CABBAGES should be sown in a full breadth some time this month, as the July sowing is of great importance, and, indeed, may be made to suffice for the whole year. In common with the sowing of Broccoli, the particular date must be determined by the climate and by the latitude of the place. In the North, the first week of July is none too early; in the Midlands, the 10th to the 20th of the month is early enough; and in the South, the seed need not be sown until quite the end of the month. Two or three large sorts may be sown with advantage in almost any garden, and there must also be a sowing of Coleworts, for these are in request from the moment the Peas and Beans grow scarce, and they make a most delicious dish. The seed-bed should be nicely prepared, and any old plaster, or other rubbish containing lime, should be dug in. Sow thinly, for a thick sowing makes a weak plant, no matter how severely it may be thinned afterwards. Red Cabbage must be sown now to produce large heads for pickling next year.

CARDOONS to be thinned to one plant in each station, and that, of course, the strongest.

CARROT.—Frame culture of small sorts should commence, to produce a succession of young Carrots for table.

CELERY to be planted out in showery weather. It is too late to sow now except for soups, and for that purpose only a small sowing should be made, as it may not come to anything.

CHARDS.—Those who care for Chards must cut down a number of Globe Artichokes about six inches above ground, and, if necessary, keep the plants well watered to induce new growth, which will be ready for blanching in September.

CUCUMBERS on ridges generally do well without water, but they must not be allowed to suffer from drought. If watering must be resorted to, make sure first of soft water well warmed by exposure to the sun, and water them liberally three or four evenings in succession, and then give no more for a week or so.

ENDIVE to be sown for winter. It will be well to make two sowings, say on the first and last days of the month.

GARLIC AND SHALLOTS to be taken up in suitable weather, and it may be necessary to complete the ripening under shelter.

LEEKS to be planted out; and on dry soils, in trenches prepared as for Celery.

PARSLEY to be sown for winter use. It is a most important matter even in the smallest garden to have a constant supply.

PEAS seldom do much good when sown later than June, but those who care to risk a little labour for a late dish may sow one or more of the early varieties.

POTATOES to be lifted when a good crop is secured without waiting for the shaws to die down. The skins, being tender, will suffer damage if the work is done roughly, but will soon harden, and the stock will ripen in the store as perfectly as in the field. It needs some amount of courage to lift Potatoes while the tops are still green and vigorous, and it should not be done until the roots are fully grown and beginning to ripen. Quick-growing sorts may be planted to dig as new Potatoes in the autumn.

RADISH.—Sow Black Spanish for winter use.

SPINACH.—Sow the Prickly-seeded to stand the winter, selecting for the seed-bed ground lying high and dry that has been at least twice dug over and has had no recent manure. The twice digging is to promote the destruction of the 'Spinach Moth' grub, which the robins and thrushes will devour when exposed by digging. These grubs make an end of many a good breadth of Winter Spinach every year, and are the more to be feared by the careless cultivator.

TURNIPS to be sown in quantity in the early part of the month; thin advancing crops, and keep the hoe in action amongst them.

WINTER GREENS of all kinds to be planted out freely in the best ground at command, after a good digging, and to be aided with water for a week or so should the weather be dry.

AUGUST

THE work of this month is not severe, but a few of its details are of great consequence. The matter of chief importance is to see that whatever should be done is well done, because the winter is coming, and the weak joints in the harness may be made manifest when it is too late to repair them. The supplies of the garden during the next winter and spring will in great part depend upon good management now, for we have to make the utmost of the few weeks of growing weather that remain. Autumn sowings of seed must not only be attended to, but with particular care, to insure a regular and rapid growth, and yet not a single seed should be sown a day too soon, because if the plants become succulent before winter they may be destroyed by frost. One great difficulty in connection with sowing seed now is the likelihood of the ground being too dry; yet it is most unwise to water seeds, and it is always better if they can be got up with the natural moisture of the soil alone. However, in an extreme case the ground should be well soaked before the seed is sown, and after sowing covered with hurdles, pea-sticks, or mats until the seed begins to sprout.

ARTICHOKES, GLOBE, to be cut down as soon as the heads are used.

BROCCOLI to be planted out. As the Sprouting Broccoli, which belongs to the class of 'Winter Greens,' does not pay well in spring unless it grows freely now, plant it far enough apart, or if crowded where already planted to stand the winter, take out every alternate plant and make another plantation.

BRUSSELS SPROUTS may be sown early in the month, part to stand the winter in the seed-bed, and part to be pricked out ready for planting in the spring. This plan insures a fine plant and an early supply of buttons.

CABBAGE to be sown in small quantities, the large sorts being suitable to sow now. Plant Coleworts without delay, and clean up plots from which Cabbages have been cut.

CARDOONS.—Commence blanching if the plants are ready.

CAULIFLOWER must be sown to stand the winter, and there is no better place for them than a sheltered spot on an open, sunny border. The time to sow must be determined by the climate of the district. In cold, late localities, the first week is none too early; from the 15th to the 25th is a good time for all the Midland districts; and the end of the month, or the first week of September, is early enough in the extreme South. In Devon and Cornwall the sowing is later still. In any case, the seed should be sown on a good bed, and with care, in order that a healthy growth may be promoted from the first. It is important to have the plants as hardy as possible by free exposure, and therefore they must not be sheltered or shaded until frost threatens them, and then the glasses must be put on, but they must have air at every opportunity.

CELERY to be carefully earthed up as required. It takes five weeks or more to blanch Celery well, and as the earthing up checks growth, the operation should not be commenced a day too soon. Take care the earth does not get into the hearts.

CORN SALAD should be sown during this month and September to produce plants fit for use in early spring. In the summer months the whole plant is edible, but in winter or spring the outer leaves only should be used.

CUCUMBER.—For a supply of Cucumbers during the winter months the general principles of management are identical with those given under January and March, with one important exception. At the commencement of the year a continued accession of light and warmth may be relied on. Now there will be a constant diminution of these vital forces. Hence the progress of the plants will gradually abate as the year wanes, and due allowance must be made for the fact. So much will depend on the character of the autumn and winter, that it will be unwise to risk all on a single sowing. Seed put in on two or three occasions between the end of August and the end of October, will provide plants in various stages of growth to meet the contingencies of the season. The production of Cucumbers will then depend on care and management. In very dull cold weather it may be dangerous to syringe the foliage, but the necessary moisture can be secured by sprinkling the floor and walls.

ENDIVE.—Make a final sowing, and plant out all that are large enough, selecting, if possible, a dry, sloping bank for the purpose.

LETTUCE to be sown to stand the winter; the hardiest sorts, such as Black-seeded Bath Cos and Winter White Cos, being the best. In cold districts the middle of the month is a good time to sow; in favoured places the end of the month will be better.

ONIONS are things to be reconsidered. For many years the Tripoli section enjoyed pre-eminence for sowing at this season, the opinion prevailing that other kinds were unsuitable. But it is found that Improved Reading, and others that may with propriety be described as English Onions, are as hardy as the Tripolis, and therefore as well adapted for sowing at this season. Thus, instead of sorts that must be used quickly, we may command for summer sowing the best of the keepers, and the result will be heavier crops and earlier ripening, with plentiful supplies of 'thinnings' for salads all through the autumn and winter. Two sowings—one at the beginning, the other at the end of the month—may be adopted with advantage. The storage of Onions is often faulty, and consequently losses occur through mildew and premature growth. If any are as yet unripe, spread them out in the sun in a dry place, where they can be covered quickly in case of rain. In wet, cold seasons, it is sometimes necessary to finish the store Onions by putting them in a nearly cold oven for some hours before they are stored away.

PEA.—It is mere waste of seed to sow now, but crops coming forward for late bearing should have attention, more especially to make them safe against storms by a sufficiency of support, and in case of drought to give abundance of water.

STRAWBERRY PLANTS may be put in should the weather prove favourable; but next month will answer. In burning weather it is well worth while to bed the plants closely in a moist shady place until rain comes, and then plant out.

TOMATOES to be gathered as soon as ripe. If bad weather interferes with the finishing of the crop, cut the full-grown fruit with a length of stem attached, and hang them up in a sunny greenhouse, or some other warm spot in full daylight.

TURNIP may be sown in the early part of the month. The best sorts now are Jersey Navet, or Snowball. All the Year Round will please those who like a yellow Turnip.

SEPTEMBER

WEEDS will be troublesome to the overworked and the idle gardener, while the best kept land will be full of seeds blown upon it from the sluggard's garden, and the first shower will bring them up in terrific force. All that we have to say about them is that they must be kept down, for they will not only choke the rising crops in seed-beds and spoil the look of everything, but they very much tend to keep the ground damp and cold, when, if they were away, it would get dry and warm, to the benefit of all the proper crops upon it. Neglect will make the task of eradication simply terrible, and, in the meantime, every crop on the ground will suffer. The two great months for weeds are May and September; but often the September weeds triumph, because the mischief they do is not then so obvious to the casual eye. As there are now many used-up crops that may be cleared away, large quantities of Cabbage, Endive, Lettuce, and even thinnings of Spinach may be planted out to stand the winter.

CABBAGE.—We advocate crowding the land now with Cabbage plants, for growth will be slow and the demands of the kitchen constant. Crowding, however, is not quite the same thing as overcrowding, and it is only a waste of labour, land, and crop to put the plants so close together that they have not space for full development. The usual rule in planting out the larger sorts of Cabbage at this time of the year is to allow a distance every way of two feet between the plants. But we carry the crowding principle so far as to put the small growing Coleworts and other miniature Cabbages in the interspaces thus : ⦂⦂⦂⦂⦂⦂⦂ the large dots being large Cabbages, and the small dots Coleworts. The latter are to be all got rid of before spring growth commences.

CAULIFLOWER.—Plant out for the winter, and sow another small pinch of seed in a frame or in a pan in the greenhouse.

CELERY.—Continue to earth up, selecting a dry time for the task.

CHARDS take quite six weeks to blanch by means of straw, covered with earth.

CUCUMBERS for the winter need careful management and suitable appliances. See the remarks on this subject under August.

ENDIVE to be planted out as directed last month. Plant a few on the border of an orchard-house, or in a ground vinery, or in old frames for which some sort of lights, however crazy, can be found.

LETTUCES should be coming in from the garden now in good condition, but the supply will necessarily be running short. Sowings of two or three sorts should be made partly in frames and partly on a dry open plot from which a crop has been taken. The ground should be well dug, but no manure put on. Sow thinly, so that there will not be much need for thinning, and confine the selection to sorts known to be hardy. The Bath Cos is one of the best of these. The Hammersmith is of poor quality, but valuable for its hardiness. The August sowings will soon be forward enough for planting out, and it will be advisable to get the work done as early as possible to insure their being well established before winter.

PARSLEY.—The latest sowing will require thinning, but for the present this must not be too strictly carried out; between this and spring there will be many opportunities. Thin the plot by drawing out complete plants as Parsley is demanded for the kitchen. If no late sowing was made, or having been made has failed, cut down to the ground the strongest plants, that a new growth may be secured quickly. A few plants potted now may prove exceedingly valuable in winter.

POTATOES that are ready should be taken up with reasonable care. It is not wise to wait for the dying down of the shaws, because, when the tubers are fully grown, they ripen as well in the store, out of harm's way, as in the ground, where they are exposed to influences that are simply destructive.

SORREL to be removed to final position, allowing a distance of eighteen inches between the plants each way. When growth ceases for the season, give a liberal dressing of rich decayed manure.

SPINACH.—In favourable seasons and forward localities Winter Spinach sown in the first half of this month will make a good plant before winter. Thin the plants that are already up to six inches apart.

TOMATOES are in request the year through. Seed sown now will produce plants that should afford fine fruit in March, and it will need care and judgment to carry them safely through the winter.

OCTOBER

WEEDS and falling leaves are the plagues of the season. It may seem that they do no harm, but assuredly they are directly injurious to every crop upon the ground, for they encourage damp and dirt by preventing a free circulation of air amongst the crops, and the access of sunshine to the land. Keep all clean and tidy, even to the removal of the lower leaves of all the Cabbages, where they lie half decayed upon the ground.

The heavy rains of this month interfere in a material degree with outdoor work, and are often a great impediment to the orderly management that should prevail. The accumulation of rubbish anywhere, even if out of sight, is to be deplored as an evil altogether. The injury to the vegetation in which we have an interest is as great as that inflicted on our own health when dirt poisons the air and damp hastens the general dissolution. On clay soils the accumulation of dead leaves and other vegetable detritus is productive of miasma. It is therefore above all things necessary to keep the garden clean from end to end. All decaying refuse that can be put into trenches should be got out of sight as soon as possible to rot harmlessly instead of infecting the air, and leaves should be often swept up into heaps, in which form they cease to be injurious, although, when spread upon the ground and trodden under foot, they are breeders of mischief. If in want of work, ply the hoe amongst all kinds of crops, taking care not to break or bruise healthy leaves, or loosen the roots of anything. Dig vacant plots, and lay the land up in ridges in the roughest manner possible. Heavy land may be manured now with advantage, but it is well not to put manure on light land until spring.

CABBAGES to be planted out as advised last month.

CARDOONS.—Blanching to be continued.

CARROTS to be taken up and stored in sand. Thin and weed late-sown crops.

CAULIFLOWERS to be prepared for the winter.

CELERIAC.—Part of the crop should be lifted and stored in sand; the plants left in the ground to be protected by earthing over.

CELERY must be earthed up, and protecting material got ready to assure its safety during frost.

CHICORY.—Lift about a dozen at a time as required, cut or wrench off the foliage, and pack the roots, crowns upwards, in boxes with moist leaf-mould or soil. They must be stored in absolute darkness in some cellar, or Mushroom-house which is safe from frost, but a forcing temperature is detrimental to the flavour. Gathering may commence about three weeks after storing. The yield is abundant, and is of especial value for salading through the autumn and winter months.

ENDIVE to be blanched for use as it acquires its full size, but not before, as the blanching makes an end of growth.

GARLIC AND SHALLOTS may be planted on dry, warm soils; but on cold, damp soils to plant now is to throw roots and labour away.

LETTUCE.—Continue to plant as before advised, and make a final sowing in frames not later than the middle of the month.

PARSNIPS may be dug all the winter as wanted. Although a slight frost will not injure them when left in the ground, protection by rough litter is needful in very severe weather. It often happens that they grow freely soon after the turn of the year, and then become worthless.

POTATOES to be taken up and stored with all possible speed. In times when work is slack, the seed potatoes for next season's planting may be got ready, by putting them in baskets and boxes preparatory to their being spread out in the daylight in lofts and sheds when the New Year has turned.

RHUBARB for forcing should be taken up and laid aside in a dry, cool place, as much as possible exposed to the weather. This gives the roots a check, and constitutes a kind of winter, which in some degree prepares them for the forcing pit.

ROOTS, such as Beet, Salsify, and Turnip, to be taken up as soon as possible, and stored for the winter.

WINTER GREENS may still be planted, and it is often better to use up the remainder of the seed-beds than to let them stand there. In the event of a severe winter, these late-planted Greens may not be of much value; but in a mild growing winter they will make some progress, and may prove very useful in the spring.

NOVEMBER

THE remarks already made on the necessity for tidiness and the quick disposal of all decaying refuse, apply as forcibly to this month as to October. The leaves are falling, the atmosphere is moist, and there should be the utmost care taken not to make things worse by scatterings of vegetable rubbish. Now we are in the 'dull days before Christmas' the affairs of the garden may be reviewed in detail, and this is the best period for such a review. Sorts that have done well or ill, wants that have been felt, mistakes that have been made, are now fresh in one's memory, and in ordering seeds, roots, plants &c. for next season's work, we can much better now than at any other time bring experience and observation to bear upon our procedure, with a view to future benefit. Consistently with the revision of plans by the fireside, revise the work out of doors. Begin even now to prepare for next year's crops by trenching, manuring, planting, and collecting stuff to burn in a 'smother.' Land got ready now for spring seeds and roots, and kept quite rough, will only require to be levelled down and raked over when spring comes to be ready for seed at a day or two's notice, and will produce better crops than if got ready in a hurry. Be prepared with protecting material for all the needs of the season, remembering that a few nights of hard frost may destroy Lettuces, Endives, Celery, and Cauliflowers worth many pounds, which a few shillings'-worth of labour and litter would have saved completely. Earthwork can generally be pushed on, and it is good practice to get all road-mending and the breaking up of new ground completed before the year runs out, because of the hindrance that may result from frost, and the inevitable pressure of other work at the turn of the spring. The weather is an important matter; but often the month of November is favourable to outdoor work, and the labour can then be found more readily than at most other seasons.

ARTICHOKES, GLOBE, must be protected ere frost attacks them. In the first place cut off the stems and large leaves to within a foot of the ground, and then heap up along each side of the rows a lot of dry litter consisting of straw, pea haulm, or leaves; taking care in so doing to leave free access to light and air; the hearts must not be covered, or decay will follow.

ARTICHOKES, JERUSALEM, may be dug as wanted, but some should be lifted and stored in sand for use during frosts.

ASPARAGUS beds not yet cleaned must have prompt attention. Cut down the brown grass and rake off all the weeds and rubbish, and finish by putting on a dressing of stable manure, about half-rotten, or sea-weed. It matters not how rank the manure used for a mulch.

BEANS.—It is customary on dry warm soils to sow Beans now for a first crop, and the practice is to be commended. On cold damp soils, and we may say on clay lands everywhere, it is a waste of seed and labour to sow now, but every district has its peculiar capabilities, and each cultivator must judge for himself; our business being to remind all alike according to our knowledge of facts and consideration of the interest of our readers. In any case, Beans sown now should be put on well-drained land in a sheltered spot.

CARROT to be sown in frames, and successive sowings made every three or four weeks until February.

CAULIFLOWERS will be turning in now, and possibly those coming forward will be all the better off for being covered with a leaf to protect the heads from frost. If the barometer rises steadily and the wind goes round to north or north-east, draw all the best Cauliflowers and put them in a shed or any out-of-the-way place safe for use.

CELERY.—Hard frost coming after heavy rain may prove destructive to Celery; and it is well, if there is a crop worth saving, to cut a trench round the plantation to favour escape of surplus water. If taken up and packed away in a dry shed, the sticks will keep fresh for a long time.

HORSE-RADISH to be taken up and stored ready for use, and new plantations to be made as weather permits and ground can be spared.

PEA.—The sowing of Peas now is not recommended for the community at large, but for those only who are so circumstanced that they may adopt the practice with some prospect of success. If it is determined to sow, select for the purpose a nice, dry, light, well-drained sunny border, and make it safe from mice, slugs, and sparrows. Any of the first earlies will serve the purpose, and it will be advisable to sow two or three sorts rather than one only.

POTATOES may be planted on dry, sandy soils, in very sheltered quarters, but not on damp, heavy land.

SEA KALE to be lifted for forcing. This delicious vegetable may, indeed, be forced for the table in this month; but it is not advisable to be in such haste, for a fine sample cannot be secured so early. It is the easiest thing in the world to force, the only point of importance is to have strong roots to begin with. Any place can be utilised for the purpose where a temperature of 45° or 55° can be maintained, such as Mushroom-houses, cellars, pits, or old sheds. The plants may be put thickly into pots, boxes, or they may be planted in a bed; but in any case light must be excluded to insure thorough blanching. By these simple means a regular supply may be obtained until the permanent beds in the open ground come into use.

DECEMBER

THE best advice we can give now is, that a look-out should be kept for heavy rain and sharp frost, that the losses they entail may be reduced to a minimum. Let the work be ordered with reference to the weather, that there may be no 'poaching' on wet ground, or absurd conflict with frost for doing what should have been done on halcyon days. In fine weather and during hard frost wheel out manure; and as long as the ground can be dug without waste of labour, proceed to open trenches, make drains, and mend walks, for these are the times for improving, and the place must be very perfect which affords no work for winter weather. Dispose of all rubbish by the simple process of putting it in trenches when preparing plots for early seeds. In sheds and outhouses many tasks may be found to keep the hands employed, such as making large substantial tallies for the garden; the little paltry things commonly used being simply delusive, for they are generally missing when wanted, from their liability to be trodden into the ground or kicked anywhere by a heedless foot. Make ready pea-sticks, stakes of sizes, and at odd times gather up all the dry stuff that is adapted for a grand 'smother.' A careful forecasting of the next year's cropping will show that even now many preparations may be made to increase the chances of success.

WARM BORDER to be prepared for early work by digging and manuring. All the refuse turf and leaf-mould from the potting-shed and the soil knocked out of pots may be usefully disposed of by adding it to this border, which cannot be too light or too rich, and a good dressing of manure will give it strength to perform its duties.

BEANS to be earthed up for protection and support.

CELERY to be earthed up for the last time. In case of severe weather, have protecting material at hand in the shape of dry litter or mats. Pea-sticks make a capital foundation on which to throw long litter, mats &c. for quickly covering Celery, the protection being as quickly removed when the frost is over, and costing next to nothing.

ENDIVE will be valued now, and must be blanched as required. Place a few in frames and other protected spots; even if in the unused corners of sheds and outhouses, they may be safer than out of doors.

Parsley.—In all cold districts it is wise to secure a bed of Parsley, in a frame or pit, or if a few plants were potted in September, they may be wintered in any place where they can have light and air freely. It is so important to have Parsley at command as wanted, that it may be worth while now to put a frame over a few rows as they stand in the open quarter, rather than risk the loss of all in the event of severe weather.

Radish.—Sow one of the long sorts for a first supply in some warm spot, to secure quick growth.

Underground Onions to be planted in rows one foot apart. They should not be earthed up, for the young bulbs form round the stems in full daylight.

THE ROTATION OF CROPS

IN THE

VEGETABLE GARDEN

THIS is a subject worthy the attention of those who aim at the largest possible production and the highest possible quality of every kind of kitchen garden crop, for it concerns the natural relations of the plant and the soil as to their several chemical constituents. The principle may be illustrated by considering the demands of two of the most common kitchen garden crops. If we submit a Cabbage to the destructive agency of fire, and analyse the ashes that remain, we shall find in them, in round numbers, eight per cent. of sulphuric acid, sixteen per cent. of phosphoric acid, four per cent. of soda, forty-eight per cent. of potash, and fifteen per cent. of lime. It is evident that we cannot expect to grow a Cabbage on a soil which is destitute of these ingredients, to say nothing of others. The obnoxious odour of sulphur emitted by decaying Cabbages might indicate, to any one accustomed to reflect on ordinary occurrences, that this mineral is an important constituent of Cabbage. If we submit a Potato tuber to a similar process, the result will be to find in the ashes fifty-nine per cent. of potash, two per cent. of soda, six per cent. of sulphuric acid, nineteen per cent. of phosphoric acid, and two per cent. of lime. Now the lesson for the cultivator is, that to prepare a soil for Cabbage it is of the utmost importance to employ a manure containing sulphates, phosphates, and potash salts in considerable quantity; as for the lime, that can be supplied separately, but the Cabbage must have it. On the other hand, to prepare a soil for Potatoes it is necessary to employ a manure strongly charged with salts of potash and phosphates, but it need not be highly charged with soda or lime, for we find but a small proportion of these elements in the Potato. There are soils so naturally rich in all that crops require, that they may be tilled for years without the aid of manures, and will not cease to yield an abundant return. But these soils are exceptional, and those that constantly need manuring are the rule. One point more, ere we proceed to apply to practice these elementary considerations. In almost every soil, whether strong clay, mellow loam, poor sand, or even chalk, there are comminglings of all the minerals required by plants, and, indeed, if there were not, we should see no herbage on the downs, and no Ivies climbing, as they do, to the topmost heights of limestone rocks. But usually a considerable proportion of those mineral constituents on which plants feed are, as it were, *locked up* in the staple, and are dissolved out slowly as the rain, the dew, the ever moving air, and the sunshine operate upon them. As the rock *slowly* yields up its phosphates and alkalies and solutions of silica to the wild vegetation that runs riot upon it, so the cultivated field (which is but rock in a state of decay) yields up its phosphates and alkalies and solutions of silica for the service of plants *quickly*, because it is the practice of the cultivator to stir it about and continually expose fresh surfaces to the transforming power of the atmosphere. It has been said that the air we breathe is a powerful manure. So it is, but not in the sense that is applicable to stable manure or guano. The air may and does afford to plants much of their food, but it can only help them to the minerals they require by dissolving them out of pebbles, flints, nodules of chalk, sandstone, and other substances in the soil which contains them in what may be termed a locked-up condition. The importance of frequent and deep stirrings of the soil is seen in this, that every fresh surface exposed to the air, and especially to frost and snow, is as the opening of a new mine of fertilisers for the service of those plants on which man depends for his subsistence.

The application to practice of these considerations is an extremely simple matter in the first instance, but it may become very complicated if followed far enough. Here we can only touch the surface of the subject, yet we hope to do so usefully. Suppose, then, that we grow Cabbage, or Cauliflower, or Broccoli, on the same plot of ground, one crop following the other as rapidly as possible for a long series of years, and take care never to refresh the soil with a scrap of manure. It must be evident that we shall, some day or other, find the crop fail through the exhaustion of the soil of its available sulphur, soda, phosphates, lime, and potash. But if this soil were allowed to lie fallow for some time, it would again produce a crop of Cabbage, owing to the liberation from the locked-up state of mineral matters which, when the crops were failing, were not liberated fast enough, but, owing to the rest allowed the soil, have accumulated sufficiently to sustain a crop. Obviously this mode of procedure is unprofitable, to begin with, and tends of necessity to exhaustion of the soil, although we must confess that utter exhaustion of any soil is a thing at present unknown. However, instead of following an exhaustive practice, we enrich the soil with manure, and change the crops on the same plot, so that when one crop has largely taxed it for one class of minerals another crop is put on which will tax it for another class of minerals. Let us take for a moment's consideration one of the necessary constituents of a fertile soil, common salt. In the ash of a Cabbage there is about six per cent. of this mineral, in the Turnip about ten per cent., in the Potato two to three per cent., in the Beet eighteen to twenty per cent. On the other hand, the Beet contains very little sulphur, but both Turnip and Beet agree in being strongly charged with potash and soda. It follows that if we crop a piece of ground with Cabbage, and wish to avoid the failure that may occur if we continue to crop with Cabbage, we may expect to do well by giving the ground a dressing of common salt and alkalies, and then crop it with Beet.

The whole subject is not exhausted by this mode of viewing it, for, in the first place, all the facts are not yet fully understood by the ablest of our chemists and physiologists, and, in the next place, crops differ in their modes of seeking nourishment. We might find two distinct plants nearly agreeing in chemical constitution, and yet one might fail where the other would succeed. Suppose, for instance, we have grown Cabbage and other surface-rooting crops until the soil begins to fail, even then we might obtain from it a good crop of Parsnips or Carrots, for the simple reason that these send their roots down to a stratum that the Cabbage never reached; and it is most instructive to bear in mind that although the Parsnip will grow on poor land, and pay on land that has been badly tilled for years, yet the ashes of the Parsnip contain thirty-six per cent. of potash, eleven per cent. of lime, eighteen per cent. of phosphoric acid, six per cent. of sulphuric acid, three per cent. of phosphate of iron, and five per cent. of common salt. How does the Parsnip obtain its mineral food in an exhausted soil? Simply by pushing down for it into a mine that has been but little worked, though the Cabbage might fail on the same plot through trusting to the overworked superficial stratum.

Having attempted a general, we now proceed to a particular application. In the first place, it is proper to say that good land, well tilled and abundantly manured, cannot be soon exhausted; but even in this case a rotation of crops is advisable. It is less easy to say why, than to insist that in practice we find it so. The question then arises—What is a rotation of crops? It is the ordering of a succession in such a manner that they will successively tax the soil for mineral aliments in a different manner. A good rotation will include both chemical and mechanical differences, and place tap-roots in a course between surface roots, as, for example, Carrots, Parsnips, and Beets, after Cabbage, Cauliflower, and Broccoli; and light, quick surface crops, such as Spinach, to serve as substitutes for fallows. The cropping of the kitchen garden should be, as far as possible, so ordered that plants of the same natural families never succeed one another; and, above all things, it is important to shift from place to place, year after year, all the Cabbage and the Potatoes, because these are the most exhaustive crops we grow. In a ton of Potatoes there are about twelve pounds of potash, four pounds of sulphuric acid, four pounds of phosphoric acid, and one pound of magnesia. We may replace these substances by abundant manuring, and we are bound to say that the best rotation will not obviate the necessity for manuring; but even then it is well to crop the plot with Peas, Spinach, Lettuce, and other plants that occupy it for a comparatively brief space of time, and necessitate much digging and stirring; for these mechanical agencies combine with the manure in preparing the plot to grow Potatoes again much better than if the land were kept to this crop only from year to year. If we could mark out a plot of ground into four parts, we should devote one plot to permanent crops—such as Asparagus, Sea Kale, and Rhubarb—and on the other three keep the crops revolving in some such order as this: No. 1, short-lived crops, such as Peas, Spinach, and saladings, to be followed by Cabbage; No. 2, tap-roots, such as Carrots, Parsnips, and Beets; No. 3, Potatoes, Turnips, and Onions. In the next season the original No. 2 would be cropped as the original No. 1, and the original No. 3 as No. 2. In the next year the original No. 3 would be cropped as the original No. 1; and so on: every crop to be prepared for by vigorous stirring of the ground and liberal manuring; and if the subsoil were good, we should trench it two spits deep for every root crop.

The 'Rotation of Crops' is so intimately associated with the 'Chemistry of Garden Crops,' that it has been impossible to avoid touching the latter subject in this article. Much, however, that is useful remains to be said, and we therefore purpose devoting another article to its further elucidation.

THE
CHEMISTRY OF GARDEN CROPS

A CONSIDERATION of the chemistry of the crops that engage attention in this country will afford an explanation of one great difference between farming and gardening. And this difference should be kept in mind by all classes of cultivators as the basis of operations in tillage, cropping, and the order and character of rotations. The first thing to discover in the cropping of a farm, is the kind of vegetation for which the land is best adapted to insure in a run of seasons fairly profitable results. If the soil is unfit for cereals, then it is sheer folly to sow any more corn than may be needful for convenience, as, for example, to supply straw for thatching, and oats for horses, to save cost of carriage &c. &c. On large farms that are far removed from markets, it is often necessary to risk a few crops that the land is ill fitted for, so as to satisfy the requirements of the homestead, and to save the outlay of money and the inconvenience of hauling from distant markets. But everywhere the cropping must be adapted to the soil and the climate as nearly as possible, both to simplify operations and enlarge to the utmost the chances of success. In the cropping of a garden this plain procedure cannot be followed. We are compelled certainly to consider what the soil and climate will especially favour amongst garden crops, but notwithstanding this, the gardener must grow whatever the household requires. He may have to grow Peas on a hot shallow sand; and Potatoes and Carrots on a cold clay; and Asparagus on a shallow bed of pebbles and potsherds. To the gardener the chemistry of crops is a matter of great importance, because he cannot restrict his operations to such crops as the land is particularly adapted for, but must endeavour to render his land capable of carrying more or less of all the vegetables and fruits that find a place in the catalogue of domestic wants. That in certain cases he must fail at certain points is inevitable; nevertheless his aim will be, and must be, of a somewhat universal kind, and a clear idea of the relations of plants to the soil in which they grow will be of constant and incalculable value to him.

We are bound to say at the outset that a complete essay on the chemistry of vegetation is not our purpose. We are anxious to convey some useful information, and to kindle sufficient interest to lead those who have hitherto given but slight attention to this subject to inquire further, with a view to get far beyond the point at which we shall have to quit the subject.

Plants consist of two classes of constituents—the Inorganic, which may be called the foundation; and the Organic, which may be considered the superstructure. The first alone concerns us now. A plant must derive from the soil certain proportions of silica, lime, sulphur, salt, phosphates, alkalies, and other minerals, or it cannot exist at all; but given these, and its manufacture of fibre, starch, gum, sugar, and other organic products will depend very much upon the action of light, heat, atmospheric air, and moisture upon it, for these have to be produced by chemical (or vital) action within the structure, or, as we sometimes say, the tissues of the plant itself. To a very great extent the agencies that conduce to the elaboration of organic products are beyond our control (though not entirely so), whereas we can directly, and to a considerable degree, provide the plant with the minerals it more particularly requires; first, by choosing the ground for it, and next by tilling and manuring in a suitable manner. A clay soil, in which, in addition to the predominating alumina, there is a fair proportion of lime and silica, may be regarded as the most fertile for all purposes; but we have few such in Britain, our clays being mostly of an obdurate texture, retentive of moisture, and requiring much cultivation, and containing moreover salts of iron in proportions almost poisonous to plants. But there are profound resources in most clays, so that if it is difficult to tame them, it is also difficult to exhaust them. Hence a clay that has been well cultivated through several generations will generally produce a fair return for whatever crop may be put upon it. Limestone soils are usually very porous and deficient of clay, and therefore have no sustaining power. Many of our great tracts of mountain limestone are mere sheep-walks, and would be comparatively worthless except for the metals that may be extracted from them, or the lime that may be obtained by burning. On the other hand, chalk, which is a more recent form of lime, is often highly productive, more especially where, through long cultivation, it has been much broken up, and has become loamy through accumulation of humus. Between the oldest limestone and the latest chalk there are many intermediate kinds of calcareous soils, and they are mostly good, owing to their richness in phosphates, the products of the marine organisms of which these rocks in great part, and in some cases wholly, consist. For the growth of cereals these calcareous soils need a certain proportion of silica, and where they have this we see some of the finest crops of Wheat, Trifolium, and Peas and Beans in all these islands. If we could mix some of our obdurate clays with our barren limestones, the two comparatively worthless staples would probably prove remarkably fertile. Although this is impossible, a consideration of the chemistry of the imaginary mixture may be useful, more especially to the gardener, who can in a small way accomplish many things that are out of the region of practice on a great scale. Sandy soils are characterised by excess of silica, and deficiency of alumina and phosphates. But here the mechanical texture is as serious a matter as it is in the case of clay. The sand is too loose as the clay is too pasty, and it may be that we have to hold the estate as it were in our hands to prevent it from being blown away. It is especially worthy of observation, however, that sandy soils are the most readily amenable of any to the operation of tillage ; and if we cannot take much out of them, we can put any amount into them, and must always calculate nicely where the process of enrichment is to stop. It is not less worthy of observation that sandy soils can be rendered capable of producing almost every kind of crop, save cereals and pulse, and even these can be secured where there is some basis of peat or loam or clay with the sand. The parks and gardens of Paris, Versailles, Haarlem, and Berlin are on deep sands, that are blown away when left exposed for any length of time with no crop upon them to prevent direct contact of the wind with the soil ; and not only do we see the finest of Potatoes and the most nutritious of herbage produced on these soils, but good Cauliflowers, Peas, Beans, Onions, fruits, and big trees full of sound timber. It would be inaccurate to say that any soil is beyond improvement, for the plough has found its way to the foot of Stonehenge, where only a hundred years ago cultivation was declared impossible, and on the granite of Dartmoor we may now see a fine grass sward where not long since the only vegetation comprised lichens and mosses. The farming and gardening at Prince Town owe their success in great part to the judicious use of sewage, and thus illustrate the immense importance of the subject before us.

Garden soils usually consist of loam of some kind, the consequence of long cultivation. Natural loams are the result of the decay and admixture of various earths, and they are mostly of a mellow texture, easily worked and highly productive. They are, as a rule, the best of all soils, and their goodness is in part due to the fact that they contain a little of everything, with no great predominance of any one particular earth. Cultivation also produces loam. On a clay land we find a top crust of clayey loam, and on a lime or chalk land a top crust of calcareous loam, where cultivation has been long pursued, for the staple is broken and manures are put on, and the roots of plants assist in disintegrating and decomposing, and thus there is accumulation of humus and a decomposition of the rock proceeding together, and a loam of some sort is the result. Hence the necessity of caution in respect of deep trenching, for if we bury the top soil and put in its place a crude material that has not before seen daylight, we may lose ten years in profitable cropping, because we must now begin to tame a savage soil that we have been at great pains to bring up to cover a stratum of a good material prepared for us by the combined operations of Nature and Art during, perhaps, several centuries. But deep and good garden soils may be safely trenched and freely knocked about, because not only does the process favour the deep rooting of the plants, but it favours also that disintegration which is one of the causes of fertility. Every pebble is capable of imparting to the soil a solution—infinitesimal perhaps, but not the less real—of silica, or lime, or potash, or phosphates, or perhaps of all these; but it must be exposed to light and air and moisture, to enable it to part with a portion of its substance, and thus it is that mechanical tillage is of the first importance in all agricultural and horticultural operations.

The principal inorganic or mineral constituents of plants are potash, soda, lime, sulphur, chlorine, silica, and phosphates of lime and iron. Clays and loams are generally rich in potash, sulphur, and phosphates, but deficient in soluble silica and lime. Limestone and chalk are usually rich in lime and phosphates, but deficient of humus, silica, sulphur, and alkalies. Sandy soils are rich in silica, and are rarely deficient of lime, but are generally poor in respect of phosphates and alkalies. Therefore, on a clay or loam, farmyard manure is invaluable, because it not only contains ingredients that all crops appreciate, but is helpful in breaking up the texture of the soil. The occasional application of lime also is of importance, and not seldom this produces an almost magical effect on an old garden soil that has been heavily cropped and liberally manured. Calcareous soils are greatly benefited by a free application to them of manure from the stable and cow-byre; but it would be (generally speaking) like carrying coals to Newcastle to dress these soils with lime. Clay may be put on with advantage; and nothing benefits a hot chalky soil more than a good dose of mud from ponds and ditches, which supplies at once humus, alumina, and silicates. In the manuring of sandy soils, great care is requisite, because of their absorbing power. In the bulb-growing districts of Holland, manure from cow sheds is worth the enormous price of one shilling per barrow-load, for digging into loose sand for a crop of Potatoes, to be followed by bulbs. This is an exceptional case, but it illustrates the subject usefully. As a rule, sandy soils are deficient of phosphates and alkalies, and hence, instead of employing manure, which may often be more advantageously bestowed upon the loamy pieces and reserved for special purposes, it will be found that kainit (a rough form of potash) and superphosphate of lime will conjointly produce the best results, more especially in raising Potatoes, Onions, and Carrots, which are particularly well adapted for sandy soils. Probably one of the best fertilisers is genuine farmyard manure from stall-fed cattle, for it contains phosphates, alkalies, and silicates, in available forms and suitable proportions. Artificial manure should be selected by analysis, and with a view both to correct the deficiencies of the soil, and to satisfy the requirements of the crops to be grown on it.

For the present purpose, the principal garden crops may be grouped in two classes, in accordance with the predominance of certain of their mineral constituents. The figures show the average proportions of the several minerals per cent. in the ashes that are left after burning a sample.

In Class I. PHOSPHATES and POTASH predominate. This class includes the following: The Pea, containing phosphates, thirty-six; potash, forty. The Bean: phosphates, thirty; potash, forty-four. The Potato (tubers only): phosphates, nineteen; potash, fifty-nine; soda, two; lime, two; sulphuric acid, six. The Parsnip: phosphates, eighteen; potash, thirty-six; lime, eleven; salt, five. The Carrot: phosphates, twelve; potash, thirty six; soda, thirteen; sulphuric acid, six. The Jerusalem Artichoke: phosphates, sixteen; potash, sixty-five.

In Class II. SULPHUR, SODA, and SALT predominate. This class includes the following: The Cabbage: phosphates, sixteen; potash, forty-eight; soda, four; lime, fifteen; sulphuric acid, eight. The Turnip: phosphates, thirteen; potash, thirty-nine; salt, ten; lime, ten; sulphuric acid, fourteen. The Beet: phosphates, fourteen; potash, forty-nine; soda, nine; salt, twenty; lime, six; sulphuric acid, five.

As a matter of course, Lentils and other kinds of pulse agree more or less with Peas and Beans in the predominance of phosphates and potash. So, again, all the Brassicas, whether Kales, Cauliflower, or whatever else, agree nearly with the Cabbage in a predominance of lime and sulphur; ingredients which fully account for the offensive odour of these vegetables when in a state of decay. Fruits as a rule are highly charged with alkalies, and are rarely deficient in phosphates; moreover, stone-fruits require lime, for they have to make bones as well as flesh when they produce a crop. As regards the alkalies, plants appear capable of substituting soda for potash under some circumstances, but it would not be prudent for the cultivator to assume that the cheaper alkali might take the place of the more costly one as a mineral agent, for Nature is stern and constant in her ways, and it can hardly be supposed that a plant in which potash normally predominates can attain to perfection in a soil deficient in potash, however well supplied it may be with soda. The cheaper alkali in combination with salt may, however, be usually employed in aid of quick-growing green crops; and more or less with tap-roots and Brassicas. As regards Potatoes, it seems worthy of observation that they contain but a trace of silica, and yet they generally thrive on sand, and in many instances crops grown on sand are free from disease and of high quality, although the weight may not be great. The mechanical texture of the soil has much to do with this; and when that is aided by a supply of potash and phosphates, whether from farmyard manure or artificials, sandy soils become highly productive of Potatoes of the very finest quality. On the other hand, Potatoes also grow well on limestone and chalk, and yet there is but little lime in them. Here, again, mechanical texture explains the case in part, and it is further explained by the sufficiency of potash and phosphates, as also of magnesia, which enters in a special manner into the mineral constitution of this root.

Thus far we have not even mentioned nitrogen, or its common form of carbonate of ammonia; nor have we mentioned carbon, or its very familiar form of carbonic acid. These are important elements of plant growth; and they account for the efficacy of manures derived directly from the animal kingdom, as, for example, the droppings of animals, including guano, which consists, in part at least, of the droppings of sea-birds. The nitrogen in these substances however, is of an evanescent character, and rapidly flies away in the form of carbonate of ammonia ; hence, a heap of farmyard manure, left for several years, loses much of its value as manure, and guano should be kept in bulk as long as possible, and protected from the atmosphere, or its ammonia will disappear. One difficulty experienced by chemists and others in preparing artificial manures is that of 'fixing' the needful ammonia, so that it may be kept from combining with the atmosphere, and at the same time be always in a state in which it can be appropriated by the plant. We cannot supply plants with nitrogen directly, but in all good manures there is a certain proportion of it in combination, and in many instances the percentage of nitrogen is made the test of the value of a manure.

The importance of humus—the black earthy substance resulting from the decay of vegetation—in a soil is that it contains in an assimilable form many of the ingredients essential to plant life. Humus is also highly charged with carbonic acid, which decomposes the crude minerals in the soil and renders them available as plant food. When vegetable refuse is burned, the nitrogen—one of the costliest manures—is dissipated and lost. But by burying the refuse the soil gets back a proportion of the organic nitrogen it surrendered and something over in the way of soluble phosphatic and potassic salts ; and as this organic nitrogen assumes the form of nitric acid, it is assimilated by the growing plant to the great benefit of whatever crop may occupy the ground.

The practical conclusion is that in the treatment of the soil a skilful gardener will endeavour to promote its fertility by affording the natural influences of rain, frost and sun full opportunity of liberating the constituents that are locked up in the staple ; by restoring in the form of refuse as much as possible of what the soil has parted with in vegetation ; and by the addition of such fertilising agents as are adapted to rectify the natural deficiencies of the soil. Thus instead of following a process of exhaustion, the resources of the garden may be annually augmented.

THE CULTURE OF FLOWERS
FROM SEEDS

INTRODUCTORY REMARKS

WE have seen within the past few years many useful applications of the principles, as well as the work, of the florists to the general decoration of the English garden. Our commonest flowers have partaken of the improvement, of which the Aster, Stock, Phlox, Poppy, and Mignonette afford striking examples. We have but to look through the horticultural picture-books of forty or fifty years ago to become convinced that a splendid revolution has been accomplished.

It is interesting to note that while the florists are concentrating their attention on such subjects as the Auricula, the Carnation, the Pelargonium, and the Gladiolus, they are abandoning some of their old favourites, or at all events altering their ways in accordance with their altered views in respect of them. It is not long since immense pains were taken to perpetuate named varieties of Primulas, Cinerarias, Antirrhinums, Gloxinias, Pansies, Lobelias, Verbenas, and other subjects that gave trouble out of proportion to results. These and kindred subjects are still grown to name, and prized for quality, as we hope and believe they ever will be, for the standards of quality must be maintained and advanced. But for the general work of the country a better method has been developed, and the need for an abundance of beautiful flowers is, in respect of many of the subjects, readily met by a simple process of growing them from seeds, instead of the laborious mode of perpetuation by cuttings. In no one department of floriculture has there been accomplished a more remarkable advance, or one tending more directly to the public advantage, than in the improvement of the strains and races and stocks of the seeds of florists' flowers. For all the ordinary, and for the highest of the ordinary, purposes of the floriculturist, the raising of these plants from seed is sufficient, provided always that the seed is produced and saved with the aid of all the knowledge that experience has brought to bear upon the business. Why should a man who has to decorate a conservatory and a set of flower-beds be subjected to the worry of working up a stock of soft-textured plants from offsets and cuttings, when the sowing of a pinch of seed will insure to him all he can desire at a tenth part of the trouble, and with a greater degree of certainty? Why encumber pits and frames and houses with stores of troublesome plants that might be thrown away with advantage, leaving the glass at liberty to produce winter Cucumbers and Kidney Beans and Mushrooms, or to shelter the nobler forms of permanent vegetation, and encourage plant beauty of the highest interest? The growth of florists' and decorative flowers from seed is a gain every way to the community, for the process liberates glass and garden room, labour, time, and money for better work than the perpetuation of named varieties, the beauty of which can, for all practical purposes, be equalled by stock raised from seed. The return to old methods will soon be made whenever it shall be found that the seed stocks have degenerated.

As the true florist is the best friend of the floral decorator, so he is the right-hand man of the producer of flower seeds of high quality. It is to him we must look for maintaining in all their integrity the true canons of floral perfection, and to these canons our stocks and strains must conform less or more, and the more the better. And beyond this the florists are our friends. By their severe rules of criticism they assist us subjectively, and by the actual results of their agreeable labours they bring objective aid, their finest flowers serving not only as our types, but as the actual stud to breed from. Thus the decline of floriculture implies the deterioration of flowers, and, on the other hand, the prosperity of floriculture is concurrently reflected in the improved and improving quality of flowers of all kinds, including such as the florists have never taken any special notice of. They constitute the school in which the public taste is formed, and they provide the ideas and the materials which aid in the gratification and advancement of the taste which finds in flowers an intellectual as well as a sensuous exercise. Let us not, therefore, be unmindful of the importance of the study of technical details and hereditary characters, and the requirements of the artistic instinct in the flower garden. The study of a flower may help us to a knowledge of the world, and we may see cause to thank the florist who has detected beauties before unknown to us, and who has proved his capability of perpetuating those beauties by means within the embrace of all.

There can be no doubt that a revolution in the method of producing many flowers has been slowly but surely progressing, and is not yet complete ; but as we know nothing of the future, we may be content to deal with the facts of the past, and these justify us in saying that a real revolution has been introduced in the economy and complexion of the English Flower Garden. The immediate result has been to reduce and simplify the gardener's labours, augment considerably the number and beauty of garden flowers, and effect a very great annual saving in the costs that accompany garden pleasures. To illustrate the nature of this revolution we will begin with one well-known fact. The Cineraria, at a certain date reaching not far back, was a troublesome plant to grow, by reason of the necessity that was felt for keeping the named varieties, and propagating them by divisions and suckers. The restricted system was reflected in restricted cultivation, for there were not many then who made the venture in a task known to be hedged in with difficulties. But by degrees it was discovered that all the kinds of Cinerarias, comprising all the qualities of the finest named examples, might be secured by simply sowing a pinch of seed, and giving it the usual cultivation of a tender annual. There was one thing wanting to complete this item in the revolution, namely, seed good enough for the purpose, a thing not everywhere at command. The attention of cultivators was now diverted from the tedious task of keeping stocks of named varieties from which to propagate stock, to the more important one of raising the seed in a scientific manner. Now that this has been accomplished, the cultivation of the Cineraria has been brought within the reach of all, and this lovely flower is grown by thousands who would not attempt it under the old system, and the consequent gain to society is immense.

The foregoing is offered by way of illustration only. What has been done with the Cineraria has its parallel in the case of a considerable proportion of the most important garden flowers. It has ceased to be needful to keep such large stocks of bedding and other tender plants under glass through the winter, and very much of the accustomed labour in striking and potting cuttings, as well as the expense of glass, fuel, labour, and the frequent purchase of high-priced varieties have become unnecessary.

The wide range of this revolution enhances its importance. We can not only grow the finest Cinerarias from seed in one season, but also the finest Begonias, Cyclamens, Gloxinias, Primulas, Geraniums, Pansies, and Verbenas. In fact many of the so-called perennial flowers conform to the new rule, and become veritable annuals or biennials, and produce the most delightful display of flowers with the very simplest treatment.

There is one most important point in this transfer of the business from the potting-shed and the crowded frames and plant-houses to the seed-bed, and a few pots and pans for flower growing. The important point is, that when the thing is well done we not only save time and money, but we have equal quality to the named sorts and greater variety—and variety is constantly desired. We have instanced the Cineraria, and now for another illustration we will take the Hollyhock. It is not long since the named varieties were perpetuated by the troublesome process of cuttings, or by grafting buds on roots of seedlings in houses heated to tropical temperature. In many places it was the custom to lift the old plants and pot them, and keep them through the winter in pits. All this was found necessary to insure fine flowers. While the burden of the work was thus rendered heavy, the constitution of the plant was enfeebled; it became a prey to disease, and at one time the fear was entertained that its annihilation was at hand. But the new system has saved the Hollyhock, and at the same time afforded a striking example of the important point just referred to, for seed saved scientifically is found to reproduce the varieties it was taken from, and seedling Hollyhocks grown as annuals give double flowers of the finest quality, and, what is of utmost consequence, the seedling plants are less liable to disease. The constant law of Nature, that progeny take after their parents, is as clearly manifested in the flower garden as anywhere; and the finest flowers, however peculiar and delicate in their colours, markings, and forms, are found to be reproducible from seed with remarkable certainty, provided the seed has been secured by methods that skill and experience have shown to be necessary for sustaining the qualities of a breed or the characteristics of an individual. The Verbena may be cited as another example of the same class as the Hollyhock. This beautiful bedding plant has been propagated from cuttings forced in heat, and systematically debilitated, so that now we have a Verbena disease. But from suitable seed we can raise plants that will produce the most resplendent flowers, and instead of propagating a stock to keep over winter, to plague us with mildew and cost no end of care, only to become diseased at last, we sow a pinch of seed in January or February, and soon have a nice stock of healthy young plants with the vigour peculiar to seedlings, and these, being bedded out at a proper time, flower as freely as plants from cuttings, and produce trusses of flowers twice the size.

It must be understood, however, that trifling variations occur when a certain standard has been fixed on ; but there is, notwithstanding, a remarkable constancy of type secured, so that the cultivator may calculate to a nicety on the effects that are at his command for parterre colouring and planting in masses. The *Phlox Drummondii* may be mentioned in illustration of this. We have it now in almost endless variety, and the different types are maintained with a surprising constancy. This fine annual Phlox, which is certainly one of the loveliest and most useful plants of its class we possess, reminds us of the perennial Phlox, which may also be grown from seed as easily as the annual Phloxes.

There appear to be no bounds or limits to further progress. All we can do is to experiment and gather knowledge, and those who love flowers and would multiply them for the enjoyment of mankind, may assist in extending the area of this new and cheap system of growing some of the grandest garden flowers in one season from seed alone.

RAPID FLOWER CULTURE

NOTES ON RAISING THE CHOICEST FLOWERS AS ANNUALS AND BIENNIALS FROM SEEDS

The sowing of the seed will have to be regulated by considerations of its nature. Seeds of tender plants are usually sown in pots or pans and placed on a moderate hot-bed or in a propagating house early in spring, and in this case the plants have greenhouse cultivation until the time arrives for hardening them off preparatory to final planting. But seeds of many hardy flowers may be treated in the same way, when a long season of growth is necessary for their development. Thus Phloxes, Verbenas, and Hollyhocks, plants that differ immensely in habit and constitution, may all be sown in February, and put side by side in the same warm pit or vinery, or even in the warmest corner of any greenhouse, and the very same treatment will suit them equally well. The soil should be principally loam and sand, with a little old thoroughly well-rotted manure from a hot-bed or compost heap; and light, air, and moisture must be regulated with a view to insure a free and vigorous growth from the first, and with the least possible amount of artificial heat. In some cases, however, the sowing should be deferred to March or April, and the result will be far more satisfactory than the growth made under the stimulus of artificial heat earlier in the season. In any case, however, *the plants must have time enough*; for although we have developed this rapid system, we have not in any great degree changed the constitution of the plants, and those that have heretofore been classed as biennials and perennials may be regarded as needing a long season when treated as annuals.

A considerable proportion of the finest flowers may be raised from seed by the aid of a frame and a little careful management. We will suppose a case of a very restricted garden, so as to write below instead of above the mark. Here is a smallish frame and some packets of seed, and the month of February or March has arrived. The pans and pots are made ready with nice sweet sandy compost, and the seeds are sown and labelled, and the pots and pans are packed together in the frame on a bed of clean coal ashes, or some slates, or tiles, or bricks laid on the soil, to promote warmth and cleanliness, and to prevent the intrusion of worms amongst the seeds. Now, by simple management we may secure almost as quick a growth of seeds in this frame as with the aid of a hot-bed, and the secret consists in careful storage of the heat of the sun. Lay over the seed-pans sheets of glass to prevent evaporation, and let the sun shine full upon them. Be careful as to moisture; they must never be wet, never dry, and the water must not be slopped about carelessly. It is a good rule to immerse the pots or pans in a vessel containing soft water, slightly tepid. When the seedlings begin to appear, give a little air and lay sheets of paper tenderly over them during the hour or two at midday when the sun may be shining brightly. But keep them from the first as 'hard' as possible with plenty of light and air, always taking care they are not roasted, nor blown away by the cruel east wind, nor nipped at night by a killing frost. A few old mats or light loppings of trees laid over the frame from sundown to sunrise will be sufficient protection at those trying times; and when spring frosts are making havoc with the tender sprouting leaf and bloom in every part of the garden those little things will be safe under their glass cover, and slight experience will show that a common frame may become a miniature hot-house in the hands of one who has not yet learned to utter the word 'failure.' We must not omit to mention that the owner of such a garden, or, indeed, of any garden, will be prudent to take advantage of the first fine weather to sow in the open ground whatever flower or vegetable seeds should be sown at that season. The frame garden can be reserved, if needful, for wet weather, because it is of the utmost importance to sow a good breadth of seeds in the open ground as early as possible in the month of March.

Turning from this example to the great garden, we cannot but reflect how immense are the advantages to the busy gardener, who has heavy work always on his hands, of this transference of labour from the old system to the new. There cannot be a doubt that to employers and gardeners the advantages are of equal importance; the propagation of bedders by cuttings, and of florists' flowers by suckers and divisions and layers and pipings, will not, of course, be suddenly and completely abolished; but for all ordinary purposes it is evident that the ends in view may be accomplished more simply, more expeditiously, and more cheaply than heretofore. The pits hitherto appropriated to bedders, and the like, may to a great extent be liberated, and there will be no difficulty in finding for them more profitable occupants. While Mushrooms and early Potatoes and winter salads are in request, it will be a gain to many a garden to have reduced the summer display of flowers to a simple system of seed-sowing, at an expense that may be described as merely nominal.

Before dealing specifically with certain flowers, it may be advisable to say a few words generally concerning the culture of Annuals— Hardy, Half-hardy, and Tender—and also on Hardy Biennials and Perennials.

ANNUALS

ALTHOUGH the most popular kinds of annuals are largely employed in the embellishment of flower gardens, they are adapted for many uses to which they have as yet never been applied. A few misconceptions prevail as to the relative merits of this class of plants, as, for example, by some they are regarded as 'weedy' and 'short-lived,' and their very cheapness, and the comparatively small amount of skill required in their cultivation, tend in some degree to their detriment in public estimation. We will not be so rash as to say that a more extended use of annuals would render unnecessary the cultivation of what are especially known as 'bedding plants'; but there is something to be said in behalf of annuals, that may be worth the consideration of all who are interested in the development of freshness, variety, and richness of colour in the flower garden. In the first place, these plants come into flower within a comparatively short period of time from the sowing of the seed, and it is a matter of considerable importance that a large proportion of the best continue beautiful until the very close of the season. Sometimes in the autumn, Geraniums become literally washed out, while Tom Thumb Nasturtiums may be ablaze with colour, and continue so when the Geraniums are housed for the winter. A number of showy and long-lasting annuals may be selected for employment in the bedding system, and by a little management those that do not last the season out may be replaced by others for succession; thus affording the advantage of increased variety, and making no demand for glass and fuel to keep them through the winter as the ordinary bedders do. We have had great and glorious sheets of Candytufts, snow-white, rich crimson, bright carmine, and deep purple; and when they began to wane they were removed, and the ground planted with Asters, and very soon there was another display, so fresh and bright and various, that no greenhouse bedders could surpass them. Great hungry banks, that would have swallowed many pounds' worth of greenhouse plants to cover them, have been made delightfully gay at a very trifling cost, by sowing upon them Tropæolums, Sweet Peas, Tom Thumb Nasturtiums, *Bartonia aurea*, *Lupinus nanus*, Virginian Stock, *Collinsia bicolor*, Limnanthes, Convolvuluses, Candytufts, Eschscholtzias, Poppies, and Clarkias; and damp, half-shady borders have been delicately tesselated by means of Forget-me-nots, Venus's Looking-glass, Pansies, the Rosy Oxalis, Nemophilas, and German Scabious.

For the more important positions in the flower garden, we have choice of many really sumptuous subjects, such as Stocks, Asters, Balsams, *Phlox Drummondii*, Lobelias, Tom Thumb Antirrhinums, *Dianthus Heddewigii*, Portulacas, Zinnias, Erysimums, the lovely Scarlet Flax (*Linum grandiflorum rubrum*), Godetias, Silenes, Nasturtiums (the true 'Tom Thumb' race, offering a variety of colours), and a score more things equally beautiful and lasting. We do not hope by these brief remarks to change the prevailing fashion—indeed, we have no particular wish that way—but we feel bound to observe that it is sufficient for the beauty of the garden that the greenhouse bedders should be confined to the parterre proper, for it is waste of space and opportunity to place them in the borders everywhere, as is too commonly done. In the sunny borders, annual and perennial herbaceous plants are far more appropriate.

Some time since, while walking over a large garden, we left the rich colouring of the geometric beds to discover what should make the wondrous glow of crimson on a border far away ; and to our surprise it proved to be a clump of our good old garden friend the Indian Pink, which had been sown as an annual with other annuals, and was there shining—not alone—but in the midst of a constellation of the loveliest flowers of all forms and hues, the result simply of sowing a few packets of seed. No one can despise the Wallflower in the spring, and the innocent gauze-like flowers of *Nemophila insignis* in early summer will tempt many a one to walk in the garden who would care little for sheets of scarlet and yellow that in full sunshine make the eyes ache to look upon them. It must be remembered, too, that amongst annuals are found many most richly-scented flowers ; others, like the everlastings and the grasses, are valuable to dry for winter use for employment in bouquets, and garlands in Christmas decorations ; and the Sweet Peas, and *Tropæolum canariense*, and Convolvulus may be employed to cover arbours and trellises with the best effect possible, and may even be allowed to hang in festoons about the sunny parts of rockeries, or trail over the ground to make genuine bedding effects. Another important matter must have mention here, and we commend it to the consideration of all classes of cultivators, and especially to gardeners who are severely taxed to secure extensive displays of flowers during the summer season. It is that a number of plants of highly ornamental character, usually treated as perennials, are really more effective, besides occasioning less labour to produce them, when cultivated as annuals. Some of the Campanulas are examples of this. The Dianthus, again, and its several splendid varieties, do better as annuals than perennials. For all the ordinary purposes of display, Lobelias may be as well grown from seed as from cuttings, and in every garden will be found proof of the small amount of care it requires ; for we find stray, self-sown plants in pots of Geraniums and other places, and these if left alone become perfect bushes, and are a mass of flowers all the summer. We have indeed made a fine bed by planting out in May all the self-sown Lobelias we could find in pits and frames and greenhouses, taking some from brickwork and woodwork, where, like happy vagrants, they had cast their lot on the best of terms with themselves and Nature. More than this, it must be observed that many annuals commonly reputed tender, and needing to be raised in heat, do very well indeed on a more rough and ready method. In proof of this, sow *Perilla nankinensis* in the first week of May where it is required, and in the month of July you will probably determine that Perilla does not greatly need the careful nursing it usually obtains in heated houses through the spring. Even the really tender Castor-oil Plant (*Ricinus*) will thrive amazingly if sown in the open ground the first week in May. Having no check, as plants put out from pots must have, the growth will be regular and sturdy, and they will attain magnificent dimensions, and flower freely if the season is favourable.

We cannot afford space to say all we should wish on this interesting subject; but we will add a remark for the benefit of such as desire to derive from their gardens a maximum of entertainment and instruction. We recommend not only a free use of annuals, where they can be appropriately employed for purposes of embellishment, but also the setting apart for a collection of them a border or plot, one part of which is sunny and another part somewhat shaded. On this border sow clumps of annuals, of as many kinds as possible, and affix to each clump a label that will last the season out, or enter the names in a book in the order in which the clumps are arranged, for purposes of ready reference. This border will afford immense delight, for many annuals that are not popular because not particularly showy will be found to be worthy of admiration for their subdued and refined appearance, their elegant forms, and their delicate blendings of colour. Amongst them are many magnificent subjects that might well emblazon the terrace garden, but the less showy ones will probably be held in highest esteem by the genuine lover of floral beauty. We know of nothing more pleasing, especially as an incident in a quiet garden walk, than to pass along a border where such gems are to be found as *Saponaria calabrica, Leptosiphon roseus, Platystemon californicus, Calandrinia grandiflora,* White, Yellow, and Purple Sweet Sultan, *Erysimum Perowskianum, Eucharidium concinnum, Eutoca viscida,* Double Sanvitalia, *Gypsophila elegans, Kaulfussia amelloides, Silene pendula compacta,* and *Viscaria oculata.* These, however, are but a few, selected almost at random, from amongst dozens that are equally beautiful, that might be had to make the ground glitter from earliest spring to latest autumn.

HARDY ANNUALS

THE seeds should be sown on carefully prepared soil from which large stones have been removed, and the clods must be broken, but the surface should not be so smooth as to be liable to become pasty after rain. Sow thinly, cover with a very slight coat of fine dry earth—the smallest seeds needing but a mere dusting to cover them—and, from the first, keep the plants thinned sufficiently to prevent over-crowding, which weakens them, and tends to a poor instead of a bountiful bloom. The soil into which they are transplanted for blooming should be deeply dug, thoroughly broken up, and if at all poor should be liberally manured. Spring-sown annuals are worthy of a better soil than they usually have allotted them, and also of more careful treatment. It is not wise to sow earlier than March or later than the middle of April. The most important matter in the after culture is to keep the clumps well thinned, for not only will the bloom of crowded plants be comparatively poor and brief, but by early and bold practice in thinning the plants will become so robust, and cover such large spaces of ground with their ample leafage and well-developed flowers, as really to astonish people who think they know all about annuals, and who may have ventured, after much ill-treatment of them, to designate them 'fugacious and weedy.' It is an excellent practice, also, to sow hardy annuals in autumn, but it is needless to say more on this subject here, as a chapter is devoted to it at page 273.

HALF-HARDY ANNUALS

GIVE these as long a period of growth as possible to insure a vigorous plant before the season of flowering. The best time for sowing is February, or the beginning of March, for although some kinds may with advantage be sown earlier, it is safer, as a rule, to wait for sunshine and full daylight, so as to keep up a steady and continuous growth. The soil for the seed-pans should be rich and fine. Good loam, improved by the addition of thoroughly decayed manure and leaf-mould, with sufficient sand to render the texture porous, will suit all kinds of annuals that are sown in pans under glass. Sow the seed thinly, cover very slightly, and lay squares of glass over to keep a uniform degree of moisture without the necessity of watering. Should watering become necessary, take care to avoid washing the seeds out. If the pans or pots are stood for an hour in a vessel containing several inches depth of water, they will absorb sufficient, and there will be no occasion to pour water on the surface. A gentle heat is to be preferred, as a too rapid germination of the seed tends to the production of weak plants. As soon as the young plants appear, remove the glasses and place the seed-pans in the fullest light, where air can be given without danger to them. A dry east wind blowing fiercely over them will prove a blast of death. If they have no air at all, they will be puny, rickety things, scarcely worth planting out. Choice varieties should be carefully pricked out into pans and pots as soon as large enough; this will promote a fine, stocky growth, and a splendid development of flowers. Take care not to plant out until the weather is favourable, for any great check will undo all your work, and make starvelings of your nurslings. If you cannot command heat for half-hardy annuals, sow in the first week in April, put the pans in a frame facing south, and the seeds will soon grow and do well. If that is too much trouble, sow in the open border early in May, making the border rich and friable, that they may have a good chance from the first.

TENDER ANNUALS

THESE require the same general treatment as advised for half-hardy annuals. But it is desirable to sow earlier, and in a stronger heat than is necessary for annuals that are to be planted out. It is also requisite to be in good time in pricking out the young plants, for if they get much drawn they cannot make robust pot plants. A light, rich, perfectly sweet soil, containing a fair proportion of sharp sand, will alone insure plants worth having. It is also important to get them into separate small pots as soon as possible, and to shift them on to larger and larger pots, until they have sufficient pot room for flowering, after which shift no more. As soon as these pots are filled with roots, give very weak manure-water constantly until the plants are in flower, and then discontinue it, using instead pure soft water only. Many of the commonest annuals are worthy of careful culture for flowering early in the greenhouse, but we have in view in this paragraph such fine subjects as Camellia-flowered Balsam, Globe Amaranth, Ipomœa, Thunbergia, &c.

HARDY BIENNIALS AND PERENNIALS

These are often sown in pans or boxes, and are pricked off when large enough into other pans or pots before they are transferred to beds or borders. The system has certain advantages in insuring safety from vermin and proper attention, for it is an unfortunate fact that too many cultivators consider it needless to thin or transplant sowings made in beds or borders. The plants are frequently allowed to struggle for existence, and the result is feeble attenuated specimens which, with trifling care and attention, might have become robust, and capable of producing a bountiful bloom in their season. Still, it should be clearly understood that all the hardy biennials and perennials may be grown to perfection by sowing on a suitable seed-bed in the open ground in the early part of the summer, protecting the spot from marauders of all kinds, and by early and bold thinning and transplanting. As a rule, we advocate one shift before placing the plants in final positions.

ABUTILON

Half-hardy greenhouse perennial

Handsome plants, two feet or more in height, can be produced from seed, and flowered in a single season. They are useful for training to greenhouse walls, and they may also be transferred to open borders for the summer. When employed for the latter purpose, the plants should be lifted and put into pots again about the end of August, after there has been a penetrating shower. In the absence of rain a soaking of water on the previous day will prevent the soil from falling away from the roots.

February and March are the right months for sowing seed, and pots filled with any fairly light potting compost will answer. Prick off the seedlings when about an inch high, putting the plants in down to the seed-leaves. They must not be allowed to suffer for want of water, nor should they be starved in small pots. The growth had better not be hurried at any stage, and the plants will then develop into shapely specimens with very little care.

ANEMONE

The Windflower.   Hardy perennial

THE discovery that it is easy to flower the Anemone from seed within about seven months from the date of sowing, has given a great impetus to the culture of this plant, especially as it possesses a high value for decorating vases, in addition to its great usefulness in beds and borders.   From seed sown in February, the plants should begin to bloom in September or October of the same year, and continue to flower until the following June, when it is unprofitable to retain them longer.   No coddling of any kind is necessary.   Dig a trench in a sheltered, sunny spot, and fill it with rich soil freely mingled with decayed cow-manure.   If the land happens to be somewhat tenacious, Anemones will take kindly to it, but it should be well worked, and perhaps it may be needful to add a little fine sandy compost to the top as a preparation for the seed.   Sow thinly in lines on the surface, and merely rake the seed in with a very light hand. The seed being woolly should be rubbed with sand, and the two may be sown together.   The germination is decidedly slow, so that until the seedlings appear the removal of weeds requires care.   The plants should be thinned until they stand six inches apart.   The thinnings will bear transplanting if carefully handled and helped with water afterwards.   Of course boxes or seed-pans can be resorted to, but the plant from its earliest stage is eminently capable of braving the weather in all but our bleakest districts.   Seed may also be sown in July or August for plants to flower in the following year, and the results will probably be even more satisfactory than from the spring sowing.

ANTIRRHINUM

Snapdragon.   Hardy perennial

As border flowers these will thrive almost anywhere, and they may be treated as annuals by sowing the seed early in the spring.   They prefer, however, a dry soil and the most breezy sunny situation that can be found for them.   They are often seen on ruins, producing flowers of varied colours, and seemingly indifferent to the starving conditions that surround them.

There are three distinct classes—dwarf, medium, and tall—ranging in height from six inches to two feet, and all are worth growing. From sowings in heat in January or February, the seedlings may be flowered in the same year without any difficulty. Pot singly, and gradually harden by the middle of May. The Antirrhinum is, however, strictly hardy, and may be sown in drills during the summer for flowering in the following season. Leave the plants in the seedbed until large enough for transplanting to final positions, and select a moist day for the operation.

AQUILEGIA

Columbine. Hardy perennial

This flower has acquired considerable importance of late years owing to the introduction of many fine varieties, all of which are thoroughly hardy. Sow early in March, in a frame, and plant out when strong enough; or sow in June, in an open border. If the season is favourable, most of those sown in March will flower the first year; the remainder will bloom in the year following, and the severest winter will not kill one of them.

ASTER

Half-hardy annual

To secure a long-continued display of bloom there must be several sowings, and the earliest will need the aid of artificial heat. One secret of successful culture is to give no check to the plant from its first appearance until the time of flowering; and if there is to be a grand display of bloom, instead of the poor sickly things frequently seen, a suitable bed must be prepared, whether the seed be sown there or plants be transferred from other quarters.

Asters do not readily accommodate themselves to violent alternations of heat and cold, particularly in the early stage of growth, and therefore the most sheltered position in the garden should be chosen for them; but avoid a hedge or shrubbery, where strong-growing trees rob the soil of its goodness. Begin the preparation of beds during the previous autumn by deep digging, and incorporate a liberal dressing of well-rotted manure as the work proceeds. On light and shallow soils it will do more harm than good to bring the raw subsoil to the surface, but the subsoil may with advantage be stirred and loosened by the fork, and if a little loamy clay or even pure clay in small portions can be worked into it, the land will be permanently benefited.

A very stiff soil will, however, present greater difficulties; but if by free working it can be made sufficiently friable, Asters will revel in it and produce flowers of a size and colour to reward the cultivator for all his trouble. Throw the ground up roughly in October. The more it is exposed to the action of wind and snow and frost, the more thoroughly will the winter disintegrate its particles and render it fertile. Early in spring give another digging, and then work in a good supply of decayed manure, together with grit, charcoal, wood ashes, or other material that will help to render the soil rich and free. Aim at inducing the roots to go down deep for supplies—there will then be a cool moist bottom even in dry weather, and these conditions will do much toward the production of fine stocky plants, which are the harbingers of an imposing display of flowers.

For sowings from the end of March to the middle of April, prepare a compost, consisting principally of decayed leaf-mould, with sufficient loam to render it firm, and sharp sand to secure drainage. Either pots or seed-pans may be used. Place these in a cool greenhouse, or in a Cucumber or Melon pit, or even on a half-spent hot-bed. Sow thinly; a thick sowing is very likely to damp off. Just hide the seed with finely sifted soil, and place sheets of glass at the top to prevent rapid evaporation. Give no water unless the soil becomes quite dry, and then it is better to immerse the pot or pan for half an hour rather than to apply water on the surface. When the plants attain the third leaf they can be pricked off round the edges of 60-pots ($3\frac{1}{2}$-inch). From these they may either have another shift singly into small pots, or may be transferred direct to blooming quarters. A high temperature is not requisite at any stage of growth, indeed it is distinctly injurious. From $55°$ to $65°$ are the extreme limits, and the happy medium should, if possible, be maintained. Give air on every suitable occasion, and as the time of transfer to the open ground approaches, endeavour to approximate nearly to the outside temperature. The plants will then scarcely feel the removal.

Another and simpler proceeding will produce fairly good results, and we give it for the benefit of those whose resources may be small, or who do not care to adopt the more troublesome method. In some spot shaded from the sun make a heap of stable manure rather larger than the light to be placed upon it. Level the top and cover with four or five inches of rich soil. Place a frame upon it with the light a trifle open. When the thermometer indicates 60°, draw drills at six inches apart; sow the seed and cover with a little sifted soil. The light had better not be quite closed, in case of a rise of temperature. As the plants thrive, gradually give more air, until, in April, the showers may be allowed to fall directly upon them in the daytime. When the Asters are about three inches high, they will be quite ready for the open ground, and a showery day best suits the transfer. After the bed has served its purpose, the manure will be in capital condition for enriching the garden.

In the event of there being no frame to spare, drive a stake into each corner of the bed. Connect the tops of the stakes, about one foot from the surface of the bed, with four rods securely tied, and upon these place other rods, over and around which any protecting material at command may be used. With this simple contrivance it is quite possible to grow Asters in a satisfactory manner.

The finest Asters are frequently grown in the open air, entirely without the aid of artificial heat, and indeed without any of the usual horticultural appliances. Those who possess the best possible resources will find additional advantage in resorting also to this mode of culture. It gives another string to the bow, and prolongs the seasoning of flowering. For open-air sowings in April, make the soil level and fine, and about the middle of that month draw drills three inches deep. In these place an inch of finely prepared rich soil, and if it is largely mixed with ashes from a smother, so much the better. The distance between the drills should be regulated by the variety. For tall-growing sorts, such as Giant French or Victoria, twelve to fifteen inches between the rows will not be too much. Ten inches will suffice for the dwarfs. Sow the seed thinly and evenly, and cover carefully with fine soil. Commence early to thin the plants, always leaving the strongest, and do this so that finally they will be left at from eight to fifteen inches apart according to the sort.

Keep the ground clean, and before the flowering stage is reached, gently stir the surface, but not deep enough to injure the roots. A thick top dressing of well-decayed manure operates beneficially in keeping the surface cool and moist, and it also promotes the growth of the plant. On no account use fresh manure, or in a few days the plants will look scorched. In that case further trouble will be wasted, and they may as well be destroyed at once. An occasional application of weak manure water will be advantageous, but it must not be allowed to touch the foliage.

For tall varieties it may be needful to provide support. If so, place a neat stick on that side of the plant towards which it leans, as this takes the strain off the tying material, and saves the plant from being cut or half strangled. In a dry season, and especially on light soils, there must be a bountiful supply of soft water, alternated every few days with the manure water already alluded to. Evening is the best time to apply it.

Plants reserved for show purposes require rather more room than we have stated. Only about five buds should be matured by each, and these, of course, the finest. To bring the various shades of colour to perfection on the same day, it is necessary to remember that dark colours, such as purple and red, come to maturity rather earlier than the lighter tints: hence the former should be shaded a few days in advance of the latter. To prepare flowers for exhibition is in itself an art, and each cultivator must be guided by his own resources and experience.

Asters in pots make excellent decorative subjects. It is only necessary to lift them carefully from the borders with balls of earth surrounding the roots, and pot them just before the buds expand.

The plants are liable to the attacks of aphis, both green and black. While under glass the pest can be destroyed by tobacco smoke; but in the open, a solution of some good insecticide may be administered with the syringe at intervals of about three days, until a clearance is effected. Other foes are the various grubs which attack plants at the collar. On the first sign of failing vigour, gently remove with a pointed stick the soil around the plant, and in doing this avoid any needless disturbance of the roots. Do not be satisfied until the enemy is destroyed.

Aster seed is not an easy thing to harvest well, particularly in damp weather. The flat-petalled varieties are especially liable to injury, for the massive flowers retain so much moisture that the organs of fructification are easily damaged or destroyed. In certain seasons it is next to impossible to secure seed which is really strong in germinating power, and we advise the cultivator not to risk all in one venture, but to make at least two sowings. Frequently when one sowing fails, success may be obtained with a second attempt from the same packet of seed.

AURICULA

Primula Auricula. Hardy perennial

DEEP is the enthusiasm of the Auricula amateur. Said a rising member of the fraternity: 'If people only knew the delight with which I look forward to the flowering of my two hundred seedlings next spring, I believe that Auricula growers would be numbered by thousands where now there are tens.' The only complaint we ever heard about the flower is, that its most devoted admirer cannot endow it with perpetual youth and beauty.

It is well to bear in mind that seed from a worthless strain requires just as much attention as that saved with all a florist's care from prize flowers. Some growers advocate sowing immediately the seed is ripe, but this intensifies the irregular germination which characterises seed of all the Primula species. Either February, March, or April may be chosen, and we give preference to the end of February. Use 6-inch pots, and as there must be no doubt about drainage, nearly half fill the pots with crocks, to be covered with a layer of coarse cocoa-nut fibre; add rough, fibrous loam mingled with broken charcoal, and on the top a mixture of loam, decaying leaves, and sharp sand. Press the soil firmly down, sow thinly and regularly, putting the seeds in about half an inch apart; just cover them with fine soil, and place the pots in a cool frame or greenhouse with sheets of glass over to prevent evaporation. Watering in the ordinary way is apt to wash out the seeds, and it is therefore advisable to immerse the pots for about an hour in a vessel filled with water to the requisite depth. Wait patiently for the plants. When they show four or six leaves, prick out into pans or boxes about two inches apart, and before the seedlings touch each other transfer to small pots. The surface soil in the pots may be lightly stirred occasionally to keep it free from moss. The plants must never be allowed to go dry, but as winter approaches water should be given more sparingly, and during sharp frosts it may be wise to withhold it entirely. There really is no need of artificial heat, for the Auricula is a mountaineer, and can endure both frost and snow. But we prize its beauty so highly that frames and greenhouses are properly employed for protecting it from wind, heavy rain, soot, dust, and all the unkind assaults of a lowland atmosphere, to which it is unaccustomed in a natural state. Still, the plants should be kept as nearly hardy as possible.

The Auricula is a slow-growing plant, and although there will probably be some flowers from seedlings in the following year, their value must not be judged until the second season. To the trained eye of the florist the Show Auriculas take precedence over the Alpine section. But for general usefulness the Alpines hold the first place. They may be fearlessly put into the open border, and especially the north border, where, with scarcely any care at all, they will endure the winter, and freely show their lovely flowers in spring.

BALSAM

Impatiens Balsamina. Half-hardy annual

BALSAMS were but rarely well grown until within the past few years, for the popular works on floriculture prescribed a false system, comprising disbudding, stopping, and other interferences with the natural growth of the plant. But an observant writer, who has grown these flowers in various ways, made the declaration that there was only one way worth attention, that being the natural way, and now the rule prevails, and we are quite accustomed to see in gardens abundance of beautiful Balsams. The old rule of pinching back the leader to promote the growth of side shoots, and removing the flower buds to increase the size of the plants, was altogether vicious, because the natural growth is more elegant and effective, and the finest flowers are produced on the main stem, and these are completely sacrificed by disbudding. It is desirable to make two or three sowings of Balsam, say, from the middle of March to the middle of May, the earlier sowings to be put on a sweet hot-bed, although March sowings will soon germinate in a frame, and the May sowing may be made in the open ground on a prepared bed. The soil at every stage should be rich and light, but not rank in any degree. The plants should be pricked out from the seed-pans when they show their first rough leaves, and soon after should be shifted to encourage a stout dwarf habit. A sunny position should be chosen for the bed, in which they may be planted out about the first week of June, or earlier if the weather is particularly favourable. Heat, moisture, and a strong light favour a fine bloom, and, therefore, water must be given whenever dry weather prevails for any length of time. If kept sturdy while under glass, they will need no support of any kind, and although they are peculiarly fleshy in texture, it is most unusual for even a hurricane to injure them. When grown in pots throughout, the chief points are to shift them often in the early stages, to promote free growth in every reasonable way, and to cease shifting when they are in pots sufficiently large to sustain the strength of the plants. Generally speaking, 8-inch pots will suffice for very fine Balsams, but 10-inch pots may be used for plants from an early sowing. They will probably not show a flower bud while increased pot room is allowed them; but as soon as their roots touch the sides of the pots the bloom will appear, and the work will be completed. It is occasionally the practice to lift plants from beds when pot Balsams are wanted, and it has the advantage of being the least troublesome method, and, moreover, we see exactly what we shall have, because the plants are lifted when the flowers show.

BEGONIA, TUBEROUS-ROOTED

Begonia tuberosa. Half-hardy perennial

BEGONIAS are generally grown for greenhouse and conservatory decoration, and for this purpose are particularly useful, as their graceful habit and beautiful colours form a pleasing contrast to other plants, and greatly add to the attractiveness of the greenhouse. When grown in pots, the soil required is a compost of sandy loam, leaf-mould, and well-rotted manure. The bulbs should be allowed to remain during the winter in the same pots in which they have bloomed, and when they begin to 'start' in the spring, they should at once be re-potted in a small-sized pot, and almost on the surface of the soil. Shift into larger sizes as the increased growth may render necessary, and at each operation insert the bulb a little deeper until the crown is covered. The plants do much better if they have been allowed to 'start' naturally, instead of being forced into growth early in the spring. It is desirable always to have a fresh stock of plants coming on to take the place of the older ones, and as seed can now be obtained which has been saved from the finest named flowers, there is every probability of obtaining some striking novelties amongst a batch of seedlings at least equal in merit to named Begonias sold at high prices. Seed may be sown during the months of February and March, and the seedlings will then, with generous treatment, come into flower in June and July, and make fine healthy plants during the autumn, to be ready for early blooming again in the following spring. Sow also in July and August; the seedlings will make good young bulbs before the winter, and come into flower in the following spring and summer.

In any case, the seed should be sown in pots, in an even temperature of about 65°, the pots being well drained, and containing a good compost at the bottom, with fine sandy loam on the surface, pressed down. Before sowing, sprinkle the soil with water, and sow the seed evenly, barely covering it with fine earth. As the seed is always a considerable time, as well as irregular, in germinating, the plants should be pricked off into pans or small pots as they become large enough to handle, and for some time afterwards other seedlings will appear in the seed-pots and require transferring. They may be shifted on as the growth of the several plants may require. Begonias need more attention with reference to an even temperature during this stage than at any other period.

As bedding plants, Begonias are not nearly so much grown as they deserve to be. They may be planted out in June, and remain till the middle or end of October, without suffering any injury from frost. In the open ground they produce abundant supplies of flowers for cutting at the end of September, and early in October, when many other flowers are over. The plants should be put out when they show themselves sufficiently strong, and it is better to be guided by the plants than by any fixed date. Let the beds be made very rich with well-rotted manure and decayed vegetable matter, and for Begonias this can scarcely be overdone.

The earliest plants to flower will probably be retained in the greenhouse, as they follow in succession the Cinerarias and Calceolarias. Those that start later may be turned out as they come into bloom, which will probably be in June. By deferring the planting out until there is a show of bloom, a selection of various shades of colour may be made, and this will greatly enhance the beauty of the beds. Begonias are hardier than is generally supposed; they need no protection, and require no heat, except in the stage of seedlings, when first forming their tubers.

For autumn decoration, Begonias should be taken up from the beds during September and potted, when they will continue to bloom in the greenhouse or conservatory for a considerable time, and form a useful addition to the flowering plants of that period.

If not required for autumn decoration, let the plants remain out as long as may be safe; then pot off, and place in the greenhouse. Be careful not to hasten the drying-off of the bulbs. When the stems fall, Begonias may be stored for their season of rest, allowing them to remain in the same pots in which they have flowered. They can be put away in a dry cellar, or on the ground covered up with cocoa-nut fibre, in any shed or frame where the bulbs will remain dry and be protected from frost. Both damp and cold are very injurious to them. The temperature during their season of rest should be kept as near 50° as possible. Nothing more remains to be done till they start naturally in the spring, and it is always best to leave them undisturbed till they show signs of growth.

BEGONIA, FIBROUS-ROOTED

Half-hardy perennial

FIBROUS-ROOTED BEGONIAS are exceedingly valuable either for bedding in summer, or greenhouse decoration during the autumn and winter. They produce a continual succession of flowers, rather small in size, but very useful for bouquets. The directions for sowing and after-treatment recommended for the Tuberous-rooted class will be suitable also for the Fibrous-rooted varieties.

CALCEOLARIA, HERBACEOUS

Greenhouse biennial

THE importance of subordinating garden practice to the teaching of Nature is exemplified in an interesting manner in the history and cultivation of this flower. It was for many years the custom for cultivators to obtain their stocks of fine varieties of Calceolaria, Cineraria, and other plants of similar habit, by means of cuttings and divisions, rooted portions of mature 'stools' being most in favour because the most certain. But this tedious procedure made an immensity of trouble, and consequently there were but few successful growers. Nature certainly does not multiply these plants by cuttings and divisions, but by scattering the seed broadcast, and leaving every seed to find for itself a resting-place. Since the growing of such plants from seed has obtained the attention it deserves, the number of cultivators has been augmented indefinitely, and so also the varieties, which in truth are beyond numbering, while the range of variation appears also to be without limit. Therefore, when it is asked how can the splendid Herbaceous Calceolarias be best grown, we answer that the simplest and safest system is to raise them from seed ; this being the method of Nature herself, and the least fraught with difficulties. In its present magnificent state, both as to constitution and the beauty of its flowers, the Calceolaria is a hybrid plant, the result of much cross-fertilisation of the finest types, hence its capability of affording ever new surprises and delights. The finest collections that have been exhibited of late years, and that have made lasting impressions on the public by their form and brilliancy of colour, have invariably been raised from seeds of selected varieties, saved on scientific principles that insure vigour, variety, and splendour in the progeny.

In the cultivation of these flowers, it should be borne in mind that they cannot endure without injury any extreme conditions of atmosphere or temperature. They must not be exposed to undue heat, or to frost, or to a dry parching air at any time. Damp will harm them less than drought ; what they require is careful cool-house cultivation. But Calceolarias cannot be grown in a careless haphazard fashion. From the very beginning the work must be thoroughly well done, and the attention be ceaseless. The result will more than justify the care and labour bestowed upon them.

May is early enough to commence operations, and July is quite late enough for the final sowing. As a rule, the June sowing will produce the quickest, strongest, and most robust plants.

The soil, whatever be its composition, should be rich, firm, and above all porous. Press it well into the pots or pans, and make the surface slightly convex and quite smooth. A compost that has been properly prepared will not need water, but should it become needful to moisten it, this must be done by partially submerging the pans in water. The seed is as fine as snuff, and requires delicate handling. It is easily lost or blown away, and therefore it is wise not to open the packet until perfectly ready to sow. Distribute the seed evenly, and sift over it a mere dusting of fine earth. Place a sheet of glass upon each pot or pan, and the glass must either be turned or wiped daily. This not only checks rapid evaporation, but prevents the attacks of vermin. Germination is always slower on an open than on a close stage. Perhaps the best possible position is a moist shady part of a vinery, if only care be taken when syringing the vines to prevent the spray from falling upon the seed-pans.

Under favourable circumstances, from seven to nine days will suffice to bring the seedlings up in force, and very few will appear afterwards. Immediately they are through the soil, remove the sheet of glass, and give them prompt attention, or they will rapidly fade away. So soon as the second leaf appears, tiny and difficult to handle as the plants may be, commence pricking them off into other pots prepared to receive them, for it is unsafe to wait until they become strong. Allow about two inches between each plant. The occupants of each pan may generally be pricked off in about three operations, and there should be only the shortest possible intervals between.

With many subjects it is a safe rule to use the robust seedlings and throw the weakly ones away. That practice will not do in the case of Calceolarias, or some of the most charming colours that can grace the conservatory or greenhouse will be lost. The strongest seedlings generally produce flowers in which yellow largely predominates. This can easily be verified if the plants are kept under separate numbers. But it must not be inferred that because the remainder are somewhat weaker at the outset, that ultimately they will not make robust plants.

Freely mix silver sand with the potting mould, and raise the surface higher in the centre than at the edge of the pot. From the first appearance of the seedlings shading is of the utmost importance, for a brief period of direct sunshine will prove certain and speedy destruction. Do not allow the plants to become dry for a moment, but give frequent gentle sprinklings of water, and rain-water is preferable. As the soil hardens, stir the surface with a pointed stick, not too deep, and give water a few hours after. About a month of this treatment should find each plant in the possession of four or five leaves. Then prepare thumb pots with small crocks, cover the crocks with clean moss or coarse cocoa-nut fibre, and fill with rich porous soil. To these transfer the plants with extreme care, lifting each with as much soil adhering to the roots as a skilful hand can make them carry. Place them in a frame, or in the sheltered part of a greenhouse, quite free from dripping water. Always give air on suitable days, and on the leeward side of the house.

Keep a sharp look-out for aphis, to the attacks of which Calceolarias are peculiarly liable. Tobacco smoke is the best remedy, and it should be given in the evening; a still atmosphere renders the operation more certain. Water carefully on the following morning, and shade from the sun.

By September the plants should be in large 60-pots, and it is then quite time to begin the preparation for wintering. Some growers put them on heat and are successful, but the heat must be very moderate, and even then we regard the practice as dangerous. Place the plants near the glass, and at one end of the house where they will obtain plenty of side light as well as light from above. During severe frosts it may be well to draw them back or remove them to a shelf lower down and towards the centre of the house, but they must be restored as soon as possible to the fullest light obtainable, as they have to do all their growth under glass. The more air that can safely be given the better, and dispense with fire-heat if a temperature of 45° to 55° can be maintained without it. Remove every decayed leaf as it appears.

When growth commences in the spring, which will generally be early in March, give each plant its final shift into 8- or 10-inch pots. This must be done before the buds push up, or there will be more foliage than flowers. The following is the compost we advise : one bushel good yellow loam, half-bushel leaf-soil, one gallon silver sand, quarter pint Sutton's Concentrated Manure, quarter pint soot — well mixed a few days before use. Any sourness in the soil will be fatal to flowering. The mould must be carefully 'firmed' into the pots, but no severe pressure should be employed, or the roots will not run freely. Neglect as to temperature or humidity will have to be paid for in long joints, green fly, red spider, or in some other way. But there are no plants of high quality that grow more thriftily if protected from cold winds and kept clean by free use of the syringe. A light airy greenhouse is their proper place, and they must have ample head-room.

Until the pots are filled with roots give no manure water of any kind, but then it may be administered until the blooms show. Tie out the plants about a fortnight before flowering ; and during the period of full display, give pure soft water only.

It may be that a few large specimens are required. In this case shift the most promising into 6-size pots, and when the pots are filled with roots, not before, give regular supplies of liquid manure until the bloom is well up. If the drainage is good and the plants thriving, a rather strong beverage will suit them. The size of the leaves will in great degree indicate and correspond with the size and quantity of the flowers. For all ordinary purposes, however, plants may be allowed to flower in 10-inch pots, and for these one shift after the winter is sufficient.

CALCEOLARIA RUGOSA

Shrubby Calceolaria. Half-hardy perennial

NOTWITHSTANDING the ease with which cuttings of the Shrubby Calceolaria can be carried through a severe winter, there is a growing disposition to obtain the required number of plants from seed sown in February; and seedlings have the advantage of great variety of colour. A frame or greenhouse, and the most ordinary treatment, will suffice to insure a large stock of attractive healthy plants for the embellishment of beds and borders.

CAMPANULA

Bell Flower. Annual and perennial; hardy and half-hardy

CAMPANULAS vary much in habit, and the quick-growing annual kinds may be disposed of by saying that they only need to be sown on the borders where they are required to flower. But the Canterbury Bell, the Chimney Campanula (*C. pyramidalis*), and some few others, require more careful cultivation. By sowing early on a gentle heat, and nursing the plants with a little care, most of the biennial and some of the perennial kinds will flower the same season. It must be remembered, however, that hardy plants will not endure much heat, and therefore when the seedlings have made a little progress in comfortable quarters, they must have as much light and air as they can endure without giving them a check, and be planted out early, unless it is intended to flower them in pots, for which the Chimney Campanula is well adapted. A light rich soil and secure drainage are essential at all stages, and they should never suffer for want of water, as this will not only impoverish the growth, but render them a prey to green fly or red spider. To raise a fine stock of the varieties of Canterbury Bell, sow the seed any time from March to July in a frame or border, and get the plants pricked out early to become strong and short, and transplant into rows in August or September to stand the winter, or bed them in a frame. In the ensuing spring transplant with care to flowering positions.

CANNA

Indian Shot.   Half-hardy perennial

THE popular name is descriptive of the seed, which is nearly round, black, and so hard that it has been used instead of shot in the West Indies. Hence it will occasion no surprise that there should be some difficulty in raising it; or that sometimes many weeks elapse before the seedlings appear; and then they generally straggle up one or two at a time. Some growers file the seeds to facilitate germination, but we prefer to soak them in water for about twelve hours before sowing. It is also advisable to record the number put in, so that it may be known when they are all up. We find that as a rule they germinate more rapidly in retentive than in porous soil. In January start the seed in a rather strong heat, and as fast as the seedlings become ready, transfer them singly to small pots. Cannas do not make leaves rapidly in a young state, and it is useless to be impatient with them; if the plants are scorched they will take a long time to recover. Besides, if they have been raised in reasonable time, there really is no hurry, for they cannot be put out until June.

Cannas are exceedingly handsome in form and colour, and they may prove useful for decorative purposes before the time arrives for transferring them to the open ground. They vary in height from four to seven feet, and stakes in proportion will have to be provided for their safety. In warm districts, and in dry, sheltered situations, they may be left in the open ground all the winter, under a covering of ashes. But from a damp soil or an exposed garden they must be lifted and stored in a frame through the cold months.

CARNATION

Dianthus Caryophyllus fl. pl.   Hardy perennial

THESE favourite flowers make a most satisfactory return when grown from first-class seeds, and the saving of trouble is very great. The proverb that what is worth doing is worth doing well, is peculiarly exemplified in the cultivation of these bright and fragrant flowers, the difference between the results of good and bad work being immense. We therefore advise the preparation of a compost consisting of about three parts of turfy loam, to one part each of cow-manure and sweet leaf-mould, with a small addition of fine grit. A compost that has been laid up for a year, according to the orthodox practice of florists, is very much to be desired; but it may be prepared off-hand if care be taken to have all the materials in a sweet, friable state, free from pastiness, and as far as possible free from vermin. By laying it in a heap, and turning two or three times, the vermin will be pretty well got rid of. Sow from April until August in 4½-inch pots, which must be thoroughly drained. The seed must be very lightly covered, and sheets of glass should be laid over to check evaporation. Place the pots in a closed frame, or if the season be genial a sheltered border will suffice. Immediately the plants are large enough to handle, prick them off into seed-pans, or round the rim of 48-size pots. Place these in a cold pit or in a quiet part of the greenhouse. Give shade and water until the plants have formed six or eight leaves, and then choose a moist day for planting out.

To insure the seedling plants flowering in the following summer, it is necessary to have them strong and robust before the winter sets in. As the blooming stems rise they must be carefully tied to tall sticks, stout enough to carry a cover for the bloom, if the plants are not flowered under glass. When the buds show they should be thinned, leaving as a rule the top, third, and fourth buds. The second is often too near the first, and some will not carry the fourth with vigour. When the pods are swelled nearly full of petals, each one must be carefully tied with a thin strip of matting a little below halfway down, or the petals will burst the pod, which spoils the flower and disqualifies it for exhibition.

CELOSIA PLUMOSA

Plumed Cockscomb. Greenhouse annual

THE conditions which suit a liberally grown Cockscomb will produce long graceful plumes of *Celosia plumosa*, but the starving system will not answer with this plant. Sow in February or March, and by means of a steady heat, regular attention with water, and a rather moist atmosphere, the specimens should be grown without a check from beginning to end. When they reach the final pots an occasional dose of weak manure water will help them, both in size and colour, but it must be discontinued when the flowers begin to show their beauty. As a rule it will be found more easy to manage this plant in a moderate-sized hot-bed than in a greenhouse. Repotting should always be done in time to prevent the roots from growing through the bottom of the pots.

CHRYSANTHEMUM

Hardy perennial and hardy annual

THE florists' class (*C. indicum*) can be as easily raised from seed as any flower grown, but hitherto perennial Chrysanthemums have not obtained much attention except as grown from cuttings. As seedlings will flower the first year if the seed is sown in February or March, the pleasant excitement of a peculiar pastime is at the command of the humblest, and gardeners who require large numbers of plants for decorative purposes may turn seedling Chrysanthemums to good account, and sometimes obtain flowers worth naming. To raise the plants and pot them is easy enough, and they will bear a moderate heat in the early stages, which is fortunate, as it is equivalent to a gain of time. They should be liberally grown, and put out of doors to keep them dwarf and healthy, as soon as it can be done with safety. It is of great importance to allow all seedling Chrysanthemums to grow naturally, without any stopping, and they should be flowered in smallish pots, say, 6- to 8-inch, according to growth, for over-potting may defer the blooming season. Those that do not flower in the first season should if possible be kept a second year, as they may in the end prove to be the best of all, and are sure to flower if grown in the usual way from divisions or cuttings.

The section of perennial Chrysanthemums includes the well-known Marguerite, or Paris Daisy (*C. frutescens*), which is not quite hardy. It should be sown in February or March, and be gradually hardened for the open ground by the end of May.

Several of the annual Chrysanthemums make superb displays in borders, especially when planted in large clumps. There is a considerable choice of colours, which come quite true from seed, and the plants may be treated in all respects as hardy annuals.

CINERARIA

Greenhouse annual

The comparative ease with which the Cineraria can be well grown, together with the exceeding beauty and variety of its flowers, will always insure for it a high position in public favour. It is now so generally raised from seed that no other mode of culture need be alluded to. The plant is rapid in growth, very succulent, thirsty, requires generous feeding, and will not endure extremes of heat or cold. A compost of mellow turfy loam, either yellow or brown, with a fair addition of leaf-mould, will grow it to perfection. If leaf-mould be not obtainable, turfy peat will make a fairly good substitute. Soil from an old Melon bed will also answer, with the addition of sharp grit such as road sand, or the sifted sweepings from gravel walks; the disadvantage of a very rich soil is that it tends to the production of too much foliage.

The usual period for sowing is during the months of May and June, and, as a rule, the plants raised in May will be found the most valuable. A June sowing must not be expected to produce flowers until the following March or April. It is quite possible to have Cinerarias in bloom in November and December, and those who care for a display at that early period should sow in April. Cinerarias grow so freely that it is not necessary to prick the seedlings off round the edges of pots or pans; but immediately the plants begin to make their second leaves, transfer direct to thumb pots, using rather coarse soil, and in doing this take care not to cover the hearts of the plants. Place the pots in a close frame; attend to shading, and sprinkle with soft water both morning and evening until well established. In the second week after potting, gradually diminish the heat and give more air. Too high a temperature, and even too much shade, will produce thin and weakly leaf-stalks. If the plants are so crowded that they touch one another it will almost certainly be productive of mischief, and render them an easy prey to some of their numerous enemies. It is far better to grow a few really fine specimens that will produce a handsome display of superb flowers, than to attempt a large number of feeble plants that will prove a constant source of trouble, and in the end yield but a poor return in bloom. Endeavour to grow them as nearly hardy as the season will allow, even admitting the night air freely on suitable occasions. Immediately the thumb pots are filled with roots, shift to a larger size, and it is important that this operation should not be delayed a day too long. To the practised eye the alteration of the colour of the leaves to a pale green is a sufficient intimation that starvation has commenced, and that prompt action is necessary to save the plants. It is the custom of some growers to transfer at once to the size in which they are intended to bloom. There is, however, some danger to the inexperienced in over-potting, and therefore we advise one intermediate shift. As a rule 32-size pots are large enough, but the 16- or even the 8-size is allowable when very fine specimens are required. The plants should be in their final pots not later than the end of November.

It will help to harden and establish the plants if they are placed in the open air during August and September. A north border under the shelter of a wall or building is the most suitable spot, but avoid a hedge of any kind. Clear away suckers, and if many buds are presented, every third one may be removed when very fine blooms are wanted. From the first appearance of the buds, manure water can be given with advantage once or twice a week until the flowers show colour, and then it should be discontinued.

Although Cinerarias are thrifty plants, they are fastidious about trifles. If possible give them new pots, or see that old ones are made scrupulously clean. Even hard water will retard free growth, oftentimes to the perplexity of the cultivator.

A host of enemies attack Cinerarias; indeed, there is scarcely a pest known to the greenhouse but finds a congenial home upon this plant. Mildew is more common in some seasons than in others. As a rule it appears during July and August, especially after insufficient ventilation, or when the plants have been left too long in one place, or too near to each other. Obviously weakness invites attack, and the necessity of robust and vigorous growth is thus effectually taught. On the first appearance of a curled leaf, dust the foliage and soil with sulphur, and give no water overhead until a cure has been effected. The aphis is easily killed by a dense cloud of tobacco smoke administered on a quiet night. For this operation the leaves should be quite dry, and when the house is well filled with smoke, remove the embers. Attention to these points will save the plants from being scorched. Some gardeners find it difficult to avoid injuring the plants when tobacco smoke is employed, and they prefer to give an hour or two once a week to the removal of the pest by means of a soft brush. From three to four dozen plants are easily cleansed by hand in the time named.

COCKSCOMB

Celosia cristata. Tender annual

THIS fine old-fashioned oddity appears to have advanced in popularity of late years, probably as the result of a number of well-grown plants at public exhibitions. Those who can produce handsome Cinerarias, Balsams, and Calceolarias, will be likely to turn out grand combs strongly coloured and on dwarf leafy plants. Liberal culture is essential, and the first start should be made in a compost consisting mainly of rich light friable loam. Sow the seeds on a rather brisk heat in February or March, a newly-made but sweet hot-bed being the best place for the seed-pans. Prick out early into very small pots, and shift on so as to encourage growth without a check, and keep the plants on the hot-bed until the combs are formed. It is well not to shift beyond the 8-inch size; then, by allowing the roots to become pot-bound, the combs are soon produced. This routine may be varied at convenience. In the first place, you may have some grand combs on tall plants. The command of a brisk hot-bed will easily enable you to improve these specimens. Prepare some pots one size at least smaller than those they are in, and cut off the heads with a sufficient amount of stem attached, remove a few of the lowest leaves, plant firmly in the new pots, put them on the hot-bed, and they will make roots with surprising rapidity, and then you will secure what is admitted to be desirable—large, symmetrical, richly-coloured combs upon dwarf stems. Another mode of procedure consists in pricking the young plants into boxes, and starving them somewhat, so as to promote premature production of combs, and then choosing the best to grow in pots for decorative purposes. It matters not how select the seed, or how careful the culture, a certain proportion of unsymmetrical combs will appear; but these, if richly coloured, will be useful for decorative purposes, and should have all the attention needed to keep their leaves fresh and the combs pure in colour.

COLEUS

Stove perennial

THERE is so much difficulty in carrying Coleus through the winter in vigorous health, that the modern plan of treating it as an annual is advantageous for the saving of trouble and fire-heat in winter, and also because it offers the charm of constant diversity. The fact is that our winter days are too brief and gloomy to maintain the splendour of colouring which makes Coleus so attractive and valuable; and seed from a good strain may be relied on to produce plants which will delight the eye all through the summer and autumn. Some experienced men sow in February and succeed, but the majority of cultivators will show prudence by waiting until March, when increased daylight favours the rapid growth of the plants. Flower pots are better than pans, as the greater depth affords opportunity of securing effectual drainage. The pots should be nearly half filled with crocks, covered with a layer of moss to prevent the soil from being washed away. Fill them with light turfy loam, mingled with almost an equal bulk of sharp sand. Make an even surface, on which sow thinly, and shake over the seed a slight covering of fine soil. Place the pots in a temperature of not less than 65°. Watering needs particular care, because of the peculiar liability of the young plants to damp off, especially in dull weather. The strongest seedlings are pretty certain to be those in which green and black predominate, and therefore they may without scruple be removed to make way for the slower-growing but better coloured specimens. These should be transplanted round the edges of pots while quite small; and such as show delicate tints, especially those having pink markings on a golden ground, are worth nursing through the early stage with extra care. The pots must be shaded from direct sunshine, but should be kept near the glass. In May the plants will be large enough for 48-sized pots, beyond which there is no occasion to go. When the pots become full of roots the foliage increases in brilliancy, whereas larger pots encourage free growth to the detriment of colour. An occasional dose of concentrated manure administered in water will maintain the plants in health.

COLUMBINE. *See* AQUILEGIA

CYCLAMEN

Half-hardy perennial

CYCLAMENS afford a striking example of the advantages of the rapid system of cultivation. Seed may be sown at any time of the year, and the plants will not only flower within twelve months, but if properly grown will produce more bloom than can be obtained from old bulbs. We do not advise more than two or three sowings, the first and most important of which should be made in October or the beginning of November, and to obtain a succession of plants sow again in January or February. The best soil for the purpose is a rich, sound loam, with a liberal admixture of leaf-mould, and sufficient silver sand to insure free drainage. Press this mixture firmly into pots or seed-pans, and dibble the seed about an inch apart and a quarter-inch deep. Covering the surface with a thin layer of sifted cocoa-nut fibre checks rapid evaporation, and keeps the soil free from moss. The autumn sowings may at first be placed in a frame having a temperature of not less than 45°. At the end of a fortnight, transfer the pans to any warm and moist position in the greenhouse, or propagating house. The January sowing should be placed in heat at once.

Although the Cyclamen is a tender plant, it does not need a strong heat, and will not endure extremes of any kind. Sudden changes are always fatal to its growth. In winter the temperature should not be allowed to fall below 56°, or to rise above 70° at any time. The more evenly the heat can be maintained the better, and it is desirable to give all the light possible. In summer, however, although a warm and humid atmosphere is still necessary, the light may with advantage be somewhat subdued, but shading must not be overdone, or the constitution of the plant will suffer.

Cyclamen seed not only germinates slowly, but it also grows in the most capricious manner; sometimes a few plants come up long after others have made a good start. Do not be impatient of their appearance, but when some seedlings are large enough for removal, transfer to thumb pots, taking care not to insert them too deeply. As the plants develop, shift into larger pots, ending finally in the 48-size. In the later stages mix less sand with the soil, and when potting always leave the crown of the corm clear. Keep the plants near the glass, and as the sun becomes powerful it will be necessary to provide shade and prevent excess of heat. Never allow the seedlings to suffer from want of water, or to become a prey to aphis. To avoid the latter, occasional, or it may be frequent, fumigations must be resorted to. About the end of May should find the most forward plants ready for shifting into 60-pots. Give all the air possible to promote a sturdy growth. In doing this, however, avoid draughts of cold air. From the end of June to the middle of July, the finest plants should be ready for their final shift into 48-pots, in which they will flower admirably. The growth during August and September will be very free, and then occasional assistance with weak manure water will add to the size and colour of the flowers. As the evenings shorten, save the plants from chills, which result in deformed blossoms.

The whole secret of successful Cyclamen culture may be summed up in a few words : constant and unvarying heat, a moist atmosphere, and abundant supplies of water without stagnation ; free circulation of air, avoiding cold draughts ; light in winter, and shade in summer, with freedom from insect pests. These conditions will keep the plants in vigorous growth from first to last, and the result will be so bountiful a bloom as to prove the soundness of the rapid system of cultivation. This routine may be varied by the experienced cultivator, but the principles will remain the same in all cases, because the natural constitution of the plant gives the key to its management.

DAHLIA, DOUBLE

Half-hardy perennial

DOUBLE DAHLIAS are scarcely known as annuals raised from seed, but it is an extremely simple matter to produce any quantity, and Show Dahlias are like Hollyhocks in giving a large percentage of fine flowers from seed. Sow in February in a warm house or pit, and treat in the ordinary way of half-hardy annuals, planting out about the end of May when the weather is favourable. These rapid-growing and noble plants require a rich soil ; indeed, if the soil is rank with manure, the growth and flowering will be all the finer for it. Slugs and snails are terribly partial to newly-planted Dahlias, but the vermin soon cease to care about them ; therefore it is advisable to plant Lettuces plentifully at the same time, or previously, on the same ground, and to dust around the Dahlias with lime.

DAHLIA, SINGLE

Half-hardy perennial

OF late there has been a growing interest in plants producing single flowers, and many old acquaintances have been restored to popular favour after a long period of neglect. Perhaps none deserve this revived attention more than the Single Dahlia, especially since a few intelligent cultivators have taken it in hand, and produced many varieties which are remarkable for intense and brilliant colouring, combined with great beauty of form.

The plant may be propagated from tubers in the same manner as the double variety, but it will save both time and space during winter to raise the required number from seed. The seedlings grow freely and quickly, and will flower quite as early as those grown by the more lengthy and troublesome method. Even those who possess a stock of named sorts may with advantage raise a supply from seed, especially as there is a probability of securing some charming novelty, which is in itself no small incentive.

Although the Dahlia is a tender plant, it is easily managed in a greenhouse, or in a frame resting on a hot-bed. The seed may be sown as early as January, but unless sufficient space is at command to keep the plants stocky as they develop, it will be wise to wait until February. A sowing then will produce plants forward enough to bloom at the usual time. Even March will not be too late; but whatever time may be chosen, when the start has been made it must be followed up with diligence, so as to avoid giving any check from first to last. Sow thinly in pots or pans filled with ordinary light rich compost, and cover the seed with a mere sprinkling of fine earth. When the first pair of leaves attain the height of an inch, pot off each plant singly close up to the base of the leaves. It is not advisable to throw the weakly seedlings away; these are the very plants which are most likely to display new shades of colour or marking, and therefore they are worth some additional trouble. Although weak at the outset, they may, by judicious treatment, be grown into a thriving and healthy condition.

When potted, place the plants in heat, giving a little extra care until growth has fairly started. In due time shift into larger sizes as may be necessary, and then it will be wise to consider whether there is space to grow the whole stock well. If not, do not hesitate to sacrifice the surplus, and in doing so reject the rankest-growing specimens, for these are least likely to produce a fine display of bloom. It is mistaken practice to take out the top shoot, as this checks the plant for no good end; but when about six inches high, each one will need the support of a stick. Give water freely, and air on all suitable occasions. The least tendency to curled leaves indicates something amiss, and demands immediate attention. A cold blast may have stricken the plants, or the soil may be poor; lack of sufficient water will produce the mischief, or it may arise from the presence of aphis. If the last-named assumption prove correct, fumigate with tobacco on the first quiet evening, and omit watering on that day. The mere mention of the other points will be sufficient to show the remedy for them.

As the time for transfer to the open air approaches, all that is possible should be done to harden the plants for the change. They may be placed for a few days under the shelter of a wall or hedge, but on the least sign of frost be prepared to protect with hurdles or mats. Full exposure during genial showers and fair weather is advisable, and an occasional examination of the plants will prevent their rooting through the pots into the soil.

The border for Dahlias can scarcely be made too rich, for they are hungry and thirsty subjects, and will amply repay in a profusion of bloom the manure that may be lavished upon them. Insert at least one stake, about a yard long, near each plant to give support, and two or three others will have to be given before the branches spread far. Secure the first shoot when planting is completed, and follow up the tying as growth demands.

Dahlias bloom continuously for a long time, and appear to be especially at home in the shrubbery border, or in the centre of a bed. They are also valuable for training against buildings having a southern aspect, and here the flowering period is much prolonged, for an early frost will scarcely reach them. A light wall is an admirable background for deep-coloured varieties, and the white or yellow flowers are displayed to advantage against a dark building. Dahlias may either be used alone or in company with the climbing plants which are usual in such positions.

The flowers possess a value quite unique for indoor decoration, and any odd corner of the garden can be utilised for producing a supply for this purpose. Cutting should invariably be done in the early morning, while yet the dew is upon them. They will then retain their beauty for a longer period than those taken at a later hour from the same plants. This remark is true of all flowers, but it applies with especial force to the Single Dahlia.

DELPHINIUM

Hardy perennial

NEARLY all the perennial varieties may be raised from seed, and where large numbers are required this is the best method of obtaining them. They make handsome border flowers, and *D. cœlestinum* is without a rival for its delicately beautiful shade of blue. Sow in drills in the open ground in March, and do not allow the seedlings to become crowded. If mixed seed has been sown, it will not be wise to thin out all the weakly plants, or it may happen that only one colour will remain. Transplant to final positions when strong enough to bear removal. One stake behind each plant will suffice to support the flowers during the first season, but in the second year three neat sticks placed in a triangle are advisable. The first flowers will be over by midsummer, and if the stalks are promptly cut down instead of being allowed to seed, there will be a second display later in the year.

The scarlet variety (*D. nudicaule*) is rather more delicate than the others, and it is wise to raise the plants in well-drained seed-pans, and to take care of them through the first winter in a cold frame; indeed, in a heavy soil there is a risk of losing them in any winter which is both cold and wet. It is not necessary to employ pots, but immediately after flowering take them up and store in a mixture of peat and cocoa-nut fibre until the following April, when they can be returned to the open ground.

As slugs are exceedingly partial to Delphiniums, the crowns should be examined in spring, and the seed-beds may be dressed with soot and surrounded with ashes to save the seedlings from injury.

DIANTHUS

Pink. Hardy biennial

MANY varieties of Dianthus claim attention for their elegant forms and splendour of colouring. They have been so wonderfully improved by scientific growers that they almost supersede the old garden Pinks, and have the great advantage of coming true from seed. *D. Heddewigii* (Japan Pink) and its varieties, *D. chinensis* (Indian Pink) and *D. imperialis*, make interesting and sumptuous beds, and may all be flowered the first year from sowings made in heat in February. Immediately the seedlings are through the soil, it is important to shift them to a rather lower temperature than is necessary for insuring germination, or the plants become soft and worthless. Be very sparing with water, especially if the soil is at all retentive. When two leaves are formed, transfer to seed-pans, allowing about an inch between each plant, and place in a sheltered position. Gradually introduce them to cool treatment, and in March pot off singly. They will thus have a much better start, when planted out in May, than if taken from the seed-pans direct.

Where there are no facilities for raising Dianthus in heat, it is quite easy to grow them in an open spot from a sowing in June or July, and they will flower freely in the following year. Place finely sifted soil in drills drawn about six inches apart, and cover the seed very lightly. Shade must be given during germination, but when the seedlings are up it should be gradually withdrawn. Transfer to final positions in August. If this is impossible, prick the plants out, and shift them again a little later. It will only do harm to leave them crowded in the seed-bed, and the second move will enable them all the better to withstand winter frosts. Dianthus thrive in a sandy or loamy soil, with full exposure to sunshine, and they scarcely need water or any attention the whole season through.

DIGITALIS

Foxglove. Hardy perennial

BESIDES the native Purple Foxglove, largely grown in gardens, there are several very handsome varieties that are valuable for adorning borders, shrubberies and woodland walks. Specially worthy of attention are *D. grandiflora*, a most beautiful yellow variety; also *D. maculata superba*, producing spotted flowers, rich and varied in colour, on dense spikes three feet in height; and the still taller white variety with its abundance of charming ivory-white bells.

Any deep rich soil suits the Digitalis, and seed sown in May, June or July will produce plants which, with very little attention, will yield a fine display of flowers in the following summer. Sow in the open in pans, or on a prepared border, and put the young plants into permanent positions during showery weather in August or September.

FUCHSIA

Greenhouse shrub

To raise Fuchsias from seed will be new practice to many; but it is both interesting and inexpensive, and every year it secures an increasing number of adherents. Seed may be sown at almost any time of the year; if a start be made in January or February, the plants will bloom in July or August. The soil for the seed-pots should be somewhat firm in texture, but a light rich compost ought to be employed later on, when the plants come to be potted off, and the final shift should be into a mixture containing nearly one-third of decayed cow-manure. For the early sowing we have named, a rather strong heat will be necessary to bring up the seed. When large enough to handle, prick off the seedlings round the edges of 60-pots, putting about six plants into each pot. Shade and moisture are requisite to give them a start after each transfer. Subsequently they must be potted on as growth demands, until the final size is reached; and flowering will not commence so long as increased pot-room is given. The growth must not be hurried, and the plants should at all times be kept free from vermin. The seedlings which have narrow pointed leaves may be consigned to the waste-heap without scruple; but plants with short rounded foliage, especially if it be dark in colour, are almost certain to prove of high quality.

GERANIUM

Crane's-bill. Half-hardy perennial

GERANIUMS of all kinds are most valuable if treated as annuals. In their seedling state the plants are peculiarly robust and tree-like, and charmingly fresh in leafage and flowers, even if amongst them there does not happen to be one that is welcome as a novel florist's flower. When grown from first-class seed, however, a large proportion of fine varieties and a few real novelties may be expected. The seed may be sown on any day throughout the year, but February and August are especially suitable. Sow in pans filled with a good mixture, in a somewhat rough state—if the surface nodules are as large as horse-beans it will be none too rough. Cover with a fair sixteenth of an inch of fine soil. Put the seed-pans in a temperature of 60° to 70° if sown in February, but heat will not be necessary at all unless it is desired to bring the plants into flower early in the ensuing summer. We have been accustomed to place the seed-pans on a sunny shelf in a cool greenhouse, and have fine plants by the end of June, many of which begin to flower in August.

GESNERA ZEBRINA DISCOLOR
Tender perennial

AN extremely beautiful stove or conservatory plant, with mottled velvety foliage, and bright orange and scarlet flowers. Although a perennial, it can be treated as an annual, and if seed be sown in January the plants will flower in about nine months. Very rich soil, a warm and even temperature, and plenty of water, are requisite to promote luxuriant growth. The culture advised for Gloxinias will exactly suit the Gesnera also.

GLADIOLUS
Corn Flag. Half-hardy perennial

THE Gladiolus is comparatively unknown as raised from seed, but that is probably because the seed which was formerly obtainable was not worth sowing. Now it is saved with so much care that, like many other plants, it will give a splendid display of flowers, a large proportion of which will be equal to named sorts, and some may show a decided advance.

The use of large pots—the 32-size will answer—is advantageous for many reasons, and they should either be new or scrupulously clean, for they will have to remain unchanged for many months, so that a fair start is the more necessary. For the same reason special care should be taken to insure free drainage. Over the usual crocks place a layer of dry sifted moss, and a compost of fibrous loam and leaf-mould in equal parts, with sufficient sharp sand added to make it thoroughly porous. Press the soil firmly into the pots, making the surface quite even, and in February dibble the seeds separately about an inch apart and half an inch deep. This will render it needless to disturb the seedlings during the first season. Put the seed-pots in a steady temperature not exceeding 65° or 70°. After watering, it will help to retain the moisture if the top of each pot is covered with a layer of cocoa-nut fibre, or *old* moss, until the plants show. When the seedlings are about an inch high remove to a lower temperature, and begin to harden off by giving air on suitable occasions. Take care, however, that in the process no check is given to growth. Soon after the middle of May the seedlings should be able to bear full exposure, and it will then be time to renew the surface of the soil. With the aid of a pointed stick, gently remove the upper layer, and replace it with rotten cow-manure, or some other rich dressing. Water must be given regularly until about midsummer, when the pots may be plunged up to the rim in a shady border, and this will keep them tolerably moist until, in September, the seedlings begin to ripen off, which they must be allowed to do. When the leaves have died down, sift out the bulbs and place them on a shelf to dry. They are then too small to bear exposure safely during the winter. A mixture of equal parts of peat, cocoa-nut fibre, and pine sawdust, placed in a box or seed-pan, will make the best possible store for them ; the box or seed-pan to be stored in any spot which is safe from heat or frost. After about six weeks, each bulb should be examined, and decayed specimens removed. If any of them have commenced growing, pot them and place them in a pit or greenhouse. In March take the bulbs out of store, pot each one singly, and prepare for planting out. The transfer to the open must not be made until all fear of frost is past, even though it be necessary to wait until the first week of June.

It must be clearly understood that flowers are not to be expected or allowed from seedling Gladiolus during the second season. Should some of the bulbs send up spikes they must be removed, or the corms will be weakened for making a display in the following year.

Further remarks on Gladiolus will be found at page 288, under 'The Culture of Flowering Bulbs.'

GLOXINIA

Tender perennial

GLOXINIAS can now be flowered in the most satisfactory manner within six months from the date of sowing seed. Hence there is no longer the least temptation to propagate these plants by the lengthy and troublesome method formerly in vogue, especially as seedlings raised from a reliable strain produce flowers of the finest quality, both as to shape and style of growth. One great advantage to be obtained from seedlings is an almost endless variety of colour, for the careful hybridisation of the choicest flowers not only perpetuates those colours, but produces other fine shades also. Those who have never seen a large and well-grown collection of seedling Gloxinias have yet to witness one of the most striking displays of floral beauty.

There are three distinct types of Gloxinia, and all need exactly the same treatment. The drooping strain is the oldest, and is gradually giving place to the horizontal and the erect classes. These display their flowers to so much greater advantage than the drooping class, that there is good reason for the increasing favour shown to them. It is not generally noticed that quite as much has been done for the foliage of the Gloxinia as for its flower, and the best strains now produce grand leaves which turn downwards and inwards in such a manner as almost to hide the pot, so that the foliage has an extremely ornamental appearance.

By judicious management it is possible to produce Gloxinias the year through. Those who care for a display at Christmas can have it from seed sown in June, and a further sowing in January or February should produce plants to flower successively in almost every month of the year.

The soil most suited to Gloxinias is a light porous compost of fibrous loam. If that is not obtainable, leaf-mould will answer, mixed with peat and silver sand in about equal parts. New pots are advisable, or old ones must be thoroughly cleansed, and free drainage is essential to success. Fill with soil to within half an inch of the top. Sow thinly, and slightly cover the seed with very fine earth. Place the pots in a warm, moist position, carefully shading from the sun. A light sprinkling of water daily will be necessary. Immediately some plants are large enough for shifting, lift them from the seed-pot by the aid o a pointed stick, so as to least disturb the rest, and prick off into large 60-pots in which the soil has a convex surface. Follow this process as plants are ready, until all the seedlings have been transferred. When potting allow the leaves to rest on the soil, but avoid covering the hearts. On the first warm day give air on the leeward side of the house, briefly at first, and increase the time as the flowering period approaches. A clear space between each plant is necessary to prevent the leaves of neighbours from meeting. The final shift should be into 48-pots, unless extra fine specimens are required, and then one or two sizes larger may be used. An occasional dose of weak manure water will prove beneficial, taking care that the foliage is not wetted. A moist atmosphere, with the temperature at about 60° to 65°, greatly facilitates the growth of Gloxinias. With care, however, they may be well grown in either greenhouse or pits heated by hot water. But although the plants love a humid atmosphere while growing, this ceases to be an advantage, and, in fact, becomes positively injurious, when the flowers begin to expand. At that time, also, the manure water should be discontinued.

GREVILLEA ROBUSTA

Australian Oak. Greenhouse shrub

IN its native country (New South Wales) this is a stately tree, but here it is grown as a pot plant; and although there is no brilliant colour to recommend it, yet the finely cut, drooping, fern-like foliage produces one of the most graceful decorative subjects we possess. And its value is enhanced by the fact that it withstands the baneful influences of gas, dust, and changes of temperature better than the majority of table plants.

Seedlings are easily raised by those who can exercise patience; and afterwards the simplest cool culture will suffice to grow handsome specimens. But we do not know any seed—not even the Auricula—which is so long and so capricious in germinating. In all cases where seed is sown in fairly rich soil, which has to be kept constantly moist and undisturbed for a long period, there is a tendency to sourness, especially on the surface. Free drainage will do something towards preventing this. Another aid in the same direction is to cover the seed with a layer of sand, and the sand with a thin coating of ordinary potting soil. When the surface becomes covered with moss, the coating of soil can be gently removed down to the sand, and be replaced with fresh earth, without detriment to the seeds.

Sow at any time of the year, in 48-sized pots, filled with rather firm soil; and as the seedlings struggle through and show two pairs of leaves, pot them off singly, and give the shelter of a close pit or frame until they become established. They must not be allowed to suffer for lack of water, but there is no necessity to give them manure-water at any stage of growth. An occasional re-potting is the only other attention they will require until they reach the final size, and this need not be large.

HOLLYHOCK

Althæa rosea. Hardy perennial

GENERATIONS of unnatural treatment had so debilitated the Hollyhock, that disease threatened to banish it from our gardens. Just at the critical time it was discovered that the plant could be grown and successfully flowered from seed. Florists at once turned their attention to the production of seed worth growing, and with marked success. The best strains may now be relied on to produce in the first season a large proportion of perfectly formed double flowers, imposing in size, colour, and substance. The seedlings also possess a constitution capable of withstanding the deadly *Puccinia malvacearum*, and there is no longer a danger that this stately plant will become merely one of the pleasures of memory.

In growing the Hollyhock, it is necessary to remember that a large amount of vegetable tissue has to be produced within a brief period, so that the treatment throughout its career should be exceptionally liberal. Sow in January in well-drained pots or seed-pans filled with rich soil freely mixed with sand, and cover the seed with a slight dusting of fine earth. Place in a temperature of 65° or 70°, and in about a fortnight the plants will be an inch high, ready to be pricked off round the edges of 4½-inch pots, filled with a good porous compost. Put the seedlings in so that the first leaves just touch the surface. At the beginning of March transfer singly to thumb pots, and immediately the roots take hold remove to pits or frames, where they can be exposed to genial showers and be gradually hardened. Defer the planting out until the weather is quite warm and settled.

The shrubbery border is the natural position for the Hollyhock, but the regular occupants keep the soil poor, and for such a rapid-growing plant as we are now considering there is obviously all the greater need for deep digging and liberal manuring. If put out during dry weather, complete the operation with a soaking of water, and repeat this twice a week until rain falls. Give each plant a clear space of three or four feet to afford easy access for staking and watering. By midsummer offshoots will begin to push through the soil. The removal of these will throw all the strength of the plant into one stem. To insure its safety a strong stake will be required, which should be firmly driven into the ground, and rise six or seven feet above it. In case of an accident at any time to the central stem the hope of flowers for that year is gone, and it is therefore worth some pains to prevent a mishap. The tying must be done with judgment, and as the plants increase in size an occasional inspection will save the stems from being cut. Several inches of half-decayed cow-manure placed round the stems, with a shallow saucer-like space in the centre to retain water, will be helpful to the roots, and if the flowers are intended for exhibition, the treatment can scarcely be too generous.

It is easy to grow and flower Hollyhocks without the aid of artificial heat. On a south border in June prepare drills about two inches deep and a foot apart. Place an inch of rich sifted soil in each drill, and upon this sow the seed very thinly, covering it about a quarter of an inch. If the weather be dry, give a gentle soaking of water, and finish with a dusting of soot to prevent vermin from eating off the seedlings. Thin the plants to six inches apart, and they may remain in the seed-rows until the end of September. Whether they are then transplanted straight to blooming quarters, or put into a cold frame for the winter, depends on soil and climate. In the southern counties, and on light land, it will generally be safe to winter Hollyhocks in the open, with merely a shelter of dry fern or litter. But in heavy loam or clay the risk is too great, and the cold frame must be resorted to. In this they will be secure, and can be ventilated as weather permits. As the season advances give more air, until they are planted out in May.

IMPATIENS SULTANI

Sultan's Balsam.   Tender annual

EARLY sowing should be avoided for two reasons. The seed germinates but slowly in dull weather, and the seedlings when raised are almost certain to damp off. We do not advise a start before March, and not then unless a steady heat of 60° or 65° can be relied on. Sow in well-drained pots, filled with soil composed of two parts of turfy loam and one part of leaf-soil, with very little sand added. The seedlings are exceedingly brittle at the outset, and re-potting should not be attempted until they are about an inch high. Even

·then they need delicate handling, and after the task is accomplished they should be promptly placed in a warm frame or propagating pit for a few days. In June or July the plants should reach 48-sized pots, but they must not be transferred to the conservatory without careful hardening, or the whole of the flowers will fall.

JACOBEA. *See* SENECIO

LOBELIA

Annual and perennial; half-hardy

THERE are several distinct classes of Lobelia, differing materially in height and habit. For dwarf beds or edgings the *compact* varieties should alone be used. These grow from four to six inches high, and form dense balls of flowers. The *spreading* class, such as *L. speciosa* and *L. Paxtoniana*, is in deserved repute for positions which do not demand an exact limit to the line of colouring. The *gracilis* strain is displayed to advantage in suspended baskets, window boxes, rustic work, vases, and any position where an appearance of graceful negligence is aimed at. The *ramosa* section grows from six to twelve inches high, and produces much larger flowers than the classes previously named.

All the foregoing can be treated as annuals; and from sowings made in February or March, plants may be raised in good time for bedding out in May. Use sandy soil, and place the seed-pans in a temperature of about 60°, taking care to keep them moist. By the end of March or beginning of April the seedlings will be ready for transferring to pots, pans, or boxes. The last named are very serviceable for this flower, for they afford opportunity of pricking off the seedlings at moderate distances, which produces a tufty habit of growth well adapted to the end in view. A gentle heat will start them, and they will give no trouble afterwards, except on one point, which happens to be of considerable importance. It is that the plants should never be allowed to produce a flower while in pots or boxes. Pick off every bud until they are in final positions, and then, having taken hold of the soil, they will bloom profusely until the very end of the season.

Lobelias make elegant pot plants, yet they cannot be grown satisfactorily in pots. The difficulty is easily surmounted by putting them out a foot apart in a good open position, and if possible in a rather stiff soil. When they have developed into fine clumps, lift them with care and place them in pots, avoiding injury to the roots. This method will produce a display of colour which cannot be attained by exclusive pot culture.

From the best strains of seed it is almost certain that some plants will revert to long-lost characters. Florists are striving to obviate this, but it will require time. Meanwhile there are two ways of dealing with the difficulty. Some growers prefer to raise plants from seed, and take cuttings from approved specimens for the next season. This plan insures almost the robust growth and free-flowering qualities of seedlings, combined with exactitude in height and colour. But it necessitates holding a stock through the winter, and this may be a serious matter to many. The simpler proceeding, and one which answers well in practice, is to remove any plants from the pans or boxes which show the least deviation from the true type. A few kept in reserve in pots will supply the place of any 'rogues' which may be detected after planting out.

The handsome perennial section of Lobelias remains for consideration, and we are bound to remark that it obtains less attention than it deserves, especially as the most ordinary routine culture will suffice for these plants. They are partial to moisture, and also to a deep rich loam. A sowing on moderate heat in March will secure plants fit for bedding out in May. They may also be grown entirely without the aid of artificial heat from sowings in June or July. Employ pots or seed-pans, and pot off singly immediately the plants are large enough to handle. The protection of a cold frame or hand-light is all that is necessary during winter, and the planting out may be done in May. These Lobelias reach two feet in height, and make excellent companions to such flowers as *Anemone japonica alba*, *Gaura Lindheimeri*, and *Hyacinthus candicans*. The dark metallic foliage and dazzling scarlet flowers also have an imposing effect as the back row of a ribbon border. Both *L. cardinalis* and *L. Victoria* come true from seed.

MARIGOLD

Tagetes. Half-hardy annual

MARIGOLDS of several classes are valued for the profuse display of their golden flowers in the later summer months. The choicest are the so-called French, or *Tagetes patula*, whice have richly coloured and striped flowers, and are judged by the florists' standards because of their high quality. The most generally useful are the African or *Tagetes erecta*, which make large bushy plants with flowers 'piled high' in the centre; the colours are intense orange and yellow in various shades. The bedding section is represented by *Tagetes signata*, a very neat plant, with fine foliage and rather small orange-coloured flowers produced in great plenty. In hot seasons and on dry soils this proves an admirable substitute for the Calceolaria, which does not thrive when short of food, whereas the Tagetes bears drought and a poor soil with patience, and up to a certain point with advantage. Sow all these in March in a moderate heat, and prick the plants out in the usual way, taking care finally to allot them sunny positions. The section of Pot Marigolds, *Calendula officinalis*, comprises many fine varieties, one of which ('Meteor') is delicately striped, and may be regarded as a true florist's flower, worth a place in the choicest garden. These may be sown on the open border in March, April, and May, and the best place for them is in the full sun on a rather dry poor soil, but they are not particular, provided they are not much shaded.

MARVEL OF PERU

Mirabilis Jalapa. Half-hardy perennial

THIS flower may be treated either as an annual or as a biennial. As an annual the plants are small, but very compact and effective, the leaves and flowers forming round glittering masses in the late summer and autumn months. When the roots are saved and planted out in April larger plants are obtained, but there is no advance in quality over the very neat and sparkling specimens raised from seed. Sow on heat in March and April, and treat as Balsams until the time arrives for planting out. A rich sandy loam suits them, and they like full exposure to sunshine.

MIGNONETTE

Reseda odorata. Hardy annual

MIGNONETTE is so much prized that we must devote to it a paragraph, although there is little to be said. As in many places it appears from year to year from self-sown seeds, it will be evident that Mignonette may be grown with the simplicity of a farm crop. And it should be so grown where bees are kept and space can be afforded it, for Mignonette honey is of the finest quality in flavour and fragrance. As a border plant we have but to sow where it is to remain, at different times from March to midsummer. It is important to thin early and severely, for any one plant left alone will soon cover a square foot, and in some circumstances a square yard. In pot culture it should be remembered that Mignonette does not transplant well ; therefore, having sown, say, a dozen seeds in each of a batch of 48- or 32-sized pots, the young plants must be thinned down to five, or even three, in each pot, as soon as they begin to grow freely. If small plants are wanted early, leave five in a pot ; if larger plants are wanted later, leave only three, or even only one. So accommodating is this plant that it may be forced for early flowers, or be grown as a hardy annual without any care at all, or even to a tree of great dimensions, and tree-like specimens can be kept for any number of years if the cultivator is careful never to allow them to ripen seeds. But it is better practice to raise young plants and grow them to specimen size by regular and moderate shifts, nipping out all blooms that show until the plants are large enough, and then having flowered them, it is more profitable to destroy than to keep them. A rich friable soil is requisite, and plenty of light. But the plant will bear a close atmosphere, and even damp in winter fairly well, so that there are but few difficulties in the way of producing handsome specimens. For winter and spring, sow in 32- or 48-pots in August, and keep them as hardy as possible until it becomes necessary to put them under glass for the winter. Several strains of different tints are now at the command of cultivators of this favourite flower.

MIMULUS

Monkey Flower.   Hardy perennial

THIS flower will grow in almost any soil, although a moist retentive loam and a shady situation are best adapted for it. There are many varieties, differing in height, and all are worth growing, both in pots and borders. *M. Roezli*, from its dwarf habit and golden yellow flowers, makes an effective edging plant. If sown in February or March, and treated as greenhouse annuals, they will all flower in the first year. Sowings in the open ground during summer will supply plants for blooming in the following season. The Mimulus is quite hardy, and the most ordinary care will suffice for it. Water in plenty it must have, or the flowering period will be curtailed.

The well-known Musk is a Mimulus (*M. moschatus*), and is as easily grown from seed as other varieties. It makes a valuable pot plant.

MYOSOTIS

Forget-me-not. Perennials, hardy and half-hardy

AN impression prevails that all the varieties of Myosotis are semi-aquatic, and can only be grown satisfactorily in very damp shady places. Now, it is quite true that most of them bloom for a longer period in a moist than in a dry soil. Still they will all flower freely, and last a considerable time in any garden border, and *M. azorica* requires no special degree of moisture to bring it to perfection. This plant is scarcely hardy, and perhaps the fact is not entirely to be regretted, for it possesses a high value for indoor decoration, both on the score of its habit and of its beauty. When grown in pots, the most simple frame or greenhouse treatment will insure success. In the open border it can be employed in the same manner as half-hardy annuals. If required to bloom in spring or early summer, sow in the preceding July or August in a rather light compost. Prick off the seedlings into boxes or pans about an inch apart, and winter them in a cold frame by plunging in ashes or cocoa-nut fibre. Free exposure whenever practicable will promote a sturdy growth. In March the plants should be transferred to fresh soil, still using pans or boxes, but allowing a little more space between the seedlings, and in May they should be planted in flowering positions. Sowings in February and March will produce a display of bloom from July to September. These sowings must be made in gentle heat, and will require nursing under glass until all danger of frost is over.

All the hardy varieties may be sown from June to August for a brilliant display in the following spring. The seed should be put into a prepared seed-bed under the shelter of a wall or hedge; and when winter is over, the plants should be transferred to blooming quarters at the earliest opportunity.

PANSY

Viola tricolor.   Hardy perennial

PANSY growing is no longer a mystery, as it was by some regarded in years not far removed.   Seed, too, is now of such a quality, and is saved in so many distinct colours, that for all ordinary purposes the trouble of striking cuttings and keeping stocks in pots all the winter through is mere waste of labour and pit-room.   The Pansy is a little fastidious, but not severely so.   It thrives in a cool climate, with partial shade in high summer, and in a rich, moist, sandy soil.   But stagnant water at the roots is unfavourable, as also is a burning heat on a dry soil.   Notwithstanding all this, the Pansy will grow almost anywhere and anyhow ; but as we prize fine flowers of this old favourite, it should have reasonable care to do justice to its great merits.

A thick sowing is very liable to damp off : therefore sow thinly either in pots or boxes in April.   The thin sowing, moreover, renders it possible to take out the forward plants without disturbing the remainder.   Make up the requisite number of pans, and in a short time transfer the plants to some cool corner, where the soil has been prepared with a heavy dressing of manure.   When they have become stocky, remove to beds or borders, with balls of earth attached to the roots.   Should the surrounding soil become set by heavy rain or by watering, a slight stirring of the surface will prove beneficial.

The first flowers are not a criterion of the value of a Pansy, and the plant should not be hastily cast aside because premature blossoms are comparatively insignificant.   Their removal will strengthen the plant for better results a little later.

Seed sown in the open ground during the summer months will readily germinate, and the seedlings need no attention beyond thinning to about six inches apart until they are ready for transferring to their proper positions, where they will produce a mass of bloom in the following spring.

The Pansy puts forth its buds very early in the year.   Whether they are particularly tasty, or the scarcity of other young vegetable growth gives them undue prominence, we know not, but certain it is that sparrows show a marked partiality for them.   And having once acquired a taste for the plants, these impudent marauders will not leave them alone; they evidently regard Pansy buds as the perfection of a winter salad. Their depredations can be prevented by an application of water flavoured with quassia or paraffin oil, which must be repeated after rain.

PELARGONIUM

Stork's-bill.   Greenhouse perennial

ALL kinds of Pelargonium may be raised from seed with the certainty of giving satisfaction if the work be well done. An amateur, who contributed to the production of symmetrical circular flowers in the Zonal section, found that by very simple cultivation Zonals began to bloom in one hundred days from the date of sowing the seed, and some of those that flowered earliest proved to be the finest. However, as regards this point, the cultivator will soon discover that there is only one rule, and that is to have seed of the best and wait for results. The simplest greenhouse culture suffices to raise Pelargoniums from seed. Some growers sow in July or August; others in January or February. The summer sowing necessitates careful winter keeping, and the flowers appear earlier than those from spring-sown seed. But the spring sowing is the easier to manage, and is recommended to all beginners. Any light, sandy loam will serve for these plants, and it is well to flower the principal bulk of them in 48- and 32-sized pots, for if grown to a great size the date of flowering is deferred without any corresponding advantage.

PENTSTEMON

Hardy perennial

PENTSTEMONS are treated as advised for herbaceous Lobelias. It is not needful, therefore, to keep any of them through the winter unless they will take care of themselves in the open border. As a rule, the seedling Pentstemons are hardy, and will scarcely feel the winter on a comparatively dry soil.

PETUNIA

Half-hardy perennial

THE Petunia affords another example of the immense strides accomplished in the art of seed saving. Not many years ago the colours were few, and the blossoms comparatively insignificant. Now the single strains produce large flowers, varied in colour and beautiful in form. There are striped, blotched, veined, and selfs (or whole colours) in almost endless diversity. Some are plain-edged, others elegantly fringed. The double varieties also come so nearly true to their types, that there is little necessity for keeping a stock through the winter. Plants raised from seed of the *grandiflora* strain embrace a wide range of resplendent colours, and the doubles are perfect rosettes, exquisitely finished in form and marking.

There is only one possible way of obtaining double seedlings, and it is from seed saved from the finest single blooms which have been fertilised with pollen of good double flowers. Plants raised from such seed may be relied on to produce from twenty to forty per cent. of double flowers of great beauty, and those which come single will be of the large-flowered type.

The dwarf varieties attain the height of five or six inches only, and make admirable edging and bedding plants. The taller strains reach two feet, and are handsome subjects for border and shrubbery work. Both dwarf and tall sections are sufficiently brilliant and free-flowering to produce a beautiful display as pot plants in the greenhouse and conservatory.

For indoor decoration, the third week in January will be early enough to commence operations. Two parts of leaf-mould, one of loam, and one of sharp sand, make an excellent soil for them. Fill the pots or seed-pans within half an inch of the rim, and press the soil firmly down. Sow thinly on an even surface, and cover the seed with almost pure sand. Keep the pots or pans uniformly moist with a fine rose and a light hand, and in a temperature of about 60°. Greater heat will render the seedlings weak and straggling. From this condition it will take some skill and much time to redeem them; indeed, they may not produce a good display of flowers until the season is well-nigh over. Just as the seed is germinating is a critical time for Petunias, and a little extra watchfulness then will be fully repaid.

In February the sun has not sufficient power to do mischief, so that shading is generally unnecessary. An even temperature and freedom from draughts should insure seedlings strong enough to prick off by the end of that month. Put the plants into seed-pans about an inch apart, so that the first leaves just touch the soil, still using a light compost.

In April they should be ready for transferring to small 60-pots. Subsequently they must be potted on as growth demands, until they reach the 48- or even the 32-size. After re-potting place the plants in a sheltered part of the house or frame, where shade can, if necessary, be given until the roots are established. Frequent sprinklings of water, and a temperature of 60° or 65°, will soon give them a vigorous start. The lights ought to be put down in good time in the evening, but this must be done with judgment, or the plants will lose their healthy colour and assume a yellowish tinge. Insufficient drainage has a precisely similar effect. In about ten days air may be given more freely, and then no suitable opportunity of exposing them should be lost.

In raising Petunias for bedding, the same conditions are applicable; but as it is useless to put them into the open ground until the weather is warm and settled, the sowing need not be made until the end of February or the beginning of March. And for bedding there is no occasion to put the plants into larger pots than the 60-size. It will be necessary to give these seedlings shade in their young state after they have been pricked off or potted.

The beds or borders intended for Petunias will be better without recent manure, for this tends to the excessive production of foliage, and defers the flowering until late in the season. Do not be tempted by the first sunny day to put them out, but wait for settled weather. A cutting east wind, such as we sometimes have in May, will ruin them irretrievably. Each plant of the tall class will occupy a space of two feet, and the dwarfs may be one foot apart.

For the double varieties two modifications in practice are advisable. In potting off the single seedlings those that are weakly may be discarded as worthless, but with the doubles it will be almost safe to reverse that proceeding. In proportion as the plants are robust are they likely to prove single, and the comparatively feeble seedlings will probably produce the double flowers. More space must be given the doubles in beds, and larger pots indoors. All Petunias are impatient of being pot-bound, and this applies especially to the double varieties. They will, if treated generously, do ample justice to the

8- or even the 10-inch size. The growth should not be hurried at any stage, and if the foliage has a dark healthy green colour, free from blight, there will be magnificent flowers four or five inches across. The final shift should be into a sound compost, consisting, if possible, of good loam and leaf-mould in equal parts, with sufficient sand added to insure drainage. About a fortnight later commence giving weak manure water once a week instead of the ordinary watering, and as the buds appear it may be increased in strength, and be administered twice a week until the flowers expand.

Petunias are accommodating in their growth, and may be trained into various forms. The pyramid and fan-shape are most common, and the least objectionable. We confess, however, to a feeling of antipathy to the creation of fanciful shapes by means of plants, no matter what they may be. It is a necessity of our artificial conditions of culture that many of them should be trained and tied to produce shapely specimens, but the more nearly the gardener's art approaches nature, the greater pleasure we derive from his labours.

PHLOX DRUMMONDII

Half-hardy annual

Those who are acquainted with the older forms of this annual might fail to recognise a friend under its new and improved appearance. There are now several beautiful types, each possessing characteristics of its own, and all producing flowers that are perfect in form and brilliant in colour. The *grandiflora* sections make splendid bedding plants, but the *compact* varieties are highly prized for effective massing and general usefulness. The latter range in height from six to nine inches, and are therefore eminently suitable for edgings and borders as well as for bedding. They bloom profusely for a long period, not only in the open ground, but also as pot plants in the greenhouse or conservatory, where they are conspicuous for the richness of their display.

Sow seed of all the varieties in February or March in well-drained pans or shallow boxes. Any good sifted soil made firm will suit them, and every seed should be separately pressed into it, allowing about an inch between each; then cover with fine soil. This will generally give sufficient space between the plants to save pricking off; but if the growth becomes so strong as to render a transfer necessary, lift every alternate plant, fill the vacant spots with soil, and those left will have room to develop. Pot the plants that are taken out, give them a start in a frame, and shade from direct sunshine. Phloxes should not be coddled, for the best results are always obtained from plants which are most sturdy, and have been hardened as far as possible by free access of air from their earliest stage of growth. This does not imply that they are to be rudely transferred from protection to the open air. The change can easily be managed gradually until some genial evening makes it perfectly safe to expose them fully. A space of about two feet each way is required for each plant of the *grandiflora* class, but a more modest allowance of nine or twelve inches will suffice for the dwarf compact varieties. Before they are put out, the plants must be free from aphis; if not, fumigation should be resorted to once or twice until there is a clearance of the pest.

PHLOX, PERENNIAL

Hardy perennial

To flower the Perennial Phlox during the first year is easy enough. Sow in the first week of March in shallow boxes, and put into a moderate heat. In due time prick out into boxes filled with light rich soil, and having hardened them in the usual way, plant out a foot apart in a good bed, and help if needful with an occasional watering. They will frequently begin to flower in August, and continue until the frosts of November make an end of them. Those plants which do not flower in the first season will bloom freely in the following summer.

PICOTEE

Dianthus Caryophyllus fl. pl. Hardy perennial

The remarks under Carnation are equally applicable to the Picotee.

PINK

Dianthus plumarius. Hardy perennial

This flower can be raised from seed in the manner advised for Carnations. The foliage maintains its colour during the severest winter, and is therefore worth consideration for furnishing the border, to say nothing of the abundant display of perfumed flowers which the plants afford in early summer.

POLYANTHUS

Primula variabilis. Hardy perennial

THE florists' varieties of Polyanthus are not so robust as commoner kinds; they will, however, endure more wet and shade than the Auricula, but must be protected from severe frost. Seed may be sown from May to August, on a shady border. Prick off the seedlings when large enough to handle. A sowing in February or March in pans will produce strong specimens for flowering in the following year. All the varieties can be grown in a bed with a cool shaded aspect, or in pots sunk in ashes in cold frames. They do not require a rich soil; a strong and fibrous loam with a little leaf-mould is sufficient. It is very important to pot the plants firmly and deeply, so that the roots sent out at the collar may at once catch the soil. Protect the bloom from inclement weather, and the foliage at all times from high winds. The plants should never flag for want of water, and green fly must be kept down by syringing if the plants are in beds. Some good solution will be necessary against red spider if through starvation in a dry situation it has been permitted to gain a footing. On passing out of flower the plants will split up into several heads, when they may be separated and potted singly.

POPPY

Papaver. Hardy annual and hardy perennial

THE recent developments of this flower have brought it into great and deserved popularity, and it may be safely affirmed that no other subject in our gardens affords a more imposing display of brilliant colouring during the blooming period. The delicate beauty of the Shirley Poppies is alone sufficient to create a reputation for the entire class, and the huge flowers of the double varieties make a gorgeous show. All the varieties are eminently adapted for enlivening shrubbery borders and the sides of carriage drives. Seeds should be sown where the plants are intended to flower, because it is difficult to transplant with any measure of success. During March or April sow in lines or groups, and thin to about a foot apart. Large clumps of some of the bolder colours should be sown in spots that are visible from a distance, and they will present glowing masses of flowers.

PORTULACA

Purslane. Half-hardy annual

This is a splendid subject when the weather favours it. In a dry hot season, and on a sandy soil, Portulacas can be grown as easily as Cress. Sowings are sometimes made early in the year in greenhouses or frames; but as a rule it is a vain attempt. Wait until May or June, when the weather appears settled; then put the seed into the open border, and the lighter the soil, and the hotter the season, the more brilliant will be the display of flowers. Sow on raised beds, in rows six or nine inches apart, and cover the seed with sand or fine earth. Should a period of rain ensue, the raised beds have a distinct advantage over a flat surface, and rows afford opportunity for stirring the soil and keeping down weeds.

PRIMROSE

Primula vulgaris. Hardy perennial

The mere name of this flower is sufficient to recall visions of spring, and perhaps of happy visits to its haunts in days gone by. But many ardent lovers of the Primrose may not know that the strains which are now in favour embrace a wide range of colour, from pure white to deep crimson or maroon, and various shades of yellow and orange. In fact, in a batch of seedlings nearly every plant may differ from its companions. They all agree, however, in possessing the delicate perfume which is characteristic of the hardy woodland favourite. Fancy Primroses are prized as pot and border flowers, and they fully reward florists for all the care which has been devoted to their improvement. They will bloom satisfactorily in any shady spot; but to grow them to perfection requires a stiff moist loam, on the north side of some hedge or shrubbery, where glimpses of sunshine occasionally play upon them. Here large flowers, intense in colour, will be abundantly produced far into the spring.

The seed may be sown from May until July. If inclined to take some pains in raising the plants—and they are certainly worth it—sow in seed-pans in ordinary potting soil; sprinkle a little sand over the seed, and as a finish press firmly down. Sheets of glass laid over the pans and turned daily will prevent rapid evaporation, and help to keep the soil uniformly moist. The seedlings may either be potted once, and then be planted out, or if strong enough they may be transferred straight to flowering positions. If this mode of procedure is too troublesome, prepare a shady patch of ground by deep digging; make it firm and level, and on this sow in shallow drills, covering the seed very lightly. A dressing of soot over the surface, and a cordon of ashes round it, will keep off slugs. Thin if necessary, and when the plants are strong enough, remove to their proper quarters. In February the buds will begin to show, and those intended for pots should be allowed to reveal their colours before they are taken up, so that a variety may be obtained. From a retentive soil each plant with its surrounding earth may be taken out almost exactly of the size required, and it should be rather smaller than the pot which has to accommodate it. A light soil must be watered the day before the operation, or the roots will be injuriously exposed. When potted, place the plants in a shaded cold frame or greenhouse, allowing them plenty of space, and withhold water until it is absolutely necessary. At first they should be kept close, but as the roots become established, gradually give air more and more freely. Cool, slow treatment is all that is necessary. Any attempt to hurry the growth will only weaken the plants, and ruin the colour of the flowers. Just before the buds open, one or two applications of manure water will be beneficial. When the display in pots is over, if the plants are put out in a shady border, it is not unlikely they will flower again late in the season.

PRIMULA SINENSIS

Greenhouse annual

To enjoy the bloom for a long period make successive sowings in May and June. A further sowing may be made in July if necessary. We prefer to use new pots which have been soaked in water; but if these are not at hand scrub some old ones clean, for Primulas are scrupulous from the outset, and it is by apparent trifles that some growers produce plants so immensely superior to others treated with less care. Provide free drainage, and place a little dry sifted moss over the crocks. Any fairly good rich soil will be suitable, but a mixture of equal parts of sound fibrous loam and leaf-mould, with a small addition of silver sand, is best. Press this compost firmly into the pots to within half an inch of the top. Water before sowing, and sprinkle sufficient sand over the surface to cover the soil. On this sand sow evenly and thinly, for it is well known that the finest new Primula seed comes up irregularly, and a thin sowing admits of the removal of plants that may be ready, without disturbing the remainder. Cover the seed with just enough fine soil to hide the sand, and gently press the surface. Place the pots in a sheltered part of the greenhouse, protected from draughts and direct sunlight; a small glazed frame will be useful for this purpose. While the seed is germinating, the temperature should not rise above $70°$, or fall below $50°$. Immediately the plants are large enough, prick off round the rim of small pots; these do best when placed in a propagating box. Water with care, and shade if necessary. When established give air, which should be daily increased until the plants will bear placing on the greenhouse stage. Transfer singly to thumb pots and subsequently shift into larger sizes as may be requisite, but never do this until the pots are filled with roots, and always put the plants in firmly up to the collar. During July, August, and up to the middle of September, expose freely to the air in any convenient position where shelter can be given in unfavourable weather.

Where there is no greenhouse, but only a hot-bed, it is still possible to grow good Primulas, with care and patience. The instructions given for treatment in the greenhouse may easily be adapted to the pit or frame, only there must be a little more watchfulness in affording shade on sunny days to prevent overheating.

Endeavour to give the plants a robust constitution from the first, for weak rickety things cannot produce a satisfactory bloom. Primulas need a long period of growth before they flower; hence they should never be subjected to a forcing temperature. Sufficient heat must be provided to raise the plants, but afterwards the aim should be to render Primulas as nearly hardy as possible before cold weather sets in. There must, however, be ample protection against frost, damp, and cutting winds.

Three very elegant varieties of garden Primula, *P. obconica*, *P. japonica* and *P. rosea*, are worthy of attention. Sow in pots or pans in summer and place them in a cool house or pit until the seedlings are ready for separate pots, prior to the transfer to open ground. The seed germinates slowly and irregularly.

RANUNCULUS

Crowfoot. Half-hardy perennial

THE Ranunculus can be grown either from seed or from roots. The seed is sown from January to March, in boxes four to six inches deep, and should be dibbled in separately about an inch and a half apart. A cool greenhouse or frame is the proper place for the boxes until the spring is somewhat advanced. A little extra care is requisite to insure free growth and a hardy constitution, and the roots should not be turned out of the boxes until they have ceased growing, and are quite ripe; then they may be stored for planting in November and February. For particulars on the treatment of roots, see page 304.

RICINUS

Castor-oil Plant. Half-hardy annual

ALTHOUGH this plant flowers freely, it is grown in the sub-tropical garden principally for its noble ornamental foliage, and also in the shrubbery border, either alone or in conjunction with such other fine subjects as Canna, Solanum, Tobacco, and Wigandia.

To have plants ready for making a show in early summer, they must be raised as half-hardy annuals in February or March. From the commencement a rich soil and abundant supplies of water are necessary for the production of stately specimens. The seed is large, and may be put singly into pots, or three or four in each, and the latter is the usual practice. A temperature of about 60° will bring them up. If several plants are grown in a pot, they must be separated while quite young, and put into small pots filled with very rich soil. It is almost impossible to have the compost too rich, so long as drainage is quite safe. When the pot is full of roots shift to a larger size, and commence the process of hardening, in readiness for planting out in June. This is worth some care, for if the plant receives a check when put out, it may take a long time to recover, and then part of the brief growing season will be wasted. Many gardeners never raise Ricinus in heat, but trust entirely to a sowing in the open on the first day of May. The seeds are put in three inches deep, in groups of three or four, and finally the plants are thinned to one at each station.

Prepare the soil in advance by deep digging, and the incorporation of an abundant supply of manure. The most effectual way of doing it is to take out the earth to a depth of eighteen inches or two feet, and fill the space with decayed manure and loam, chiefly the former. Upon this put out the plant, or sow seed as may be determined. If this is too great a tax upon resources, or the near presence of shrubs renders the proceeding impossible, drive a bar into the soil, which, if light, can be readily worked into a fair-sized hole. Fill this with rich stuff nearly to the top, and over it either put the plant or sow seed. A heavy top dressing round each stem is also desirable, and the application of copious supplies of water will carry the goodness down to the roots. Sub-tropical plants are only a source of disappointment under niggardly treatment, but they amply repay all the care and generosity which a liberal hand may lavish upon them. The plants will need the support of stakes to save them from injury in a high wind.

SCHIZANTHUS

Half-hardy annual

To a certain extent this flower has recovered from the undeserved neglect to which careless cultivation had in some degree consigned it. We have no more elegant half-hardy annuals for specimen culture than the varieties of this very distinct plant. The seed should be sown in heat in March, and the plants can be potted on for flowering in the conservatory, or may be planted out in the open border. But to obtain fine conservatory specimens the seed must be sown in August or September, and the plants kept through the winter in a light, airy house, sufficiently heated to exclude frost. *S. retusus* and its white variety are also extremely useful for open-air decoration, and may be treated as ordinary half-hardy annuals.

SENECIO, or JACOBEA

Groundsel. Hardy annual, and half-hardy perennial

MANY varieties of Jacobea are known to gardens, but the dwarf crimson, purple, rose and white varieties take the lead for beauty and usefulness. They are remarkably accommodating plants, adapted for beds or the greenhouse. Sow early in a moderate heat, and grow on with liberal care, and when bedded out the plants will produce myriads of bright flowers, until frost puts a stop to them. Any good soil which does not become pasty will suit, and full exposure to sunshine is essential to the production of a rich display of colour.

SILENE

Catchfly. Hardy annual

SILENES may be better grown from seed than from cuttings in every case that can be thought of. It is well to sow-in August or September the bedding kinds that are required to flower early, but for the rest a March sowing is all sufficient. As the most useful sorts are perfectly hardy, the only protection required in winter is against damp rather than frost, and a cold pit or frame will suffice for those in pans and boxes. The best soil for Silenes is that which is sandy and dry, still, they will do very well in loam, provided the situation is not damp. On heavy, damp clay lands, it is best not to grow Silenes at all, but on dry, sandy spots, they may be planted out in autumn in the beds in which they are to flower in the spring.

SOLANUM

Nightshade. Annual and perennial ; half-hardy

SOLANUMS are of importance, some as greenhouse plants, and others as sub-tropical bedders. They require good cultivation, and a light, rich soil, being somewhat tender in constitution, and liable to the attacks of the red spider. March is early enough to sow the seed, but for ordinary purposes April is to be preferred. By the middle of June, the plants will be strong enough to put out, and with genial weather will make rapid progress. Those grown for their berries may be sown from February onwards, as it is important to secure bushy plants before they begin to flower, and an early start insures an early ripening of their handsome berries.

STOCK

Mathiola. Annual and biennial ; half-hardy

STOCKS comprise three divisions—the Annual, which includes all the Ten-week and Pyramidal forms ; the Intermediate, so excellent for pot culture; and the Biennial, which includes the well-known Brompton and Queen varieties—all splendid border flowers.

ANNUAL STOCKS are a large family, and include a wonderful variety of colours, as well as considerable diversity in the habit of growth. For their brightness, durability, and fragrance, they are deservedly popular. It is usual to sow the seed under glass from the middle to the end of March. Pans or shallow boxes, filled with sweet sandy soil, make the best of seed-beds, and it may be well to say at once that no plants pay better for cultural care than the subjects now under consideration. Sow thinly, that the plants may have room to become stout while yet in the seed-bed, and from the very outset endeavour to impart a hardy constitution by giving air freely whenever the weather is suitable. This does not mean that they are to be subjected to some cutting blast that will cripple the plants beyond redemption, but that no opportunity should be lost of partial or entire exposure whenever the atmosphere is sufficiently genial to be of benefit to them. If a cold frame on a spent hot-bed can be spared, it may be utilised by pricking off the seedlings into it, or the pans and boxes may simply be placed under its protection. The nearer the seedlings can be kept to the glass, the less will be the disposition to become leggy. In transplanting to the open ground, it is worth some trouble to induce each plant to carry a nice ball of soil attached to its roots.

On light, friable land, Ten-week Stocks can be successfully grown from sowings made in the open about the end of April. The character of the season must be some guide to the time chosen, and the sowing in this case should be rather thicker than in the seed-pans. Should the seed germinate well, severe thinning will have to be practised as growth demands. This method of culture entirely prevents the loss by mildew, which so often proves fatal to young transplanted seedlings. Give the plants a thoroughly rich, friable soil; indeed, it is difficult to have it too good for them, and there is no comparison between plants grown on a poor border and those grown in luxuriance. Some growers make a little trench for each row of seed, and this affords a certain degree of protection from cutting winds, and also forms a channel for water when there is a necessity for administering it. In a showery season, the plants will appear in about twelve days, but in dry weather it will be longer, and one or more gentle morning waterings may be necessary to bring them up. The distance between the rows must be determined by the variety. Nine inches is sufficient for the dwarf sorts;

twelve or fifteen inches will not be too much for the medium and tall kinds.

Slugs may be kept off by a dusting of soot or wood ashes, and some precaution must also be adopted to prevent birds from disturbing the seed-bed.

On a heavy soil, it is next to useless to sow in the open, but with a little management it will still be possible to grow good Stocks by transplanting. Make a small hot-bed about the first week in April. Let it settle down for a week, then cover with four to six inches of the best soil at command. Upon this, draw drills, six inches apart and an inch deep. Sow in these drills, and cover the seed with fine soil. Water the whole bed gently, but thoroughly, with a fine rose. Half a brick at each corner will support a common hurdle, covered with a mat to protect from inclement weather, either by night or day. But do not keep this, or any other means of protection that may be substituted for it, upon the bed for an unnecessary hour, for Stocks should be grown as nearly hardy as possible. Before the plants are ready for transferring to blooming quarters, an attempt should be made to reduce a stiff soil to a friable state. Where the plants are to stand, cut small trenches, and fill them with any light soil enriched with decayed manure. In these rows the Stocks will thrive, and yield an ample return for the little trouble bestowed in raising them. A few plants potted separately will be certain to prove useful in filling up blanks caused by failure.

It may be well to mention a fact here which is not always remembered, although the knowledge of it is generally assumed. Seed can only be saved from single flowers, but those who have made a study of the business find little difficulty in selecting plants, and treating them in such a manner that seed obtained from them will produce a large percentage of double blossoms in the following generation. The experience of the most skilled growers has not, however, yet enabled them to save seed which will result entirely in double-flowering plants; and perhaps this circumstance is scarcely to be regretted, for should the time ever arrive when there are no single Stocks, there will be an end to this valuable class of annuals. In keeping the various colours true, there is one very awkward fact. Certain sorts invariably produce a difference in colour between the double and single flowers. This is clearly illustrated in the sulphur-yellow varieties, in which the single flowers always come white. Hence in saving seed, it is impossible so to select the plants that an occasional white does not also appear among the double blossoms

INTERMEDIATE STOCKS are most valuable for house and window decoration in spring. It is easy to grow them in pots, if the protection of a house or pit can be given during the winter to preserve them from frost. A simple plan is to sow in August or early in September five or six seeds in 48-sized pots, and plunge these in ashes under a frame until March. Thin to three plants in each, and of course a larger pot with more plants can be used when desirable. Give air whenever possible, and water regularly. There is no need for artificial heat, indeed it is not well to hurry the plants in any way. A good top dressing of rich soil is advisable before flowering, and as the buds appear, manure water, weak at first but gradually increased in strength, may be given once a week until in full bloom. If seed be sown in March the plants will flower in the succeeding autumn.

BROMPTON STOCKS are remarkable for the size of their spikes of bloom, and their striking appearance during May and June. They do well under the shelter of trees and shrubs, and on cold soils this position will save them from damage by frosts. In some seasons it may answer to sow at once in blooming quarters, but the practice is too precarious to be risked generally. A safer method is to sow in June or July, in seed-pans. Place these under shelter until the plants are an inch high, then stand them in the open for a week before transplanting. Have ready a piece of freshly dug soil, and on a dull day put them out at eight to twelve inches apart. If the growth is too rapid during September, it may be advisable to lift them and plant again, for the winter must not find them soft and succulent. There should be hard stems and sturdy growth to carry them through the cold weather. In districts that are specially unfavourable, it may be necessary to pot each plant singly in the 60-size, and plunge these in ashes in a cold frame, or under the shelter of a south wall, until severe weather is past, and they can then be turned out into the borders.

We commend these beautiful Stocks to all who love hardy and fragrant flowers.

STREPTOCARPUS

Cape Primrose. Tender perennial

THE hybrids are a very striking race, invaluable for greenhouse and conservatory decoration, producing a continuous succession of large trumpet-shaped flowers, embracing colours ranging from pure white, through lavender, purple, violet, rose, and red, to rich rosy-purple. This highly decorative plant is easily grown, and seed sown in January and February will produce plants which come into bloom the following June and July.

SUNFLOWER

Helianthus annuus. Hardy annual

THE utility of the Sunflower has been alluded to in a former page. Here we have only to regard the plant in its ornamental character, as an occupant of the shrubbery or flower border.

In addition to the common species, there are several strains which are adapted to special purposes. The dwarf variety grows about three feet high, and yet produces fine heads of bloom. The 'giant' attains the enormous height of eight or ten feet in a favourable season, and the flowers are of immense size. The double strain generally reaches six feet in height, and is valuable for its breadth of colour and enduring quality. There is no difficulty, therefore, in making a selection to suit the requirements of any border. The Sunflower can also be employed in one or more rows to make a boundary or to hide an unsightly fence, and some growers use it as a screen for flowers which will not bear full sunshine.

Seed may be raised very early in the season, and the plants can be brought forward in the manner usual with half-hardy annuals, but there is no necessity for this mode of growing them. Sow in April where the plants are to flower, on soil which has been abundantly manured to a depth of eighteen inches, and they will bloom in good time. As a large growth has to be made in a very brief period, water must not be stinted in dry weather.

SWEET PEA

Lathyrus odoratus. Hardy climbing annual

SINCE the Sweet Pea has been taken in hand by skilful hybridisers there has been a large accession of new colours, and at the same time the blossoms have been considerably increased in size without diminishing the free-flowering habit of the plant. On its decorative value in the garden we need not dwell; but as a subject for the adornment of vases and all purposes for which cut flowers are available, much has yet to be learned. Sweet Peas possess all the qualities desired in cut flowers, firm slender footstalks, brilliant and varied colours, exquisite grace and delicious perfume.

Spring sowing is usual and will continue to be generally practised, but those who have the courage to adopt autumn sowing will be rewarded with an earlier display of bloom, more vigorous growth and finer flowers. In the majority of gardens seed should be sown in August, again in February or March, followed by one or two successional sowings at intervals of a fortnight for insuring a prolonged supply of this flower far into autumnal days. Even in small gardens, where only a few clumps can be grown, it is unwise to depend on a single sowing. By a succession of sowings the risk of total loss is avoided.

Sweet Peas have two principal foes, the slug and the sparrow. Against the former the usual precautions, such as ashes, soot, lime, and various traps, are available; and the latter must by some means be prevented from doing mischief. After the buds show through the soil, it is generally too late for the adoption of remedies. Nearly all of the heads will be found nipped off and laid ready for inspection. One could almost forgive the marauders were food the object, but the birds appear to commit havoc from pure wantonness, and in the absence of precautions whole rows are sometimes destroyed in a single morning.

When two or three inches high supports should be given, and these may be primitive or decorative according to the will and pocket of the cultivator. The blooming period can be prolonged by the simple expedient of daily removing the newly formed seed-pods, a task in which children take delight—for a time. The ripening of only a few seed-pods speedily puts a stop to flowering.

TOBACCO

Nicotiana. Half-hardy annual

THE Tobacco plant is grown both for use and ornament, and in the latter capacity it is universally acceptable. The cultivation is that of half-hardy annuals, the seed being sown in heat in February or March, and the plants put out in June, or earlier. But in some places, more especially in the south of England, Tobacco seed sown on an open sunny border early in May will produce fine plants that will flower freely in August.

TORENIA

Greenhouse annual

Sow in a warm temperature in March or April. Prick off while small into pots, and subsequently pot the seedlings singly. Any fairly good compost will suit them. The branches will need support, and the plants must be kept free from green fly. The Torenias make very elegant pot plants, and they are also well adapted for hanging baskets and other ornamental contrivances.

TROPÆOLUM

Nasturtium, or Indian Cress. Hardy and half-hardy annuals

THE *Tropæolum tuberosum* is treated under the culture of flowering bulbs, so that here we have only to consider the varieties that are grown from seed. There are two distinct classes, both widely cultivated, for the seed is inexpensive, and the plants extremely showy and easily raised.

Tropæolum majus is the climbing Nasturtium, or great Indian Cress. The flower as originally obtained from Peru was a rich orange, marked with deep reddish-brown, but it has been developed into various shades of yellow and red culminating in a tint which is almost black. The leaves are nearly circular, and are attached to the long footstalks by the centre instead of at the margin. Loudon fancifully compares the leaf to a buckler, and the flower to an empty helmet. The Lobbianum section is close in habit, with smaller foliage borne on somewhat woolly stems. All the varieties bloom freely and constitute a brilliant class of climbers of great value for brightening up the backs of borders or hiding unsightly objects. After the seeds have been dibbled about an inch deep either in April or May the only attention the plants require is to nip out a straggling shoot occasionally, or prevent a stray branch from reaching over and smothering some plant which will not endure its embraces.

The well-known Canary Creeper—*T. canariense*—is a distinct variety, and as a half-hardy annual must be raised under protection. Unlike the others it needs a rich soil to insure vigorous growth. When liberally treated the entire plant will be covered with its bright fairy-like flowers, until frost ends its career.

The Tom Thumb, or Dwarf varieties make excellent bedding

plants, blooming far on into the autumn after many of the regular bedders have become faded and shabby. There is an extensive choice of colours in reds, yellows, and browns which come perfectly true from seed, and all possess the merit of flowering freely on very poor soil. They grow luxuriantly on rich land, but then the foliage becomes a mere mask under which the flowers are concealed. There is not one of the Tom Thumb class that may not be treated as a hardy annual, and all afford opportunity of making a gorgeous show of colour at a cost ridiculously disproportionate to the effect obtained. They are also admirably adapted for pot culture, making shapely plants covered with bloom for a long period.

As the flavour of the flowers and leaves somewhat resembles that of common Cress, they are frequently used in salads, and are accounted an excellent anti-scorbutic. The flowers are legitimately employed in decorating the salad-bowl, because they are not only ornamental but strictly edible.

In a green state the seeds of both tall and dwarf varieties make a first-rate pickle, which by some persons is preferred to capers.

VERBENA

Vervain. Hardy and half-hardy perennials

VERBENAS raised from the best strains of seed come true to colour, and the plants are models of health and vigour, and make resplendent beds. It is of the utmost importance to remember that the Verbena requires very little of the artificial heat to which it is commonly subjected, and which fully accounts for the frequency of disease. The seeds may be sown in boxes in January, February, and March, the earlier sowings naturally requiring more heat than the later ones. As the seedlings become large enough, they should be potted on and planted out in May, when they will flower throughout the summer, and far into the autumn.

Verbenas may also be raised from seed sown on a well-prepared bed in March, and the plants will appear towards the end of April, and should be planted out as they become fit. If this rough and ready method is thought too hazardous, the seed may be sown in March in boxes, and put into a frame, and if kept moist a lot of plants will appear in about a month, and when large enough these must be carefully lifted and potted. A rich, mellow, and very sweet soil is needed by the Verbena. Many of the failures that occur in its cultivation are not only traceable to the coddling of the plant under glass, but also to the careless way in which it is often planted on poor worn-out soil that has been cropped for years, and never refreshed with manure, or the sweetening effects of a good digging. Raising Verbenas from seed will restore this plant to the list of hardy, easily grown, thoroughly useful subjects, and will also produce one of the most effective flowers for the parterre.

The *V. venosa* and *V. pulcherrima* sections also come perfectly true and uniform from seed, and make fine sheets of colour for sloping banks, and knolls, and rockeries, as well as beds in the parterre.

VIOLA

Hardy perennial

THIS plant well merits its popularity for use in beds and borders. It is perfectly hardy, the habit is good, and it continues in bloom for nearly nine months in the year.

The treatment prescribed for Pansy is also suitable for Viola.

WALLFLOWER

Cheiranthus Cheiri.   Hardy biennial

WALLFLOWERS are often sown too late. As a result the growth is not thoroughly ripened, and the plants present but a feeble show of bloom. They should in their season be solid with bloom, not dotted with it; little mountains of fire and gold, exhaling a perfume that few flowers can equal in its peculiar freshness. Sow the seed in May or June, in a sunny place, on rather poor, but sweet, and well-prepared soil favourable to free rooting. When the plants are two inches high, transplant into rows six inches asunder, allowing three inches apart in the row. In about three weeks afterwards, transplant again, six or nine inches apart every way, aiding with water when needful to help them to new growth. Or lift every other row and every other plant, leaving the remainder untouched to supply flowers for cutting. When the beds are cleared of their summer occupants, the best plants may be transferred to them, to afford cheerful green leafage all through the winter, and a grand bloom of Wallflowers in the spring, as frost will not hurt the single varieties, but the doubles will not always endure uninjured the rigours of a severe winter.

WIGANDIA

Half-hardy perennial

THIS plant is grown for its foliage, and is extensively used in sub-tropical gardening. The instructions given for raising Ricinus in heat apply equally to this plant; but it is not wise to rely on an open-air sowing for a supply of Wigandias.

ZINNIA

Zinnia elegans.   Half-hardy annual

A MARKED change has been made in the value of this flower since the introduction of the double varieties. These are so varied in colour and beautiful in form, that they deserve to take high rank as exhibition flowers. They have so entirely eclipsed the single sorts, that even the most enthusiastic lover of single flowers would scarcely venture to institute a comparison between the value of the two for decorative purposes.

The Zinnia is a delicate subject, and if sown too soon it becomes more plague than profit. March is quite early enough to commence operations, and the first week in April will be none too late for sowing. A compost that suits Asters will answer admirably for Zinnias. Sow in $4\frac{1}{2}$-inch pots, which should have very free drainage, and cover the seed thinly with fine soil. Plunge the pots at once in a temperature of about 60°, when the seed will germinate quickly, and the plants on attaining one inch in height can be potted off separately. Place them in a close frame, shade from sunshine, and when well established gradually give air and harden off. It will not be safe to transfer to the open until the first week in June, unless the position is exceptionally sheltered, and the soil very dry. A shrubbery border is a suitable spot, and the more scorching the season the finer will be the flowers. There must, however, be shelter from the wind, for Zinnias are unusually brittle, and easily damaged by a storm.

A satisfactory display of this flower may be obtained without the aid of heat by sowing in the open ground about the middle of May. Select a sunny sloping border or bed for sowing, enrich the soil and make it fine. Press this down rather firmly, then drop three or four seeds at intervals of from fifteen to eighteen inches between each group, and lightly cover them. In due time thin to one plant at each station. If they thrive the branches will not only meet but overlap, and produce a grand display. In the event of very dry weather at sowing time the ground may be watered before the seed is put in, and then be covered with dry fine soil.

Zinnias do not transplant well, except as small seedlings. When it is necessary to undertake the task, choose, if possible, a showery day, and shade each plant with an inverted flower-pot for a few days, but take the pots off in the evening.

Zinnias intended for exhibition must be treated in a more generous fashion than plants that are grown for border decoration, or for the sake of yielding cut flowers. The seed may be raised in heat as already directed, but the border will need to be prepared with special care and liberality. If the soil is heavy, it must be reduced to a friable state during winter. Before the plants are put in raise the land into ridges about four or five inches high. Plant on the top of the ridge, and then an application of soot or lime (not too near to inflict injury) may be used as a precaution against slugs. In a wet season the plants will stand a better chance than if put on the flat, and if a scorching summer comes they will be none the worse for it. As the flowering time approaches mulch the ground with well-decayed manure.

The plants must be carefully staked and tied out, and it is not merely necessary to secure the main stem, but the branches should also be supported, or when weighted with flowers they will be very liable to give way under a moderate wind. Superfluous branches may be removed, but not so severely as to start new growth to the detriment of the flowers. Disbudding also will have to be practised for the highest class of flowers. Only one bloom should be allowed to develop on each branch at one time, and this must be protected from sun and rain after it is about half grown.

SPRING FLOWERS FROM SEEDS

DISPLAYS of spring flowers in English gardens are so much prized that it may contribute both to extend the custom and to promote economy in its observance if we offer a few remarks on the employment for the purpose of spring flowering plants which have been raised from seeds. It will, of course, occur to the reader that a

T

considerable proportion of the annuals that are usually sown in autumn are particularly adapted for producing rich and varied displays in spring. A type of this class is found in the well-known *Erysimum Perowskianum*, one of the cheapest, hardiest, and most resplendent plants of the kind, cheap enough for the humblest amateur to employ freely in his borders and beds, and at the same time so effective in its colouring as to be adapted for the most complex and highly finished examples of geometric work. Amongst the annuals are many—such as, for example, *Erysimum arkansanum*, a lighter tone of yellow than the species just named; *Nemophila insignis*, well known for its lovely blue flowers, and the white variety, *alba*, of the same; *Saponaria calabrica*, exquisite rosy pink, and the white variety, *alba*, of the same; *Silene pendula*, lively rose, and its dwarf variety, *compacta*, and white variety, *alba*; Virginian Stock, of which the distinct varieties are remarkably well adapted to form bands and masses of red, white, and yellow, and also to make a delightful groundwork for enhancing the splendour of late Tulips and clumps of Aubrietia, Yellow Alyssum, and other of the more distinctive plants that are employed in high colouring in first-class geometric gardening. A list of such plants will at once indicate that there is yet a field of enterprise for the practitioner of spring flower gardening; and while cheap and effective materials are thus brought into the service, there is no interference with the later summer bedding, because, if the annuals are well managed, they will give their plentiful bloom when the garden is most in need of colour, and may be cleared off in time to make way for the plants that are generally employed in the summer display, and which are known as 'bedding plants' *par excellence*.

In the management of annuals for an early bloom, it is of great importance to sow them at a proper time, so that they will be strong enough to perform what is required of them, and yet not so forward (or, as we may say, 'winter proud') as to suffer from the severity of the weather. In the North the middle of July is none too early for a general sowing in beds, and in the South the middle of August is none too late. In some few sheltered spots in the extreme South-West the middle of September is a suitable time. As a rule, however, the sowing should be made as early as those familiar with the soil and climate of the place may deem safe, the main point being to have the plants as forward as possible without being in such a succulent state as to be seriously injured by the weather. We prefer sowing in drills on a rather poor soil well broken up to a kindly state, and if the weather is dry at the time of sowing, the drills should be freely watered before the seed is sown, and there will be no more watering needed. The after-management is extremely simple: the plants must be kept clear of weeds, and be slightly thinned out if much crowded, for a few sturdy specimens are of more value than any number that have run up weak and wiry through overcrowding.

In sheltered gardens, having dry chalky or sandy soils, the greater part, or perhaps the whole stock, might be transplanted from the seed-beds to the flower-beds and borders in the month of October; but on heavy soils and in exposed places it will be advisable to delay the removal until March. This part of the work must be nicely done, the plants being lifted in clumps and no attempt being made to single them, and they must be carefully pressed in and aided with water, if necessary, to promote a quick 'taking hold' of their new quarters. Those planted out in October on a dry soil will not only bloom early and gaily, but will be beautiful in their different tints of green all the winter through.

But we are not restricted to annuals in seeking for spring flowers from seeds. With very few exceptions, *all* the favourite plants of the spring garden may be grown from seeds at a cost almost infinitesimal as compared with the raising of named varieties from cuttings and divisions. And this remark applies even to Daisies, which now come sufficiently true and good from seeds. Pansies, which are still unsurpassed as distinct and splendid bedders, also come true from seed, as do the several species and varieties of Arabis, Alyssum, Aubrietia, Viola, Polyanthus, Iberis, Forget-me-not, and Wallflower. The precision of style and colouring that results from raising these from cuttings is, of course, admitted; but in forming masses and ribbon lines, minute individual characters are of less consequence than a good general effect, and this may be insured by raising the plants from seed in a manner so cheap and expeditious, that we feel assured spring bedding would be more often seen in its proper freshness and fulness were the system we now recommend adopted in place of the tedious one of multiplication by offsets and cuttings.

It is of importance, however, to observe that these biennial and perennial plants require more time to prepare themselves for flowering than do the annuals. If sown in August they are likely not to bloom at all the next season, or, at least, to bloom but late and weakly. But if sown in May and June they have a long season of growth before winter sets in, and at the turn of spring they are well matured and strongly set for bloom, and will do their duty.

The sowing of biennial and perennial plants for a display of spring flowers must be carefully done. The ground should be moderately rich and quite mellow through being well broken up; in other words, a good seed-bed must be prepared. If the weather is dry, the drills should be watered before the seed is sown; and in the event of a drought, the young plants must have the aid of water to keep them growing through the summer. The seed should be sown thinly, and, as soon as the plants are large enough, they should be thinned out if at all crowded, and the thinnings should be planted in rows and shaded for a while to make extra fine plants. As a rule the whole of the work will be comprised in sowing, thinning, and weeding, for in an average season they will not require watering, and in this matter alone will be seen the advantage of raising from seeds instead of cuttings.

The roughest mode of procedure will, with such plants as we have named, insure a splendid display of spring flowers; but they will make an ample return for careful culture, and we recommend the bestowal upon them of every needful care to insure complete and early development. It may happen that plants from early sowings will show a few flowers in autumn if neglected. This is easily prevented, to the great advantage of the plants, by the simple process of 'stopping' or nipping out the points of the leading shoots to cause the production of side shoots. If a sturdy growth is thus promoted, and the plants are transferred to the flower beds in October, the result will justify the labour.

Practical gardeners will not need to be informed that the system we now propose is capable of many applications and expansions; but it may be proper to suggest to amateurs who lament the dreary aspect of their beds and borders in the month of May and early part of June, that the plants we recommend for the formation of masses in the geometric garden are equally well adapted to form beautiful clumps and sheets on borders, banks, and rockeries, as well as in many instances to serve as a groundwork to Hyacinths, Tulips, Crown Imperials, Narcissi, and other of the most famous because the most splendid of our many hardy spring flowers.

THE CULTURE

OF

FLOWERING BULBS

INTRODUCTORY REMARKS

OUR popular flowering bulbs are obtained from many lands; they are exceedingly diversified in character, and they bloom at different periods of the year. Each variety has a value of its own, and answers to some special requirement in its proper season under glass or in the open ground. In the darkest winter days we prize the glow of Tulips and Hyacinths for brightening our homes. And bleak days are not all past when Aconites and Snowdrops sparkle in beds and borders. The Anemones follow in March, and during the lengthening days of spring there are sumptuous beds of Hyacinths and Tulips. When high summer begins to decline we have stately groups of Gladiolus and many beautiful Lilies in the shrubbery borders.

Not least among the merits of Dutch Bulbs is the ease with which they can be forced into flower at a period of the year when bright blossoms are particularly precious, and they are equally available for the grandest conservatory or the humblest cottage window. They are attractive separately in pots or vases, or they can be arranged in splendid banks and groups for the highest decorative purposes. Bulbs endure treatment that would be fatal to other flowers. They can be grown in small pots or be almost packed together in boxes or seed-pans; and when near perfection they can be shaken out, have the roots washed for glasses, ferneries, and small aquaria; or they can be replanted close together in sand and covered with green moss.

Their hardiness, too, is an immense advantage, and permits of their being grown and successfully flowered without the least aid from artificial heat. Small beds and borders may be made brilliant with these flowers, and the number of bulbs that can be planted in a very limited space is somewhat astonishing to a novice. Unlike many other subjects, bulbs may be rather crowded without injury to individual specimens.

For the decoration of windows no other flowers can compare with Dutch Bulbs in variety and brilliancy of colour. Some of them are not particularly long-lived, and this need occasion no regret, for it affords opportunity of making constant changes in the character and colour of the miniature exhibition, which may easily be extended over many weeks. And a really beautiful display is within reach of those who have not a scrap of garden in which to bring an ordinary plant to perfection. Unused attics and lead flats can, with a little skill and attention in the case of bulbs, be made to answer the purpose which pits and greenhouses serve for most of our showy plants. Many of the latter cannot be grown in large centres of population, but bulbs will produce handsome blossoms even in smoky towns.

We do not recommend the attempt to grow bulbs in the actual window boxes. It is seldom entirely satisfactory. They should be treated in the manner advised under the several varieties in the following pages, and just as the colours are becoming visible, a selection can be made from pots or boxes for crowding closely in the ornamental arrangements for the window. When the first occupants show signs of fading others can be brought forward to fill their places, and this process may be repeated so long as there are materials to draw from. Winter Aconites, Snowdrops, Squills, and Glory of the Snow will furnish the earliest display; these to be followed by Crocuses, Tulips, Hyacinths, and the many forms of the great Narciss family, until spring is far advanced.

The secret of their accommodating nature lies in the fact that to a considerable extent the work has been accomplished. Within the Hyacinth or Tulip every petal of the coming flower is already stored. During the five or six years of its life in Holland all the capacities of the bulb have been steadily conserved, and we have but to unfold its beauty, aiming at short stout growth and intensity of colour. Of course there is an immense difference in the quality of imported bulbs, and they necessarily vary according to the character of the season. The most successful Dutch growers cannot insure uniformity in any one variety year after year, because the seasons are beyond human control. But those who regularly visit Holland can always obtain the finest roots of the year, although it may be necessary to select from many sources.

Such bulbs as Lilies, Iris, Montbretia, Hyacinthus, and Alstrœmeria suffer no deterioration after the first year's flowering. Indeed, it will be the cultivator's fault if they do not increase in number and carry finer heads of bloom in succeeding years. As outdoor subjects some of them are not yet appreciated at their full value. Magnificent as *Lilium auratum* and *L. lancifolium* must ever be in conservatories, they exhibit their imposing proportions to greater advantage, and their wealth of perfume is far more acceptable, when grown among handsome shrubs in the border. Very little attention is needed to bring them up year after year in ever increasing loveliness.

ACHIMENES

These showy stove bulbs have been considerably improved of late years, and the varieties that now obtain favour are remarkable for their beauty. Given a sufficiency of heat, and the cultivation is of the easiest nature, for they grow rapidly and flower freely, if potted in sandy peat, and kept in a warm greenhouse or the coolest part of a stove, in a somewhat humid atmosphere. It needs only the simplest management to have these plants in flower at almost any season of the year, for the bulbs may be kept dormant for a considerable length of time without injury, and may be started into growth as required to keep up a long succession of flowers. They are occasionally well grown in common frames over hot-beds. For suspended baskets Achimenes are invaluable.

AGAPANTHUS

It is not generally known that this noble plant is quite hardy, and succeeds admirably if planted out between September and March in a rich, deep, moist loam, either in full sun or in partial shade. When grown in pots it requires a strong loamy soil, with plenty of manure, and throughout the summer the pots should be allowed to stand in pans of water. As the Agapanthus is a gross-feeding plant, it should be re-potted annually in autumn, and be wintered in a cool pit or frame. It forms an immense mass of fleshy roots, and a little care must be taken to avoid injuring them.

ALLIUM

THE *Allium neapolitanum* is the finest white-flowered variety, and is exceedingly valuable for bouquets and vase decoration. The large umbels of blossoms are of the purest white. It is one of the earliest spring-flowering bulbs, and, although quite hardy, it comes forward quickly and easily in a cool house.

ALSTRŒMERIA

THIS elegant plant belongs to the nearly hardy group referred to in the notice of Ixia. In autumn it may be safely planted out in almost any part of Britain, provided it is planted nine inches deep, and can have a sunny position on a dry soil, for damp is more hurtful to it than frost. As a pot plant it is comparatively useless, but if allowed to remain several years in a dry border, a large clump of any of the varieties presents a brilliant appearance when in flower.

AMARYLLIS

SEE remarks under Lilies at page 298.

ANEMONE

Windflower

OUR observations on this flower will be limited to the tuberous varieties; but even with this restriction, the range of form and colour is exceedingly wide. The Anemone is an accommodating plant, and can be successfully flowered either in pots or in beds, at the option of the cultivator.

The most natural place for it is near shady woodland walks, where it can be seen to the greatest advantage. But it is also a splendid subject for masses in the mixed border, or in front of shrubberies; and alone in beds it makes a brilliant and lasting show. For all the purposes of garden decoration to which the Crocus,

Hyacinth, and Tulip are applied, the Windflower is equally well adapted. We do not advise its employment as single specimens, but it answers admirably in lines, groups, or beds, and the colours admit of numberless harmonies and contrasts.

The commoner Anemones need only to be planted about three inches deep, with the eyes upwards, at any time between September and March, and they will require little or no attention afterwards. Under trees, instead of planting in a formal pattern, it is worth while to put them in with some attempt at natural grouping, and not too close together—say from six inches to a foot apart. In such positions they may be left undisturbed for years; and if the soil happens to be a good sandy loam, they will thrive and increase. In masses or beds within the garden, however, a richer effect is wanted, and the distance between the roots should not exceed from four to six inches.

A choice collection of roots is worth more care, and florists are accustomed to prepare the beds for their reception with fastidious exactness. The soil, if not considered suitable, is taken out to the depth of two feet, and is replaced by a rich and specially prepared compost. Although the individual flowers produced by this method are generally very fine, and the total effect of the bed is exceedingly beautiful, yet the truth must be confessed that for ordinary gardening the system is extravagant and unnecessary. As a hobby, it is, of course, justifiable enough; but Anemones of high quality can be grown by a much simpler mode of procedure. One deep digging there certainly should be, and a layer of manure at the bottom of each trench is sound practice, for it supplies the roots with food and a cool subsoil. Poor land should also be enriched by incorporating a dressing of decayed manure as the work proceeds. Subsequently one or two light surface forkings will help to make the bed mellow. A rough plan, showing the name and position of every root, will be a safer record than labelling in the usual way, and it also prevents the disfigurement of the bed. There should be a distance of six inches between each root; and they may be put in singly by means of the trowel, or in drills drawn three inches deep. The former method is generally adopted for groups; but to insure regularity in flowering, the planting must be uniform in depth. For beds, drills are more reliable, and they are speedily made.

The time of planting determines to a considerable extent the date of flowering; and, as the roots may be put in during autumn, winter, and early spring, it is easy to secure a succession of Anemones from January until May. But this flower is of so much more value early in the year than at a later period, when many other subjects brighten the garden, that it is scarcely worth while to plant so late as March.

The Anemone is well worth growing in pots, both for its foliage and flowers. It does not resent forcing to the same extent as the Ranunculus; nevertheless, cool treatment is almost essential to do it full justice. The potting should be done in batches to insure a succession of flowers, and the first lot may be put in at the end of August or beginning of September. They should have the benefit of really good soil; a mixture of leaf-mould and loam, with the addition of a little powdered charcoal, will suit them exactly. In preparing the pots, place a layer of light manure above the crocks, which will assist the drainage and benefit the plants. Then fill with compost to within two inches of the top, and lay in the roots; add soil to a level with the rim, and press lightly down. The strongest roots should, of course, be selected for potting, and it will need more than a hasty glance to put them in with the eyes upwards. One or more roots may be planted in each pot, according to the size of the latter.

The early plantings can be placed in any warm position out of doors, such as under a south wall; but after the middle of October remove to a cold pit, or on to the greenhouse stage. Watering is all the attention they will require, and of this there must be no stint, especially during the blooming period. A high temperature at any stage is needless, and if they are just kept out of the reach of frost they will take excellent care of themselves.

Anemones are adapted for many decorative purposes; they make capital window plants, and their sharply cut foliage is very ornamental in the drawing-room or on the dinner table.

BABIANA

BABIANAS are delicately constituted, but extremely elegant plants when well grown, though far from showy, and appealing rather to the educated eye for appreciation of their blue and purple oculate flowers. The culture is the same as for the Ixia, and we incline strongly to the practice of keeping the bulbs at least two seasons in the same pots.

BEGONIA, TUBEROUS-ROOTED

Few flowers have a greater claim on the attention of amateurs than the Tuberous-rooted Begonia, either for the ease with which it can be grown, or for the many valuable purposes to which the plant may be applied. It can be flowered at any time from February until October, and is available for all kinds of indoor decoration, and also for growing in the open ground during the summer months.

Instead of allowing the plants to be rudely dried off, it is worth a little trouble to reduce them slowly to the dormant state by gradually withholding water. They should still be retained in pots, which may be stored under a thick layer of cocoa-nut fibre in any cellar, frame, or shed where the thermometer stands pretty uniformly at about 50°. The store should also be dry, for damp is as injurious to these roots as cold. Roughly speaking, it may be said that any store which is safe for Dahlias will also preserve Tuberous-rooted Begonias.

After the winter's rest the bulbs are invariably cup-shaped, and in the event of their being watered before growth has commenced, sufficient water will remain in the hollow to destroy the bulb. This peculiarity renders it essential not to start the plant before activity is evident. In January or February, as the bulbs show signs of life, pot them almost on the surface of a rich loamy soil, and employ the smallest pots possible. Nurse them with a little care in a warm place for about ten days, and they should then be very gradually hardened. A regular system of potting on will be necessary until the final size is reached; and at each operation the plants should be inserted rather more deeply than before. If re-potting is deferred too long, the foliage will turn yellow—a sure sign that the plant is starving. No flowers should be allowed in the early stages of growth, and this rule is imperative if fine specimens are wanted; but when the plants are transferred just as the pots are full of roots, there will be little disposition to bloom prematurely. While growing, the Tuberous Begonia delights in a humid atmosphere, but this should be avoided after flowering has commenced. When sticks are inserted for tying out the flowers, the bulbs must not be wounded.

The erect-growing varieties are valuable for low conservatory stages, and they form splendid groups in corners of drawing-rooms. The drooping kinds are seen to advantage on brackets, shelves, and in suspended baskets; and the short-jointed plants of the drooping class are specially adapted for rockeries and beds. They must not be put into the open until the danger of a nipping east wind is past. The early part of June is generally about the right time.

In the autumn it is usual to lift and pot the plants, although in mild districts, and in a light soil, they may safely be left out all the winter under the shelter of a heap of ashes or decayed manure. In beds this plan is scarcely worth adoption, because it leaves the ground bare for several months; but where Begonias are grown in the reserve border to furnish a supply of flowers for cutting, it may be a considerable advantage to leave them until the following year.

A word is necessary as to soil. The Begonia is a gross feeder, and to develop its fine qualities there must be a liberal employment of manure. As a matter of fact, it is scarcely possible to make the soil too rich for this flower.

CHIONODOXA LUCILIÆ

Glory of the Snow

THE white centre of the Chionodoxa, its more open blossoms, larger size, and graduated tint of blue, distinguish it in a marked manner from its older and justly prized rival, the Scilla. Indeed, the Chionodoxa is an exquisitely beautiful flower, and is of great value for pot culture, beds, or borders. Five bulbs may be grown in a 48-sized pot, and in the border not less than half a dozen should be planted in a group. Employed as a single or double line, it also produces a striking bit of colouring. The bulbs should be planted in autumn four inches deep, the distance between being not more than three inches. Any ordinary garden soil will grow this flower, and it is advisable to allow the bulbs to remain undisturbed for several years, as the effect in each succeeding spring will be the greater.

CROCUS

THIS brilliant harbinger of spring will thrive in any soil or situation, but to be brought to the highest possible perfection it should be grown in an open bed or border of deep, rich, dry sandy loam. The bulbs should be planted during September, October, and November. If kept out of the ground after the end of the year they will be seriously damaged, and however carefully planted, will not flower in a satisfactory manner. Plant three inches deep in lines, clumps, or masses, as taste may suggest, putting the bulbs two inches apart. If possible, let them remain undisturbed two or three years, and then take them up and plant again in well-prepared and liberally manured soil. A bed of mixed Crocuses has a pleasing appearance, but in selecting bulbs for the geometric garden, it is more effective to employ distinct colours, reserving the yellow for the exterior parts of the design to define its boundaries, and using the blue and the white in masses and bands within. In districts where sparrows destroy the flowers, they may be deterred from doing mischief by stretching over the beds several lengths of coloured twine, which will not interfere with the beauty of the display, and will terrify the sparrows for a sufficient period to save the flowers.

The named varieties are invaluable for pot and frame culture, and to force for decorative purposes, for though the flowers are short-lived, they are everywhere welcome, and in character they are quite distinct from all other flowers of the same early season. When grown in pots and baskets, the bulbs should be placed close together to produce a striking effect. A light rich soil is desirable, but they may be flowered in a satisfactory manner in a mixture of charcoal and moss, or in cocoa-nut fibre, or moss alone. When required in quantity for ornamental baskets and other decorative purposes, it is wise to plant them in shallow boxes filled with rotten manure and leaf-mould, and to lift them out separately, and pack them when in flower in the ornamental baskets. A perfect display of flowers in precisely the same stage of development may thus be secured, and successional displays may follow as long as there are suitable materials remaining in the boxes.

CROWN IMPERIAL. (*See under* LILIES, *page* 301.)

CYCLAMEN

THE lovely Cyclamen is frequently subjected to a treatment which results in the destruction of the bulbs; or, if they survive it, they never present the rich appearance of plants grown in a more sensible manner. It is commonly supposed that the bulbs should be 'dried off' as soon as they have done flowering, and accordingly we see them put out of doors in the burning sun to perish, or to be spoiled beyond recovery. A long and decided season of rest is needed certainly, but it should be in a cool, moist atmosphere, and the roots should never be quite dry. It is better to keep them in a greenhouse or pit in the resting season, because they are not then so likely to be forgotten as when put out in the open air. Pot them in August, in a compost consisting of mellow turfy loam three parts, leaf-mould one part, and silver sand one part. The corm should be placed deep enough in the pot to bring the crown about level with the rim. Specimens that show a great quantity of flower-buds should be assisted with weak liquid manure, and once a week, until they have done flowering, should be stood in a vessel of water half the depth of the pots for half an hour.

C. coum and *C. europæum* are rarely well grown, for although quite hardy, the climate of this country does not suit them in their season of flowering, which is the early spring. The cool greenhouse is the safest place for them, except in sheltered spots, where they may be planted out on a border of peat, or amongst ferns in a rockery. When grown in pots, light turfy loam and peat in equal quantities, with a fourth part of cow-manure, and a liberal addition of sand, will form an excellent compost for them. The pots should never be exposed to the drying action of the sun or wind, but should be plunged to the rim in coal ashes or cocoa-nut fibre. The best time for potting or planting them is September or October.

Instructions on raising Cyclamen from seed will be found at page 232.

DAFFODILS. (*See* NARCISSUS, *page* 303.)

DOG'S-TOOTH VIOLET

THE red and white varieties are as hardy as any plant in our gardens, and by their neat habit and elegant leaves and flowers they are admirably adapted to plant in quantities in the front of a rockery, either in peat or sandy loam and leaf-mould. They are equally suitable for edging small beds in gardens where spring flowers are systematically grown; in fact, they are true 'spring bedders.' Plant in autumn. They are also worth growing in pots, especially where an unheated 'Alpine house' is kept for plants of this class. Several bulbs may be put in a 48-size pot.

FERRARIA, or TIGRIDIA

The short-lived blossoms of the Tiger flower are most gorgeously painted, and differ from everything else of the great family of Irids to which they belong. When planted out on a dry sunny border, they are quite hardy; but on a damp soil they cannot be kept through the winter. Still, the flowers are much finer from the border than when grown in pots, and they present us with great variety, scarcely any two plants amongst hundreds producing flowers exactly alike. A bed of Tigridias makes an agreeable ornament in front of the window of a breakfast room, as the flowers are in a brilliant state in the early hours of the day. Plant in autumn.

FREESIA

The singularly graceful form and the delicious perfume of this flower have made it an immense favourite; and happily there is no Cape bulb which can be grown with greater ease in the frame or cool greenhouse. One characteristic is very marked, and it is the disproportion between the small bulb and the fine flowers produced from it.

Procure the bulbs as early in the autumn as possible, and lose no time in potting them. Any light rich soil will answer, but that which suits them best is composed of two parts loam, one of leaf-mould, and one of peat, with enough sand or grit added to insure drainage. Commence with pots of the right size, for the roots are extremely brittle, and there must be no risk of injuring them by repotting. The 3½-inch size will accommodate two bulbs placed nearly close to the rim on opposite sides of the pot; larger sizes may have three, four, or more bulbs. Place under a south wall, and cover with ashes or cocoa-nut fibre until top-growth commences, and then remove the covering.

At the end of September transfer the pots to a cold frame, and when the plants attain a height of four inches, support them with neat sticks, which should not be inserted too near the bulbs. Watering will require judgment, for too much turns the foliage yellow. When the pots are full of roots, liquid manure twice a week will be helpful.

After the blooming season has passed, encourage the foliage to wither by withholding water. The roots may be stored away in their own pots until the following August.

FRITILLARIA

FRITILLARIAS produce bell-shaped flowers, varying in colour, but generally of a purplish tint, and beautifully spotted. They thrive best in a good deep loam, but may be grown in almost any soil, and do well under the shade of trees. They are quite hardy, and like most other bulbs should be planted in autumn.

GLADIOLUS

THE Gladiolus is adapted for many important uses. It associates admirably with Dahlias, Hollyhocks, Pyrethrums, and Phloxes, in the furnishing of clumps on the lawn and in the mixed border. It is perfectly at home and in harmony with surroundings when planted in front of American beds and on the margin of the mixed shrubbery. To supply cut flowers it is invaluable, for they retain their freshness in a vase for many days, and a plentiful supply should be grown in reserved spots expressly for indoor decoration. Some flowers are resplendent in the richness of their colouring, others delicately beautiful, with markings so refined that they command the admiration of tastes the most cultivated.

The culture depends very much on the end in view. To secure a brilliant and varied display in the garden is one thing; to stage a collection of flowers capable of holding their own at some great floral exhibition is another. Treatment that will be ample for the embellishment of the garden will prove inadequate to secure success in a keen competition, and we therefore propose to give a few practical directions to assist both objects.

The Gladiolus may be grown by simply planting the bulbs in April, and leaving them to take care of themselves. A better return will generally be obtained than this neglectful method deserves. But a lover of these flowers will scarcely treat them in so primitive a fashion, and the pleasure to be derived may be entirely commensurate with the care and attention bestowed upon them. Almost any soil can be made to answer, but that which suits them best is a good medium, friable loam, with a cool rich subsoil, and each one must decide for himself how far this is within reach naturally, or can be secured by resources at command. Thus a light soil may be made suitable by placing a layer of rotten cow-manure a foot below the surface, and a heavy retentive loam can be reduced to the proper state by the admixture of lighter material. In any case it is advisable to begin preparations in the autumn. Spread a thick layer of manure and dig this in deeply, leaving the soil in a rough state to be disintegrated by frosts. Before the time of planting arrives, it is worth some trouble to free the ground from wireworms, or they will play havoc with the growth just as it is appearing above ground. Potatoes serve admirably as traps for these pests.

Gladioli are peculiarly liable to injury from wind, so that a sheltered but not a shaded position should, if possible, be chosen for them. The time of planting depends partly on the district, partly on the season; but the soil must be in suitable condition, and fine weather is necessary. From the middle of March to the middle of April should afford some suitable opportunity of getting the bulbs in satisfactorily. Give the land a light forking, not deep enough to bring up the manure, and make the surface level. The rows may be twelve or eighteen inches apart—we prefer the greater distance because of the convenience it affords in attending to the plants when growing, and nine inches space is sufficient in the rows.

There are two methods of putting in the bulbs, each of which has advocates among practised growers. One is to take out the soil with a trowel to the depth of six or seven inches for each corm, then insert about two inches of mixed sand and powdered charcoal or wood ashes; lay the root upon it, and carefully cover with fine soil. If that process is considered too tedious, draw a deep drill with a hoe, and at the bottom put the light mixture already named; place the roots at regular distances upon it, and lightly return the top soil. The operation should be so performed as to leave the crown of the corm four inches below the surface; and when planting is completed give the bed a finishing touch with the rake.

One eminent grower strips off the outer coat or skin of each bulb before planting to ascertain that there is no disease, and this cannot otherwise be discovered. No doubt the procedure prevents the bed from showing blanks, but that object can be more safely attained by growing a reserve in pots. There is, however, another practice which possesses very decided advantages, and it is to open carefully the skin at the crown of the bulb to allow the foliage free exit. The skin is so tough that it is frequently the means of distorting the plant in its attempt to struggle through.

The bed for a time needs little attention, except to keep it free from weeds, and this is best done by hand. When the shoots reach about a foot high, tying must be resorted to in earnest. The most effectual plan, of course, is to put a separate stake to each plant, and for exhibition specimens this is certainly advisable. But rows can be secured by a stake at each end, with two or three strands of strong material carried across, to which each flower must be tied. Whatever method is adopted, care should be taken to avoid cutting the plant while holding it secure from damage in a high wind. Let the material which is placed round the flowering stem be soft and wide, such as list, which answers admirably.

Water must be freely and regularly given during dry weather, either in the morning or evening; and a mulch of old manure spread over the bed will not only prevent evaporation, but also save the ground from caking hard.

Another important matter is shading. For ordinary purposes this is not essential, but as it very much lengthens the duration of the flower, it is worth attention on that ground alone, and for exhibition it is indispensable. Whether shading is accomplished by separate protectors made expressly for the purpose, or by home-made contrivances of canvas or wood, the point to be quite certain about is security, or an accident may wreck well-grounded hopes.

The lifting and storing of the corms affect the quality of the next year's flowers so much that it is important to accomplish lifting at the most suitable time, and the storing in the best manner. By the middle or end of October, on some fine day, take up the roots even if the foliage be still green, tie a label to each variety, and hang them in some airy place until they can be cleared of soil and leaves. Remove the foliage with a sharp knife, and lay out the bulbs to dry for another fortnight. They can then be stored in paper bags or in boxes on any dry shelf which is safe from vermin.

GLOXINIA

GLOXINIAS may be had in bloom almost all the year by judicious management. When required for early flowering, those that start first should be selected and carefully shifted into other pots, and be kept near the glass, as they depend much on light for a rapid and luxuriant growth. A moist atmosphere, with the temperature about 60° to 65°, greatly facilitates the growth of Gloxinias, but they may be grown well in either greenhouse or in pits heated by hot water.

The soil most suited to Gloxinias is a light compost of fibrous loam, combined with a little peat and silver sand. Watering with manure water during the growing period twice a week is helpful, but it should be discontinued when the flowers show colour. The plants love shade, and at no time should suffer from drought. Storing Gloxinias for their season of rest, *i.e.* the winter, must be carefully attended to, as losses frequently occur during this stage. It is also important that the plants should not be 'dried off' too quickly, but let them rather be placed in a light, airy position, and by a gradual reduction of moisture the leaves will fall off naturally. The bulbs may then be stored away on a shelf, in an even temperature of about 50°, each bulb being closely surrounded by cocoa-nut fibre and peat in equal parts to prevent excessive dryness, which, like too much damp, often causes the loss of the bulb.

Besides growing the same plants from year to year, it is always desirable to have a fresh stock coming on, as the old bulbs may deteriorate after two or three years. This can easily be managed by successive sowings of seed, as advised at page 241.

HEMEROCALLIS (*See page* 300)

HYACINTH

THIS most valuable of early flowering bulbs is so accommodating that it can be flowered in a variety of ways by very simple modes of treatment, and may be employed as a hardy, rough-weather plant for the garden border, or as a grand exhibition and conservatory flower. The bulbs may be planted at any time from September to the middle of December, with the certainty of their blooming well, if properly cared for; but the prudent cultivator will plant them as early as possible in the autumn, and so manage them afterwards as to secure the longest period of growth previous to their flowering. They may be forced to flower at Christmas, but the more slowly the flowers are developed, the finer in the end will they be. To obtain good bulbs is a matter of the utmost importance, and it may be useful here to remark that the mere size of a Hyacinth bulb is no criterion of its value—nor, indeed, is its neatness of form or brightness of appearance. The two most important qualities are soundness and density. If the bulbs are hard and heavy in proportion to their size, they may be depended on to produce good flowers of their kind. The bulbs of some sorts are never large or handsome, while, on the other hand, many sorts partake of both these qualities in an eminent degree.

CULTURE IN POTS.—It is not necessary to employ large pots, or pots of a peculiar shape, for Hyacinths. There is nothing better than common flower-pots, and in those of 60-size ($3\frac{1}{2}$-inch) single bulbs may be flowered in a most satisfactory manner. The pots usually employed are 48-size (5-inch), and 32-size (6-inch); the last-named being required only for selected bulbs grown for exhibition. We advise the use of small pots where Hyacinths are grown in pits and frames for decorative purposes, because they can be conveniently placed in ornamental stands, or packed close together in baskets of moss, when required for the embellishment of the drawing-room. A rich, light soil is indispensable, and it should consist of at least one-half of good rotten manure, and the remainder turfy loam, with a liberal allowance of sharp sand. The mixture should be in a moderately moist condition when ready for use. When small pots are employed, one hollow crock must suffice, but 48- and 32-sized pots must be prepared in the usual way, with one large hollow crock, and a little heap of smaller potsherds or nodules of charcoal over it. Fill the pots quite full of soil, and then press the bulb into it, and press the soil round the bulb to finish the operation. If potted loosely they will not thrive; if potted too firmly they will rise up as soon as they begin to grow, and be one-sided. In large pots the bulbs should be nearly covered with soil, but in small pots they must be only half covered, in order to afford them the largest possible amount of root-room. When potted, the coolest place should be found for them, and unless they go absolutely dry, they should not have a drop of water, until they begin to grow freely, and are in the enjoyment of full daylight. The pots may be stored in a dark, cool pit, or any out-of-the-way place, where neither sun, nor frost, nor heavy rains will affect them; but it is advisable to plunge them in coal ashes or cocoa-nut fibre, and cover them with a few inches of the plunging material. As to their removal, there are two matters to consider. They must be taken out as wanted for forcing, and certainly before they push their flower spikes through the plunge material, as they will do if they remain in the bed too long. The cultivator will be guided in respect of their removal from the bed, by circumstances; but when they are removed, a distinct routine of treatment must be observed, or the flowering will be unsatisfactory. For a short time they should be placed in subdued daylight, that the blanched growth may acquire a healthy green hue slowly, and they need to be kept cool in order that they shall grow very little until a healthy colour is acquired. The floor of a cool greenhouse is a good place for them when first taken out of the bed, and cleaned up for forcing. Another matter of great importance is to place them near the glass immediately their green colour is established, and to grow them as slowly as the requirements of the case will permit. If to be forced early, allow plenty of time to train them to bear a great heat, taking from bed to pit, and from pit to cool-house, and deferring to the latest possible moment placing them in the heat in which they are to flower. Those to bloom at Christmas should be potted in September, those to follow may be potted a month later. If a long succession is required, a sufficient number should be potted every two or three weeks to the end of the year. Those potted latest will, of course, flower in frames without the aid of heat. In any and every case the highest temperature of the forcing pit should be 70°; to go beyond that point will cause an attenuated growth and poverty of colour. If liquid manure is employed at all, it should be used constantly, and extremely weak, until the flowers begin to expand, and then pure soft water should be used instead. No matter what may be the particular constitution of the liquid manure, it must be weak, or it will do more harm than good. The spikes should be supported by wires or neat sticks in good time, and a constant watch kept to see that the stems are not cut or bent, as they rapidly develop beyond the range allowed them by their supports.

CULTURE IN GLASSES.—It is of little consequence whether rain, river, or spring water be employed in this mode of culture, but it should be pure, and in the glasses it should nearly but not quite touch the bulbs. Store at once in a dark, cool place, to encourage the bulbs to send their roots down into the water before the leaves begin to grow. When the roots are developed, bring the glasses from the dark to the light in order that leaves and flowers may be in perfect health. Let them have as much light as possible, with an equable temperature, and provide supports in good time. Hyacinths are often injured by being kept in rooms that are at times extremely cold, and at others heated to excess. Those who wish to grow the bulbs to perfection in glasses, must remove them occasionally as circumstances may require, to prevent the injury that must otherwise result from rapid and extreme alternations of temperature. It is not desirable to introduce to the water any stimulating substances, but the glasses must be kept nearly full of water by occasionally replenishing as it disappears. If the leaves become dusty, they may be cleansed with a soft brush or a sponge dipped in water, but particular care must be taken not to injure them in the process.

CULTURE IN BEDS.—The Hyacinth will grow well in any ordinary garden soil, but that which is light and rich will suit it best, and the position of the bed should be effectually drained, for though the plant loves moisture, it cannot endure to stand in a bog during the winter. It is advisable to plant early, and to plant deep. If a rich effect is required, the bulbs should be six inches apart, but a good effect may be produced by planting nine inches apart. The time of blooming may be to some extent influenced by the time and manner of planting, but no strict rules can be given to suit particular instances. Late planting and deep planting both tend to defer the time of blooming, although there will not be a great difference in any case, and as a rule the late bloom is to be preferred, because less liable to injury from frost. The shallowest planting should insure a depth of three inches of earth above the crown of the bulb, but generally speaking they will flower better, and only a few days later, if covered with full six inches of earth over the crowns. The Hyacinth is so hardy that protection need not be thought of, except in peculiar cases of unusual exposure, or on the occurrence of an excessively low temperature when they are growing freely. Under any circumstances, there is no protection so effectual as dry litter, but a thin coat of half-rotten manure spread over the bed is to be preferred in the event of danger being apprehended at any time before the growth has fairly pushed through.

As the bulbs may be taken up and dried off as soon as the leaves acquire a yellow colour, the beds will be vacant in time for the ordinary summer bedders, so that the brilliant display of the spring may be immediately followed by another, equally brilliant perhaps, but in character altogether different. When grown in beds, Hyacinths do not require water, or sticks; all they need is to be planted properly, and they will take care of themselves.

MINIATURE HYACINTHS.—These charming little sparkling gems are invaluable for baskets, bowls, and other contrivances which are adapted for the choicest decorative purposes. In quality they are excellent, the spikes being symmetrical, the flowers well formed, and the colours brilliant. But they are true miniatures, growing about half the size of the other kinds, and requiring less soil to root in. They will flower well, if planted in a mixture of moss and charcoal, kept constantly moist, and covered with the greenest moss, to give to the ornament containing them a finished appearance.

FEATHER, GRAPE, AND MUSK HYACINTHS will grow in any good garden soil, and are admirably adapted for borders that are shaded by trees. They should be planted in large clumps, and be allowed to remain several years undisturbed. They are all beautiful—the Feather Hyacinth emphatically so; indeed, numerous as beautiful flowers are, this, for delicacy of structure, has peculiar claims to our admiration, when presenting its feathery plumes a foot or more in length, all cut into curling threads of the most elegant tenuity.

ROMAN HYACINTH.—This flower is particularly welcome in the short, dark days of November, December, and January. For placing in glasses to decorate the drawing-room or dinner table, the spikes of bloom are largely grown; and the separate flowers, mounted on wire, form an important feature in winter bouquets, for which purpose their delicious perfume renders them especially valuable.

The bulbs are cheap, and can be grown with the utmost ease. Pot them immediately they can be obtained in August or September, putting three roots in each 48-sized pot, and stand them in some spare corner in the open ground, where they can be covered with a few inches of cocoa-nut fibre or ashes. This will encourage the roots to start before there is any top growth. In October remove the covering, and transfer the pots to a pit or frame, or they may even be placed under the greenhouse stage for a time, provided they will not be in the way of dripping water. A little later room should be found for them upon the stage, or the foliage may become drawn. When the buds are visible, plunge the pots in a bottom heat of 65° or 70°, and in a week the flowers will be fit for use. Like its more imposing prototype, the Roman Hyacinth may have its roots gently freed from soil for packing in bowls or vases filled with wet moss or sand; but they ought not to be subjected to a violent change of temperature. If wanted in glasses, they can be grown in water after the usual fashion, but the flower is scarcely adapted for this mode of treatment.

HYACINTHUS CANDICANS

THIS bulb produces stately spikes of flower, which make it an excellent companion to Delphiniums, Salvias, and perennial Lobelias in the mixed border. It also associates well with shrubs, and will help to enliven a bed of Rhododendrons at a period of the year when the latter is uninteresting. It may be planted in any soil from November to March; and, as the bulb is perfectly hardy, it can be left in the open ground all the year without the least misgiving as to its safety. A strong root will produce a succession of flower spikes, and this tendency will be assisted by cutting off each spike immediately it has ceased to be attractive.

IRIS

The common varieties of Iris are well-known favourites of the border, and the whole family have claims on the attention of amateurs, on account of their excellent faculty of taking care of themselves if properly planted in the first instance. The tuberous or bulbous rooted kinds do not require a rich soil, but a sandy loam suits them, and they thrive in peat. Such beautiful species as Reticulata, the Persian, the Chalcedonian, and the Peacock should be grown in pots in frames, or in a cool greenhouse. The English and Spanish varieties should be planted out in clumps in front of a shrubbery border, where they may be seen to advantage. The crown of the bulb must not be more than three inches below the surface. From September to December will answer for planting, and the roots may be taken up when the flowering period is over, or if the space is not wanted they can be allowed to remain for the following season; but they should not be grown in one spot for more than three years. After that time they must be divided, and a fresh position should be found for them.

IXIA AND SPARAXIS

These attractive Cape bulbs are hardy in favoured districts, and may be left out for years in a sheltered border next a stove or greenhouse. In places where none but the hardiest plants pass through the winter safely, they must be grown in the greenhouse or the frame, and any good sandy soil will suit them, whether peat or loam. They should be potted early in the autumn, and have plenty of air at all times when the weather is favourable, especially when they are growing freely in spring. If carefully managed, they may remain two seasons in the same pots. Use the 48-size, and plant four or five bulbs in each. A dry, deep sandy border under a wall in any of the warmer western and southern districts might be grandly furnished with such plants as Ixias, Sparaxis, Alstrœmerias, Oxalis, Tritonias, Babianas, and the choicest of the smaller kinds of Iris. It would constitute a garden of the most interesting exotics capable of withstanding the rigours of this northern clime.

JONQUIL

THE delicious fragrance and the exquisite beauty of the flowers of the Jonquil render it one of the most valuable of the Narciss family for cultivation in pots, and it is also a first-rate border and woodland flower. When forced, the treatment should assimilate as nearly as possible to that prescribed for the Narcissus. Four or five bulbs may be planted in one pot.

LACHENALIA

AN elegant plant which is not quite hardy enough to be trusted in the open ground, but it is the easiest matter possible to grow it well in the greenhouse. The bulbs should be potted as soon as they begin to grow in the autumn, and several bulbs may be put into each pot. There can be no better soil than turfy loam alone, without manure or sand. One point is of the utmost importance; it is that they should have abundance of water, when they will produce leaves two inches across, and spikes of flowers fully double the size of those commonly met with. An admirable use for these bulbs is to insert them all over the outside of hanging baskets, which they will cover with the most graceful display of aërial vegetation imaginable, the flower spikes turning upwards, and the leaves hanging down.

LEUCOJUM ÆSTIVUM

THE Summer Snowflake is a white flower slightly tipped with green. It closely resembles the Snowdrop, but is much larger than that well-known spring favourite. The bulb is perfectly hardy, and will grow in any garden soil. Plant in clumps three inches deep any time from the end of September until the middle of November.

LILIES

HARDY border Lilies are amongst the most useful garden plants known. They are peculiarly hardy and accommodating, requiring no support from sticks or ties; several of them are green all the winter, and capable of resisting any amount of frost, and, if left alone, they increase rapidly, and become more and more valuable every year. We will say nothing of their beauty, for that is proverbial; but it may be proper to add that many of the most lovely Lilies, that are regarded as only suitable for the greenhouse, and grown with great care under glass, are really as hardy as the old common white Lily, and may be grown with it in the same border. To grow the Liliums well requires a deep, moist, rich loam. A stubborn clay may be improved for them by deep digging, and incorporating with the staple plenty of rotten manure and leaf-mould. They all thrive in peat, or rotten turf, or indeed in any soil containing an abundance of decomposing vegetable matter. The autumn is the proper time to plant Lilies, but they may be planted at any season, if they can be obtained in a dormant state, or growing in pots. They should be planted deep for their size, say, never less than six inches. When they have stood some years, they should be taken up and parted, and the borders should be deeply dug and liberally manured before replanting. If the stems of Lilies become leafless and unsightly before the flowers are past, it is a sign that the roots are too dry, or that the soil is impoverished, and therefore, as soon as the stems die down, they should be lifted and perhaps planted in a more favourable spot.

AMARYLLIS.—These magnificent plants do not require the high temperature in which they are usually grown, nor should they be allowed to remain for a great length of time dust-dry, as we sometimes find them. It is important to remember that they have distinct seasons of activity and rest, but must not be forced into either condition by such rude measures as are occasionally resorted to. The proper soil for them is turfy loam, enriched with rotten manure, and rendered moderately porous by an admixture of sand. The light soil in which many plants thrive will not suit them; the soil must be firm, and somewhat rough in texture. When first potted, give them very little water, and promote growth by means of a bottom heat of 65°. Increase the supply of water as the plants progress, and shift them into 6-inch pots for flowering. While they are in flower they may be placed in the conservatory, or wherever else they may be required for decorative purposes. When the flowers have faded, take them to the greenhouse to complete their growth, after which dry them off slowly, but with the clear understanding that they are never to be desiccated. They may be wintered in the greenhouse, and should certainly be placed where they will always be slightly moist, even if a few leaves remain green throughout the winter. Frequent disturbance of the roots is to be particularly avoided in the cultivation of Amaryllis, and therefore it is desirable to allow them to remain in the same pots two or three years, or if they are shifted on, it should be done in such a way that the roots are scarcely so much as seen in the process. Top dressing and liquid manure will help them when they have been some time in the same pots.

LILIUM AURATUM.—The Golden-rayed Lily of Japan is as hardy as our common white Lily, and, like it, will grow with vigour in good loam, though, in common with the rest, it loves peat. Since it has been cheap it has been plentifully planted out, and proves to be a remarkably beautiful, and indeed noble, border flower ; but its distinctness will always insure it a high degree of favour as a conservatory plant. When grown in a pot the best soil is sandy peat, but it will flower finely in a rich light mixture, such as Fuchsias require. It is advisable to begin with the smallest sized pot in which the bulb can be placed, and then to shift to larger and larger pots as the plant progresses, and the flower-buds appear, when, of course, there must be no further shifting. In respect of temperature, this is an accommodating Lily, but as a rule a cool house is better for the plant than one which is maintained at a high temperature. The supply of water should be plentiful during the growth and flowering, but should be reduced when the flowering is over.

LILIUM HARRISII (*The Bermuda, or Easter Lily*) is of the *longiflorum* type, but the flowers are larger and are produced with greater freedom than by the ordinary *L. longiflorum*. Moreover the Bermuda Lily flowers almost continuously. Before one stem has finished blooming another shoots up. This perennial habit gives it a peculiar value for the greenhouse, and renders forcing possible at almost any season.

Immediately the bulbs are received they should be potted in rich fibrous loam—the more fibrous the better—and be placed in a cold frame. They need little water until growth has fairly commenced, after which more moisture will be necessary. So far as safety is concerned they only require protection from frost, but for an early show of bloom artificial heat is imperative. The temperature should, however, be very moderate at first and rise slowly. When the buds show, a top dressing of fresh loam and decayed manure will be helpful, and to allow for this the soil must be two inches from the tops of the pots when the bulbs are first potted. After producing two or three flowering stems it will be wise to place the pots out of doors and give less water, or the bulbs will be exhausted. But they must never be allowed to become quite dry, and after a partial rest of six weeks or two months they may be re-potted in fresh soil and started for another show of bloom.

We do not recommend the planting of this Lily in open borders during autumn, for growth will commence immediately, and a severe frost will cut it down; but if planted in spring it succeeds admirably and will produce a long succession of its handsome, trumpet-shaped flowers. For the following winter it can either be protected, or lifted for storing in a frame.

LILIUM LANCIFOLIUM.—This graceful and highly perfumed Lily is perfectly hardy, and will grow in good loam, though peat is to be preferred for pot culture. To produce handsome specimens, the same routine must be followed as directed for the cultivation of *L. auratum.* It scarcely need be added, that instead of growing the bulbs separately in pots, several may be grown in the same pot to produce a richer effect. In any case, however, it is not advisable to place the bulbs in a large mass of earth in the first instance. It is better that they should commence their growth in small pots, and be shifted on as they require more room. The varieties of *L. lancifolium* make splendid basket plants, especially if they can be displayed on a level with the eye, as the flowers are then seen to advantage. Aphis is extremely partial to these Lilies, particularly if they are badly grown, and allowed to suffer for the want of water. The simplest way to remove the pest is to dip the plants in pure water, taking care, of course, to prevent them from falling out of the pots in the operation.

JAPANESE DAY LILY (*Hemerocallis Kwanso fl. pl.*).—This beautiful plant is admirably adapted for pot culture to decorate the conservatory, the rich variegation of its graceful curling leaves affording an elegant display of colour in the early months of the year, and its fine double flowers being extremely showy during their short blooming season. As it is quite hardy, it may be planted in the select border with perfect safety, and, in common with other Day Lilies, it bears the shade of trees remarkably well. This is certainly one of the handsomest hardy plants in cultivation.

CROWN IMPERIAL (*Fritillaria imperialis*).—This noble plant requires a deep, rich, moist soil, and an open situation, to attain to its full structure and proper degree of stateliness, but it will make a very good figure in any border where it can enjoy a glimmer of sunshine. There are several distinct varieties, the flowers of which range in colour from palest yellow to the deepest shade of orange and reddish buff, and there is one which has variegated leaves.

MONTBRETIA

M. crocosmiæflora is a showy autumn-blooming plant of graceful branching habit, with large, bold, deep orange-red flowers which attain a height of about three feet. This bulb is now classed with the Tritonias, and should be cultivated in the same manner.

NARCISSUS

THE Narcissus differs from the Hyacinth, Tulip, and some other bulbs in one particular, which is important, because it furnishes the key to the management of this flower. The rootlets do not perish during the season of rest, and this fact clearly indicates that the bulbs should not remain out of ground for a day longer than is necessary.

CULTURE IN POTS.—All the Polyanthus class, and almost all the Garden varieties, thrive in pots, and can be forced with extreme ease. Pot them early in any rich, porous compost, and put them into the soil a little deeper than is usual for Hyacinths. For a few weeks keep them in a cool spot in the open ground under a thick covering of ashes or cocoa-nut fibre, which will promote root-growth without prematurely starting the tops. With all bulbs this is an important point, especially for such as are intended to be brought forward in heat. When the pots are full of roots, leaf-growth will commence, and the covering should be removed. A cool pit is then the best place for them. The after treatment will depend entirely on the date the flowers are wanted. A low temperature, long continued, means late flowering, so that within reasonable limits the grower can control the time of their appearance. For the earliest display select the Roman and Paper White, which are naturally early blooming varieties. After a few days in the cool pit, transfer to the greenhouse, and about a week or ten days before they are needed in flower, plunge them in a brisk bottom heat, and give plenty of water of the proper temperature. The forcing should not begin until the plants are sufficiently advanced, or it will injure them both in size and colour. Weak manure water will be beneficial occasionally, but when the flowers begin to open this must be discontinued, and at the same time the heat should be diminished.

A succession of Narcissi for indoor decoration can be secured by starting batches at intervals of two or three weeks; and by moderating the treatment as the season advances, the last lot will flower naturally without artificial stimulus. Large bulbs should be potted singly, but several roots of the smaller sorts may be put into one pot. Heavy heads of bloom will need support, and there is nothing neater than the wires which are made expressly for the purpose.

CULTURE IN WATER.—For growing in glasses no other bulbous flower is equal to the Narcissus. Darkness at the outset is not essential to it, and therefore the gradual development of the roots may be observed from the time they start; and contact with water will do no harm to the bulb. The glasses should, however, be kept in a low and fairly uniform temperature, to discourage the growth of foliage until the bulbs have fully formed their roots. Pure rain water is desirable, but it is not actually necessary; and for the sake of appearances, as well as on the score of health, it should be changed immediately it ceases to be quite transparent. Those who do not care to observe the growth in glasses, but like to have the plants in water during the blooming period, may grow the bulbs in pots in the usual way, and wash off the soil when wanted. In this case the roots will not be quite so regular as those which have been wholly grown in water. Perhaps we need scarcely say that it is possible to utilise this flower in many other ways; such, for instance, as in decorating épergnes, glass globes, and fancy vases. They may also be made to float on a small fountain or aquarium; indeed, it is surprising to what varied and effective purposes a little ingenuity will adapt them.

CULTURE IN OPEN GROUND.—For this purpose the Narcissus will always command attention for its graceful appearance; and this observation applies with as much force to the Polyanthus section when thus used, as to the varieties which are specially recognised as Garden Narcissus. The latter class includes many old favourites, among which is the Pheasant's Eye—one of the most exquisite flowers grown in our gardens.

We may at once admit that the Narcissus does not alone make a showy bed of flowers. The gracefulness which is its principal charm is not effective when planted in large masses. But this apparent shortcoming is more than atoned for by its elegant appearance in the positions for which it is naturally adapted. Beneath trees, by the side of a shady walk, in front of shrubberies, or in the mixed border, the Narcissus is thoroughly at home, and large groups of it cannot fail to arrest attention.

If possible, choose a position where the bulbs need not be disturbed for several years, and plant them early. When the spot they are to occupy happens to be full, pot the bulbs until the ground is vacant, and in due time turn them out. A southern or western aspect is desirable, but the nature of the soil is comparatively unimportant, provided it is dry when the bulbs are in their resting state. In sour land or in stagnant water they will certainly rot, but a touch of sea spray will not injure them. If the soil needs enriching, there is no better material than decayed cow-manure, which may be incorporated as the work goes on, or it can be applied as a top dressing. Plants which are evidently weak may be assisted with a few doses of manure water, not too strong.

In planting groups, put the smaller bulbs four or five inches apart, and the larger sorts from six to nine inches ; depth, six to nine inches, according to size. Where exposed to a strong wind, it may be necessary to give the flowers some kind of support to save them from injury.

The Double and Single Daffodils are now in marked public favour. Their bright colours make them extremely valuable for planting under and among trees, and a sufficient number should always be put in to produce an immediate effect. They thrive in damp, shady spots, and every three or four years it will be necessary to divide and replant them.

ORNITHOGALUM ARABICUM

DURING the month of June this fine variety of the *Star of Bethlehem* produces heads of pure white fragrant flowers, each having a black centre. The roots are large and fleshy, and should be planted in the autumn nine inches deep. A sheltered position, such as under a south wall, is desirable for them, and some protection in the form of dry litter, or a heap of light manure, will be necessary to carry the roots safely through severe winter weather. The bulbs are frequently potted for indoor decoration.

OXALIS

THESE frame plants are suitable for the cool greenhouse or for forcing, and they are adapted also for the open border in peculiarly favourable climates: They are particularly neat and cheerful, flowering abundantly, and requiring only the most ordinary treatment of frame plants. In winter they should be kept dry. The 48-sized pot is suitable, and about five bulbs may be planted in each, using light soil freely mixed with sand.

RANUNCULUS

To maintain a collection of named Ranunculuses demands skill and patience, but, strange to say, a few of the most brilliant self-coloured and spotted and striped varieties may be easily grown, provided only that a cool, deep, rich, moist soil can be provided for them. The best staple soil for the Ranunculus is a loam or clay in which the common field Buttercup grows freely and plentifully. The situation should be open, the bed well pulverised, and the soil effectively drained, both to promote a vigorous growth and as far as possible to save the plants from injury by wire-worms, leather-jackets and other ground vermin. Elaborate modes of manuring, such as mixing several sorts of manures together in mystical proportions, are altogether unnecessary, but a good dressing of rotten manure and leaf-mould should be dug in before planting, and if the soil is particularly heavy, sharp sand must be added. The roots may be planted in November and December in gardens where vegetation does not usually suffer from damp in winter; but where there is any reason to apprehend danger from damp, the planting should be deferred to February, and should then be completed within the first twenty days, if weather permit. Prepare a fine surface to plant on, and draw drills six inches apart and two inches deep, and place the tubers, claws downwards, in the drills, four inches apart, covering them with sifted soil before drawing the earth back to the drill. Rake the bed smooth, and the planting is completed. To keep free from weeds, and to give plentiful supplies of water in dry weather, are the two principal features of the summer cultivation. When the flowers are past, and the leaves begin to fade, take up the roots, dry them in a cool place, and store in peat or cocoa-nut fibre.

TURBAN RANUNCULUSES.—These are remarkably handsome

plants, of hardier constitution and freer growth than the edged and spotted varieties. For the production of masses of colour, and to form showy clumps in the borders, they are of the utmost value. They require a good loam, well manured, and the general treatment advised for the named varieties; but as they are less delicate, they may be dealt with in a rougher fashion.

SCILLA

THE Blue Squill may be grown in exactly the same manner as the Roman Hyacinth for indoor decoration, and it makes a charming companion to that flower. It is perfectly hardy, and for its deep, lovely blue should be largely grown in the open border, where it appears to especial advantage in conjunction with Snowdrops. It is also valuable for filling small beds, and for making marginal lines in the geometric garden.

The *Scilla sibirica* thrives on the mountains of North Italy, where masses of it may be seen growing close to the snow, and in this country it withstands wind and rain which would be the ruin of many another flower. Still we like to see it in a sheltered border, where it has a fair chance of displaying its beauty without much risk of injury. In such a position it will flower in February, and in the bleakest quarter it will open in March. It is not at all fastidious as to soil, but when planted will give no further trouble until the foliage withers, and it is time to lift the bulbs to make way for other occupants. If convenient they may remain for years in one spot.

The *Scilla campanulata* deserves more attention than it has hitherto received. After almost all other spring flowering bulbs are over, it makes a beautiful display, which lasts until nearly the end of May. It somewhat resembles the wild Blue-bell, but is much larger than that woodland flower.

SNOWDROP

SNOWDROPS are amongst the hardiest flowers known to our gardens, and are invaluable for their welcome snow-white bells in the earliest days of the opening spring. They should be planted in clumps, and left alone for years. The double-flowering variety is exquisitely beautiful : we might indeed speak of it as a bit of vegetable jewellery.

The flowers are bell-shaped, closely packed with petals, like so many microscopic petticoats arranged for the 'tiring' of a fairy: they are snow-white, and sometimes delicately tipped with light green. This variety is as hardy as the single, and the best for growing in baskets and pots. When employed in lines the planting ought to be very close together, and the line should be composed of several rows, making in fact a broad band. Such a ribbon when backed with *Scilla sibirica* is very beautiful. The best way of displaying the Snowdrop alone is in large groups densely crowded together. The effect is much more telling than when the same number of bulbs is spread over a larger area. Put the roots in drills, two inches deep, and if possible in a spot where they need not be disturbed for two or three years. Snowdrops may be grown in pots, and be gently forced for Christmas. But unless wanted very early, it will answer to lift clumps from the border in November and pot them.

SPARAXIS

SEE instructions under Ixia at page 296.

STERNBERGIA LUTEA

A HARDY yellow Amaryllis which blooms in September and October, and is one of our most useful autumnal bulbous flowers. It grows freely in a light rich loam, and may be lifted every year, or be allowed to occupy the same spot for two or three successive seasons. Plant in patches three inches deep, either in November or December.

TIGRIDIA

SEE Ferraria, page 287.

TRITELEIA UNIFLORA

THIS little gem belongs to the spring garden, and should be the companion of the Dog's-tooth Violet, the Crocus, and the Snowdrop. It will grow in any soil, and will produce an abundance of its violet-tinted white flowers, which, when handled, emit a faint odour of garlic.

As a pot plant for the Alpine house it is first-rate. In the open, plant in October two inches deep.

TRITONIA

TRITONIAS are more showy than the Ixia or Sparaxis, but belong to the same group of South African Irids, and require the same treatment. They may be planted out in April, if prepared for that mode of cultivation by potting them in small pots in November or December. It is not considered advisable to tie them to sticks, for they are more elegant when allowed to fall over the edge of the pots, and suggest the 'negligence of Nature.'

TROPÆOLUM

Tropæolum tuberosum

A FEW of the tuberous-rooted Tropæolums are hardy, but it is not advisable to leave them in the ground, for damp may destroy them if they are proof against frost. They are all graceful trailing plants, adapted for covering wire trellises, and may be flowered at any season if required, though their natural season is the summer. The compost in which they thrive best is a light rich loam, containing a large proportion of sand. The stems are usually trained on wires, but they may be allowed to fall down from a pot or basket with excellent effect, to form a most attractive tracery of leafage dotted with dazzling flowers. The sunniest part of the greenhouse should be devoted to the Tropæolums, and special care should be taken in potting them to secure ample drainage.

TUBEROSE

Polianthes tuberosa

THIS bulb is extensively grown in the South of France for the delicious perfume obtainable from its numerous pure white flowers. In this country it is widely known, but considering the beauty and exceeding fragrance of the blossoms it is astonishing that a greater number is not planted every season. Perhaps the fact that the bulbs are valueless after the first year may in a measure account for the comparatively limited culture. There are several varieties, including the African, American, and Pearl, and all are easily flowered as pot plants in a mixture of loam and leaf-mould, plunged in a bottom heat of 60° or 70°. They grow rather tall, and should be kept near the glass.

TULIP

WHEN grown in pots, Tulips are treated in precisely the same manner as the Hyacinth, but several bulbs, according to their size and the purpose they are intended for, are placed in a pot. When required to fill épergnes and baskets, and other elegant receptacles, it is a good plan to grow them in shallow boxes, as recommended for Crocuses, and transfer them when in flower to the vases and baskets. This mode of procedure insures exactitude of colouring, height, and stage of development, whereas, when the bulbs are grown from the first in the ornamental vessels, they may not flower with sufficient uniformity to produce a satisfactory display. In common with the Hyacinth and Crocus, Tulips may be taken out of the soil in which they have been grown, and after washing the roots clean, they can be inserted in glasses for decorating an apartment. As the early Tulips are extremely cheap, they are often employed in this way to light up festive gatherings at Christmas and the early months of the year. The early and medium varieties are admirably adapted for pot culture, but late Tulips are not worth growing in pots because of their lateness; otherwise, indeed, they are extremely beautiful, and the florists' varieties are highly valued as exhibition flowers.

For general usefulness the early Tulips are the most valuable of all, because of their peculiarly accommodating nature, their many and brilliant colours, and their suitability for the formation of rich masses in the flower garden. Any good soil will suit them, and they may be planted in quantities under trees if the position enjoys some amount of sunshine, because they will have finished their growth before the leafage of the trees shades them injuriously. If it is necessary to prepare or improve the soil for them, the aim should be to render it rich and sandy, and sufficiently drained to avoid a boggy character in winter. Plant in October or November, four or five inches deep, and six inches apart. The roots require no water and no supports, and may all be taken up and stored away in good time for the usual summer display of bedding plants. It is important to select the sorts with care for geometric planting, but a most interesting border may be made by planting clumps of all the best sorts of the several classes. The result will be a long-continued and splendid display, beginning with the 'Van Thols' (which are as hardy as any), then following with the early class in almost endless variety, and finishing with the noble 'Gesneriana,' and the flamed and feathered varieties of the late section.

VALLOTA PURPUREA

This brilliant plant is nearly hardy in the southern counties, and a cool greenhouse plant where it cannot be grown in the open border. To produce fine specimens, a regular system of potting on must be practised, a firm loamy soil being employed, with abundance of water all the summer, and moderate supplies all the winter. To 'dry it off' is to kill or weaken the bulb past recovery. It is a substitute for the Amaryllis, with those who cannot cultivate that plant.

VIOLET, DOG'S-TOOTH (*See page* 286)

WINTER ACONITE

The Winter Aconite is the very 'firstling' of the year, for it blooms in advance of the Snowdrop, covering the ground with gilt spangles in the bleakest days of February. Any soil or situation will suit it, and it should be planted in large patches where a winter's walk in the garden is valued. It should also be grown in quantity within view from the windows, for the benefit of those who, in the dreary season, cannot get out. The bulbs may be left in the ground for several years, or they may be taken up and stored after the leaves have perished.

ZEPHYRANTHES CANDIDA

Flower of the West Wind

A dwarf white Crocus-like flower, with foliage resembling the common rush on a small scale. Plant in clumps from November to March in borders, and it will commence blooming about the end of July, and continue in flower until frost cuts it down. Any soil will suit it, and it thrives for several years if left undisturbed.

FLOWERS ALL THE YEAR ROUND

FROM SEEDS AND ROOTS

INTRODUCTORY REMARKS

BEFORE proceeding to the duties which belong to the several months of the year, it may be worth while to consider some of the points which constitute the alphabet of pot culture. To grow any plant in a pot is an artificial proceeding, and the conditions for its sustenance and health have to be provided. Among these conditions are temperature and accommodation. Now, it is useless to attempt to grow flowers which require heat if that requirement cannot be met. And it is equally useless to pot many more plants than the space will accommodate when they attain their full size. A limited number, well grown, will produce a greater wealth of bloom, of finer quality, than many plants which are feeble through lack of space for development. Nevertheless, there are numerous varieties raised in heat in the early months of the year which can be grown and flowered in the most satisfactory manner, without any kind of artificial aid, from sowings made in the open ground during April and May. The flowering will be somewhat later than from plants brought forward under glass; but as they receive no check from the very commencement, they will not be greatly behind their nursed relations; and they may even excel them in robust beauty, if they are treated intelligently and with a generous hand.

GOOD SOIL for pot plants is not always obtainable at a reasonable cost, and sometimes the materials at hand must be made to serve the purpose. Still it is a well-known fact, that in proportion to the skill and experience of the cultivator will be his desire to secure a supply of loam, peat, and leaf-mould. Those who are capable of turning poor soil to the best account are precisely the men who will be most anxious to obtain the materials which are known to promote the luxurious growth of pot plants.

The top spit of an old pasture makes capital potting soil. If taken from light land, it need only be stacked for one year before use. A heavy loam should be kept for at least two seasons, and in any case the heap should be turned and remade several times. A slight sprinkling of soot between the layers of soil will be beneficial, and help to make it distasteful to grubs, wireworms, and other vermin. The frequent turnings will not be wasted labour, for it equalises the quality, and tends to sweeten the whole by exposing new surfaces to the atmosphere; and this is a great aid to healthy growth.

Many plants thrive in peat, or in soil of which peat is a constituent, and some flowers cannot be grown without it. The peat may have to be purchased from a distance, but there is no difficulty in obtaining it, as a considerable trade is done in this article.

A constant supply of decayed leaf-mould may possibly be arranged for on the spot; but if this is out of the question, it is procurable in most districts.

The preparation of soil for pot plants is frequently postponed until the day on which it is actually required. This is bad practice, and results too often in the use of an improper proportion of the materials, and perhaps in their defective admixture. In this, as in all other operations connected with horticulture, the men who take time by the forelock will achieve the highest results. In no pursuit of life is it more necessary to forecast coming duties, than in the culture of flowers. We will suppose that three or four weeks hence many pots are to be filled with Primulas. The man who grows them with any degree of enthusiasm will not defer the preparation of the soil until the day arrives for potting the plants. He will determine in advance the proportions of loam, leaf-mould, and sand, have the whole thoroughly incorporated, and possibly sifted to remove stones. With these may come away some undecayed fibres, which make excellent material for laying over the crocks at the bottom of each pot. Forethought of this kind is certain of an ample reward.

Potting soil should also be in the right condition as to moisture. This is not easy to describe, but it should handle freely, and yet there should be no necessity for the immediate application of water after sowing seeds or planting bulbs. In the event of the compost being too dry, give it a soaking and allow it to rest for one or more days, according to the time of year and the state of the atmosphere.

Pots NEW OR OLD should be soaked in water before use. They are very porous, and by absorbing moisture from the soil they may at once make it too dry, although in exactly the right condition before being placed in the pots. And old pots ought never to be used until they have been scrubbed quite clean. These may appear to be trivial matters, unworthy of attention. They have, however, an influence on the health of plants, and experienced growers know that a few apparent trifles make all the difference between success and failure. Pots which are dirty, or covered with green moss, prevent access of air, and tend to bring about a sickly growth. Cleanliness in horticulture is valuable for its own sake, and for the orderly routine it necessitates on the part of the cultivator.

Pots are known both by number and by size. They are sold by the 'cast,' and a cast always consists of the distinguishing number. The following are the numbers and sizes:—

Number in Cast			Inches
72	Inside diameter across top		$2\frac{1}{2}$
Small 60	,,	,,	$2\frac{3}{4}$
Mid. 60	,,	,,	3
Large 60	,,	,,	$3\frac{1}{2}$
Small 54	,,	,,	4
Large 54	,,	,,	$4\frac{1}{4}$
Small 48	,,	,,	$4\frac{3}{4}$
Large 48	,,	,,	5
40	,,	,,	$5\frac{1}{2}$
32	,,	,,	$6\frac{1}{4}$
28	,,	,,	7
24	,,	,,	$7\frac{1}{2}$
16	,,	,,	$8\frac{1}{2}$
12	,,	,,	$9\frac{1}{2}$
8	,,	,,	11
6	,,	,,	$12\frac{1}{2}$
4	,,	,,	14
2	,,	,,	$15\frac{1}{2}$
1	,,	,,	18

WATERING is sometimes conducted on the principle that the usual time has arrived, and therefore the plants must have water. But do they need it? Press the fingers firmly on the surface; if particles of soil adhere it is too dry. Or tap the pots smartly with the knuckles or with a stick, when a clear and unmistakable answer will be obtained. Plants differ widely in their demand for water. Some are very thirsty, others require less frequent attention. The season of the year and the state of the atmosphere have also to be considered, as well as the fact that a heavy soil is more retentive of moisture than a lighter compost. A watchful eye and a willing hand will seldom err on this point. The water should always be of the same temperature as the house, otherwise the plants will be constantly checked. A tank in the greenhouse meets this requirement. In its absence, the watering pots should be kept full under the stage, and they will be ready when wanted.

In the open ground, it is better to water a few plots thoroughly for two or three successive evenings, and then have an interval, rather than moisten the surface daily. The effect of constantly applying small quantities of water is to encourage the surface growth of roots. Then if the sun shines fiercely upon the soil, the first day of neglect results in immense mischief.

DRAINAGE is easily managed. Into each pot put a crock almost the size of the bottom, with the convex side upwards. There need be no niggling to remove sharp angles, or to make the fragment shapely. Cover this with smaller crocks, and these with moss, cocoa-nut fibre, or in some cases with small pieces of charcoal. If the compost has a proper admixture of sharp sand or grit, free drainage will be insured, and yet the soil cannot be washed through the pot. Silver sand is employed in districts near a supply, and there is nothing better for the purpose. But road grit, and the sweepings from gravel walks, finely sifted, are substitutes not to be despised.

VENTILATION is important, for a house full of plants cannot long be kept close with impunity. The lights should be opened whenever the state of the weather admits of it, and by doing this on the side opposite to the quarter whence the wind blows, it is frequently safe to give air when it may be dangerous from other points of the compass; and it should be done early in the day before the sun gets hot. Often the lights remain closed on a sunny morning, until the atmosphere becomes stifling; and then perhaps plants which have been made sensitive by excess of heat are subjected to a killing draught.

IN MANAGING TEMPERATURE, there should be no violent alternations of heat and cold, for these bring speedy disaster; and it is unwise to employ more heat than is actually necessary. Deviations from this rule are generally traceable to neglect. If the proper season for sowing seed of some important flower has been allowed to pass, an attempt is made to compensate for lost time by hurrying the growth in a forcing temperature. Every needless degree of heat will be harmful and result in attenuated growth, poverty of colour, or in the attacks of some insect plague which the weakly plant seldom invites in vain. It is wise always to employ the lowest temperature in which plants will flourish. This necessitates the proper time for their full development, and will result in a sturdy growth capable of yielding a bountiful display of bloom. Occasionally it is requisite to force some special subject, such as bulbs for Christmas festivities. Even then it is advisable to augment the temperature very gradually, and to defer the employment of its highest power until the latest possible moment.

Plants are frequently taken straight from the forcing pit into some cold room, to their utter ruin. A moment's reflection will show the folly of such a proceeding. They should be prepared for the change by gradual transfer through lower temperatures; and if only a few hours are occupied in the process it will help them to pass the ordeal with less injury.

It should be an established custom to examine the seed-pans at least once every day, and morning is the best time for the task. If work has to be done, there is the whole day to arrange for its accomplishment. Whereas if the visit is not made until evening, there may not remain sufficient daylight to do what is necessary. Just as seedlings are starting, a few hours' neglect will render them weak and leggy.

When transferring plants from seed-pans, it is usual to put them round the edges of pots. This is no mere caprice, but is founded on the well-ascertained fact that seedlings establish their roots with greater readiness near the edge of the pot than away from it.

In years gone by, tan was very much in demand for covering newly potted bulbs, and for many other purposes in connection with horticulture. But the use of chemicals in the process of tanning has rendered the tan deleterious, and it should be avoided. Cocoa-nut fibre is an efficient substitute, light, clean, and beneficial to plant life.

In the following monthly notes, one principal object is to offer a series of reminders which will insure the sowing of various flower seeds and the planting of bulbs at their proper periods, and thus save the disappointment of losing some important display for a whole season. Those who have command of large resources will sow certain seeds a month earlier than we recommend, and their intimate knowledge and great facilities justify their practice. But we have especially in view the possibilities for an amateur, and of gardens moderate in extent, where appliances may not be of the most perfect kind.

When seeds are once sown or bulbs potted, the work is before the cultivator, and appeals mutely for attention. Therefore it is not our purpose to give detailed and continuous instructions month by month for every flower. We shall limit our remarks to hints at the time for sowing or planting, and to some few points which may subsequently appear to demand notice.

For convenience of reference, the subjects are arranged alphabetically under each month.

JANUARY

IN the open ground there is little or nothing of interest in the way of flowers, but the greenhouses and pits are full of promise. A constant watch must be kept upon the barometer, and the materials for repelling frost or bleak winds should be at perfect command, so that there may be ample provision for saving plants from biting weather.

ACHIMENES are stove bulbs, which cannot be grown without a sufficiency of heat. A warm greenhouse will answer for them, and some gardeners produce fair specimens in frames over hot-beds. The bulbs will lie dormant for a considerable time, so that it is easy to have a succession of flowers. A few should be started now, employing sandy loam for the pots. Follow up with others at intervals.

ANEMONE.—See remarks under October.

ANTIRRHINUMS raised in heat now will flower later in the year. Pot off singly, and gradually harden for planting out in May. There are dwarf, medium, and tall varieties, of many beautiful colours.

CANNA.—From the popular name of Indian Shot, it will naturally be inferred that the seed is extremely hard and spherical. It needs soaking in water for twelve hours before sowing. Even then it will probably be a considerable time in germinating, and there will also be longer or shorter intervals between the appearance of the seedlings. A high temperature is necessary to insure a start; but after the young plants are transferred to single pots, they should be kept steadily going in a more moderate heat until ready for the border or sub-tropical garden in June. Meanwhile they will need re-potting two or three times, and should have a rich and rather stiff compost.

CINERARIAS should have air whenever it is possible. For watering choose the middle of the day, and do not slop the water about carelessly, or mildew may result. In houses which are not lighted all round, the plants should be turned regularly to prevent them from facing one way. Such specimens are worthless for the dinner table, and will be diminished in value for decorating the drawing-room.

CYCLAMENS are still in the height of their beauty. The pots have become so full of roots that ordinary watering partially fails of its purpose. An occasional immersion of the pots for about half an hour will result in marked benefit to the plants. The flowers, when taken from the corm, should be lifted by a smart pull. If cut, the stems bleed and exhaust the root.

Where a succession of this flower is valued, a sowing should be made either in this month or in February. Dibble the seed, an inch apart and a quarter of an inch deep, in pots or pans firmly filled with rich porous soil; and place in heat of not less than 56° not exceeding 70°; the less the temperature varies the better. Cyclamen seed is both slow and irregular in germinating, and sometimes proves a sore trial even to the patient. As the seedlings become ready transfer to small pots, and shift on as growth demands, always keeping the crown of the corm free from soil. The increasing power of the sun will render shading essential; yet a position near the glass is most advantageous to the plants.

GESNERA ZEBRINA DISCOLOR.—Those who have once grown this handsome conservatory plant will not afterwards consent to be without it. The richly marked foliage contrasts admirably with the orange and scarlet flowers. Sow in the manner advised for Gloxinia, and the two plants may be grown in the same house.

GLOXINIA.—From two or three sowings, and by a little management, it is easy to have a supply of this magnificent flower in every month of the year. There are three types—the drooping, horizontal, and erect-flowered. All are beautiful, and have their special adaptations, but the horizontal and erect classes command the majority of admirers. One routine of treatment is applicable to all. Sow thinly in new pots filled with a light porous compost, and see that the drainage is exceptionally good. Give the pots a warm moist position, and a light sprinkling of water daily will assist germination. The first seedlings that are ready should be lifted and pricked off without disturbing the remainder of the soil. Follow up the process until all are transferred. Although the leaves may rest on the surface, the hearts should never be covered. Pot off singly when large enough, and shift on until the 48-size is reached. For ordinary plants this is large enough, but extra fine specimens need more pot room, and so long as increased space is given the flowering will be deferred. Between each plant there must be a clear space, or the leaves may decay through contact. While growing, a moist atmosphere, with a temperature of 60° or 65°, will suit them, but immediately flowering commences, humidity will be a source of mischief. The forwardest plants from the present sowing will begin to flower early in June if well treated.

GREVILLEA ROBUSTA.—Seed of this exceedingly handsome shrub may be sown at any time of the year, and the pots containing it must be kept moist until the seedlings appear. How long it will be before they become visible we cannot tell. Germination may not occur until hope has died, and the pots have been contemptuously relegated to some obscure corner. But after the young plants are pricked off, they will give no trouble except to re-pot them two or three times, and see that they do not perish for want of water.

HOLLYHOCK.—The named varieties which have been continuously propagated by cuttings have become so feeble that disease has almost swept them away. But seedlings are sufficiently robust to withstand its attacks, and this grand border flower is now grown as an annual or biennial, with fine double blossoms, superb in colour and of noble proportions. Sow in well-drained pots or seed-pans, cover the seed with a sprinkling of fine soil, and place in a temperature of 65° or 70°. In about a fortnight the seedlings will be ready for pricking off round the edges of $4\frac{1}{2}$-inch pots.

PETUNIA.—About the third week of this month, a sowing should be made to produce plants for indoor decoration. Late in February or early in March will be soon enough to prepare for bedding stuff. Sow thinly in good porous soil, and give the pots or pans a temperature of about 60°. They should have a little extra attention just as the seed is germinating, for that is a critical time with Petunias. Uniformity in temperature and moisture, with shade when necessary, and plenty of pot room, are the secrets of success in growing these plants.

VERBENAS have been ruined in constitution by the needless heat to which they have been subjected for generations, and the method of raising them by cuttings has almost broken down. Seedlings have the advantage of being strong enough to withstand mildew, to say nothing of the saving effected in time and labour. The Verbena should be grown with as little artificial aid as possible In fact, the more nearly it is treated as a hardy plant, the more vigorous and free flowering will it be. A temperature of 60° is sufficient to raise the seed at this period of the year; and after the plants are established in pots, heat may be gradually dispensed with. Sow in pans or boxes filled with rich, mellow, and very sweet soil. Transfer to thumb pots when large enough, and give one or two more shifts as growth demands, until the plants are ready for bedding out in May. Green Fly is very partial to the Verbena, especially while in pots; it must be kept down, or the seedlings will make no progress. There is a choice of distinct colours, which come true from seed.

FEBRUARY

A CONSIDERABLE number of important flowers should be sown during this month. The precise dates depend partly on the character of the season, and partly on the resources of the cultivator. Should the month open with frost, or with rough wet weather, it will be wise to exercise a little patience. Where there are insufficient means for battling with sudden variations of temperature, choose the end rather than the beginning of the month for starting tender subjects. Govern the work by intelligent observation, instead of following hard and fast rules. But in no case should fear of the weather form an excuse for the postponement of any duty which certainly ought not to be deferred.

ANNUALS AND BIENNIALS, HARDY.—It is one of the merits of hardy annuals and biennials sown in late summer for blooming in the following spring, that they need very little attention. Still they ought not to be entirely neglected. They should be kept scrupulously free from weeds, and it may be evident that a mulch of decayed manure is necessary to protect and strengthen them for a rich display of colour in the spring. Such varieties as have to be transplanted should be watched, and the first suitable opportunity seized for transferring them to flowering positions.

ABUTILON is a flowering greenhouse shrub which answers well under the treatment of an annual. It does not need a forcing temperature at any stage, nor is the plant fastidious as to soil. The seed, which is both slow and irregular in germinating, may be sown in pots. As the young plants become ready they should be pricked off and kept steadily growing. When leaves drop it indicates mismanagement, perhaps starvation. A well-grown specimen, when the buds show, will be two feet high, and bear examination all round.

ANEMONE.—Against the practice of planting Dutch and French roots of this elegant flower we have not a word to say. On the contrary, there is much to be advanced in its favour. Arrangements of colour can be secured by it which are impossible of attainment from seedlings. Still there can be no doubt that the supposed necessity of depending alone on bulbs has proved a barrier to the growth of Anemones in many gardens, and on a large scale. We believe that an immense number will in future adorn borders in autumn where few or none have been grown hitherto. The culture of the plant from seed is of the simplest character, no appliances whatever beyond those at the command of the humblest cottager being necessary. The prime requisite is a rich moist soil. Where this does not exist naturally, a liberal dressing of mellow cow-manure, and, when necessary, a diligent employment of the water-can, will render it possible to grow superb flowers of brilliant colour. The best way of making the seed-bed is to open a trench, putting a layer of decayed manure at the bottom, and mingling a further quantity with the soil when it is returned. The addition of some light compost or sand to the surface may or may not be necessary to prepare it for the seed. We prefer sowing in rows, and lightly scratching the seed in. Some growers only sift a little sand over, and the practice answers well. Pains must be taken to remove weeds until the seedlings appear, and it must be confessed that they are a long time about it, because the seed is very slow in germinating. Thinning to six inches apart, and keeping the bed clean and moist, constitute the whole remainder of the work of growing Anemones.

AURICULA.—The Show Auricula is one of the reigning beauties of the floral world, and, like the Rose, has its own special exhibitions. Over its deep, soft colours, partially hidden by a veil of powder —technically called paste—enthusiasts almost lose their heads. And although the flower merits all the admiration it receives, yet it must be confessed that some amateurs indulge in a great deal of misplaced coddling in the work of raising it. One quality there must be in the grower, and that is patience; for seed saved from a single plant in any given season, and sown at one time, will germinate in the most irregular manner. Months may elapse between the appearance of the first and last plant. The lesson to sow thinly is obvious, so that the seedlings may be lifted as they become ready, without disturbing the surrounding soil. Both the Show and Alpine varieties should be sown in pans filled with sweet sandy loam or peat. They may be started in gentle heat, but it is really needless. The Auricula is thoroughly hardy against cold, and glass is only employed as a protection against wind, heavy rain, and atmospheric deposits.

BEGONIA, TUBEROUS-ROOTED.—The grace and beauty of this plant have placed it in the front rank of popular favourites. For the foliage alone it is worth growing, and the flowers are unique both in form and colour. Raising the plant from seed is not only the least expensive process, but it possesses all the charm arising from the hope of some novelty which shall eclipse previously known varieties. As a matter of fact, new attractions either in colour or in habit are introduced almost every year. From a sowing made now, plants should flower in June or July, and become fine specimens by the autumn in readiness for blooming again in the following spring.

The seed is small, and requires careful handling. It is also slow and capricious in germinating, and many growers have their own pet methods of starting it. Good results are obtained by insuring free drainage, and partly filling the pots with rather rough fibrous compost, covered with a layer of fine sandy loam made even for a seed-bed. This is sprinkled with water, and the seed is sown very thinly. Some experienced growers make a rather loose surface, and press the seed gently into it, and do not finish with a covering of soil. The majority, however, will find it safer to give a slight sifting of fine earth over the seed. Then comes a trial of patience, and as the seedlings appear at intervals, the wisdom of thin sowing will be apparent, for each one can be lifted and potted as it becomes ready, without wasting the remainder. An even temperature of about 65° is essential during germination.

Begonia bulbs which have been stored through the winter will need careful watching. Not until they start naturally should there be any attempt to induce growth, or in all probability it will result in the destruction of the bulb. Such as show signs of life should be potted in good soil, commencing with small pots, and afterwards shifting into larger sizes as the pots become full of roots. Until the largest size intended for them is reached, remove all flowers. A warm humid atmosphere is favourable to them while growing, but when flowering begins moisture will be injurious.

CALCEOLARIA, SHRUBBY.—Seed sown in pans placed in a frame or a greenhouse of moderate temperature will insure plants for out-door summer decoration. Transfer the seedlings to pots quite early.

CELOSIA PLUMOSA.—Seed may either be sown now or in March, and the routine recommended for Cockscombs will develop splendid plumes, but in this case the dwarfing practice by means of the knife is neither practicable nor desirable.

CHRYSANTHEMUM INDICUM can be raised easily from seed, and if sown now in a moderate heat, the plants will flower the first season. Pot the seedlings immediately they are ready, then harden and put them out of doors as early as may be safe. This treatment will keep them dwarf and robust. Seedlings should not be stopped, but be allowed to grow quite naturally. Those that do not flower the first season, will do so in the second year. The well-known Paris daisy (Marguerite) is a perennial Chrysanthemum, and it is the only one which is not quite hardy.

COCKSCOMB.—The ideal Cockscomb is a dwarf, well-furnished plant, with large, symmetrical, and intensely coloured combs. Seed of a first-class strain will produce a fair proportion of such plants in the hands of a man who understands their treatment. Sow in seed-pans filled with rich, sweet, friable loam, and place in a brisk temperature. Transfer the seedlings very early to small pots, and shift on until the size is reached in which they are to flower. Directly they become root-bound the combs will be formed, and having been grown entirely in heat, it is not improbable that the plants may be much too tall. If so, fill pots with suitable soil, using a size smaller than those already occupied; cut off the heads with a sufficient length of stem, remove a few of the lower leaves, and insert the stems firmly in the new pots. Place them on a hot-bed kept close and shaded for a few days, and if the specimens have been judiciously chosen and skilfully treated, there will be grand combs on dwarf plants.

DAHLIA, DOUBLE, can be grown and flowered from seed as a half-hardy annual, and the best strains will produce a good proportion of double flowers of fair quality. Either in this month or early in March, sow in a warm house or pit. When the seedlings are large enough transfer to single pots, and thoroughly harden them in readiness for removal to the open ground in May. With very little trouble and expense, it is easy to raise a large stock of this fine border flower from seed.

DAHLIA, SINGLE.—After many years of neglect, the Single Dahlia almost suddenly attained to great popularity, mainly through the improvement it has undergone in the hands of a few able growers. The immense demand for it is easily met by raising large numbers from seed, and this mode of growing it will naturally increase, because of the small cost of seedlings, especially as a good strain produces flowers of great excellence. A sowing in this month will supply plants sufficiently forward to bloom at the usual time. Some growers begin in January, and provided they have room, and the work can be followed up without risking a check at any stage, no objection can be raised to the practice. For most gardens, however, February is safer, and March will not be too late. Sow thinly in pots or pans, filled with light rich soil, and finished with a very thin covering of fine leaf-mould. When the seedlings are about an inch high, pot them separately, taking especial care of the weakly specimens, for these in point of colour may prove to be the gems of the collection. After transplanting, a little extra attention will help them to a fresh start.

DIANTHUS.—All the varieties may be raised in about 55° or 60° of heat, but immediately the seed has germinated, it is important to put the pots in a lower temperature, or the seedlings will become soft. They should also be transferred to seed-pans when large enough to handle.

FUCHSIA.—It is not generally known that Fuchsias can be satisfactorily flowered from seed in six or seven months, and from a good strain there will be seedlings well worth growing. Sow thinly on a close soil, and give the pots a temperature of about 70°. While quite small, transfer the plants to the edges of well-drained pots, and later on pot them singly into a compost consisting largely of leaf-mould until the flowering size is reached, when a proportion of decayed cow-manure should be added. The Fuchsia is a gross feeder, and must have abundance of food and water. Aphis and Thrips are persistent enemies of this plant, and will need constant attention.

GERANIUM seed may be sown at any time of the year, but there are good reasons why the months of February and August should be chosen. Seedlings raised now will make fine plants by the end of June, and they will begin to flower in August. They are peculiarly fresh and robust in habit, and from a reliable strain there will be a considerable proportion of handsome specimens, with the possibility of some valuable novelty. Sow in pans filled with soil somewhat rough in texture, and the surface need not be very smooth. Lightly cover the seed with fine loam. To have plants ready for flowering in the summer, it will be necessary to give the seed-pans a temperature of 60° or 70°, and follow the usual practice of pricking off and potting the seedlings.

GLADIOLUS.—It is not common to grow this noble flower from seed, but the task is simple, and seed good enough to be worth the experiment is obtainable. In large pots, well drained and filled with fibrous loam and leaf-mould, dibble the seeds separately an inch apart and half an inch deep. A temperature of 65° or 70° will bring them up, and when they reach an inch high the heat should be gradually reduced. The seedlings need not be transplanted, but may remain in the same pots until the grass dies down, and the corms are sifted out in September or October. Flowers must neither be expected nor allowed until the third season.

GLOXINIAS.—There is yet ample time to secure a brilliant summer display from seed. The directions under January are applicable, but it will be necessary to provide shade for the seedlings as the sun becomes hot, especially after they have been re-potted.

LOBELIAS occupy a foremost place for bedding, and are sufficiently diversified to meet many requirements. Indeed, there is no other blue flower which can challenge its position. The compact class is specially adapted for edgings; the spreading varieties answer admirably in borders, where a sharply defined line of colour is not essential; the *gracilis* strain has an elegant effect in suspended baskets, window boxes, and rustic work; and the *ramosa* section grows from six to twelve inches high, producing large flowers. All these may be sown now as annuals, to produce plants for bedding out in May. Put the seed into sandy soil, and start the pans in a gentle heat.

MIMULUS, if sown now and treated as a greenhouse annual, will flower in the first year. It is one of the thirstiest plants grown in this country, and must have unstinted supplies of water.

MYOSOTIS AZORICA.—Moisture and shade are almost inseparably associated with the name Forget-me-not. But so far as *M. azorica* is concerned, the idea is altogether erroneous. It will flower admirably in the border if treated as a half-hardy annual, and it also makes a very elegant pot plant. Sown in this and the succeeding month, it will bloom from July to September. Use a light compost, and when large enough put the seedlings into boxes or pans, from which they can be transferred to flowering positions. For pot culture get them early into small-sized pots, and give additional room as they develop.

PELARGONIUM.—In raising seedling Pelargoniums, it is well to bear in mind that worthless seed takes just as much time and attention as does a first-class strain. The simplest greenhouse culture will suffice to bring the plants to perfection. A light sandy loam will suit them, and the pots need not go beyond the 48-, or at most the 32-size. Flowering will be deferred until re-potting ceases.

PETUNIA.—Towards the end of the month, the seedlings raised in January for pot culture will be ready for transferring to seed-pans, and they should be put in about an inch apart. It will also be time to sow for bedding plants, although the beginning of March is not too late for the purpose.

PHLOX DRUMMONDII.—The attention which has been devoted to this flower has rendered it one of the most varied and brilliant half-hardy annuals we possess. The *grandiflora* sections make splendid bedding subjects, for they flower freely, and continue in bloom for a long period. These and others are also valuable as pot plants, and even in the greenhouse or conservatory they are conspicuous for their rich colours. All the varieties may be sown now in well-drained pans or shallow boxes. Press the seeds into good soil about an inch apart, and as a rule this will save transplanting; but if transplanting becomes necessary, take out alternate plants and put into other pans, or pot them separately. The remainder will then have room to grow until the time arrives for bedding out.

POLYANTHUS.—Either now or in March sow in pans filled with any fairly good potting soil, and do not be impatient about the germination of he seed. Many a good lot of seed has been thrown away because it was not known that Polyanthus partakes of the slow and irregular characteristics of his class of plants. As the seedlings become ready, lift them carefully, and transplant into pans or boxes from which a little later they may be moved to any secluded corner of the border, until in September they are put into flowering quarters. While in the seed-pans they must be kept moist, although excessive watering is to be avoided. Should the summer prove dry, they will also need water when in the open ground.

PRIMROSES of good colours are admirably adapted for indoor decoration, and there is no occasion to grow them in pots for the purpose. Lift the required number from the reserve border without exposing the roots; pot them, and place in a cool frame until established. Plenty of space, no more water than is absolutely essential, and progressive ventilation comprise all the needful details of cultivation.

RANUNCULUS.—Although it is not usual to grow this flower from seed, it is both easy and interesting to do so. Sow in boxes containing from four to six inches of soil, and as there need be no transplanting, each seed should be put in separately, about an inch and a half apart. A cool greenhouse or frame will supply the requisite conditions for growing the seedlings. When the foliage has died down, sift out the roots, and store in dry peat or cocoa-nut fibre for the winter.

To secure an immediate display of Ranunculuses, it is necessary to plant mature roots. The soil in which they especially thrive is an adhesive loam or clay. This happens to be unfavourable to their safety in the winter, and therefore it is wise to defer planting in such soils until this month. In light land the roots may be put in during November or December, and a valuable collection should be protected through severe weather by litter. The culture of the Ranunculus was formerly regarded as somewhat of a mystery, and amusing recipes as to the sorts and proportions of certain manures have been occasionally disclosed by the learned in such matters. A very simple procedure, however, will suffice to produce handsome, richly coloured flowers. If possible, choose for the bed a heavy soil in an open situation, and dress it liberally with decayed manure. Give the land a deep digging, and lay it up rough that it may be benefited by frosts. In January and February fork it lightly over several times, with the double purpose of making it mellow, and of enabling birds to clear it of vermin. Traps made of hollowed potatoes will also assist the latter object. Not later than February 20, the roots should be planted in drills drawn six inches apart, and two inches deep. Put them four inches apart in the rows, with the claws downwards, and cover with fine soil. Keep the bed free from weeds, and give abundant supplies of water in dry weather. When the foliage is dead, lift the roots and store through the winter.

The Turban Ranunculuses are not so delicate as named varieties, and there need be less hesitation about autumn planting.

RICINUS.—The Castor-oil Plant is largely cultivated for its striking ornamental foliage, and under generous treatment it will attain from four to six feet in height. It is a half-hardy annual, and should be grown in the same manner as Tobacco.

SOLANUM.—The varieties which are grown for winter decoration are much prized when laden with their bright-coloured berries. Sow the several kinds in heat, and transfer the seedlings straight to single pots filled with very rich soil.

TOBACCO.—Where sub-tropical gardening is practised this plant is indispensable. To develop its fine proportions there must be the utmost liberality of treatment from the commencement. Either in this month or early in March sow in rich soil, and place the pans in a warm house or pit. Put the seedlings early into small pots, and promote a rapid but sturdy growth, until the weather is warm enough for them in the open ground.

VALLOTA PURPUREA.—This handsome bulbous plant is not quite hardy, but in several of the southern counties it may be grown in the open ground, with only the shelter of dry litter or a mat. In pots the bulb should not be allowed to go dry through the winter; and when growth commences in spring, water must be given freely. Good loam suits it, and in re-potting disturb the roots as little as possible.

VERBENA, if not sown last month, should be got in promptly, for it is important not to hurry the growth of this plant by excessive heat.

WIGANDIA is a half-hardy perennial, grown exclusively for its noble tropical foliage. If started now, it will attain a large size as an annual. Like all similar plants, it is impossible to grow it too well. A lavish employment of manure and water will secure stately specimens. The instructions given for Tobacco apply equally to the Wigandia.

MARCH

THE first duty is to ascertain that there are no arrears to make good, or failures to replace. If any sowing has gone wrong, do not waste time by repining over it, but sow again. Growing flowers under artificial conditions is a prolonged struggle with Nature, in which the most experienced and skilful need not be ashamed of an occasional failure. But although it is useless to 'cry over spilt milk,' the cause of the failure should, if possible, be ascertained for future guidance. We say if possible, because the secret cannot always be discovered. There may have been every apparent condition of success, and yet for some inexplicable reason there has been failure. As a rule, however, the hidden source of mischief will be brought to light by the man who is determined to make every disappointment the stepping-stone to future success.

The lengthening days and the growing power of the sun bring enlarged responsibilities demanding increased vigilance and activity.

Danger of frost remains, and worse still there may come the withering influence of the north-east wind, which scorches delicate seedlings as with a breath of fire.

ANNUALS, HARDY, may all be sown in the open during March and April. Perhaps a list of the principal flowers comprised under this denomination may aid the memory. Some of the following are not strictly hardy, but for practical ends they may be so regarded.

Alyssum	Gypsophila	Nolana
Asperula	Hawkweed	Œnothera
Bartonia	Helianthus	Papaver
Cacalia	Helichrysum	Phacelia
Calandrinia	Hibiscus	Poppy
Calendula	Jacobea	Prince's Feather
Campanula	Kaulfussia	Sanvitalia
Candytuft	Larkspur	Saponaria
Centaurea	Lavatera	Silene
Centranthus	Leptosiphon	Sphenogyne
Chrysanthemum, annual	Limnanthes	Sunflower
Clarkia	Linaria	Sweet Pea
Collinsia	Linum	Sweet Sultan
Convolvulus minor	Love-lies-bleeding	Tropæolum
Coreopsis	Lupine	Valerian
Erysimum	Malope	Venus's Looking-glass
Eschscholtzia	Mathiola	Virginian Stock
Eucharidium	Mignonette	Viscaria
Eutoca	Nasturtium	Whitlavia
Gilia	Nemophila	Xeranthemum
Godetia	Nigella	

These flowers are worth better treatment than they sometimes receive. They may be sown at once where they are intended to bloom, and for Larkspur, Lupine, Mignonette, and Poppy this method is a necessity, because they will not bear transplanting. For the majority, however, the transplanting system is an advantage. A comparatively small space has to be prepared as a seed-bed, and more care can be devoted to it than is always possible over a larger area. In every case sow thinly, and afterwards thin boldly, for many of the flowers named will occupy a space of one or even two feet, if the soil is in a condition to do them justice. Give the ground a deep digging and incorporate plenty of manure, except where

Nasturtium and Tropæolum are to be planted. A rather poor soil is necessary for these, or the flowers will be hidden by excessive foliage.

ABUTILON.—There is yet time to raise plants to flower during the current year. The seedlings must be potted on regularly to render them robust and free flowering.

AQUILEGIA sown in the early part of this month in a frame will produce plants which may flower later in the year, provided the season is favourable, but they will certainly pay for this early sowing in the succeeding spring. The plant is quite hardy, therefore seed may be sown later on in the open for flowers in the following year.

ASTER.—Only those who are closely acquainted with the modern development of this handsome flower can have any conception of its varied forms and colours. There are dwarf, medium, and tall varieties, in almost endless diversity, and nearly all of them will be a credit to any garden if well grown. Too often, however, flowers are seen which are a mere caricature of what Asters may become under the hands of men who understand their requirements. To grow them to perfection, the ground should be trenched in the previous autumn, where the soil is deep enough to justify the operation. If not, dig deeply, and make it rich with decayed manure; a layer should also be put at the bottom of each trench as the work proceeds. Leave the land roughly exposed to the disintegrating effects of winter frosts; and in spring it should be lightly forked over once or twice to produce a friable condition, in which the roots will run freely, and go down to the buried manure for stimulating food. If by such means stiff land can be made mellow, it will grow Asters of magnificent size and colour. In sowing, it is not wise to put all the eggs in one basket. We advise at least two sowings; and three are better, even if only a few plants are wanted. This diminishes the risk of failure, and prolongs the flowering season. Prepare a compost of leaf-mould and loam, mixed with sharp sand to insure drainage. Towards the end of the month, sow in pots or in seed-pans on an even surface; and we lay stress on a thin sowing to avoid the danger of the seedlings damping off. Barely cover the seed with finely sifted soil, and place sheets of glass over to check rapid evaporation. If water must be given, immerse the pots for a sufficient time, rather than apply it to the surface. A cool greenhouse, vinery, or a half-spent hot-bed is a good position for them, and a range of temperature from 55° to 65° should be regarded as the outside limits of variation.

AURICULA.—There is yet time to sow seed, indeed April will not be too late. Partially submerging the pans when water is needed, saves many seeds from being washed out and wasted.

BALSAM.—Although this flower comes from a tropical climate, it is not very tender; a gentle hot-bed is quite sufficient to bring up the seed. Two or three sowings are advisable to secure a succession of bloom; and for the first, the middle of this month is the proper time. It is important that the soil for this plant should be light, rich, and very sweet. When the seedlings show their first rough leaves, lose no time in pricking them off, and they should afterwards be potted early enough to promote a dwarf habit.

BEGONIA, TUBEROUS-ROOTED.—Seed may still be sown for a summer display. Transplant seedlings which are ready, and later on pot them singly.

CALCEOLARIA.—Plants from last year's sowing will begin to move, and should be shifted into their final pots before the buds show. The 8- or 10-inch size ought to contain very fine specimens. The compost for them should be prepared with care. For our own plants we use the following proportions: one bushel good yellow loam, half-bushel leaf-soil, one gallon silver sand, quarter pint concentrated manure, and a quarter pint of soot, prepared several days before use. Put the plants in firmly, and place them in a light airy greenhouse. When the pots are filled with roots, an occasional dose of manure water will be beneficial until the flowers begin to show colour, when pure soft water alone will be required. Tie out the plants some time before the buds attain full size.

CAMPANULA.—The hardy annual varieties, such as *C. attica*, should be grown in the manner advised for hardy annuals. The half-hardy perennials, such as *C. fragilis* and *C. pyramidalis*, if sown during this month, will flower later in the year. Raise them in pans in a gentle heat, and pot off when large enough. *C. macrostyla* is an exceedingly beautiful variety, producing large flowers curiously marked. It should be sown now or in April, and be treated as a half-hardy annual.

COLEUS is strictly a stove perennial, but as our winters generally make the plants look sickly and unwholesome, it will in almost every instance give more satisfaction if treated as an annual, enjoying the beautiful and varied foliage during summer and autumn, and consigning the plants to the waste-heap as wintry days draw near. We do not advise the sowing of seed earlier than March, because a considerable amount of daylight is necessary to the development of rich tints and diversified markings in the foliage. The essentials for raising plants from seed are good drainage, a temperature which does not fall below 65°, the careful employment of water, and the early transfer of the seedlings. The green plants may be thrown away immediately they reveal their character, but those which show delicate tints in the small leaves will abundantly compensate for all the care bestowed upon them.

DELPHINIUM.—Sow the perennial varieties on a prepared bed. Thin early, without removing all the weaker seedlings, and when sufficiently advanced to bear removal, transplant to borders where the plants are to flower.

DIANTHUS.—Put the seedlings into single pots, and harden in readiness for transplanting to the open in May or June.

GLADIOLUS.—This is one of the most stately and beautiful flowers grown in our gardens, and it commands admiration from persons differing in taste as widely asunder as the poles. The secret is in a measure traceable to the varied colouring of the different varieties. Some are strikingly brilliant; others are exceedingly delicate in tint, and refined in their markings. The culture may be of the most primitive kind, or it may become one of the fine arts of horticulture. Simply put into the ground and left to fight their own battle, the corms sometimes produce splendid spikes of flower, although not so imposing as better culture might have made them. Or they may receive the connoisseur's skilful care, resulting in flowers of a size and splendour worthy the adornment of a royal garden.

The main work of preparing the ground should be done in autumn. Now, it is only necessary to give it two or three light forkings, and those not deep enough to bring the buried manure to the surface. This frequent stirring is beneficial in itself, and it promotes the destruction of the foes which prey upon Gladiolus roots. Small Potatoes roughly hollowed out, pieces of Carrot, and Rape Cake, may be used as traps for wireworm and other vermin. Planting may be done at the end of this month, but as a rule it is better to wait until the beginning of April.

GLOXINIA bulbs which have been stored through the winter need attention. Where these flowers are wanted early, and there is plenty of room, a commencement will probably be made in February; but in the greater number of gardens March is soon enough. Assuming the bulbs to be sound, they should be potted in a mixture of loam, peat, and sand. Those which start first must be re-potted for a forward supply. While growing, manure water twice a week will help to produce fine flowers, intense in colour; but when the flowers open, the liquid manure must be abandoned. Pure, soft water must be given as often as necessary, for Gloxinias cannot endure drought. Shading is an important matter from the commencement and particularly during the flowering period.

Propagation is effected by making an incision on the underside of the midrib of a leaf. A crock is laid on the surface to press the wound upon the soil, and from this a bulb is gradually formed. But flowers of such fine quality are now obtained from seed, that fewer bulbs are stored every winter, and there is a growing disinclination to make use of the tedious process of propagation.

HOLLYHOCK seedlings will be ready for putting into thumb pots. Directly they are established, begin to prepare them for planting out in May.

IMPATIENS SULTANI.—Some growers find a little difficulty in raising this elegant flower from seed. Probably it arises from sowing too early. In March no trouble should be experienced, but it is essential to sow very thinly for two reasons. Crowded seedlings are liable to damp off, particularly in dull moist weather, and they are so fragile that it is well-nigh impossible to transfer them from the seed-pots until they are about an inch high. The humid atmosphere which suits tender Ferns will grow them freely.

LOBELIA.—The perennial varieties (*L. Victoria* and *L. cardinalis*) make splendid border plants, and are easily grown from seed. Sow in moderate heat, and in due time transfer to a deep rich loam. Their dark metallic foliage and intense scarlet flowers give them a conspicuous appearance, and admirably fit them for the back row of a ribbon border. They are also valuable in the mixed border.

MARIGOLD.—Both the African and French varieties are of importance late in the season, for they continue to bloom until cut down by frost. The former reaches the height of from eighteen to thirty inches, and the colour is limited to yellow in several shades, from pale lemon to deep orange. The latter is more varied in habit as well as in colour, and the Miniatures make excellent bedding plants. In hot dry seasons Marigolds entirely eclipse Calceolarias, because they can well endure drought and a short supply of food; whereas the Shrubby Calceolaria does not thrive under such conditions. All the varieties of Tagetes may be sown now on a moderate heat, and they should be pricked off into pans or boxes in readiness for transferring to the open ground in May.

MARVEL OF PERU.—The treatment prescribed for Balsam will suit this plant also. In the first year it will grow to a considerable size, but will not, as a rule, attain to its full dimensions until the second season. It is a half-hardy perennial, and when saved through the winter will need protection from frost.

MIGNONETTE finds a welcome in every English garden ; and to add to its attractiveness, there are now yellow, red, and white varieties, in addition to such forms as dwarf, pyramidal, and spiral. Mignonette can be grown without the least difficulty ; indeed, it will reproduce itself from seed shed in the previous year. Nevertheless, it is true that in the majority of gardens justice is seldom done to it, for the simple reason that there is not sufficient faith in its capabilities. Each plant will cover a space of at least one foot, and we have seen specimens a yard across, bristling with flower spikes, and fragrant as only Mignonette can be. The soil for it should be made firm, just as an Onion bed is treated. Except for this one point, the culture of a hardy annual is all that is necessary. Mignonette does not well bear transplanting, but otherwise it is very accommodating. It may be grown as a tree, and kept for a number of years by removing the seed-pods in their young state, but it is more satisfactory and less troublesome to raise plants annually. Mignonette is frequently taken off by fly as fast as it appears above ground. Soot and wood ashes applied in good time are the best remedies ; but a second sowing may be necessary, and it should be made immediately the mischief can be discovered.

PENTSTEMON.—The treatment recommended for the perennial section of Lobelias will exactly suit this flower.

PHLOX DRUMMONDII.—There is still time to sow. Established seedlings should be gradually hardened by free access of air, until they are ready for the open ground.

PHLOX, PERENNIAL, is easily raised from seed, and flowered in the first year. Sow in shallow boxes in the early part of this month, and place them in moderate heat. Transplant the seedlings when ready, gradually harden, and plant out in rich soil one foot apart, or put them into vacant places in the shrubbery. Help them with water if necessary.

POPPIES do not well bear transplanting, especially from light soils, and therefore, as a rule, it is advisable to sow where the plants are intended to bloom. All the varieties make conspicuous lines and clumps among shrubs ; and this is especially the case with the huge flowers of the double class. Sow in March and April, and commence thinning the seedlings while they are small. They should ultimately be left about one foot apart.

SCHIZANTHUS.—An elegant class of half-hardy annuals, which can be grown as specimens for the conservatory, or in quantity for open borders. Sow in gentle heat, and pot on the seedlings.

SENECIO SPECIOSUS is a half-hardy perennial of great beauty and value, both for the greenhouse and for beds. Raise the seed in a temperature of about 60°; and when the plants are bedded out, give them a position exposed to full sunshine, where the bright magenta flowers will be seen to advantage to the end of the season.

SOLANUM.—For a succession of the berried varieties sow again in heat, and make a sowing of the ornamental foliaged kinds for sub-tropical gardening. The latter are rather more tender, and need a somewhat higher temperature than the former. They must all have liberal culture to bring out their fine qualities.

STOCK, TEN-WEEK.—Within the past few years Annual Stocks have obtained a marked increase of favour. In part this is no doubt attributable to the growing appreciation manifested for all kinds of flowers. But it is traceable in a still greater measure to the augmented purity, brilliance, and variety in colour of modern Ten-week Stocks, as well as to the enhanced reliability of seed in producing double flowers. A certain proportion of single blossoms there will always be, even from seed saved with the highest skill. It is well this should be the case, for double Stocks produce no seed, and the race is perpetuated by single flowers. We need say nothing of its perfume, for this is a quality which the most unobservant can scarcely fail to appreciate.

Although the Ten-week Stock is half-hardy it must not receive the treatment of a tender annual; indeed, one of the most important points in growing it is to avoid any excess of artificial heat. A little assistance at the commencement it must have, but the aim should be to impart a hardy constitution from the moment the seedlings appear. We are not advocating reckless exposure to chill blasts, but the necessity of giving air freely whenever there may be a fair opportunity The best of seed-beds can be made in pans or shallow boxes filled with sweet sandy soil. In these sow thinly, so that the young plants may have abundant room. Even a little apparent wastefulness of space will be repaid by stout and vigorous growth. From the middle to the end of the month is a suitable time for sowing.

VERBENA.—It is possible to raise Verbenas in the open air from seed sown in drills on light soil, but the attempt is a little hazardous.

There is, however, no danger at all in sowing in pans placed in a cool frame. The plants should be potted immediately they are large enough to handle. The flowering from this sowing will be rather late, but not too late for a good show of bloom.

ZINNIA.—The double varieties are now grown almost to the exclusion of single flowers. The former are so incomparably superior, that they are judged by the severe rules of the florist. It is useless to start this plant too early. Towards the end of the month a commencement will be made by experienced growers, but the comparative novice will be wise to wait until the beginning of April. Sow in pots filled with a compost of leaf-mould, loam, and sand, and be quite sure there is effectual drainage. Plunge the pots in a temperature of about 60°.

APRIL

MANY half-hardy flowers, such as *Acroclinium roseum*, *Convolvulus major*, *Linum rubrum*, and others, which at an earlier period can only be sown with safety under protection, may now be consigned to the open ground without the least misgiving. This fact is of immense value to owners of gardens that are destitute of glass, for it enables them to grow a large number of flowers which would otherwise be impracticable. Of course, the flowering will be a little later than from plants raised earlier in heat, but the difference will not be very conspicuous after all.

ANNUALS, HARDY, which were not sown last month, should be got in during the first half of this, and Coreopsis, Helichrysum, Hibiscus, Leptosiphon, Mathiola, Mignonette, Sanvitalia, and Sunflower, will do quite as well now as from sowings in March.

ASTER.—When the seedlings attain the third leaf, they should be pricked off round the edges of 60-sized pots; later on, put them singly into small pots, from which the transfer to the open ground will not cause a perceptible check. As the plants do not thrive in a close atmosphere, it is important to give air freely on every suitable occasion, or they cannot be maintained in a healthy growing condition. A second sowing should be made about the middle of the month, following the routine already advised. A sowing in drills on a carefully prepared bed in the open ground is also desirable, and in some seasons it may produce the most valuable plants of the year. Asters come so true from seed that the bed may be arranged in any desired pattern. Thin the plants early, and continue the process until they are far enough apart for flowering. A distance of eight inches is sufficient for the miniatures, ten inches for the dwarfs, and twelve or fifteen inches for the tall varieties. A top dressing of thoroughly decayed manure will strengthen the plants, and help to keep them cool and moist.

BALSAM.—About the middle of this month will be the time for a second sowing, and the seed may be raised in a frame without artificial heat.

CARNATION.—Any time from now until August will be suitable for sowing, and if the seed has been saved with judgment, a good proportion of very fine flowers will be produced in the following year. For these plants florists have always considered it important that the potting soil should be prepared months before use, and there are good reasons for the practice. If this is impossible see that the compost is sweet, friable, and above all free from that terrible scourge of Carnations, the wireworm. Even sifting will not rid the soil of its presence with certainty, but by spreading thin layers of the mould evenly upon a hard level floor, and passing a heavy roller over it east and west, then north and south, the wireworm will be disposed of. Turfy loam three parts, leaf-mould one part, decayed cow-manure one part, with an addition of sharp sand, make a first-class compost. Sow in well-drained 48-size pots, cover the seed very lightly, and place in a frame. Transplant the seedlings immediately they can be handled, when a cool shaded pit will help to keep them in hard condition. After six or eight leaves are formed, it will be time to plant them out. In the following spring, the usual routine of staking and tying must be followed.

CYCLAMEN.—The bulbs which have been flowering in pots through the winter are now approaching their period of rest, and they must not be neglected if they are to make a satisfactory display next season. Water should be gradually diminished until the foliage dies off, and then the corms will require shade or they will crack. Dry treatment generally results in an attack of thrips, and each root must be painted with some good insecticide to destroy the pest. Cyclamen should never be allowed to become actually dust-dry; but if the pots can be plunged in a shaded moist pit, watering will rarely be necessary. In June the pots may be buried to the rim in a shady spot until August, when it will be time to re-pot and start the bulbs into growth. The chief enemies of Cyclamen are aphis and thrips. Tobacco smoke will settle the former; for the latter, dip the plants in a solution of tobacco-water and soft soap.

DAHLIA seedlings must have plenty of water, and be kept free from aphis while in pots. Instead of taking out the leading shoot, as is often done, give it the support of a neat stick. The plants should also be potted on as growth demands; the important point being to maintain steady progress without a check until they can be planted out. At the same time they must be hardened in readiness for removal to the open ground; and if the work is carried on with judgment the plants will be dwarf, and possess a robust constitution capable of producing a brilliant display of flowers until frost appears.

GLADIOLUS.—Assuming that the beds have been properly prepared, we have now only to consider the question of planting, and no better time can be chosen than the beginning of April. Some eminent growers are at the trouble of taking out the soil with a trowel for each bulb. In the opening, a bed of sand and wood-ashes or powdered charcoal is made, on which the root is placed. Others lay them in deep drills, partly filled with a similar light mixture. Whichever method is adopted, the crown of the corm should be left about four inches beneath the surface. The distance between them may vary from twelve to eighteen inches, and we favour the greater space, because of the facility it affords in attending to the plants subsequently. The same rules apply to the planting of clumps.

LOBELIA.—Early in the month transfer the seedlings to pans or boxes, and the latter are preferable. Not a single flower should be allowed to show until the plants are established in the open ground. Although Lobelias have an elegant appearance in pots, they cannot be satisfactorily grown in them. The object is easily attained by potting plants from a reserve bed after they have developed into good tufts. From a stiff soil they can be lifted and potted with facility; and a light soil will cause no difficulty if the bed be soaked a short time in advance. After potting, the plants will give no trouble except to supply them with water.

MARIGOLDS can now be raised in a cold frame, and towards the end of the month there will be no risk in sowing in the open ground. The plants thrive in a sunny position, even in a scorching season.

MARVEL OF PERU.—If not sown last month there is no time

to lose, and with a little care seed can now be germinated without artificial heat. When the plants come to be transferred to the open, put them, if possible, in sandy loam, exposed to full sunshine.

MIGNONETTE.—Successional sowings may be made up to the end of June. Give each plant plenty of room. By removing the seed-pods as fast as they are formed, flowering is greatly prolonged.

PANSY.—Although the Pansy will grow almost anywhere, a moist rich soil, partially shaded from summer sun, is necessary to do the plant full justice. Many distinct colours are saved separately, and the quality of the seedlings is so good that propagation by cuttings is not now so much in vogue as in years gone by. Sow thinly in pots or pans, and when the young plants have been pricked off, put them in a cool safe corner until large enough for bedding out. The soil should be plentifully dressed with decayed cow-manure.

PETUNIA.—Plants from the first sowing will be ready for small pots, and they must be kept going until the 48- or 32-size is reached. All Petunias rebel if root-bound, and the double varieties are especially impatient in this respect. After each transfer give them a sheltered, shady position, and attention with water until they start again. Good drainage and careful ventilation are essential, or the foliage will lose colour. Seedlings intended for beds may be transferred direct from the seed-pans into 60-sized pots.

PICOTEE AND PINK.—See the culture prescribed for Carnation.

RICINUS.—At quite the end of the month or the beginning of May, seed put into the open ground may be made to produce splendid specimens, if treated with a lavish hand. Where the seeds are to be sown, take out the soil for a depth of eighteen inches or two feet, and fill the space to within three inches of the surface with a mixture of rich soil and well-decayed manure. Upon each bed thus made place three Ricinus beans in a triangle, and when they are up thin to one plant at each station, and this, of course, the strongest. This mode of growing Ricinus will astonish those who have been accustomed to allow the plant to struggle through existence in the ordinary soil of a garden border. Plentiful supplies of water must be given in dry weather, and stakes will be necessary to save the specimens from injury by wind. It is too early for putting out those raised in heat.

STOCK, TEN-WEEK.—Where the requisite quantity of seed has not been sown, it must be done promptly. If there happens to be a cold frame on a spent hot-bed to spare, it will exactly suit the seedlings when they are ready for transferring. Make the surface fresh by adding a little rich soil, and put the plants in rows three or four inches apart, and three inches between them in the rows. In seed-pans, however, space cannot be afforded in this liberal fashion, but they will make a full return for rather more than the usual spacing. To maintain a dwarf habit, it is imperative that the plants should be kept near the glass.

Where there are no facilities for growing Stocks in the manner described, seed may be sown at the end of the month in the open ground, and with a little care there may be a handsome show of bloom. The seedlings are exposed to the attacks of Turnip fly, which is a terrible foe to them in the seed-leaf stage; in fact, the plants may be up and gone before danger is suspected. A light sprinkling of water, followed immediately with a dusting of wood-ashes, just as they are coming through, will save them, but it may be necessary to repeat the operation two or three times until they are out of peril. A rich and friable seed-bed is one remedy for the fly, for it promotes rapid growth, which speedily places the plant beyond the power of its insect adversary. But if open-ground culture exposes Stocks to one hazard, it saves them from another, as mildew does not attack them unless they have been transplanted. Stocks come so true from seed, that it is easy to arrange a pattern in any desired colours. Sow in drills from nine to fifteen inches apart, according to the height of the variety, and cover the seed very lightly with fine soil. The bed must be protected from birds, and a dressing of soot will keep off slugs. Begin to thin the plants early, but do not forget that some single specimens will have to be taken out when the flowers show, and that is the time for the final thinning.

SUNFLOWERS do not well bear transplanting, hence the seed should be sown where the plants are intended to flower. During its brief season of growth the Sunflower taxes the soil very severely, and to develop its full proportions decayed manure must be freely employed to a good depth, and there must also be unstinted supplies of water in dry weather.

VIOLA.—For treatment, see Pansy.

ZINNIA.—The first week of this month is as good a time as any to sow seed, and the conditions named under March should be followed. When the seedlings are an inch high pot them separately, and place in a close shaded frame while they become established. Then give air more and more freely until the plants will bear full exposure.

MAY

THIS is the chief month for bedding, and the crowded state of pits and houses creates a natural anxiety to push forward the work, yet the exercise of a little patience may save many a valuable lot of plants from being injured past recovery. Although the days are long, and perhaps sunny, the nights are often treacherous, especially in the early part of the month. The first business is to prepare the plants gradually for the change, by free exposure whenever there is a favourable opportunity. Take off the lights on genial days, and by degrees open them at night, until they can be dispensed with altogether. About the second week of the month it will generally be safe to put the most hardy subjects on a bed of ashes, under the shelter of a hedge or wall, before planting them. Begin with Antirrhinum, Dianthus, Phlox Drummondii, Stock, and Verbena. A little later on, others which are rather more delicate, as, for instance, Balsam, Begonia, Dahlia, Petunia, Zinnia, &c., can be treated in the same way, until the great bulk of them are in final quarters. Sub-tropical plants, such as Ricinus, Solanum, Tobacco, and Wigandia, had better be kept under control till the first or second week of June.

ANTIRRHINUM is admirably adapted for a dry and sunny position, in which it will thrive and flower freely.

BALSAM.—A final sowing early in the month may be made with safety in the open ground. Former seedlings will need potting on until they reach the 8-inch size, and at each transfer put the plants in rather deeper than before, for this encourages the growth of roots from the stems. While increasing the pot room not a bud will show; but immediately the roots are checked by the pots, flowering will commence. The old method of stopping and disbudding not only spoiled the plants, but robbed them of the finest flowers, which are invariably produced on the main stem. Since the natural method of growing Balsams has been in favour, it is usual to see grand specimens covered with immense flowers.

CINERARIA.—Those who care to have Cinerarias in bloom during November and December, may do so from a sowing made at the beginning of April, but it is not usual to begin so early. Our own practice is to sow twice, choosing the present month for the first—and from this we look for our finest plants—and again in June to insure a succession. The Cineraria is easy to raise and to grow, but it will by no means take care of itself. It has so many enemies, that unusual vigilance is necessary to flower it to perfection. It thrives in a compost of turfy loam, with a little peat or leaf-mould added ; but the soil should not be over-rich, or there will be much foliage and few flowers. Still, as the plant is a rapid grower, it must not be starved, neither must it suffer for lack of water. Pots or pans may be employed for the seed ; and as the young plants grow freely, they may go straight to thumb pots without the usual intermediate stage of pricking off.

COLEUS should receive their final shift into 48-sized pots. If signs of decline become manifest, some weak liquid manure-water occasionally will revive the plants, and intensify their colours. As the weather grows steadily warm, any ordinary greenhouse or conservatory will suit them provided they are shaded from fierce sunshine.

CYCLAMEN.—The strongest seedlings should now be ready for 60-sized pots. Abundant but judicious ventilation, plenty of water, and freedom from aphis, are the conditions to be secured.

DAHLIA.—Make the ground on which this flower is to be planted thoroughly rich. It is a rapid grower, and cannot attain to fine proportions on a poor soil. If the plants are carefully prepared for the change by free exposure on genial days, and also during warm nights, they will scarcely feel the removal. When first put out, dress the surrounding soil with soot to prevent injury by slugs, which show a decided partiality for newly planted Dahlias. Give water freely when requisite, and in staking the plants take care that the ties will not cut the branches. These ties will require attention occasionally during the summer and autumn.

HOLLYHOCKS may be put into the borders when the weather is quite warm and settled. Wait until the end of the month or even the beginning of June, rather than have them nipped by an untimely frost. Like the Dahlia, this plant must have unstinted supplies of water and abundance of manure. A tall stake, firmly fixed, will also be necessary for each plant.

PETUNIAS are very sensitive under a frost or cutting east wind. Therefore be in no hurry to bed the plants until quite the end of the month or beginning of June, especially if the weather appears to be at all doubtful. A good mellow soil, free of recent manure, suits them. If unduly rich, it will strengthen the foliage at the expense of the flowers, and will also postpone the blooming until late in the season.

PORTULACA.—It is useless to sow until the weather is warm and settled, for this flower will neither endure a moist atmosphere nor a retentive soil. If necessary, wait until the close of the month, or longer, before putting in the seed. Sow on raised beds of light soil, the more sandy the better; and in seasons which speedily burn the life out of other plants, Portulacas will display their beauty, no matter how fiercely the sun may beat upon them. Water will occasionally be necessary, but it should never be given until there is obvious need for it. Portulacas are easily grown in pots or window-boxes, and they will bloom profusely where many other flowers will only wither and die.

PRIMULA.—Almost every season witnesses the advent of some novelty in this flower, either in colour or in form. And the plant is now worth growing for the beauty and diversity of its foliage alone. The flowers range from pure white through all shades of tender rose up to a deep, rich, blood red. After years of earnest effort a beautiful blue has also been obtained. Then there are several elegant double strains, and these possess a special value for bouquets because of their enduring quality. They can all be grown with extreme ease in any soil which is fairly rich and friable. Equal parts of leaf-mould and loam, with a little sand, will suit them to perfection. Fill the pots firmly, and have them well drained. A thin layer of silver sand sifted over the soil will aid an even sowing by showing up the seed. As a finish, shake over just enough fine soil to hide the sand. Thin sowing is important, because the most reliable new seed is almost certain to germinate at intervals, and the plants which come first can then be lifted without imperilling the remainder. Prick off as fast as ready round the edges of small pots, and shade until established. Then give air more and more freely.

STOCK, TEN-WEEK.—The preparation of the soil is the first business; and whether the Stocks are intended to be grown in small groups or alone in beds, the treatment should be the same in either case. With light land there is no difficulty; it is only needful to dig it well, and incorporate enough decayed manure. If disposed to incur a little extra trouble to give the plants a start, take out some soil with a trowel, and fill the space with compost from the potting shed. This course is indispensable on heavy land; and assuming it to be rich enough, the quickest and most effectual way is to make drills six inches deep at the proper distances, and nearly fill them with prepared soil, in which the Stocks can be planted. For a short time afterwards, provide shelter from the mid-day sun, but do not keep them covered a moment longer than is necessary. In planting, it must not be forgotten that an uncertain proportion of single specimens will have to come out. On this account we put them in small groups, and remove the surplus, even if they are double.

TOBACCO.—On an open sunny border seed may be sown, but it is a waste of seed and labour to put it into poor soil. Prepare the ground beforehand by deep digging, and by incorporating plenty of manure. If this course cannot be adopted because of the near presence of other plants, drive a bar into the soil and work a good-sized hole. Fill it with rich stuff to within a few inches of the surface, and finish with fine soil as a seed-bed, upon which sow the seed. This method can only be adopted for light land. In the event of a cutting east wind after the seedlings are up, improvise some kind of shelter until the danger is past.

VERBENA.—Beds for Verbenas should be rich, mellow, and very sweet. A poor soil not only produces poor flowers, but it materially shortens the blooming period. Peg the plants down from the outset, and allow them to cross and recross each other until there is a sheet of glowing colour.

WALLFLOWER.—This fragrant spring flower is not always grown as well as it might be. It is often sown too late to become established before winter sets in. Sow now in drills nine inches apart on friable loam. Thin to three inches apart, and transplant the thinnings. A little later repeat the operation, so as to leave the plants at a distance of six inches in the rows. Assist them with water if necessary.

ZINNIA.—A sowing in the open ground about the middle of the month will provide plants in gardens where there are no means of raising them artificially at an earlier date. Even those who possess a stock will be wise to put a final sowing in the open. If possible choose a sunny border sloping to the south, and make the soil rich, fine, and rather firm. Drop seeds in little groups of three or four at each spot, allowing fifteen or eighteen inches between the groups. Cover the seed lightly, and ultimately thin the plants to one at each station

JUNE

THE days are now at their longest, and plants in pits and houses should have the full benefit of it. By opening the lights early, and shading in good time, the flowering period will be greatly prolonged. Ply the syringe over plants infested with aphis until they are quite clean. In some instances, it may even be wise to pinch off young shoots which are covered with the fly.

Keep Verbenas, Petunias, and the taller varieties of Phlox Drummondii pegged down; this furnishes the beds, and helps to check evaporation. Rain and watering alike tend to harden the ground; and as this condition does not favour growth, the surface should be stirred frequently. A dressing of cocoa-nut fibre gives a nice finish to beds, with the additional advantages of retaining moisture and discouraging the growth of weeds.

AQUILEGIA seed will germinate now in the open ground, and the plants need no protection during winter.

BALSAM.—As a rule it is unwise to put Balsams into beds or borders before the first week of this month. The plant revels in warmth and light, and should therefore have an open sunny position. Its succulent nature will indicate the necessity of giving abundant supplies of water. For so fleshy and apparently fragile a plant, it is astonishing how well it stands in a strong wind; and if the growth in pots has been kept dwarf and stout, there will be no need for supports of any kind. When Balsams are wanted in pots, they are often grown in the open ground, and lifted for potting. This plan has the advantage of rendering a choice of colours possible when mixed seed has been sown. The colours are, however, saved separately, and the Camellia-flowered strain comes so true from seed that the pattern of a bed can be accurately arranged.

BEGONIA, TUBEROUS-ROOTED.—A bed filled with this flower will prove a pleasant surprise to those who have never seen one. The plant should also be freely grown in the reserve border to produce flowers for cutting. Employ specimens that are large enough to make a show at once, and select plants of the short-jointed class for out-door work. They must have unusually rich soil.

CALCEOLARIA.—For wealth of bloom, combined with richness and intensity of colouring, the Herbaceous Calceolaria has no rival among biennials. A greenhouse filled with fine specimens in their full splendour is a sight which will not soon be forgotten. One great source of interest lies in the annual changes in shades of colour, and the variations in the markings of individual flowers. From a good strain of seed, high expectation will not be disappointed. Indeed, the excellence of seedlings is so fully recognised, that there is not the smallest disposition to propagate the plant by the tedious method of cuttings. There is no difficulty whatever in raising the seed, or in growing the plant. And it is as easy to grow a good specimen as a poor one. But Calceolarias will not be trifled with. They must have an even temperature and unremitting attention to maintain a thriving condition. The careless gardener had better leave them alone, for he is almost certain to wreck them at some stage in their growth; but there is no flower which gives a more abundant reward for watchful attention. Fill the seed-pans or pots with a compost which is rich, firm, and porous; the last point is of great consequence in helping to secure free drainage. Make the surface perfectly even, and whiten it with silver sand; this answers the double purpose of revealing the seed, and afterwards of showing when it is sufficiently dusted over with fine soil. Whether or not this method be adopted, the seed must be sown thinly and evenly, and as it is exceedingly fine, the task is rather a delicate one. Sheets of glass placed over the pans and turned daily will check rapid evaporation. Place the pans in a moist shady spot, where the temperature is even, and germination will take place in from seven to nine days, when the glass must be promptly removed. Then comes a critical stage, and a little neglect may result in the loss of past labour, and necessitate a fresh start. Still keep the pans in some sheltered corner which can be thoroughly shaded from the sun. This question of shade needs much vigilance. So also does the supply of water, which must not be rudely administered, but rather by frequent gentle sprinklings. On the appearance of the second leaf, promptly prick off the seedlings in carefully prepared pots, allowing about two inches between each. They will need dexterous manipulation because of their small size, but a skilful hand will transfer them without injury, and perhaps with a little soil adhering to the roots. As all the seedlings will not be ready at one time, it will probably require about three operations to clear the seed-pans, and the early removals should be so made as to avoid injuring the remainder. Retain them in a sheltered position, and continue the attention as to shade and watering. In about a month the plants will be ready for thumb pots.

CANNA.—In the mixed border, and also in the sub-tropical garden, Cannas are much valued for the exceeding grace and beauty of their foliage. They should be put into very rich soil; and, like all other plants of rapid growth, they will need copious supplies of water in dry weather. Most of the varieties grown in this country reach the height of about four feet, but *C. gigantea major* will, if well treated, attain the magnificent proportions of seven feet. In mild districts and on dry soils the plants may remain out all the winter, under the protection of a heap of ashes. But as a rule it will be necessary to store them in frames until spring; and they may be finer in the second than in the first season.

CINERARIA.—Where a sufficient stock is not already provided, another sowing should be made, following the method advised last month. The seedlings, when transferred to small pots, should be put into a close frame, and be sprinkled with water morning and evening, until the roots take hold. At first it is desirable to keep them fairly warm, but in a fortnight the heat may be gradually reduced, and more air be given until hardy treatment is reached. The plants will need potting on up to November, when they should go into the final size ; and, except for special purposes, $6\frac{1}{4}$ or $8\frac{1}{2}$ pots are large enough. Cinerarias are sought after by every pest which infests the greenhouse. We need only say that by fumigation, sulphur, or by syringing with a suitable insecticide, the plants must be kept clean, or they cannot be healthy.

DIANTHUS.—For a display next summer, sow in drills drawn six inches apart in an open situation, and cover the seed lightly with fine soil. Shade the spot until the plants show.

GERANIUM.—Sometimes a difficulty is experienced in bringing Geranium seedlings into flower. They possess so much initial vigour, that the production of wood continues to the very end of the season. Plants which show signs of excessive growth should be put into the border without removing the pots. This check to the roots will throw the plants into luxuriant bloom.

GLADIOLUS are very liable to injury by high wind, and stakes should be put to them in good time. Each plant may have a separate support, and this is the most perfect treatment ; or the stakes may be at intervals, or at the ends of rows, connected by lengths of strong, soft material, to which intervening stems can be secured. The work should be done carefully, and if the flowers are intended for exhibition they must also be shaded by some means. This may be a cheap or a costly proceeding ; but in whatever manner it is carried out, security is essential, or the whole bed may be ruined.

HOLLYHOCK.—A sowing in the open ground will produce plants for wintering in the cold frame ; and if generously treated, they will make a fine show in the following year.

MYOSOTIS.—During this month or in July sow the hardy varieties on a prepared seed-bed in a shady spot. August will not be too late. Transplant when ready.

PANSY.—From the end of May to the end of July seedlings may be raised in the open ground. Thin and transplant when ready.

PORTULACA.—The weather may have been too cold and wet for

sowing in May, or seed then sown may have failed in consequence, but there is yet ample time for raising this flower either in beds or pots.

PRIMROSE.—It will astonish a good many lovers of the garden to learn that this fine old favourite may be grown from seed in almost any shade of colour from white to deep crimson, and in various tints of yellow. They make beautiful pot and border flowers. Now is as good a time as any to sow seed, but May or July will answer. Seed-pans can be used, or the sowing may be made in drills in the open. In the latter case, a free dressing of soot must be employed to render the spot distasteful to slugs. When transplanting, give the plants a deep retentive loam if possible, and a shady position.

PRIMULA.—To insure a succession of flowers next spring, make another sowing as advised under May. Seedlings which are ready should be got into small pots, and afterwards they must be re-potted when necessary; but never shift them until the pots are full of roots, and always put them in firmly up to the collar.

SOLANUM.—The berried varieties may be grown entirely in pots, or they can be put into beds for the summer, from which they will lift for potting again just as the handsome berries are turning colour. The spiny-leaved varieties are valuable for sub-tropical gardening. Small plants are of little worth, hence they should be put into very rich soil, with a thick layer of manure on the surface, and have copious supplies of water to induce free growth.

STOCK, BROMPTON.—Magnificent spikes of this flower may be seen in May and June, even in cottagers' gardens. Seed is sometimes sown where the plants are to flower, but a certain degree of risk attends this mode of procedure, and the plant is so valuable that it is worth more careful treatment. Either now or in July sow in pans, and place them under shelter until the Stocks are an inch high; then stand them in the open for a week before planting out.

TOBACCO.—To expose Tobacco plants before warm weather is established will give them a check from which they may not recover until the summer is half over, if they recover at all. Spare frames with movable lights will prepare them admirably and save labour. The second week of this month is generally warm enough for the planting; and they must have a very rich soil, and abundance of water in dry weather. A heavy mulch of decayed manure will help to supply them with food, and also check evaporation.

WALLFLOWER.—There is still ample time to sow seed. Follow the instructions given under May.

ZINNIA.—The first week of June is about the right time to bed Zinnias, and there are three facts to be borne in mind concerning them. The first is that they do not transplant well, and therefore a showery day should, if possible, be selected for moving them. In the absence of rain, be liberal with water. The second fact is that Zinnias are very brittle, and should have a position somewhat sheltered from the full force of the wind. And the third fact is that they revel in sunshine, and the more roasting the season the finer will be the flowers.

JULY

ANEMONE.—Those who grow this flower from seed should make another sowing at the end of July or beginning of August, even if they have thrifty plants from the February sowing. By this arrangement the flowering period is prolonged, and the finer blossoms will probably come from the present sowing.

ANTIRRHINUM.—A sowing in drills will supply plants for flowering next year. Transfer direct from the seed-bed to the positions where they are intended to bloom.

BEGONIA, TUBEROUS-ROOTED.—Seedlings raised now will become established before winter, and commence flowering in spring, as a succession to the plants obtained from the sowing made in February last.

CALCEOLARIA.—If more plants are wanted, sow again. Among the seedlings which we left last month just as they had been pricked off, it will soon be evident that there is a wide difference between the strength of the plants. As a rule, the most robust are those in which yellow largely predominates. These make bright and showy decorative plants, but the colours that are especially valued by lovers of this flower will probably come from the seedlings which are weakly in the early stage. Hence these should be specially prized, and under skilful management they may be grown into grand specimens. The thumb pots for Calceolarias should be carefully prepared with crocks covered with clean moss or cocoa-nut fibre, and be filled with rich porous compost. Transfer the plants with extreme care, and place them in a sheltered part of the greenhouse or in a shaded frame, allowing free access of air on the leeward side. If aphis has to be dealt with—and it is very partial to Calceolarias—tobacco smoke is the best remedy. Choose a quiet evening for the work; next day, syringe with pure water, and shade the plants.

CAMPANULA.—All the perennial varieties may be sown during the summer, either in pans or in the open, the former for preference. Protected in a frame during the winter, they will flower freely in the following spring. Give them a good light soil, and do not stint the supply of water.

CYCLAMENS which are forward enough should be shifted into 48-sized pots. Follow up the process until all are re-potted.

LOBELIA.—The perennial varieties may be raised from seed in pots or pans for planting out next year. Pot off singly when ready, and protect in a cold frame through the winter.

MIMULUS sown in the open ground will flower in the following spring. If possible, make the seed-bed in a moist retentive soil, and in a shaded situation.

MYOSOTIS AZORICA.—For a display next spring sow now in light soil, and when ready transfer the seedlings to pans or boxes. Plunge them in ashes or cocoa-nut fibre in a cold pit or frame until next March. Then prick them off again, allowing rather more space between the plants, and in May they will be ready for the open border. *M. azorica* is so attractive in the greenhouse or conservatory, that a number should be grown every year in pots.

POLYANTHUS may be sown from May to August on a shaded border. Thin the seedlings boldly, and bed the thinnings. Those raised early will flower next spring, but the later seedlings cannot be depended on for blooming in the first year.

PRIMULA.—To force the growth of this plant is to ruin it. The most satisfactory results are invariably obtained from specimens which have matured slowly, and have been treated as nearly hardy after the seedling stage. From this month up to the middle of September it will be quite safe to expose them freely, day and night, except in inclement weather. Even in the winter, protection is only needed from frost, damp, and keen winds.

AUGUST

ANNUALS AND BIENNIALS, HARDY.—In the majority of English gardens the spring display of bulbous flowers is too often followed by a dreary blank, which is almost unredeemed by a touch of colour, except that afforded by the late Tulips and a few other flowers which are comparatively unimportant. The very brilliance of the Crocuses, Hyacinths, and early Tulips serves to throw into relief the comparative barrenness which follows. And the contrast is rendered all the more striking by the cheerful spring days. It is at this juncture that annuals and biennials from autumn sowings light up the garden with welcome masses and bands of fresh and vivid colouring. They are then so valuable that it is surprising they are not more commonly grown, especially as the cost of seed is very trifling. Even the transitory character of some of them is an element in their favour, for they do not interfere with the summer bedding arrangements. Such flowers as Pansy and Viola, however, produce a brilliant and long-continued show of bloom.

The following list contains the varieties which are best adapted for the purpose :—

Alyssum, Sweet
Asperula azurea setosa
Calandrinia grandiflora
Calendula officinalis fl. pl.
Candytuft
Centaurea Cyanus minor
Chrysanthemum segetum gr.
Clarkia
Collinsia
*Coreopsis tinctoria
Erysimum
Eschscholtzia
Eucharidium concinnum
Gilia tricolor
Godetia, Duchess of Albany
Godetia, Lady Albemarle
Larkspur, dwarf rocket
Leptosiphon androsaceus
Limnanthes Douglasii
Nemophila
Nigella, double dwarf
*Pansy
Phacelia tanacetifolia
Saponaria calabrica
Scabious, German
Silene
Sweet Pea
Venus's Looking-glass, purple
*Viola
Virginian Stock
Viscaria
Whitlavia grandiflora
*Xeranthemum.

Sow thinly, not later than the middle of the month in cold districts, but September will be early enough in the southern counties. Drills are preferable to broadcasting, as the beds are more easily weeded and kept in order. Those preceded by an asterisk should be sown under a south wall or other sheltered situation, and be transplanted to flowering quarters during open weather early in the new year. Transplanting must be resorted to if the plants are to be flowered in heavy soil; but on light, rich land, sow where they are intended to bloom. Thin the rows early, so that the plants may become stout and hard before winter overtakes them.

ASTERS for indoor decoration should now be lifted from beds or borders and potted. It is worth a little trouble to accomplish the task with the least possible injury or disturbance to the roots. Light soils should have a good soaking of water on the previous evening, to prevent the mould from crumbling away.

CARNATION.—Seed may still be sown as advised in April; but to carry the plants safely through the winter, it is necessary to have them strong before cold weather sets in.

CHIONODOXA LUCILIÆ can be forced with the same ease as Roman Hyacinths. A 48-sized pot will accommodate several bulbs.

CINERARIAS are frequently placed in the open during this month and September, and as it tends to impart a hardy constitution the practice is to be commended. A north border under a wall will suit them, but the proximity of a hedge should be avoided. Before the plants are put out see that they are quite clean, or it may be necessary to restore them to the house in order to rid them of some troublesome pest.

DIANTHUS.—Either now or a little later transfer seedlings to flowering quarters, and if possible put them into sandy loam in a sunny spot.

FREESIA.—Few and simple are the conditions necessary to the well-being of this beautiful and delicately scented flower. The fine specimens to be seen occasionally in cottagers' windows in the Isle of Wight attest the ease with which it can be grown in a congenial atmosphere. The bulbs are exceedingly small in proportion to the flowers, and the rootlets are so fragile that potting on is not to be attempted. A 48-sized pot will hold three bulbs, and the soil for them should consist largely of decaying vegetable fibre, such as peat, leaf-mould, and turfy loam. The pots can be stood in any sheltered position out of doors, under a covering of cocoa-nut fibre or other light material, until the foliage begins to grow.

GERANIUM.—A sowing will supply plants for flowering next summer, and the directions given in February are suitable, save that heat can now be dispensed with. These late seedlings will need more care to carry them through the winter than plants raised earlier in the year.

HYACINTH, ROMAN.—Obtain the bulbs as early as possible, and pot them promptly. Place them in any spare corner of the open ground, where they can be covered with cocoa-nut fibre or ashes until the roots are formed. A child may grow this flower; and as the bulbs are cheap, they should be largely employed for indoor decoration, as well as for bouquets, during the dark winter days.

MIGNONETTE.—For winter flowering sow in 48- or 32-sized pots, filled with light rich soil. Put the seed in little groups, thin to three or five plants in each pot, and give them the benefit of full daylight close to the glass. When flowering commences do not allow seed to form. If the spikes which have passed the hey-day of perfection are cut off, the plants will break again and flower a second time.

PELARGONIUM.—The remarks under Geranium apply with equal force to this flower also.

PICOTEE.—See Carnation.

SCHIZANTHUS.—To do full justice to this flower, seed should be sown now for plants to be kept through the winter in any house which is sufficiently warm to exclude frost.

SCILLA SIBIRICA is quite hardy, and the treatment which suits Roman Hyacinths will also answer for this bulb. The two form an admirable harmony in blue and white.

SILENE.—All the most useful varieties of Catchfly are hardy against cold, but not entirely so against damp. They possess a special value for their sparkling appearance in spring. Sow in light sandy soil, in which they will pass the winter safely. On a heavy loam the transplanting system must be resorted to in February or March.

STOCK, BROMPTON.—A bed prepared under trees or shrubs will afford some shelter from winter frost. Make it thoroughly rich, and in it plant the seedlings. Should the growth be very rapid in September, the plants will probably become too succulent to endure the stress of winter. If so, lift them and plant again on the same spot.

STOCK, INTERMEDIATE, is principally grown for indoor decoration in spring. No artificial heat is necessary to raise the seed; in fact, it is not wise to employ it. Either in this month, or early in September, sow the required number of pots and plunge them in ashes in a frame until March. Thin the seedlings to three in each pot Before flowering, a rich top dressing will be beneficial; and manure water—weak at first, but stronger by degrees—will intensify the colours.

STOCK, QUEEN.—A distinct and valuable flower, which should be grown in the manner recommended for the Brompton class. The best strains are dwarf and branching in habit, and produce dense wide-spreading masses of bloom in several beautiful colours.

SEPTEMBER

AGAPANTHUS taxes the soil severely, and must have ample nourishment in pots. It is also one of the thirstiest bulbs known, but is quite hardy, and will thrive in the open if planted in a deep rich loam at any time from September until March.

ALSTRŒMERIA.—Although related to the Ixia, this bulb may be trusted to the open ground in all but the coldest districts of the country. It is not suitable for pot culture, but in a dry border it may be allowed to remain undisturbed for years. Plant quite nine inches deep.

AMARYLLIS.—The proper time to make a commencement with these superb flowers is during their season of rest, which ranges from September to March. Pot them in firm loam, enriched with leaf-mould, and containing a fair proportion of sand. Very little water is required until growth begins, and then it must be increased with the progress of the plant. Start them by plunging the pots in a temperature of about 65°, and when they are coming into bloom, remove to a warm greenhouse or conservatory. After the flowers have faded, allow the plants to complete their growth, and then slowly reduce them to a resting condition, without permitting the bulbs at any time to become quite dry.

ANEMONE.—The tuberous varieties are valuable as pot plants, not only for their flowers, but also for the distinctive character of the foliage. The roots may be potted from now up to the end of the year, so that a succession of flowers can be easily insured. Plunged in a pit or frame to preserve them from frost, watering is all the attention they will need, but of this there must be plenty, particularly when the plants begin to flower. Pot the roots between one and two inches deep, in rich soil, and with the eyes upwards. A large pot will accommodate several roots.

BABIANA.—Treat in the same manner as the Ixia.

BEGONIA, TUBEROUS-ROOTED.—Lift the plants which are in open ground, and pot them to complete their season in the greenhouse; but if they are not wanted for this purpose, they may remain in the beds until October. When the stems fall, still retain the bulbs in their own pots, and store them in a dry cellar or shed, under a layer of cocoa-nut fibre. They need protection from both damp and cold. Neither hurry the drying off of the roots, nor attempt to force the growth in spring, but wait for them to start naturally.

CALCEOLARIAS ought now to be in large 60-pots, placed close to the glass to insure a dwarf habit. During sharp weather they may be taken down, but should be restored immediately the danger is over. Much heat in the winter will be injurious; a range of 45° to 55° should be considered the limits of variation in temperature. Pot the plants on as growth demands.

CROCUS.—For indoor decoration, two or three separate lots should be potted at intervals of a fortnight; and the named varieties are worth this mode of treatment, both for the size of their flowers, and for the exceptional brightness and diversity of their colours. Use a light rich soil, and put four or five corms in a 48-sized pot. They may also be grown in quantity in large seed-pans or in shallow boxes. When coming into flower, the roots may be freed from soil to facilitate the packing into ornamental baskets or vases.

CROWN IMPERIAL.—This bulb requires a rich loamy soil, and an open position to bring it to perfection. Still it will flower satisfactorily in a shrubbery, or under the shade of trees; and, so far as the roots are concerned, there is no occasion to divide them more than once in three seasons. Plant during this month, and on to the beginning of November.

CYCLAMENS in pots will pay for an occasional dose of weak manure water. Shut the plants up in good time on chilly evenings.

The hardy varieties such as *C. europæum* and *C. coum* are cultivated out of doors; and in some of the warmer districts of the south of England, the Persian varieties can also be successfully grown in the open. They are suitable for rockwork, or for little nooks and sheltered corners in which some gardens abound. For their success, good drainage, a warm position, and plenty of water in dry weather are essential. September and October are the best months for planting out.

DOG'S-TOOTH VIOLET.—For small beds, or in front of a rockery, these compact and interesting little plants are valuable for spring flowering, and are worth cultivating for their foliage alone. They also succeed in pots, and thrive in peat, or in sandy loam and leaf-mould. A 48-sized pot will accommodate five bulbs.

FREESIA.—Towards the end of the month these bulbs will be ready for removal to a cool greenhouse or cold pit. No heat is required—merely protection from frost and excessive moisture. The footstalks are so slender that support must be given early. As the plants do not bear re-potting, the danger of exhausted soil can be met by administering weak manure water occasionally.

A A

FRITILLARIAS belong to the same order as the Crown Imperial, and the conditions which suit that plant will answer for all the Fritillaries. The bulbs thrive in a deep loam, and they are quite hardy.

GLOXINIA.—As the season of rest approaches, place the plants in any airy position, and gradually reduce the supply of water until the leaves fall off. The bulbs may be stored for the winter in peat or in cocoa-nut fibre, or in a mixture of both. There are, however, a great number of growers who never store a bulb, but rely entirely on seedlings raised annually.

HYACINTH.—To grow this flower successfully in glasses demands no horticultural skill, for children often produce very creditable specimens. It only requires the intelligent application of certain well-understood principles. Like all other bulbs, the Hyacinth should have its roots formed before top-growth begins. The flower is cultivated in water for two principal reasons: the pleasure derived from seeing the entire plant, and the enhanced decorative value insured by this mode of treating it. As darkness retards top-growth, but does not delay the production of roots, it is usual to place the glasses in a cool cellar; and if this happens to be airy as well as cool and dark, there is no better place in which to start the bulbs. Still it must be admitted that darkness is not essential for the development of roots. But darkness and coolness alike tend to delay the growth of foliage until roots are formed. Therefore, if the cultivator resolves to have the plants in view from the commencement, he will have to rely on a low and uniform temperature for securing these ends. The water must always be pure and bright, and it should not quite touch the bulb, or the latter will rot. Wires to support the flowers must be provided in good time; those which are manufactured expressly for the purpose being both neat and effective. A rather low temperature, and free access of pure air, should be regarded as necessary conditions of health in all stages of growth. Hence it will be obvious that a mantelpiece, with its fluctuations of heat and cold, is a most unsuitable position for the glasses. We should like to add, that notwithstanding the high qualities of the Hyacinth, it is quite a cottager's flower. Good spikes have been grown in tumblers kept in a garret.

For pot culture the Hyacinth is a grand subject. Prepare the pots carefully as to drainage, and fill them with a light, rich, porous compost. Remove a little soil from the central surface, and into this hollow lightly press the bulb, and press the soil somewhat firmly round it, leaving about half the bulb visible. If too much power is employed, the soil will be so compact that when the roots begin to grow, instead of penetrating, they will lift the bulb out of its proper position. There is always some risk of this, and it accounts for the practice of heaping over the pots a considerable weight of ashes or cocoa-nut fibre. Of course this covering serves a second purpose in checking leaf-growth until the roots are established. Any cool and safe position will answer for storing the pots at this stage. For the earliest supply of flowers, select single varieties, as these naturally come into bloom somewhat in advance of the doubles. When the tops begin to grow, remove the pots to a greenhouse or frame, and subdue the light for a brief period until the natural colour is gained. Thence transfer to the forcing pit as requirements demand, and they will need a week or ten days to prepare them for use. It is easy to secure a continuous supply of Hyacinths from Christmas onwards by forcing successive batches of roots until the final display will come naturally into flower without artificial assisttance. To augment the beauty of the flowers employ as little heat as may be necessary, and defer the finishing temperature until the latest moment possible. For general decorative purposes, small pots will be found extremely convenient when a brilliant display is wanted in a limited compass; good specimens can be grown in the 48-size, but for exhibition the 32-size must be resorted to. Neither in pots not in glasses should the bulbs be allowed to send up foliage from between the outer scales; these rob the central growth, and they should be carefully removed with a sharp knife.

HYACINTHS, ROMAN, should be potted in successive batches to provide a continuous supply. When the roots are formed the pots may be removed to a pit or frame, and thence to the forcing temperature as the buds show. If they have been brought on gradually, a very few days in a warm pit or house will throw them into flower. It is a source of astonishment to us that this flower is not more extensively grown in private gardens. Immense numbers are annually consigned to the London markets, and find a ready sale for bouquets and table decoration Of course it will not bear comparison with the splendid named varieties which come later, but the Roman Hyacinth is ready at a time when white flowers are scarce and valuable. Like other bulbs of the same class, it may be shaken out of its own pots, and transferred to ornamental contrivances.

IRIS.—The tuberous varieties are all perfectly hardy, and may be planted at any time from August to December. Put into light soil three inches deep and nine inches apart they will give no trouble, except to lift and divide them every second or third season.

IXIA.—Babianas, Ixias, and Sparaxis may all be treated in precisely the same manner. In certain warm districts of the southern counties they can be grown in the open ground; but as a rule, the culture must be in pots under the shelter of a frame or greenhouse. A 48-sized pot will hold four or five bulbs, and they will thrive in any soil which contains a large proportion of sand. In spring they may be transferred to a sandy border, or can be kept in pots even for a couple of years when well managed.

JONQUIL.—The treatment recommended for Narcissus will suit this highly perfumed flower, both for forcing and in the open ground.

NARCISSUS.—It is undesirable to hold these bulbs in a dry condition longer than is necessary, and those intended for pot culture should be got in promptly. A low temperature must be relied on for keeping back such as are intended to flower late. The Double Roman and the Paper White naturally come into bloom in advance of other sorts, and these should be selected for the earliest display. Give them a rich porous soil, and pot them rather firmly, but not so firmly as to render it impossible for the roots to penetrate, or they will raise the bulb out of the soil. Place them in a cool spot, covered with some material to keep the bulbs in their places, and to prevent the foliage from starting prematurely. When top-growth commences, the pots must go into some house or frame to progress slowly until the moment arrives for forcing them. If the buds just show, about a week in a bottom heat of 65° will suffice to bring them to perfection. A succession can be brought forward at intervals by the same means, until the final lot will flower naturally without such assistance. And for the comfort of those who do not possess heating apparatus we may add that the flowers grown without artificial aid will probably be the finer for its absence.

Narcissus may also be grown in glasses in the manner recommended for Hyacinths, and there is no bulb which surpasses the former for this special treatment.

In the open ground Narcissus should be planted in quantity, especially in those spots where it appears naturally at home, such as under the shade of trees and in shrubbery borders. There is now an awakened interest in the many forms of Double and Single Daffodil, and they are certainly most effective border flowers. All the varieties of Narcissus should be grown in clumps and patches, in every spot which is suitable and vacant. In the reserve border of many gardens large numbers of Pheasant's Eye and other Narcissus are planted to supply flowers for cutting. Their graceful appearance renders them peculiarly valuable for the purpose, and if cut when scarcely ready they will develop in water, and last for many days. In planting, be guided as to distance apart by the size of the bulb, allowing four or five inches between small sorts, and six to nine inches for large varieties ; depth, six to nine inches.

OXALIS.—Except in a few sheltered districts, it will be necessary to cultivate this exceedingly pretty flower in frames, or in a sunny, airy greenhouse. It may also be forced in the stove with success. Put several bulbs in a pot, and give them a light soil with plenty of sand in it.

SNOWDROP.—It does not improve the roots of this exquisite little favourite to keep them out of the ground, and they should, if possible, be planted early.

SPARAXIS need the same treatment as advised for the Ixia.

TROPÆOLUM TUBEROSUM.—In potting the tuberous varieties, insure efficient drainage, and use a compost of rich light loam and sand. The foliage will trail over the sides of wire baskets with graceful effect ; but the usual plan is to train it around balloon-shaped wires specially made for these flowers. The bulbs remain dormant all through the winter, and may be started at any time from September to March.

TULIP.—The early class of Tulips is of great value for forcing because of their brilliant colours and elegant forms. They take kindly to a high temperature, but forcing should not be commenced too early, nor should the heat be allowed to exceed 65° at the finish. The best means of applying it is by plunging. Several bulbs may be put into one pot, but as a rule the most convenient method is to grow them singly, so that flowers in exactly the same stage of development may be selected for use at one time. A continuous supply may be secured by potting batches at short intervals. When in flower, the roots can be washed free from soil for packing in vases. Decayed turf, with decomposed cow-manure, and a proportion of sand, make an excellent potting soil for Tulips, and it will be none the less suitable if it has been laid up in a heap for twelve months after being mixed.

OCTOBER

ANEMONE.—The tuberous-rooted Anemones may be planted in the open at any time from September to January, and by successive plantings a continuous display will be obtained from February until far into spring. For the choice named varieties it is customary for connoisseurs to make elaborate preparations, into which we need not enter here. Splendid flowers can be grown in clumps and beds in ordinary gardens by deep digging, and the employment of a liberal dressing of decayed cow-manure. Plant the roots from four to six inches apart, and at a uniform depth of about three inches. In a heavy retentive soil it is not advisable to risk a collection of named Anemones until January, unless a deep layer of light compost can be placed in the drills where the roots are to be planted.

ANNUALS, HARDY.—It will be safe to transplant these to light soils now; but on heavy land the hazard is too great, and it will be wise to wait until February or March. Lift the plants with as much soil attached to the roots as possible.

CROCUS.—Several flowers bloom in advance of, or as early as, the Crocus; but no other bulb can compare with it for brightness and effective colouring. Plant during this and the next month in groups and patterns wherever there is a vacant plot, and bulbs can be found to fill it. Put them in at a uniform depth of about three inches. Drills are easy to draw, and are better for the bulbs than the objectionable plan of dibbling.

CYCLAMEN seed may be sown at almost any time of year, but we regard this month and November as the most important period for making a start with this flower. If properly grown, seedlings raised now will bloom splendidly next autumn. Instructions for sowing are given under January.

GLADIOLUS.—By the end of the month lift roots which have flowered, even if the foliage is still green. Label them, and hang in an airy place to dry. A little later remove the foliage with a sharp knife. Then lay out the roots for about a fortnight, and when ready store them in paper bags or boxes placed on a safe dry shelf.

HOLLYHOCK.—In favoured districts and in light soil it will be safe to winter this plant in the open ground with merely the protection of a little dry litter. But in damp adhesive land it will be perilous, and a cold frame must afford the requisite protection until May returns.

HYACINTH.—Considering the magnificent appearance of this flower, its culture is a model of ease. Any fairly good garden soil which is not too damp in winter will grow it; and the bulbs may be planted in clumps or beds in any pattern or arrangement of colour that taste may dictate. At six inches apart there will be a brilliant display, but the distance is quite optional. The crowns of the bulbs should not be less than four nor more than six inches below the surface, and the deeper they are put in, the later will be the flowering. When planted they will give no more trouble until the time arrives for lifting them to make room for other occupants.

HYACINTH, FEATHER, is an exceedingly beautiful border flower during May and early in June. The stems are from nine to fifteen inches high, and carry flowers whose petals are cut into slender hair-like filaments. It will grow in pots and in the open, in any soil which suits Hyacinths. Plant a good number in each group.

HYACINTH, GRAPE, is an interesting dark blue flower, and should be freely grown in mixed borders to bloom in April. Singly it is useless; plant good-sized clumps in any soil which answers for bulbs.

HYACINTHS, MINIATURE, are the delight of children, in whose honour many of the varieties are named. Except for their diminutive size, they are in all respects equal to their larger relations. The culture in pots, glasses, and beds, is similar to that advised for the full-sized roots, save that the planting in open ground need not be quite so deep; three inches of soil over the crowns being sufficient.

HYACINTH, MUSK.—This flower derives its name from its odour of musk; but apart from the perfume, it is a charming little plant, and is worthy of a place in borders where various bulbs are grown.

HYACINTH, ROMAN.—Uncover the pots containing the earliest planting, and at first place them in a dimly lighted position. The application of heat will depend on the time the flowers are wanted; but when the plants are forward enough, plunge them for about a week in 65°, and they will be ready for use.

LACHENALIAS rarely attain the proportions they are capable of for want of water in their growing state. They thrive in peat, and may be forced into flower at almost any season. Except in warm and sheltered gardens, they must not be planted in the open. Yet only sufficient warmth is required to keep frost at bay.

LEUCOJUMS are perfectly hardy bulbs which will grow in any garden. They bloom in April and May, and the flowers resemble Snowdrops, but are much larger. Plant in dense groups.

NARCISSUS.—From the natural characteristics of this bulb it is desirable that it should be planted early. Sometimes, however, it is impossible, consistently with other arrangements, either to pot or plant Narcissus before October or November. In such cases it is consoling to know that the finest roots imported from Holland are so sound and well-ripened, that good flowers may be confidently anticipated from these late plantings.

ORNITHOGALUM ARABICUM.—In the open this bulb must have some protection during winter, to save its large fleshy roots from injury by frost. A heap of light manure or dry litter will answer the purpose. Plant nine inches deep.

SCILLAS can be grown almost anywhere, and in a light rich soil they bloom profusely. The bulbs will pass the severest winter safely in the open ground, and flower in February or March. The exact time depends partly on the climate, and partly as to whether they are put in a sheltered or an exposed position. Plant in masses or lines. A dense row makes an exceedingly beautiful background to Snowdrops. They may remain undisturbed for years.

TRITELEIA UNIFLORA is a handsome white flowering hardy bulb, which will grow freely in any garden. It is adapted for the company of any of the dwarf-growing bulbs, and may be employed either in lines or clumps. Plant the roots three inches apart and two inches deep.

TUBEROSES are valued for the purity of their white flowers, and for the powerful and agreeable perfume they exhale. The African bulbs are imported about this season of the year, and may be potted singly or three in a pot. They thrive in a compost of loam and leaf-mould, and need a bottom heat of 60° or 70° to bring them to perfection. The American varieties including Pearl are imported in December and January.

TULIPS may be planted in the open ground at any time during the month. We shall say nothing as to the arrangement of colours, nor as to the form of the beds, for both points admit of endless diversity. The mixed border may be enlivened with groups of many varieties, and if they are judiciously selected, there will be a succession of flowers for several weeks in the spring.

WALLFLOWER.—When the summer bedding plants are cleared, Wallflowers may be usefully employed to fill beds with green foliage all the winter. They will flower freely in spring, when their colour and fragrance will be especially welcome, and they can be removed in time to make way for a different display for the summer.

WINTER ACONITE is not dismayed by frost or snow, but will put forth its golden blossoms in the dreariest days of February, and after the flowers have passed away the foliage will remain as an ornament. But it is useless to put in single roots; it is far better to plant a few large patches rather than fritter away the flower in a number of small and inconspicuous groups.

NOVEMBER

CYCLAMEN.—If seed was not sown in October it must not be neglected now; and where there is a large demand for this flower, sowings in both months will be better than risking all on a single venture.

FERRARIA (OR TIGRIDIA).—In a dry border these bulbs will pass the winter safely, but it is somewhat hazardous in wet land. Pot culture under the shelter of a frame will frequently be necessary, and this is a proper time for potting them; but as the border flowers are finer than those grown in pots they should, if possible, be planted out in February. Sandy loam and peat suit them admirably.

GLADIOLUS.—The soil which answers best for this bulbous flower is a medium friable loam, with a cool rich subsoil. A light loam can be made suitable by trenching, and putting a thick layer of cow-manure at the bottom of each trench. And a heavy soil may be reduced to the proper condition by the free admixture of light loam and sand. Autumn is the proper time for doing this work, and the ground should be left rough so that it may benefit by winter frost. Wireworms are deadly enemies to the Gladiolus corms, and an effort should be made to clear them out. Happily they will flock to traps such as Potatoes and Rape cake, and their destruction is a mere question of daily attention.

HYACINTHUS CANDICANS is generally grown in the company of other flowers which attain to something like its own imposing proportions. In good soil the spikes grow three feet high. It may be planted from this time until March.

LILIES are an ornament to the cottage garden, and they grace the grandest conservatory. Many of the most superb varieties, including the king of all the race, *L. auratum*, can be magnificently flowered in the open border; and we have seen fine specimens of the *Lancifolium* varieties which had been grown in pots without the aid of pit or frame. It is therefore obvious that there are no difficulties in the culture of Lilies. In borders the best soil for them is a deep rich moist loam. Peat and leaf-mould also answer; but a stiff clay will not do unless it has been tamed and mixed with lighter stuff. Plant the roots at least six inches deep, at any time they are in a dormant state, or can be obtained in pots. Their position in the border should be clearly marked, or the roots may sustain injury when the soil is forked over.

The noble appearance of *L. auratum* will always command for it a prominent place in the conservatory or greenhouse. It will grow in sandy peat, or in a mixture of loam, leaf-mould, and sand. The bulb should be put into a small pot at first. When this is full of roots transfer to a larger size, and shift occasionally until the flower buds appear, when re-potting must cease. A cool house will bring the plant to perfection, although it will bear a high temperature if wanted early. During growth it must have plenty of water, but this should be diminished when the flowering season is over.

The *Lancifolium* varieties require the same treatment, but several bulbs should be grown in one large pot. After the flowering is ended, instead of allowing the roots to become quite dry, keep them moist enough to prevent the fibrous roots from perishing, and they will start with all the greater vigour when the time arrives for re-potting them next season.

RANUNCULUS.—On a light dry soil, where there is no danger of the roots sustaining injury during winter, this is a suitable time to plant Ranunculuses. To do them justice, the land must be made rich with decayed manure, but that which is raw should be avoided. The longer the bed can be made ready before planting, the better will it answer for this flower. Put the roots in drills drawn six inches apart and two inches deep, and cover with fine soil. For retentive land it is advisable to defer planting until February.

STERNBERGIA LUTEA.—A hardy yellow Amaryllis, which can be grown in any light rich soil. Plant three inches deep, and it will come into flower in September or October.

TIGRIDIA.—See Ferraria.

TRITONIA.—Perhaps the best way of treating this flower is to pot the bulbs now or in December, and keep them in frames until April, when they may be transferred to the open ground. A dry soil and a sunny spot should be found for them.

TULIP.—There is no better time for planting Tulips in beds than the first half of this month. The bulbs should be buried four or five inches deep according to size, and it is important that each kind should be put in at a uniform depth to insure a simultaneous display. On a heavy soil draw deep drills, and partially fill them with light compost, on which the roots should be planted. The late single varieties are the Tulips which were formerly so highly prized by florists. For these bulbs it was the custom to prepare the soil with extraordinary care when the Tulip craze was at its height. After the amazing folly of paying 300*l.* for a single bulb, the minor folly of extravagance in preparing the soil may be readily pardoned. Happily that phase of the business has passed away, and handsome Tulips are now grown without such a prodigal expenditure of money and labour. The site for this flower should be sunny, the soil fairly rich, and the drainage good. With these conditions insured, and roots which are sound and dense, it is easy to obtain a magnificent show of Tulips.

ZEPHYRANTHES CANDIDA can be grown in any soil, and if possible the bulbs should be planted in some spot where they may remain unmolested through several seasons. It flowers about the end of July, and resembles a white Crocus in form, but it will continue in bloom until cold weather puts a stop to it. The planting may be done between November and March.

DECEMBER

ONLY the idle or the half-hearted gardener will complain that he has no work to do in the short dark days of this month. Although there may be little or nothing to plant or sow, and few flowers need repotting, yet there are soils to obtain and store for future use ; former heaps to turn over and remake ; dead leaves to remove from plants in pits and houses ; stakes and neat sticks to prepare for subjects which will need support by-and-by ; beds and borders to enrich, and many other duties to perform. In the evenings, too, there are new combinations and fresh harmonies in colour to be designed for beds and groups in borders ; the requirements for the coming season to consider while experience gained during the closing year is still fresh in the memory ; the position of plants in pits and frames and houses to forecast, so that the plan of the summer campaign may be clearly understood, and all the resources of the garden be under intelligent control. The fluctuations of the thermometer have also to be watched, and means adopted to save plants from injury by a sudden fall of temperature. Altogether there are abundant sources of profitable employment for those who have a mind to work.

BULBS, such as Hyacinths, Tulips, Crocuses, &c., which have not been planted, will have commenced growing, notwithstanding the precautions taken to prevent it, thus showing that they ought to be in the ground. The growth has been made at the expense of the bulb itself, for there are no fibrous roots from which to draw support. Therefore it can scarcely be expected that the flowers from them will be quite so good as the same bulbs would have produced had they been put in at an earlier period. Still there are cases when the delay is unavoidable, and it is reassuring to know that such bulbs, when carefully set at the proper depth, will produce flowers only in a degree inferior to those from earlier plantings.

BULBS IN STORE, such as Begonia, Dahlia, Gladiolus and Gloxinia, should be passed in review. Examination will almost certainly reveal some unsound specimens, and their removal may save valuable companions from their contaminating influence. This practice should be followed up about once a fortnight until all are eventually planted.

THE FORMATION
OF
LAWNS AND TENNIS GROUNDS
FROM SEED

INTRODUCTORY.—A close and verdant lawn is a beautiful object in itself, and it enhances the charm of every flower, shrub, and tree in its vicinity. The popularity of tennis and bowls has made a piece of turf almost indispensable to every residence where a court or bowling green can by any possible arrangement be secured. It is not our business, however, to dwell upon the pleasure to be derived from lawns, nor upon the influence they have in the promotion of health. We have merely to consider the best and least expensive means of creating them.

SEED *v.* TURF.—There is a widespread impression that a velvety lawn can only be obtained by laying turf. It is an utter fallacy. Experience has abundantly proved that the finest and most enduring sward can be produced from seed, provided the requisite preparation be given to the land, and that pure and suitable grasses and clovers in sufficient quantity are sown. The expense of preparing the ground is not greater for seed than for turves, and there is no comparison between the cost of seed and the far heavier bill for turves, including the carting and laying of them. However closely turves may be laid, they always separate under a hot sun or drying wind, so that for a time the whole surface becomes disfigured with ugly seams. And there is no material difference in the period which must elapse before the lawn is fit for use. A slight advantage may, no doubt, be claimed for laid turf, but compared with the importance of complete future success it is scarcely worth consideration. We will, therefore, assume the question to be settled in favour of seed, and proceed to describe the manner of preparing land for its reception.

PREPARATORY WORK.—Whether the lawn is to lie wholly or in part at a slope more or less steep, or is to be perfectly level over the entire surface, deserves a moment's attention. Around some of the stately homes of England are vast stretches of ornamental turf, which, with their surroundings, constitute landscapes of surpassing beauty. Lawns of this magnitude need the treatment of a master hand, and they are beyond the modest limits we have now especially in view. But the principles which govern the work are applicable alike to great and small. The land to be made into a lawn must be well drained, in good condition, thoroughly firm, with a fine, friable and perfectly true surface.

GRASS SLOPES.—In small gardens it is not unusual to finish a lawn on one or more sides with a sharp ascent to a terrace. When the turf in such positions is well kept, and the arrangement in harmony with the dwelling, the effect is often extremely pleasing. But before spending money in making these steep slopes it will be wise to consider the possible disadvantages. Any slope towards the south is liable to burn in summer, and even a prodigal use of water will scarcely prevent the turf from turning brown during continued dry weather. This is true to a limited extent concerning slopes which face east and west. There is also a difficulty as to mowing. The grass is often beyond reach of machine or scythe, and has to be kept close mainly by the use of shears, and a wearisome business it is. The least neglect results in a slovenly appearance, so that, unless it is quite certain that steep slopes can be maintained in perfect order, they had better be avoided.

DRAINAGE.—Should draining be necessary, this operation takes precedence of all other work in the preparation for a lawn. It is so usual to assume the drainage in gardens to be satisfactory, that the subject is seldom thought of. If rain pass freely through the soil, leaving no stagnant pools even in wet winters, the sufficiency of the natural drainage may be inferred. But it should be clearly understood that a fine lawn cannot be established on a bog. Sour land soddened with moisture, or an impervious clay, must have pipes properly laid in before good turf is possible, and as the trenches cannot be filled in so firmly as to prevent the ground sinking afterwards, draining must be accomplished at least six months before seed is sown. The size of the pipes depends on the rainfall of the district, and the distance between the rows on the nature of the soil. The depth need not be great, as grass roots do not penetrate far into the earth. Fifteen feet between the rows, and the pipes three feet below the surface, are common measurements. No single drain should be very long, and the smaller should enter the larger pipes at an acute angle, to avoid arresting the flow of water. Near hedgerows the sockets should be set in cement, or the roots may force admission and choke the drain, and the outflow ends should be examined periodically to insure efficient working. It is, however, necessary to employ a practical man who understands the business and who will consider the peculiar requirements of the case.

LEVELLING.—When the land needs no important alteration of the surface, deep cultivation is not only unnecessary, but directly injurious. Spudding to the depth of from six to nine inches will suffice, and this affords the opportunity of incorporating such manure as may be required. It frequently happens, however, that the surface does not present the desired conformation, and that a level plot, as for a tennis lawn, can only be obtained by the addition or removal of a considerable mass of earth. Possibly the level may have to be raised, and to effect this, soil from a distance has to be procured. In the latter case it is usual to shoot the loads where needed as they arrive, tread the earth firmly down, and make the surface even as the work proceeds. This is the proper method of procedure if the whole bulk of soil come from one source, is uniform in quality, and suitable for forming the actual seed-bed. But in the event of there being much difference in the mould, it will be necessary to spread a layer of each kind over the entire plot, putting the retentive material at the bottom, and reserving the finer and more friable portion for the top. To make up one part of the ground with stiff clay, and another part with light loam, will inevitably result in a patchy appearance, because each soil fosters those grasses which possess affinities for it. In order to insure a perfectly level surface, pegs must be driven into the soil at the four corners and at regular distances between, upon which a long piece of wood having a straight edge can be adjusted by a spirit level. By shifting the wooden straight-edge from peg to peg, the level of the whole area can be efficiently tested.

WEED SEEDS IN SOIL.—A serious danger to which strange soil is liable is the presence of pernicious weed seeds. We have seen a lawn which had been made level with sifted soil taken from a neighbouring field. Upon every spot thus treated a strong colony of *Bromus mollis* was growing, and the great pale green tufts defied all efforts to extirpate them until the crowns were severely scored with a knife and salted, leaving large bare patches. The only efficient way of ridding soil of troublesome weed seeds is to burn it. This operation is well understood by agriculturists, and we should like to insist upon it as not only essential when adding strange soil upon which a lawn is to be made, but highly desirable whenever the land to be laid down as a lawn is of a very clayey character, in which case burning is often worth undertaking for the marvellous effect it has on the future growth. But we are not unmindful of the different conditions which prevail in the farm and the garden. The farm is in the open country, where smouldering fires are a nuisance to nobody. Near a town they may call forth a storm of remonstrance. If the proximity of dwellings renders burning impracticable, the only alternative as regards the weeds is to allow their seeds plenty of time to germinate, and destroy successive crops of them by light hoeings in dry weather. The disintegration of the soil, which is one of the good effects of burning clay, may to some extent be obtained by simply digging up the ground in autumn and leaving it rough for the frosts to break down and sweeten. Of course waiting for the weed seeds to start is vexatious when the land is prepared and the season is passing away. Still it will prove a real saving both of time and labour to insure a clean seed-bed. After grasses are sown the soil must not be disturbed, and atmospheric conditions may follow which retard the germination of the grasses but do not in the least hinder the growth of weeds. The latter rob the soil of its moisture, choke the rising grasses, and only too often doom the sowing to failure. Those who are practically acquainted with gardening know that land which has been regularly cultivated for years, and is supposed to be fairly clean, will always produce a plentiful crop of weeds, although no seed whatever be sown; yet many a faultless lot of grass seed has been condemned when the weeds have had their origin entirely in the soil. Delay offers the further advantage that the soil will become thoroughly consolidated—a condition which is highly favourable to grasses, and very difficult of attainment under hurried preparation.

ENRICHING THE SOIL.—In preparing for a lawn, the fertility of the soil is too often disregarded, but it is a matter of importance nevertheless. Luxuriant Peas, Beans, Broccoli, and Lettuce are not expected from poverty-stricken land; but any soil, however exhausted, is supposed to be good enough for growing grass, although grass is just as easily starved as any other crop, and the feeding of it has to be accomplished under disadvantages to which other crops are not subject. Vegetables in a well-ordered garden are changed from plot to plot so as to tax the soil for different constituents, and the land is not only frequently manured, but is broken up and exposed to atmospheric influences which increase its fertility. Grass is a fixed crop, which chiefly derives its nourishment from a few inches near the surface, and the only way of refreshing it is by harrowing and top-dressing. Hence there are obvious reasons for putting the land into good heart before sowing. Well-rotted stable manure is always beneficial, but that which is fresh should be avoided because of its tendency to make the soil hollow. Where artificial manure is more convenient, two cwt. of superphosphate of lime, one cwt. of Peruvian guano, and one cwt. of bone dust, mixed together, constitute an excellent dressing. The quantities named are sufficient for an acre, and the mixture can be sown when the processes of raking and rolling are in progress. Sutton's Concentrated Manure can also be recommended, as it contains all the constituents essential to the growth of fine grasses and clovers. Three cwt. required per acre. After the application of artificial manure not less than ten days should elapse before sowing the grasses, or some of the seed germs may be destroyed. The artificials named can also be added to three or four times their own bulk of sifted loam as a valuable spring dressing for the growing turf.

SURFACE PREPARATION.—A fine friable surface is of utmost consequence for insuring the success of the seed, and therefore in levelling the ground there must be a diligent use of the rake and roller. To go over the ground once with each implement is not sufficient. Repeated raking will clear the land of stones, unless very full of them, in which case it may have to be covered with two or three inches of fine rich earth. And after every raking the roller should follow, each time in a different direction. These operations reveal inequalities, pulverise the clods, and make the soil firm. Grasses, particularly the finer varieties, cannot germinate when covered with clods, and many seeds will be lost altogether if buried to a greater depth than a quarter of an inch.

SELECTION OF SEEDS.—The selection of grasses and clovers which are to form a sward should be regarded as in the highest degree important. They must be permanent in character, adapted to the soil, and entirely free from coarse-growing varieties. On land which is liable to burn, clovers maintain their verdure under a hot sun long after grasses have become brown. Still, the two classes of plants must be carefully proportioned, for although clovers show conspicuously in summer they almost disappear in winter when the grasses alone are visible. Again, clovers do not wear so well as grasses, and they hold rain longer, so that for tennis grounds and bowling greens it is advisable to sow grasses only, unless the soil is peculiarly liable to scorch in summer, and then an admixture of clover must be regarded as the lesser of two evils.

Several grasses and clovers are specially suitable for lawns, but it is seldom requisite to employ the whole of them in any single prescription. The following particulars will indicate the soil and purpose for which each kind is naturally fitted.

CYNOSURUS CRISTATUS (*Crested Dogstail*).—The foliage of this grass is very narrow, ribbed, slightly hairy, and possesses the great advantage of remaining evergreen. The roots are equal to the task of penetrating the hardest soil, and the capability of the plant in withstanding drought adapts it for sowing on dry loams, especially such as rest upon a chalky subsoil, for which it manifests a marked partiality. Still, it will thrive almost anywhere, and should form a prominent constituent of most prescriptions for lawns. Crested Dogstail is strictly perennial, and will increase in strength and vigour for quite two years after it is sown.

FESTUCA DURIUSCULA (*Hard Fescue*).—This grass grows freely on sheep downs, and mingled with other varieties is helpful in forming a fine close turf. It commences growing early in spring, and should be sown on all soils that are not very wet.

FESTUCA OVINA TENUIFOLIA (*Fine-leaved Sheep's Fescue*).— The dark green foliage of Fine-leaved Sheep's Fescue maintains its colour during hot dry weather, and is so slender as to make the term 'blades of grass' almost a misnomer. Although most useful in mixture with other grasses, a homogeneous turf cannot be obtained from Fine-leaved Sheep's Fescue only, as its habit when alone is to grow in dense tufts which have an antipathy to each other. The roots descend to a considerable depth in search of moisture, and as a consequence this grass will thrive on sandy or rocky soils that are incapable of supporting any other variety. In the early stage of growth it is easily overpowered by weeds, and for this reason autumn is preferable to spring sowing, because weeds are then less prevalent. But this grass cannot be dispensed with in lawns at whatever time of year a sowing may be made. After the plants are established they easily hold their own against all comers.

FESTUCA RUBRA (*Red Fescue*) often remains green when other grasses are burnt up, and on this account it is valuable for lawns on dry soils. The plant attains perfection in the second year.

LOLIUM PERENNE SUTTONI (*Sutton's Perennial Rye Grass*).—Most of the Perennial Rye Grasses are too coarse to be fit for a lawn, but this variety is eminently suitable for the purpose, alike for the fineness of its foliage and the dwarf branching habit of growth. It tillers out close to the ground, forms a compact sward, and retains its verdure throughout the year unless burnt by excessive drought, from which it speedily recovers. The quick maturity of this grass is another strong point in its favour, for it occupies the ground while slower-growing varieties are developing.

POA PRATENSIS (*Smooth-stalked Meadow Grass*).—In the United States *Poa pratensis* is often sown alone for making lawns. During the first year the effect is disappointing, but subsequently it makes a satisfactory turf, choking weeds and putting forth fresh green foliage with astonishing rapidity after the burning drought experienced in that country. In England better results can be obtained from a combination of seeds, and we cannot advise the exclusive employment of *Poa pratensis*. For a somewhat shallow-rooted grass its endurance of drought is remarkable. Light land, rich in humus, is its favourite resort, and it will also grow, although not with the same freedom, on heavy soil, but it is next to useless on sand. The plant does not develop its full proportions in the first season.

POA TRIVIALIS (*Rough-stalked Meadow Grass*) is somewhat similar in appearance to *Poa pratensis*, but instead of being adapted to dry light soils, it flourishes in strong moist situations, and unless the land contains abundance of potash and phosphoric acid the plant speedily perishes. *Poa trivialis* should be liberally employed for shaded lawns, as it endures the drip from trees with impunity.

POA NEMORALIS SEMPERVIRENS (*Evergreen Meadow Grass*).—From the perpetual greenness and dwarf close-growing habit of this grass it is admirably suited for lawns and pleasure grounds. It commences growing very early in spring, and although it is one of the best grasses for enduring drought it will thrive under the shade of trees.

TRIFOLIUM REPENS PERENNE (*Perennial White Clover*) is indigenous all over the country, and may be seen growing freely by roadsides; indeed, it grows better in poor than in rich land. The seed will lie dormant at some depth in the soil, and yet germinate freely when brought to the surface. Warm moist summers favour its development, and then, if too abundant, it may spread so much as to prove injurious to other herbage which can ill be spared. It must be employed with great judgment.

LOTUS CORNICULATUS (*Birdsfoot Trefoil*).—A strictly perennial plant which thrives in the poorest soils, and is capable of enduring the most extreme drought. It does not attain maturity until the second year after sowing. This clover possesses the merit of succeeding upon land which is 'clover-sick.'

TRIFOLIUM MINUS (*Yellow Suckling*).—The very small foliage of this clover gives it an especial value for lawns. It is a quick-growing plant and will succeed on dry and gravelly soils. In summer it shows abundantly just when the grasses are thin and the dense foliage of clover is most welcome. The habit is trailing.

ACHILLEA MILLEFOLIUM (*Yarrow, or Milfoil*) is neither a grass nor a clover. It is indigenous in many districts, and may be seen in some of the finest and most beautiful lawns in the kingdom. When all other herbage is brown Yarrow remains green. Still we cannot recommend it for general use. Unless the turf is kept down with scrupulous care, Yarrow soon becomes coarse and unsightly, and its employment in a lawn must be considered quite exceptional.

QUANTITY OF SEED.—We need scarcely allude to the necessity of sowing new and pure seed, strong in germinating power. The grass and clover seeds which are suitable for producing a lawn are nearly all expensive, some of them very expensive. But there must be no stint of seed on that account, for fine grasses do not tiller out to anything like the same extent as the larger pasture varieties, and therefore a much more liberal seeding is imperative; never less than three bushels per acre, and we do not consider a sowing of four bushels per acre to be excessive. The outlay for this quantity of seed will be well repaid by the rapid clothing of the ground; and there is this fact in favour of thick seeding, that the more closely the plants are crowded the finer will be the herbage. A plot of land measuring 100 feet by 50 feet will give a useful margin round a full-sized tennis court, and this area will be liberally seeded with half a bushel of grasses, assuming that the requisite time can be allowed for the development of the plant. But it generally happens that a tennis court is wanted almost before it is sown, and the only known means of insuring the rapid formation of a fine sward is by very thick seeding. In such cases the sowing of a bushel of grasses on the space just named is quite reasonable, and even this quantity may be exceeded without being open to the charge of extravagance.

TIME OF SOWING.—Grass seeds may be sown at any time between the middle of March and the end of September. But from the latter half of May on to about August 10, dry or hot weather often proves too much for the young plants. They cannot acquire sufficient stamina to endure continued drought or fierce heat unless constant watering is possible, and it is exceedingly annoying to see a good plant wither away. From the middle of March to the first week of May is the best period for spring sowing, the earlier the better; and from about August 10 to the middle of September for summer or autumn sowing. The clovers from an autumn sowing run the risk of destruction by a severe winter even if slugs spare them. Should there be failure from any cause, more seed must be sown in the following spring.

MODE OF SOWING.—The seed is more likely to be evenly distributed by two sowings than by one, however skilful and practised the sower may be; and the second sowing should cross the first at right angles. As lawn grass seeds are small and light they are readily blown to a distance by a high wind: a quiet time should be chosen, and the workman should keep his hand low. After the seed is sown the whole plot must be raked once more with the object of slightly covering as many seeds as possible. Those which are deeply buried will not germinate, and those which are exposed may be scorched by the sun, or consumed by birds. As a finish put the roller over twice, crossing the land, and it must be done carefully, for on every spot which the roller misses the grasses will fail. The result of good work will leave the surface as smooth and true as a billiard table.

WORM CASTS.—In a very short time a thick sprinkling of worm casts will be observed. We have no intention of calling in question the services rendered by worms in fertilising the soil. Darwin's work on earthworms has set that point at rest. But the operations of worms in soils newly sown down for a lawn are an unmitigated nuisance, and the mischief they accomplish will be greater in proportion to the looseness of the soil. Upon an old lawn the cast is thrown up from a well-defined orifice seldom exceeding a quarter of an inch in diameter. On newly made ground the soil becomes loosened for a considerable distance all round, and on this broken earth not a grass seed will germinate. It would be comparatively unimportant if the casts only appeared at wide intervals, but generally hundreds of them may be seen on a pole of ground. The lesson is obvious. The land must be made firm before sowing, and it must be kept firm by the early and frequent use of the roller.

WATER AND SHADE.—When severe and prolonged drought succeeds the sowing, there is a possibility that the seeds may be 'malted.' In spring the soil is generally moist enough to start seed-germs into life, but in continued dry weather growth is arrested, and the fragile shoots wither away. As a rule the watering of newly sown land is to be avoided, but it may become a necessity if the plant is to be saved. A small plot can easily be watered by means of the hose, or even by the water-can fitted with a fine rose. A large area will present greater difficulties especially in the absence of hose, or if water has to be carried a considerable distance. In any case there must be no rude trampling on the soil. Flat boards laid at intervals, and ordinary care, will prevent injury from the traffic. The water must be delivered in a fine spray, and for a sufficient time to save the necessity of a second application. Still, watering is an evil at best, and one means of avoiding it altogether is to cover the entire surface with a thin layer of cocoa-nut fibre, which will screen the soil from burning sunshine, check rapid evaporation, and foster the slender blades of grass as they rise. There is no occasion to remove this slight protection, for it will prove an advantage long after the grass has grown through it. To some extent the fibre is also a defence against the depredations of birds, and if it cannot be adopted some other precaution must be taken to save the seeds.

BIRD SCARES.—Sparrows and several of the finches are partial to grass seeds, and must be kept off until the plant is up. Small meshed nets are, of course, a certain preventive, but except over a very small area this mode of defence is almost out of the question. Strands of cotton are fairly effectual, but perhaps the best cheap bird scare is a number of lengths of twine, with feathers or strips of bright glittering tin suspended at intervals in such a manner as to turn freely in the wind.

MOWING.—As great benefit results from early cutting, the plant should be topped with a sharp scythe while it is quite young. The roots are thus encouraged to tiller out, and the surface speedily becomes clothed with fine herbage. At brief intervals the cutting should be repeated, and for this early work on the tender blades of grass the scythe is unquestionably preferable to the mower. Indeed the risk of injury from the latter is so great that many practical men condemn its employment until the plant is fairly established. But the condition of the machine must be taken into account. We have successfully used a mower for the very first cutting of a newly sown lawn, having previously ascertained by a trial on old grass that the machine was in perfect order.

In the judicious use of the mower lies one secret of a close sward. During severe winter weather the implement may not be wanted for several weeks, but as spring advances the ragged plant will demand attention, and the necessity for more frequent cutting will be evident, until in warm moist weather twice a week, and possibly for a brief period every other day may not be too often. No rigid law can be laid down on this point. The grass should never wear a neglected appearance, nor should the work on any account be postponed to a more convenient season. Except perhaps on a few occasions when the herbage is too dense to permit the machine to run freely, the collecting box need not be used. The scattered grass is no disfigurement to the lawn, and by leaving it some return is made for the vegetation produced. Setting the mower requires the exercise of judgment. It should never be so low as to graze the surface, and in summer, during scorching sunshine, it will be advisable to raise the cutter a trifle higher than for a luxuriant spring growth.

ROLLING.—Next in importance to mowing comes the use of the roller, without which it is impossible to create a lawn, or to maintain the turf in high condition. After the first cutting of the young grass, the whole surface should be gently compressed with a rather light roller, and the work needs care, bearing in mind that the soil is easily broken by a heedless foot. Subsequent cuttings to be followed by the roller until the plant is so far established as to bear a heavier implement, which should not always be used in the same direction. When the soil becomes hard through dry weather, of course rolling can do no good, and during frost it will be injurious;

but in spring and autumn frequent use of the roller will have a visibly beneficial effect on the grass. The best rollers are now constructed with two cylinders, having the outer edges rounded. The division of the cylinder facilitates turning, and the rounded edges prevent unsightly marks.

DESTRUCTION OF WEEDS.—After the most careful preparation of the land, annual weeds are certain to appear, and every weed if left alone will choke a number of the surrounding grasses. Frequent mowing checks these weeds, but there may be other and more serious pests which demand individual attention. Plantains, thistles, and dandelions must be taken up, each one singly, about an inch below the surface. A pinch of salt or 'daisy destroyer' dropped upon the cut root will effectually prevent new growth. It is worth while to see that the lad who does this work understands what he is about, for a plantain cut off just below the collar will send out half a dozen shoots, in the same manner as Sea Kale, and prove a greater nuisance than the original crown; and the careless use of salt will kill a lot of grass plants. Daisies also need separate treatment. Each plant should be lifted with its root entire, and although new growth will here and there appear for a second or even a third time, the plants will be weaker, and a little perseverance will speedily rid a large grass plot of every daisy.

IMPROVING OLD LAWNS.—Old lawns become thin and bare from various causes, such as poverty of the soil, over-wear, or because the seeds originally sown were not suitable for the land. Three remedies are easily adopted, and they almost invariably result in marked improvement. The first remedy is to stimulate the surface by a vigorous use of the rake. The immediate effect is apparent ruin, but the grass will speedily recover and be the better for the rough treatment. Then over the loosened surface sift or lightly spread a mixture of fine loam mixed a few days before use with Sutton's Concentrated Manure in the proportion of seven pounds of the manure to a medium-sized barrowful of soil, and lightly rake the surface to insure even distribution. And finally, after an interval of ten or fourteen days sow a renovating prescription of suitable seeds; rake these in and put the roller over the entire surface twice in different directions.

The work can be commenced at the end of January or beginning of February, supposing the weather renders it possible; and as the old turf will protect the young grasses from injury by frost, the seed may be sown early in March. An autumn sowing of renovating seeds can, however, often be made immediately the grass can be spared from play at the end of the season, but it certainly must not be later than the middle of September. The possibility already alluded to of losing the clovers in winter applies here also, and the sward should be examined in spring to ascertain whether another sowing of seed is necessary.

A weak-growing sward may be stimulated by the application of a pound of Concentrated Manure stirred into ten gallons of water. This quantity will suffice for a rod or perch of land, and it should invariably be administered in the evening. . Dry artificial manure scattered over the surface in hot weather will certainly scorch the grass.

We have occasionally been asked whether a lawn which is thin might not be allowed to thicken its herbage by seeding. A more disastrous course could not be pursued. It has exactly the opposite effect to that desired, by weakening the standing plant without resulting in any corresponding advantage. The little seed that is produced comes from the coarser varieties alone, and the benty growth will take years to overcome.

Moss in lawns is generally a sign of poorness of soil, and sometimes indicates the need of drainage. But before laying in drain pipes, remedial measures may be tried, especially as the work of draining sadly cuts the place about. There may also be a difficulty as to the disposal of the outflow. To improve the grass either put the rake heavily over the sward, or if the lawn be large enough employ a toothed harrow to drag out as much moss as possible. Then spread over the turf a compost, previously prepared, of lime mixed with rich soil, in the proportion of one load of lime to four loads of soil. Ten cartloads required per acre. At the same time, a sowing of seed will fill the ground with young healthy plants, which will assist in preventing a reappearance of the moss.

Cricket and Recreation Grounds scarcely fall within the limits of our present subject, and we must therefore restrict ourselves to a brief statement.

All that has been said respecting the preparation for, and the sowing and after management of lawns applies to cricket and recreation grounds. Unfortunately, these are not invariably prepared with the requisite care, nor are they always sown over their entire surface with the finest and most appropriate grasses. On the playing square of a cricket ground the necessary cost of labour and seed is justly regarded as imperative. The more important club grounds are levelled with utmost precision, and are maintained with scrupulous care to insure the ball travelling evenly to the boundary. When the work is in progress it costs so little more to prepare the whole area perfectly, and to sow it with the finest possible prescription of grasses in adequate quantity, that any saving which may be effected in the outlay for seeds is usually repented of subsequently.

THE
PESTS OF GARDEN PLANTS

WHEN adverse weather operates injuriously on vegetation, the insect plagues that infest the garden usually acquire increased power in proportion to the degree of debility to which vegetation is reduced. This circumstance perfectly accords with the general scheme of Nature, and is full of instruction as to the means of eradicating vermin, for it suggests that one way at least is to augment, if we can, the vigour of the vegetation about which we are most concerned. The subject is, however, too important to be disposed of in general observations, and we propose to enter into a few particulars.

Agencies that weaken plants usually promote the increase of vermin upon them. The keen, dry, east wind that so often jeopardises our fruit crops is usually followed by outbreaks of fly and maggot, and in the case of pot plants neglect of watering and air-giving will cause them to be quickly covered with Aphis, Mealy Bug, and other of their insect enemies. As prevention is better than cure, so in the case of plants good cultivation not only insures fine specimens, but in a great measure keeps insects at bay. It should always be borne in mind that insects, one and all, are among the frailest of living creatures, and their very frailness places them within our power. They perish at a touch. As they breathe through the pores of the skin, water alone—the grand promoter of life and cleanliness—is death to them, and they are, of course, still more subject to sure destruction when to the water is added an active poison such as tobacco, or a substance that adheres to them and stops the process of breathing, such as glue, clay, sulphur, and so forth. We repeat that good cultivation is to a considerable extent a sure preventive of vermin; but it is a wide term, and comprehends in every instance the conditions requisite to the most complete development of any particular plant. The sickly plant is the first to be attacked by insects, and in many cases air and water will do much to extinguish the plague and restore the plant to health.

APHIS in some form or other is the most persistent and perplexing of the common plant pests. The Green Fly is the enemy of the softer kinds of vegetation, and the Blue and the Black Fly are common plagues of the Peach-house and the orchard. The tender body of the Aphis is instantly affected by conditions unfavourable to its life, and hence it is one of the easiest to destroy, but its marvellous power of reproduction renders its extinction impossible, for in every instance a few escape and very soon re-establish their race. The two best remedies against Aphis are hot water and tobacco smoke. In the case of a few small pot plants, such as Fairy Roses in pots, hot water is the best eradicator of Green Fly. The water must in no case exceed 150° of Fahrenheit, but for soft-textured plants, such as Chinese Primulas, 140° is the maximum allowable, for to dip the plants in very hot water will be to cook them as well as the fly. With a pail or tub filled with water sufficiently hot, take the plant in the right hand and place the fingers of the left hand over the surface of the mould to prevent an accident, and then turn the plant over and plunge it into the water, and move it up and down briskly two or three times, when the whole of the insects will be removed into the water, the heat of which will kill them. When a houseful of plants is affected, lose no time in fumigating. The plants should be quite dry, and the house closely shut. If none of the modern appliances for this purpose are at hand, take a large flower-pot, and make a hole in the side of it about an inch above the bottom. Throw into the pot a few hot cinders, and then a few fragments of brown paper. When the paper begins to burn freely, put on it a little dry tobacco, and then add shag tobacco or tobacco paper in smallish pieces and slightly damped, and place the pot in the house —it ought to give off a dense cloud of smoke without bursting into a flame—and watch from the outside. If you are soon unable to see what is going on, you may conclude that all is right; but if a flame occurs, you must open the house at once and extinguish it, and begin again. If all goes well, no air should be given, but the smoke must be allowed to do its deadly work. Early the next morning syringe the plants freely, and in the course of an hour or so give air.

Plants may be fumigated out of doors by the aid of a tarpaulin, but it is a troublesome business, and either tobacco powder or a wash may be employed to advantage. To prepare a wash, steep shag tobacco in hot water at the rate of four ounces to the gallon, and add a little size. To economise this mixture, it is advisable to dip the plants; but if this is not practicable, syringe the plants, taking care to wet the under as well as the upper sides of the leaves. We have seen Plum trees literally blue with Aphis rendered perfectly clean by a solution of common glue, at the rate of a quarter of a pound to the gallon of water, with a little flowers of sulphur added. After being well wetted with this cheap mixture, the trees shone as if varnished, and the mixture was not washed off, because it soon cracks and peels off naturally, and trees being freed from fly begin to grow again vigorously. Rose trees may generally be cleansed of fly by means of the garden engine and pure water only, the essential point being to direct the water on the trees with some amount of force for several evenings in succession, at the time when the fly threatens to get ahead. Quassia is often used instead of tobacco, but it is uncertain in its operation, and therefore, although we know it is at times effectual, we cannot give it a general recommendation. The same may be said of Socotrine Aloes, which sometimes kills the fly, and sometimes leaves it unhurt. These drugs vary in quality, but strong tobacco never fails to do its appointed work.

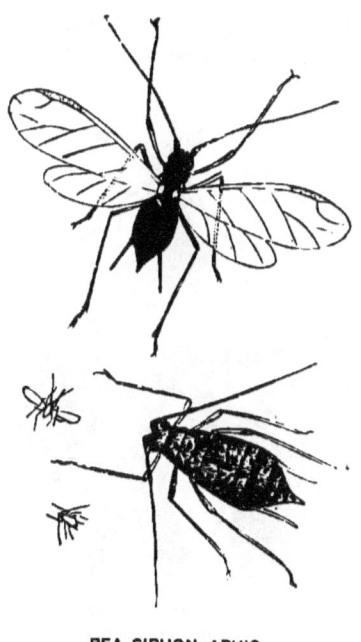

PEA SIPHON-APHIS
Siphonophora pisi

THE PEA SIPHON-APHIS (*Siphonophora pisi*, Kalt).— Amongst the aphides peculiar to vegetables, this is one of the most common. Our illustration shows natural size and enlarged figure of the greenish-winged and green-tinted wingless females, as produced, not from eggs, but alive and developed. This insect is occasionally very destructive to Pea crops.

THE BEAN APHIS—the Bean Plant Louse, or Black Dolphin (*Aphis fabæ*, Scop.).—Our illustration shows the wingless female and pupa natural size and magnified. The pupa is black, with greyish white mottlings, whilst the female is deep greenish black in colour. This insect commonly attacks the young shoots and tops of Broad Beans. It is well to cut off the infected tops and burn them.

BEAN APHIS
Aphis fabæ (pupa and female)

AMERICAN BLIGHT should never be allowed to get ahead, for neglect of it may result in the ruin of the orchard. Generally speaking, it comes first on trees that are grafted on dwarfing stocks, especially the bad forms of the Paradise Apple; but it soon spreads, and the healthiest trees acquire the taint, and once affected it is difficult to restore them to health. We have seen old trees restored to youth by scrubbing them with dandy brushes dipped in hot brine. This must be done during winter, or before the trees come into leaf in spring, and mats must be spread to catch the splashes, or they will kill the grass under the trees. A careful pruning should accompany the washing, and the prunings should be burnt. In the course of the summer the woolly pest will appear again, and should be extirpated by carefully washing the patches with methylated spirit. Fir Tree Oil Insecticide is a sure remedy for Woolly Aphis; and pure water will go some way towards cleansing the trees if well brushed into the wounds this destructive insect produces in the bark of the trees.

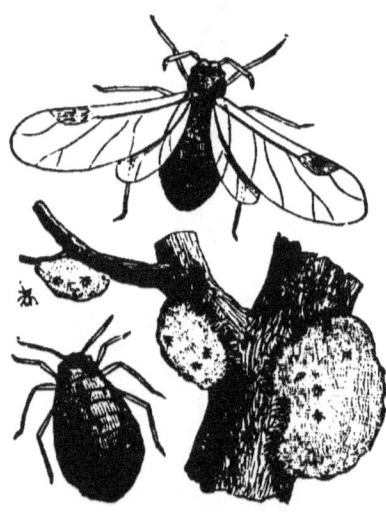

AMERICAN BLIGHT
Schizoneura lanigera

A good paint for Apple trees may be made with Gishurst Compound, at the rate of eight ounces to the gallon of water, with a little fine clay added to render it adhesive. This should be applied before the trees begin to grow in spring. Our illustration shows a piece of Apple twig with the aphides and their woolly material natural size. The enlarged figures represent the winged female and the wingless larva of the Apple Blight Aphis (*Schizoneura lanigera*). The insect is deep purplish brown in colour, and the well-known bluish white cottony material naturally exudes from the insects. Andrew Murray recommends that in bad cases of American Blight it is sometimes necessary to root up and burn all the trees, and let the ground remain unplanted for a year or two.

THE CARROT FLY (*Psila rosæ*, Fab.), with its larva, pupa, and perfect insect, is here illustrated natural size and enlarged. The ochreous, shining larvæ live upon the tap-roots of the Carrot, and by eating into them cause them to rot. The body of the fly is intensely dark greenish black, with a rusty ochreous head. The presence of the larvæ in the tap-root is made known by the change of the colour in the Carrot leaves to yellow. The plant should be immediately taken up, and the grubs destroyed by dipping the Carrots into hot water. It is well to trench in the autumn, so that the pupœ in the earth may be exposed to the frosts of winter and the attacks of birds.

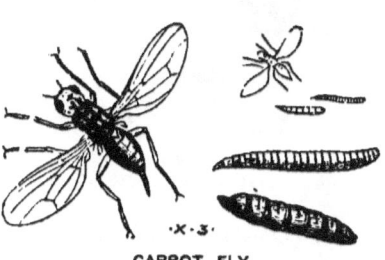

CARROT FLY
Psila rosæ (with maggot and chrysalis)

CATERPILLARS cannot often be treated in a wholesale way, because to reach them effectually is apt to endanger the plant. Hence we are usually compelled to rely on hand-picking, and we are bound to observe that, tedious as this may be, a little patient perseverance will accomplish wonders. We have seen a fruit garden, literally hideous with clusters of Caterpillars in spring, completely cleared by a few days' steady work, costing but a trifle, and only needing to be directed so that in removing the vermin there should be no harm done to the trees. In the same way the Gooseberry grub should be disposed of. A remedy against Caterpillars does not exist, but the careful cultivator will in good time look for patches of eggs and clusters of young Caterpillars on the under sides of leaves, and will carefully nip off the leaves on which the colonies are seated, and make an end of them. This enemy cannot be raked in rank and file, but must be taken in detail, as in guerilla warfare.

CELERY FLY is not amenable to any medicaments, for its larva harbours within the blade of the leaf, in which it causes apparent blisters, which, however, are not blisters, but places deficient of parenchyma or leaf-green, which the insect eats while making itself a home. Dusting newly-planted Celery with lime or soot may do something to prevent the fly laying its eggs ; but when once the grub appears, it should be crushed by pinching the leaf, or the leaves should be picked off and burnt. It should always be remembered, however, that the leaves are as much needed by the plant as the roots, and every leaf removed tends to the diminution of its vigour. Our illustration shows the Celery Fly (*Tephritis onopordinis*, Fab.) natural size and magnified. This fly is also destructive to the leaves of Parsnips, and it is called *onopordinis* from its habit of frequenting the Cotton Thistle (*Onopordon Acanthium*).

CELERY FLY AND LARVA
Tephritis onopordinis

The larva is pale green, the fly is shining tawny. An Ichneumon Fly detects the larva of the Celery Fly in the Celery and Parsnip leaves, and lays its eggs in the body of the larva. These parasites, named *Alysia Apii*, therefore tend to reduce the numbers of the Celery Fly. A second insect, named *Pachylarthrus smaragdinus*, is also frequently destructive to the pupæ of the Celery and Parsnip Fly.

ONION FLY AND LARVA
Anthomyia ceparum

ONION FLY. — Onion crops are sometimes totally destroyed by the larvæ of the Onion Fly, here illustrated, with the perfect insect, natural size and magnified. The flies lay eggs in the Onion, close to the earth, and when these eggs are hatched the larvæ emerge and eat their way at once into the Onions. In this position they frequently destroy the hearts of whole crops of Onions. This fly also

ONION FLY—DADDY LONG LEGS—POTATO BEETLE

attacks the wild Alexanders (*Smyrnium Olusatrum*). The scientific name of the Onion Fly is *Anthomyia ceparum*, and a close ally is found in the Cabbage Fly (*A. brassicæ* and *A. trimaculata*), the destroyer of Cabbage roots.

Parsnips are often attacked by the larva of a Carrot Moth named *Depressaria cicutella*. The larva spins webs about Carrot flowers and leaves for security whilst feeding, and sometimes works fearful havoc amongst Carrots and Parsnips.

DADDY LONG LEGS, in its perfect form of a fly (*Tipula*), does no harm, but it lays its eggs in grass turf and in garden soil, and its dark sausage-like grubs are terribly destructive. When this pest occurs in grass turf, it is a good plan to roll the turf late at night and early in the morning. This will crush them wholesale when feeding. A bush harrow used at the same hours will sweep them up, and whenever they can be got together in a bulk, a heavy sprinkling of salt will kill them, although they are proof against mild poisons, whether liquid or solid, when applied diffusively. Where song birds are scarce, the *Tipula* is capable of utterly destroying grass turf, and of seriously ravaging the kitchen garden; but cultivation, aided by the robins, thrushes, nightingales, and other insect-eating birds, will keep the insect within bounds, even after a hot summer favourable to its increase. When a few choice plants are found to be eaten through at the 'collar,' that is, where root and stem meet, it is good practice to scrape the earth away from them, so as to leave a shallow saucer-like hollow round every plant. This should be done with care, to avoid injuring the roots. In the process of scraping with a bit of pointed stick, the black grub will probably be found and can be killed; but if not seen by human eye, it will be exposed to the sharper eye of the robin, to whom it will prove a welcome meal, for which the scraper will be doubly repaid, first by the saving of the plants, and next by the sweet song of this best of feathered gardeners.

THE POTATO BEETLE OR POTATO BUG (*Lygus solani*) is a destructive and common insect that lives upon Potato foliage. At one time this insect was considered by many agriculturists

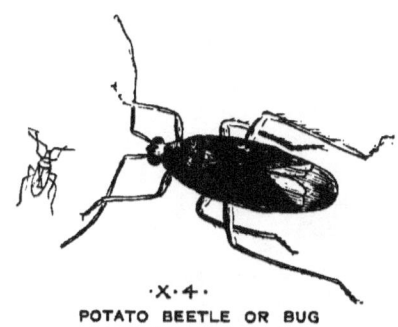

·X·4·
POTATO BEETLE OR BUG
Lygus solani

to be the cause of the Potato murrain; at another time the puncture of *Aphis rapæ* was stated to be the undoubted cause of the Potato disease. Our illustration shows the insect natural size and magnified. Its body is green, and its head ochreous. The Colorado Potato Beetle is a totally different insect.

BEAN WEEVIL.—This insect not only attacks Beans, but it at times ravages Peas, Turnips, Savoy, Kale, Broccoli, Raspberries, Apples, Pears, Vines, wall-fruit, &c. Its scientific name is *Curculio* (*Otiorhynchus*) *picipes*, and our illustration shows the larva, chrysalis, and perfect insect. These Weevils hide in the ground during the day, and commit their depredations entirely during the night hours; hence one of the common names of the pest is the Night-feeding Weevil. These insects eat holes through the stems and leaves of Beans, and the larvæ during the autumn, winter, and spring months devour the roots of garden and field crops. The beetle is clay-brown in colour, so that when it is resting on the ground during the day-time it is impossible for the sharpest eye to distinguish it from the surrounding earth. No means are known for effectually protecting gardens against these pests; the best plan may possibly be to make the ground disagreeable to them by dressings of soot or lime.

BEAN WEEVIL
Curculio (*Otiorhynchus*) *picipes*
(with larva and chrysalis)

THE PEA WEEVIL OR BUG (*Bruchus pisi*).—This pest attacks Peas at the time of flowering or while setting the pods; the beetles pair at this time and deposit their eggs in the newly formed Peas. The Peas when gathered appear to be undamaged, although they really contain the larva of the Pea Weevil. This larva eats part of the seed and changes to the chrysalis form in the spring; the chrysalis then changes to a beetle, and creeps out of the Pea as shown in our illustration. It then flies

PEA WEEVIL
Bruchus pisi

away and lays its eggs on other Pea blossoms. Our illustration shows the Pea Weevil, natural size and magnified. It occasionally happens that the beetles do not emerge from the Peas until after the sowing time in spring, so that the pest is actually planted with the seed. The early sowing of Peas has been recommended as a preventive against the Weevil, as by early sowing the insects are subjected to adverse conditions of weather. Another recommendation is that infected Peas should be plunged into boiling water for one minute before sowing; but care must be exercised, or the Peas will be killed with the Weevils.

EARWIGS are the dread of the florist, for they spoil his best Dahlias and Hollyhocks, and are too partial to Chrysanthemums. They are easily trapped, as they like to go up to a high, dry, dark retreat; hence a bit of dry moss in a small flower-pot, inverted on a stake, will entice them into your hands; and if you are determined to keep down Earwigs, this way is sure, though, perhaps, not easy, because it must be followed up morning and evening from the beginning of June onwards. The hollow stems of the Bean make good Earwig traps, as indeed do hollow stems of any kind, for they love to creep into close, dark retreats after their nocturnal meal—and the cultivator who has resolved that he will not be eaten up by Earwigs needs only to persevere, and he may depend on trapping every Earwig within the boundaries. Unfortunately, they use their wings freely, and so travel from the sluggard's garden to find 'fresh fields and pastures new.'

WOODLICE are terrible destroyers, but are easily caught, and may be completely eradicated by perseverance. When a frame or pit is infested, they may be destroyed wholesale by pouring boiling water down next the brickwork or the woodwork in the middle of the day. If this procedure does not make a clearance, recourse must be had to trapping. In common with Earwigs, they love dryness, darkness, and a snug retreat; but as a mere home suffices for Earwigs, a home with food is demanded by Woodlice. Take a thumb pot, quite dry and clean. In it place a fresh-cut slice of Potato or Apple, fill up with dry moss, and turn the whole thing over on a bed in a frame or pit. Thus you have devised a Woodlouse trap, and next morning you may knock the vermin out of it into a vessel full of hot water, or adopt any other mode of killing that may be convenient. Fifty traps may be prepared in a hundred minutes;

and those who are determined to get rid of Woodlice may soon make an end of them.

MEALY BUG.—This plague is by no means confined to plants under glass. In the case of a lot of stove plants badly affected, the desperate course of committing the whole to the fire, and then repairing and painting the house, is often the cheapest in the end. We have known a Pine-grower compelled to destroy a houseful of plants that have been infested by the introduction of a plant from a buggy collection. Mealy Bug may be known by its mealy, floury, or cottony appearance. It has a great fancy for Grape vines. One of the best remedies is Gishurst Compound, prepared at the rate of eight ounces to a gallon of water, with clay added to give it the consistence of paint. Miscellaneous stove plants may be cleansed by washing with a brush and soft soap. Our illustration shows a group of Mealy Bugs natural size, with one insect magnified.

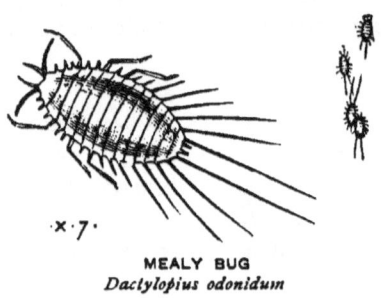

MEALY BUG
Dactylopius odonidum

RED SPIDER is encouraged by a dry hot atmosphere. It occurs in almost every vinery, however well managed. A moist atmosphere is a great, though not a certain, preventive; indeed we cannot, without injury to the vines, keep the air of the house always so humid that the Spider is unable to obtain a lodgment. Syringing operates in aid of a moist atmosphere, for, like other vermin, the Red Spider (which is in reality a mite) thrives best in heat and dryness. But the most decided repellent of Spider is a painting of sulphur on the hot-water pipes. This may be done by sprinkling dry sulphur on the pipes, or by making a paint of sulphur, clay, and water, with which the pipes should be painted.

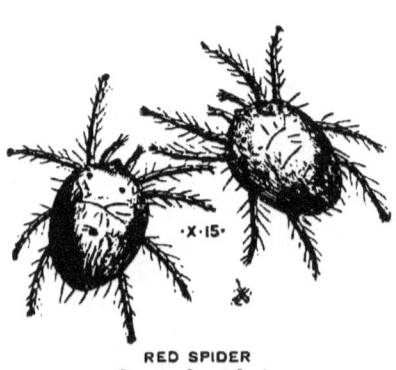

RED SPIDER
Tetranychus telarius

Be careful not to raise the heat at the same time, for if the pipes are hotter than the hand can bear, fumes destructive to vegetation will be given off. Melons and Cucumbers may generally be kept clear of spider by means of the syringe only ; but when Melons are ripening they must be kept rather dry, and it is very difficult indeed to finish a crop without having the plants attacked by Red Spider. Gishurst Compound answers admirably to remove spider from house plants. The mixture should consist of one and a half or two ounces to the gallon, and should be applied with a sponge. The scientific name of the Red Spider is *Tetranychus telarius*. Our illustration shows one of these destructive red mites, natural size, and two individuals greatly magnified.

SCALE.—The commonest and best known of the Scale insects is the *Lecanium hibernaculorum*, here illustrated on a twig, natural size and magnified. This Scale infests many plants. It is brown, tumid, rounded, and commonly somewhat more than hemispherical in shape. Besides this very common species there is the *L. filicum* of Ferns, the *L. hemisphæricum* of Dracænas, the *L. rotundum* of the Peach, and the common *L. hesperidum* or Orange-tree Bug ; this is one of the flat species, and it spreads to a great variety of plants.

COMMON SCALE
Lecanium hibernaculorum
(natural size and enlarged)

The Scale insect sucks the sap from plants, and to such an extent is this the case that in some instances the ground beneath the foliage is wet and soddened by the falling sap. Fir-tree oil is said to be a good remedy for Scale, when mixed with water in the proportion of half a pint of oil to two gallons of water. It is, however, advisable (as in other remedies) to test this on a small number of plants at first. A near relative, a large brown *Coccus*, infests pomaceous trees, and is especially partial to the Pyracantha, which it often kills outright. The Scale of the Vine is *Pulvinaria* or *Coccus vitis*. Careful washing with soap and water has been recommended for the extirpation of this pest, and the destruction of each separate Scale as soon as seen.

THRIPS may pursue their mischief to a great extent before they are discovered by the novice, for their minute size and their habit render them inconspicuous. But the black deposit they make reveals their existence to the experienced eye, and the debilitated condition of the plants they have attacked would soon compel attention were there no such deposit to tell the tale. The Indian Azaleas are apt to be beset by Thrips, as the Grape-vine is by the Scale, the Pine-apple by Mealy Bug, and the Rose by Green Aphis. Atmospheric humidity is a powerful preventive, as is also the promotion of vigorous growth by a plentiful supply of water to the roots of the plants; in fact, starvation and a dry, hot air will bring Thrips as soon as anything. The usual and, generally speaking, the best remedy is fumigation by tobacco, and, in common with every other insect plague, tobacco water and a solution of soft soap, together or separately, will soon make an end of Thrips, if carefully applied. A special preparation may be made as follows: Take six pounds of soft soap, and dissolve in twelve gallons of water, add half a gallon of strong tobacco water, and dip the plants in the mixture. Before they become dry, dip again in pure rain water to remove the mixture. If too large to dip, apply the mixture with the syringe, and in the course of a quarter of an hour or so syringe with pure rain water. Our illustration shows the Thrips in the larval and winged state, natural size, and greatly magnified.

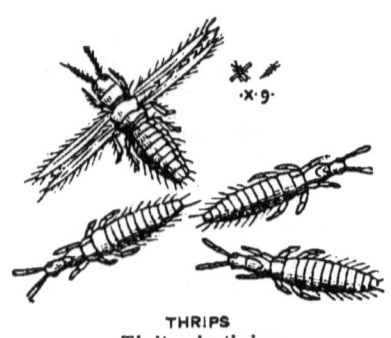

THRIPS
Thrips minutissima

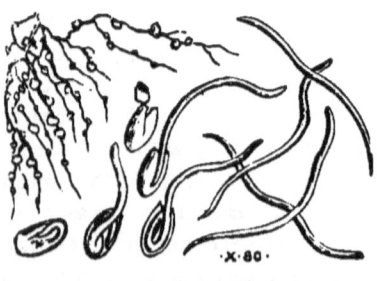

CUCUMBER WORMS AND EGGS
Anguillulæ

CUCUMBER DISEASE.—One of the most terrible pests that a Cucumber grower has to deal with manifests itself by the presence of minute warts or nodosities, chiefly on the rootlets. These warts range from the size of a pin's head to that of a pea, and when they are present in large numbers the total failure of the Cucumber crop is the invariable result. These nodosities are caused by the presence of innumerable and excessively small thread-like worms named

Anguillulæ. Each worm is about one-hundredth of an inch in length. At first the worms are coiled up inside transparent eggs; at maturity the eggs crack open and the worms emerge. Although only one-half the size, this *Anguillula* is closely allied to the well-known Vinegar Eel, and to the minute worms found in 'cockled' Wheat. The worms are probably introduced to Cucumber houses in infected water: when once introduced, they bore into the most tender rootlets and there lay their eggs. These eggs speedily hatch inside the plant and new worms are produced, which traverse the rootlets in every direction.

These *Anguillulæ* are by no means peculiar to the Cucumber plant; they attack the roots of Melons, and the roots, stems, and foliage of many other plants, notably of late years the Carnation. Our illustration shows some very small rootlets, natural size, with the worms in the eggs, the worms emerging and free of the empty egg-shell, enlarged eighty diameters. The only recommendation for cure that has at present been published, is that all infected plants should be removed and burnt, and the compost entirely cleared away and replaced by fresh earth.

SLUGS are serious plagues to the gardener, and it appears sometimes as if the little Slugs came down in showers, so suddenly and so plentifully do we find them distributed. The crops are, when young and growing freely, peculiarly liable to injury by Slugs, and it is not easy to subdue the pest, even in gardens. Here, however, as in the case of many other kinds of vermin, means may be adopted that will accomplish the double purpose of destroying the plague and benefiting the land; for lime, salt, soot, and nitrate of soda are certain Slug killers, and will usually pay for their employment by their enrichment of the ground. The nice point always is to employ them advantageously. Land made ready for sowing may be pretty well cleared of Slugs by broad-casting it with salt. When a rising crop is much infested by them, recourse must be had to trapping. Cabbage leaves, sliced Turnips and Potatoes, and other tasty traps must be employed; whatever in the nature of waste material that may be at hand of a suitable kind being, of course, preferable. These should be scattered about at dusk, and be gathered up in the morning, and given to the pigs, or buried in pits, or destroyed by fire. Sawdust is a capital bait for Slugs. It should be borne in mind that a Slug, slightly touched by lime or salt, has the power of throwing it off by means of the slimy exudation with which the creature is endowed. But if again and quickly assailed in a similar manner, death is certain to follow. Therefore if one salting or liming does not answer, a second is likely to prove completely effectual.

RATS AND MICE are irrepressible garden vermin, and we must consider ourselves fortunate if we can keep them somewhat in check. Traps are good while they are new, and almost any reasonably good contrivance will answer for a time, but will fail at last, or at least for a season. To keep down Rats and Mice effectually, there must be invented a succession of new modes of action, for these creatures—Rats especially—are so clever that they soon see through our devices, which then fail of effect. Generally speaking, two rules may be prescribed. In the first place, we think it imprudent to fill up their holes or stop their runs; let them have their way. If you stop them, they will make new thoroughfares, to the further injury of the foundation; and, besides, when you know of their runs you know where to put traps and poison for them. As for the best poison, there is nothing so effectual as arsenic; but it should be employed with great care, and the safety of the bulk should be considered before it is brought on the premises. A fat bloater split down and well rubbed with common white arsenic will kill a score of Rats, provided only that they will eat it. Cut it into four parts, and place these in or near their runs, and cover them with tiles or boards to prevent dogs and cats obtaining them. If this fails, try bread and butter dressed with oil of rhodium and phosphorus. The oil of rhodium seems to possess an irresistible attraction for these vermin. When dry food is preferred, there is nothing so good as oatmeal, and it is a golden rule to feed the Rats for a few days with pure oatmeal, and then to mix about a fourth part of arsenic with it. A correspondent of *Chambers's Journal* (Part 235, page 473) disposed of a colony of Rats by catching two in a wire trap and well smearing them with tar. They were then restored to their runs. Every Rat migrated to other quarters, and not one of them returned. A good fox-terrier will keep a large garden free from Rats and Mice.

TURNIP FLY is well known to the gardener, and is the most important of all the aërial pests of the farm, and one with which it is most difficult to cope, not only because of its general diffusion and numbers, but because it produces a succession of broods throughout the summer, and is therefore always in force, and ready to devour the crop when the crop is ready. The so-called 'Fly' is a beetle named *Haltica nemorum*, a little jumping thing, strongly made and decidedly voracious. The larvæ are not to be feared, except that, of course, they in due time become beetles. In its perfect state as a winged jumping insect this creature makes havoc of the Turnips, and the crop is only in danger while in the seed-leaf stage. It is in the spring and early summer chiefly that their ravages occasion perplexity, for they awaken from their winter torpor active and hungry, and have a ready appetite for almost any cruciferous plant. Hence we see the leaves of Radishes pierced by them, and all such weeds as Charlock, Cuckoo Flower, Hedge Garlic, and Water Cress serve them for food until the Turnip crops are on the move, when they will travel miles, even against the wind, to make havoc of the farmer's hopes. Very many preventive and remedial measures that are sound in themselves are nevertheless not generally practicable. We shall enumerate them briefly as they occur to us, leaving the ultimate choice of weapons to those whom fate may condemn to use them.

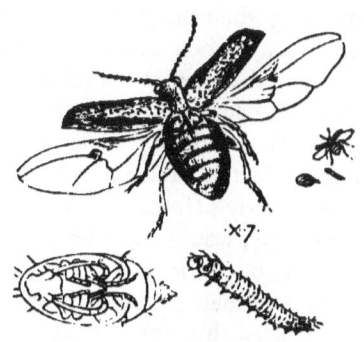

TURNIP FLY OR BEETLE
Haltica nemorum (with larva and chrysalis)

The safest course against Turnip Fly is to promote a quick germination of the seed and strong growth of the plant in its first stage of the seed-leaf. The cotyledons are tender and tasty, perhaps sugary from Nature's process of malting; and while the seed-leaf is assailable, the *Haltica* makes the best of the shining hour. It is of no use to dress the seed with any mixture, and it is a mistake to regard the spots on the seed as the eggs of the insect. This, however, may be said with safety, that the seed sown should be all of one age, and the newest possible, because of the need for a quick and strong growth. When a powerful manure is sown with the seed, the quantity of seed should be increased, because of the considerable portion that will be killed by the manure. It is important always to drill in Turnip seed, for broad-casting seems to invite the Fly; at all events, a drilled crop is generally the safest.

The sprinkling of slaked lime over the young plant is at once a safe and an effectual process, and possesses the additional advantage of being beneficial to the plant. We are aware that it does not always succeed, but we are inclined to attribute the failure to a bad quality of the lime, or a careless method of employing it. There should be enough put on to make the plants white, and they will be none the worse for the whitening. Dustings of ashes and soot are scarcely less effectual, but salt must not be used, for it injures the plants and does not hurt the Beetle. All such dustings should be done in the morning while the plants are still wet with dew. To apply a dusting at midday, when the sun shines gaily, is to waste time in merely amusing the Beetles. Probably many of the recorded failures might be explained if we knew at what hour and in what sort of weather the work was done. Nets and sticking boards have been tried and found effectual, and yet it is but rarely we see such things used. A board newly painted with white paint, drawn over the plant on a still sunny day, would soon become a black board by the attachment of myriads of *Halticas* that would jump at it and remain upon it, the victims of their extravagant love of light and of jumping towards it.

Finally, this, in common with all other insects in the winged state, needs a dry air and some degree of warmth for its health and happiness. Many kinds of larvæ need moisture, but no winged insect can abide moisture long, and herein perhaps we may find a clue to the eradication of Turnip Fly. By the simple process of irrigating the plant overhead three or four times a day, until the plant is out of the seed-leaf and the danger is over, it is possible to wash out the *Haltica*; and any kind of insecticide or flavouring may be mingled with the water to render the plants distastefu to the insects. The illustration shows the Turnip Fly in its three stages, and in each case of the natural size and magnified seven diameters.

Wasps are a terrible scourge in some gardens. They spoil a large quantity of fruit, and jeopardise the remainder by forcing the harvest before the crops are ready for gathering. When the positions of the Wasps' nests are known, it is a simple task to dispose of them. Turpentine, gunpowder, and tar have their advocates, especially among the younger members of the community, to whom a spice of danger is an attractive element in the fun. But these are clumsy methods of destruction after all, and will not compare with the far easier remedy of poisoning the colonies by means of cyanide of potassium. Dissolve one ounce of the drug in a quarter of a pint of water. This will be sufficient to destroy several nests, but it is a deadly poison, and must be kept in a place of safety. Soak a piece of rag in the fluid, and lay it over the entrance to the nest. There is no occasion to run away; not a Wasp will venture out, and those which return from foraging will not lose their tempers and find yours, but at each successive attempt to enter their home they will become feebler, until they fall near or beneath the drugged rag. After an hour or two the nest may be dug out, when every insect, including queen and pupæ, will be found dead.

If the colonies lie without your frontier, or their positions cannot be ascertained, the enemy must be disposed of by stratagem and in detail. One of the best modes of trapping them is to put some injured fruit beneath one of the trees, and over it a hand-light raised about three inches above the ground by stones or pieces of wood placed at the four corners. This light must have a rather large hole at the top. Upon it should rest another light from which all means of egress is prevented, except through the apex of the lower light. After the Wasps have visited the fruit, they will rise into the first light, and gradually find their way through the opening into the upper one, from which not one insect in a hundred will escape. In this trap we have seen an enormous number of Wasps and Hornets which had been allured into it within a few hours.

WIREWORM is the most persistent and destructive of all the ground vermin. There are fully a dozen species of beetles, the larvæ of which are known as 'Wireworms,' and of these the 'Spring-Jacks' and 'Click-Beetles' and 'Blacksmiths'—*Elater obscurus, E. lineatus,* and *E. ruficaudis*—are the most prevalent, and demand the most serious attention. The female beetle deposits her eggs in the earth in the height of the summer, and in due time the worms emerge and commence their depredations. These worms have a tenure of five years in their subterranean homes, during which time they feed voraciously and are not very particular as to what they eat, and are well protected by their horny jackets and the muscular power which renders them expert in burrowing. When their term of five years' feeding is completed, they descend to a considerable depth and change into the chrysalis state, from which they come forth as jumping beetles in the course of July and August, a certain proportion remaining in the ground to complete their final change in spring. Now their power to destroy is at an end. They resort to flowers, lead a merry life for a short time, and when they pass away leave plenty of eggs to continue the race of Wireworms. The history of the Meal worm (*Tenebrio molitor*) does not greatly differ from that of the true

Wireworm, and it is in the larva state as long-lived. These, however, are pests of the granary, and give us no trouble in the garden.

For practical purposes the Wireworm may be regarded as inhabiting every kind of soil and consuming every kind of crop. The crops it is most partial to are Grass, Potatoes, Turnips, and the juicy stems of all kinds of cereals. The first step towards its destruction must consist in stirring the earth by spade or other agency. Lands that have been long undisturbed, as fallows and pastures, for instance, are usually crowded with Wireworm, and these, as a matter of course, prey upon whatever crop is put upon the land when first it is broken up. Soot, lime, salt, nitrate of soda, and sulphuric acid are cheap and useful manures suitable to many soils and circumstances, and directly destructive to Wireworm.

The most convenient food is Potatoes; the Wireworms seek these out instantly upon their being committed to the soil, and thus they serve as traps admirably. Chat Potatoes that have not been greened might often be used advantageously to clear a piece of land of Wireworm.

CLUB, ANBURY, AND FINGERS AND TOES.—These affections of the roots of brassicaceous plants, more especially Cabbages and Turnips, are produced by various causes, insect agency being certainly concerned, but the selection of the seed and the method of cultivation have also their several influences to induce or prevent them. The supposed cause of one common form of Club is a little midge called *Trichocera hiemalis*, and certain Weevils, one of which is known as *Ceutorhynchus sulcicollis*. These lay eggs on the ground or amongst weeds, and the resultant maggots find their way to the roots of brassicas, which they puncture, and a gall or excrescence is soon produced. This grows rapidly at the expense of the entire plant, and it soon becomes hollow and putrescent, when Beetles, Wireworms, Millipedes, and Slugs find their way to it; and when we cut open a large offensive Club it is no unusual thing to find it packed full of strange creatures like a travelling menagerie. In certain soils Club is almost unknown; in others it is so persistent a plague that it is with difficulty a crop of Cabbage or Turnip can be produced. According to the observations of a famous Russian botanist, M. Woronin, the Fingers and Toes disease is caused by the attack of a fungus named by him *Plasmodiophora brassicæ*. The opinion of that authority has to a considerable extent been confirmed by botanists in this country; but it is desirable that further experiments should be made. The Cabbage, Charlock, Mustard, and many cruciferous weeds are attacked by the same pest, and in some districts this malady of Turnips is equally bad with the ravages of the fungus of the Potato disease. The protoplasm, or gelatinous formative living material of the fungus, is said to first ramify amongst and within the tissues of the roots of the plants attacked, and to ultimately produce an abundance of spores so small, that more than thirty millions would be required to cover a superficial inch. Diverse opinions have been expressed as to whether the Turnip is first in a bad condition of health, and then easily attacked by the fungus, or whether the fungus makes its attack upon perfectly healthy plants. As a rule, unhealthy and weakly plants are the earliest to fall. The *Plasmodiophora* belongs to an order of fungi, the *Myxomycetes*, which, as a rule, live upon decaying vegetable material. Some botanists assert that this fungus will only live on the healthy tissues of cruciferous plants, but this opinion needs confirmation. Very young seedlings are soon attacked by Fingers and Toes, if the seedlings are isolated and treated with water in which the tissue of old Fingers and Toes has been macerated. The attack of the disease arrests the growth of the plant. The spores are capable of resting in a state of vitality for a long time, and can easily withstand the frosts of winter. The illustration at A shows the fungus in its protoplasmic condition, and at B its ultimate sporiferous or seed-producing condition, or when the protoplasm has changed to a mass of minute spores, enlarged 520 diameters. The spores on germinating throw out an amœba, an animal-like mass furnished with a fine thread-like tail, as at C, D, E, and capable of a creeping motion in moisture. When quite free

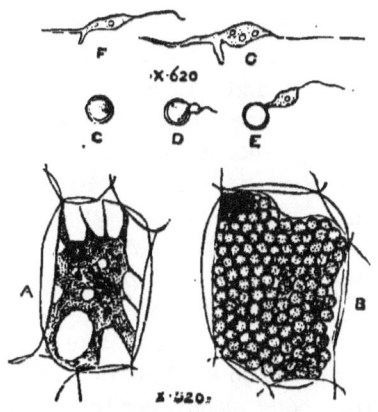

FUNGUS OF FINGERS AND TOES DISEASE
Plasmodiophora brassicæ

from the spores, transparent expansions or limbs extend from the bodies of the amœbæ, as at F, G, and when these amœbæ reach the roots of cruciferous plants, they take the protoplasmic condition shown at A, and live within the cells, and at the expense of the nurse plant. Charlock, Mustard, and numerous weeds are less seriously damaged by the pest than are Turnips and Cabbages; but it is evident that if diseased Charlock is near Turnips, the Turnips are very likely to fall a prey to the disease. We advise the planting of the best seeds, the eradication of cruciferous weeds, and the destruction by fire, wherever possible, of all decaying Fingers and Toes material, for it is in this material that the spores of the disease rest ready for opening, and reproduce the disease in the following season. It is also desirable that cruciferous plants should not be continuously planted in the same quarter.

Thoroughly good cultivation will doubtless tend more directly to eradicate this pest than any special treatment. A complete change in the order of cropping, the free use of soot and lime, and systematic subsoiling, will go far towards clearing the land so that in two or three years it may be safe to grow Turnips again. As regards the occurrence of Anbury in seed-beds, frequent transplantation is a very effectual mode of stopping its progress, for the little galls can be pinched off by the workman, and burnt as he proceeds; and the plant, being invigorated by change of soil, will soon grow away from the affection; indeed, it is no uncommon thing to see the formation of new healthy roots above the Club, showing the disposition of the plant to grow away from it without help. It is worthy of special remark, that in market gardens Anbury is by no means so prevalent as to interfere with the routine of cultivation, although the Cabbages, Broccoli, and Cauliflowers grown in these grounds are under other circumstances especially liable to attack. By 'other circumstances' we mean that market gardens are generally kept under high cultivation, the land being perpetually turned about and heavily manured; and these measures appear to keep Anbury away, while, on the other hand, they make heavy crops. But on land less energetically tilled, Anbury may prevail to such an extent as to seriously interfere with the order of cropping.

Seed-beds of Cabbage may be in a material degree protected against Club by scattering fine dry dust or road scrapings amongst the young plants; for this, at any rate, checks the progress of the midges and weevils that cause the root-galls. Another very important mode of keeping down the pest consists in burning instead of burying the stumps and all other refuse of the crop that cannot be turned to account. Where burning is inconvenient, the burying should be deep to be effectual.

Fingers and Toes are usually associated with Anbury, but the cause is probably in the plant and its conditions, and has no special relation to insect agency. Instead of forming a shapely solid bulb, the feeding fibres swell into useless tap-roots, or what should be the bulb divides into Fingers and Toes in a manner suggestive of degeneracy—the result of poverty in the soil, careless cultivation, or degenerated seed. Those who save their own seed during a series of years are pretty sure to become well acquainted with this malady. We advise such to obtain a change of seed, and to consider at the same time where the routine of work is defective. A healthy, vigorous plant derived from a pure seed-stock does not make Fingers and Toes, but a sound plant that stands for food and money.

ERADICATION OF GARDEN VERMIN

THE expense of preparing mixtures and washes may be in some degree lessened by economy of application. A drenching board, fitted on a firm frame, should be provided in every place where plant-growing is carried on to any extent. The board should slope from a resting ridge at the base. The plant in its pot may be laid on the board, with the bottom of the pot against the resting ridge, and a pail should be put to catch the liquid used as it drains from the plant after syringing. Every general washing or fumigating should be followed by another at an interval of from a week to a fortnight, because, although the first operation may kill every insect, there will be many living eggs left, and these renew the race, and very soon bring the plants into as bad a state as ever, unless consigned to a happy despatch as their parents were. In some cases, it will be more economical to feed than to destroy the vermin; and, as a rule, feeding vermin does not add to their numbers, in the same or any future season, for insect life is so strangely dependent on certain conditions of temperature &c. that if the season is not favourable to a particular kind it will be scarce, no matter how plentiful it may have been in a former generation. In the case of the Turnip Fly, feeding is frequently the cheapest and surest way of saving the crop. It is customary with Dahlia growers, and indeed with the growers of florists' flowers generally, to sow Lettuces where the flowers are to be planted, for as long as Lettuces are on the spot Slugs and Snails will prefer them to other food, and the Lettuces themselves serve as traps; so that as evening approaches, we may find pretty well all the Snails and Slugs that are in the garden congregated about the Lettuces and may catch and destroy *ad libitum*; greasy Cabbage-leaves, and heaps of brewers' grains, are also good traps for Slugs and Snails.

In using a mixture or preparation for the first time, it is advisable to try it on one plant only, and that, of course, the worst in the collection affected. If the preparation is too strong or too weak, the truth will be declared by the state of the plant within twenty-four hours; thus a little caution may save a great loss. Another good rule is to employ the several preparations rather less powerful than advised, until experience has been gained, for we have not only the strength of the medicine to consider, but the management of the patient before and after it is administered. It is above all things important to be thorough in the cleansing of plants, for they succumb rapidly to the attacks of insects, and should be effectually and promptly cleaned or consigned to the fire; if left in a foul state they spread the infection to all around.

Several very excellent preparations are now offered for the extermination of insect plagues. The following articles are also of value for the same purpose.

ALCOHOL is a deadly poison to every species of insect, and, diluted with water, might often be employed to advantage. Common methylated spirit, if carefully used, is one of the cheapest of insecticides, and may be made the more efficacious by the addition of camphor.

ARSENIC is a deadly and dangerous mineral, that may be employed with great advantage by a careful person for the destruction of Mice, Rats, and Crickets. It should be mixed in small quantities with dry oatmeal and powdered sugar, and, to avoid injury to any, except the animals intended to be killed, it must be placed in the runs under cover of a large hollow tile, or in a dry drain-pipe, or in some other way rendered inaccessible to any except burrowing animals.

CLAY is largely used to mix with various washes, to give them the consistence of paint. Now clay has a virtue of its own, and is an effectual insecticide, for when the soft body of an Aphis is covered with wet clay, its death is certain.

SALT may be usefully employed in a variety of ways, but needs care because it is a destroyer of vegetation. Ground vermin may be eradicated by sowing salt on the surface, and in such a case it would be well to wait until rain has fallen before sowing or planting. The larvæ of the Tipulæ are all easily destroyed by salt, but the difficulty is to apply it without at the same time injuring the crop they are feasting on. A weak solution of salt may be used to cleanse Cabbage, Cauliflower, &c., when much infested by Caterpillars, for it acts instantly on their tender bodies, and does not injure the plant.

SOFT SOAP is much employed in mixtures, but is efficacious when used alone in solution to remove Mealy Bug and Aphis.

SULPHUR is employed in mixtures and also alone. When injudiciously handled, it is a terrible destroyer, and many a house of Vines has been ruined by an unskilful use of it. It is customary to paint the hot-water pipes in vineries with sulphur, and the philosophy of the proceeding is that the moderate heat causes it to sublimate slowly, and mix with the air in sufficient quantity to destroy Red Spider, and yet in insufficient quantity to injure the Vines. Seeing the salutary effects of sulphur wisely employed, it is no unusual thing for a novice in Grape-growing to *burn* sulphur in the house, and the result is shrivelling of the leaves and loss of the crop; and if the Vines recover in the next season, the owner may consider himself fortunate. Dry flowers of sulphur may be sprinkled on plants with safety, and is a valuable remedy in the case of mildew; but this mode of using it requires care.

TOBACCO is the most extensively used of all insecticides, for in truth no insect can withstand its poisonous power, and if employed with reasonable caution, it does not in the least injure vegetation. In the form of dry powder, it is at once a cheap, cleanly, convenient, and efficacious destroyer of soft vermin, such as Aphis &c., and under Excise regulations is sold free of duty for horticultural purposes, being first doctored with sulphur, as alcohol is for a like reason doctored with naphtha. In purchasing tobacco, the strongest shag should always be preferred; but tobacco paper and tobacco liquor are useful, and in every case it is advisable to purchase the best.

TURPENTINE is used in mixtures and also separately. It is not safe to touch plants with pure turpentine, but the vapour is a destroyer of insects, and does no harm to vegetation. In the case of delicate plants, such as Orchids, Ferns, &c., growing in closed cases, spirits of turpentine may be introduced in an open vessel, and the vapour diffusing in the atmosphere of the case will soon make an end of insect life there.

THE FUNGUS PESTS
OF
GARDEN PLANTS

THE plants of our gardens and farms are very liable to attacks from destructive fungi. Cures are in most instances unknown, but preventives seem to be in many cases within reach. When first-class seed is sown, and receives good cultivation, a strong and robust growth will probably be the result. Well-grown and healthy plants are known to be less liable to the attacks of fungus than ill-grown and weakly ones. It is amongst the ill-tended and weakly that disease generally begins, and from these centres of contamination it too often spreads to well-cultivated places. It is therefore a matter of the first importance in the prevention of disease that the best seeds should be sown, and that they should be developed by good cultivation into robust and vigorous plants.

POTATO DISEASE.—Every cultivator of Potatoes must have noticed the white flocculence which grows on the discoloured patches of diseased Potato foliage. This white flocculence is the dreaded Potato fungus—or rather fungi, for there are two distinct species. When the flocculence cannot be seen on the patches, the fungus spawn is growing inside the leaf, and has not yet emerged in a flocculent form from the organs of transpiration of the foliage.

That the two fungi are capable of causing the disease, is proved by the following fact. When the fungus spores are taken from an infected plant, and placed upon the leaves of a healthy one, they immediately germinate, penetrate into the interior of the Potato leaf, and at once reproduce the parent fungus and with it the Potato disease.

The names of the Potato fungi are *Peronospora infestans* and *Fusisporium Solani*. They are both microscopic in size, and require the highest powers of the microscope for their proper examination. Both are shown in the accompanying illustration magnified seventy-five diameters. The *Peronospora* is shown at A, the *Fusisporium* to the same scale at B. The *Peronospora* is like a finely branched thread of spun glass. It is seen at the bottom of the illustration emerging from one of the organs of transpiration of the Potato leaf. As the thread grows it rapidly branches, and produces spores or seeds at the end of each branch. As these spores drop off one by one, the branches extend by joints, and produce other spores, till seven or eight are produced by each branch. The spores in the act of falling from the branches are shown in the illustration. When the spores fall, they commonly discharge their contents in the form of smaller spores, from three to nine in number, as shown at C, C. When the spores and their contained secondary spores are further magnified to four hundred diameters, as at D, the secondary spores or zoospores are seen to be furnished with two lash-like tails, with which they can rapidly propel themselves through water or upon any damp surface.

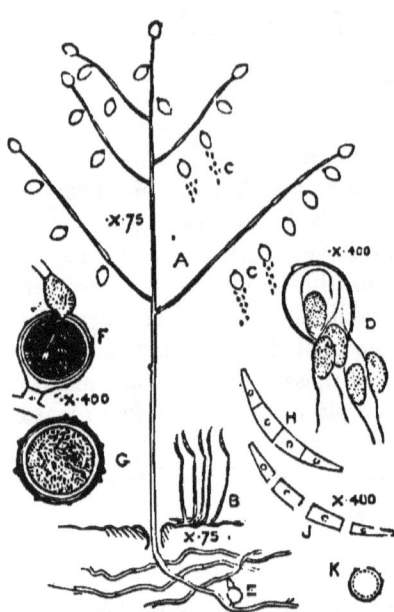

THE FUNGI OF THE POTATO DISEASE
A *Peronospora infestans*
B *Fusisporium Solani*

Inside the leaf, as seen at E, are other organs belonging to the Potato fungus, but further enlarged to four hundred diameters at F; the larger of these two bodies is comparable with an ovule or seed, and the smaller to an anther with its pollen. The smaller commonly comes in contact with the larger, in a similar way to an anther coming in contact with a stigma. The fertilising contents of the smaller body are poured into the larger through a small beak, as illustrated at the top of F, and the result is a resting-spore or seed capable of living in a resting or seed-like condition for one or more years. When the resting-pore is mature, as at G, it is glossy and rich brown in colour. It does not germinate when first formed, but reserves its power for a fitting time during some future autumn.

The second fungus, named *Fusisporium*, illustrated at B, almost invariably accompanies the *Peronospora*. Under the microscope its growth looks like dense fields of transparent wheat. When the separate ears are magnified to four hundred diameters, they are like the illustration at H; each ear is divided into four parts. At maturity these parts fall asunder into four oblong spores, as at J; but when these spores fall on a damp place, they speedily take a globular form, as at K, and then they rest for a few days, weeks, or maybe months, and at length reproduce the *Fusisporium*. Like the last, this smaller fungus decomposes the host plant by contact.

These explanations show the immense power of increase possessed by these two fungi. The number of reproductive bodies these pests are capable of producing is simply marvellous, and quite incomprehensible to the mind. When weather conditions tend to destroy the fungi outside the leaves, stems, and tubers, then the parasites carry on their existence in the resting-spore stage, or by perennial spawn or mycelium.

As the resting-spores and perennial mycelium hibernate in decaying Potato refuse, it is of the highest importance, with a view to the prevention of the Potato disease, that no bad Potatoes or foliage should be allowed to rot on the ground or on manure-heaps through the winter. Diseased Potatoes, stems and leaves, should, as far as practicable, be burnt. If burning is inconvenient, deep burying should be resorted to.

LETTUCE DISEASE.—This mould is sometimes of the most destructive character; it is a close ally of the Potato mould, and is named *Peronospora gangliformis*. It covers Lettuce leaves with a fine white bloom, and this bloom decomposes the leaves, and makes them adhere together in one putrescent mass. It should be looked for in its earliest stages, and hand-picked and burnt.

ONION DISEASE.—This is also caused by an ally of the Potato mould; it is named *Peronospora Schleideniana*, and it is occasionally very destructive to Onions; in some districts it is almost unknown; in others it is common. It occurs at uncertain intervals of time with extraordinary virulence, and then utterly destroys the crops. Autumn sowing is considered a good preventive by many growers, as the disease is frequently fatal to spring seedlings.

PARSNIP DISEASE.—This is also caused by a *Peronospora*, named *P. nivea*. When it attacks Parsnips, it causes the roots to become putrescent in the style of bad Potatoes.

There is also a *Peronospora* peculiar to the Pea tribe, another on Spinach, one on Clover, one of the most destructive character on Roses, and others on the many diverse plants of our fields and gardens. We do not illustrate any of these, because they all more or less resemble (though undoubtedly they are quite distinct from) the fungus of the Potato plant. The resting-spores are known in several instances, and where known they fairly agree in size, colour, and general habit with each other.

PEA DISEASE.—Although garden Peas often suffer badly from the attacks of a *Peronospora*, yet the most deadly foe to Peas, especially late Peas, is a fungus of a totally different character. To such an extent does the Pea blight sometimes devastate the later Peas round London in dry summers, that the whole crop is in some gardens completely destroyed. The name of the fungus of the Pea blight is *Erysiphe Martii*. Its attack is often made suddenly ; the leaves then lose their natural green colour and become yellowish, and densely coated with a fine white bloom; this bloom becomes at length dusted over with innumerable minute black bodies, which look, under a lens, like tiny spider's-eggs in the web. These little black bodies are filled with extremely small transparent bladders, and each bladder contains from four to eight spores or seeds. Our illustration shows the *Erysiphe* enlarged one hundred diameters, with the bladders containing the spores removed from the globular spots and further enlarged. The fungus of the Hop blight is a close ally of this ; its name is *Sphærotheca Castagnei*. The Grass blight, *Erysiphe graminis*, is still nearer. Many other species of fungi belonging to the same order attack our fruit trees, vegetables, and garden flowers. It is, however, unnecessary to illustrate them, as they bear a more or less close resemblance to the fungus of Pea blight. They all arise from an *Oidium* condition, similar to the *Oidium* or mildew of the Vine, and it is in this condition alone, as in the case of the Vine, that they can be reached by any preventive.

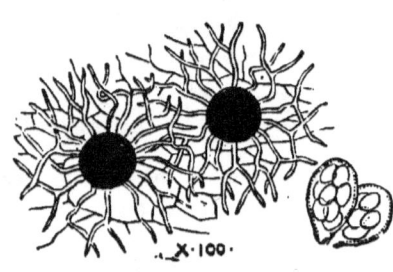

FUNGUS OF PEA MILDEW
Erysiphe Martii

TOMATO DISEASES.—Of late years Tomatoes have been extensively destroyed by several virulent forms of disease. The first to attract attention was a disease of the leaves in which these organs became entirely enveloped in a dense pearly white or pinkish mass of powder or mould. In bad cases of this disease the leaves are twisted, thickened and distorted; they next quickly rot and fall off, so that the Tomato plants are ruined. When this mildew—for such it is—is examined under the microscope and magnified 300 diameters, it is seen as in the accompanying illustration, one vast mass of thickly compacted, transparent fungus threads with an infinite number of pale rose-coloured spores: the spores are often jointed, and so break up into two, three, or four pieces, and every piece germinates as shown at A, B, C, D, and reproduces the fungus. The spore production is so profuse that in moderately bad cases the spores may be seen dispersed in the air like a vapour or mist when the leaves are touched. The spores germinate not only on the Tomato plants but in the air, on the glass and on the shelves, pots, &c., which go to furnish a greenhouse. The name of the fungus is *Dactylium roseum*, and it has been described as a distinct species or variety under the name of *D. lycopersici*.

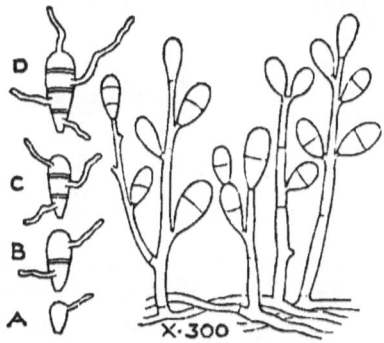

THE LEAF DISEASE OF TOMATOES
Dactylium roseum, var.
(enlarged 300 diameters)

Another too familiar disease of Tomatoes is popularly known as 'Black Spot.' This disease is also caused by a fungus, much smaller in size than *Dactylium roseum*, and named *Cladosporium lycopersici*. The peculiar habit of this fungus is to first attack the pistil of the very young fruit; when once the minute pistil is destroyed, as at A, the fungus radiates from this point as a centre and gradually invades the substance round the pistil in circles, one circle beyond another, as seen in the illustration: the dead part of the Tomato now becomes jet black and quite flat as shown. The black stain is not confined to the exterior, it spreads deeply into the interior and turns the substance of the fruit into a putrid but generally firm and sometimes hard mass. As with the *Dactylium* of the leaves, the fungus spreads from one plant to another with great rapidity, but the growth is never profuse with the *Cladosporium*; although the fungus is sparingly produced, it is, however, certain and deadly in its effects; when it is enlarged 300 diameters under the microscope it is seen as at B. The habit resembles that of the *Dactylium*, but the whole growth, including the spores, is much smaller, and the spores themselves are pale brown, not pink.

Up to the present time both fungi have defied all attempts at extirpation; they are both parasites, their roots or *mycelia* grow within the plants attacked, and so are virtually beyond reach. Good ventilation and hand picking when the diseases are in the earliest states may sometimes prevent the entire destruction of the Tomato plants, and the dissemination of *Sulfosteatite coprique* is believed to be useful, but we know of no conclusive experiments.

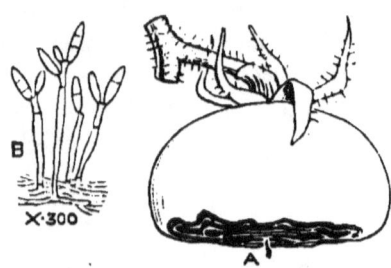

THE 'BLACK-SPOT' DISEASE OF TOMATOES
Diseased fruit, natural size; the parasitic fungus *Cladosporium lycopersici* enlarged 300 diameters

Tomatoes are sometimes seriously attacked in the roots by eel-worms, which are in every way identical with the eel-worms of the Cucumber disease. And the Potato fungus, *Peronospora infestans*, sometimes attacks Tomatoes.

The black patches often seen on Tomato stems and leaves are not due to the fungus which causes the black spot on the fruit, they appear to be due to some cultural defect, possibly in reference to the root growth, but the eel-worms of the roots are not associated with the black spots on the stems.

THE FUNGUS PESTS

OF

CERTAIN FLOWERS

CINERARIA AND SENECIO DISEASE.—*Senecio pulcher* has only been in cultivation in England for a few years, yet during this time it has in some gardens been completely destroyed by a fungus named *Puccinia glomerata*, or rather the *Uredo* state of this fungus with simple, not compound, spores. The fungus is well known, and very common on the wild species of Groundsel in England, being especially frequent and virulent on the Ragwort Groundsel, *Senecio Jacobea*.

FUNGUS OF SENECIO DISEASE
Uredo senecionis

The leaves of infected plants are covered with rust-coloured dusty pustules, the *Uredo* condition of the fungus, and known in this state as *Uredo senecionis*, sometimes termed *Trichobasis senecionis*.

At A is illustrated a fragment of a leaf of *Senecio pulcher*, natural size, and covered with the orange fungus ; at B a small part of a *Uredo* pustule as seen bursting through the cuticle of the Senecio leaf.

The fungus has a *Puccinia* stage of growth very similar to that of the Hollyhock fungus.

No remedial measures for the extirpation of this fungus are known, but as garden Senecios and Cinerarias are infected by diseased plants of Wild Groundsel, it is desirable that weeds of the latter (especially when diseased) should be destroyed. Weeds in and about gardens are a common cause of disease in cultivated plants. It often happens that a weed, being sturdy, is only slightly inconvenienced when attacked, whilst a cultivated plant will speedily succumb if attacked by the same fungus. This is the case in the *Sempervivum* disease. In this country the common House Leek is the nurse plant, and is seldom much injured; but if the disease *Endophyllum sempervivi* gets amongst greenhouse species, every plant may be utterly destroyed.

GLADIOLUS, CROCUS, NARCISSUS, AND LILY DISEASES.—In certain soils and situations where the ground is heavy and the atmosphere inclined to be humid, the Gladiolus is very subject to a destructive fungoid disease. This is especially the case in this country, and during unusually wet summers. The disease attacks the corm, and corrodes and decomposes the tissues, so that on cutting open a corm, the whole interior, or such parts as are diseased, will be found permeated with a deep, foxy colour. It is believed by some persons that one stage of this disease is identical with the disease named 'Tacon' by the French and in this country known as 'Copper Web,' *Rhizoctonia crocorum.* The *Rhizoctonia* is a mere spawn or mycelium, a mass of rusty-brown material like a thick coating of spider's web of a red tint. The *Rhizoctonia* attacks the Crocus (especially *C. sativus*), the Narcissus, Asparagus, Potato, and

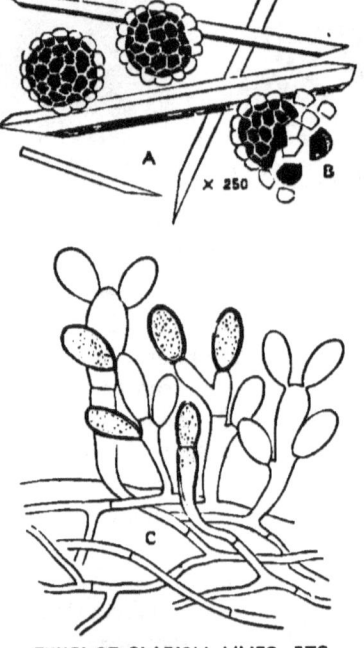

FUNGI OF GLADIOLI, LILIES, ETC.
Urocystis Gladioli and *Ovularia elliptica*

other plants. Immersed in the softer and damper portions of the red substance of the corm, may frequently be found great numbers of large compound spores, as illustrated at A, enlarged two hundred and fifty diameters. These bodies belong to the fungus named *Urocystis Gladioli*; but whether they really belong to the spawn named *Rhizoctonia* there is no conclusive evidence, as the spores have never been seen on the threads or upon any spawn. The spores are very ornamental objects, consisting of from three to six compacted inner brown bodies, surrounded by an indefinite number of transparent cells. At maturity these spores break up as at B, and both the inner dark bodies and the outer transparent ones are capable of germinating and reproducing the fungus.

The *Colchicum* is attacked by a closely allied but different species of *Urocystis*—viz. *U. colchici*. The Ranunculaceæ are attacked by another ally in *U. pompholygodes*, and Rye is attacked by a third in *U. occulta*. No method of cure has yet been published for this pest; it is, however, desirable that only sound and good corms should be planted, for if infected corms are placed in the ground it is one certain means of propagating the disease. The bars shown across the illustration of this disease are magnificent crystals, very common in Gladiolus corms.

Lilies, especially during late years, have been very subject to a disease in early summer: the leaves get spotted and damp and rot off; the flower-buds speedily follow and leave the bare stalk. The Rev. M. J. Berkeley, who has studied this disease, and whose illustration we have copied from the *Gardeners' Chronicle*, says the disease of Lilies is caused by a fungus closely allied to the fungus of the Potato disease, and named *Ovularia elliptica*. The spores are large, and produce zoospores, or spores with hair-like tails, capable of sailing about in water or upon moist places, as illustrated in the figure of the Potato fungus, page 404. This pest attacks a large number of species of Lilium, both before and after flowering. *Hyacinthus candicans* and some Tulips suffer from a very similar, if not the same, production. This fungus has lately been described as a true Peronospora. Bulbs are subject to many fungus growths, as *Volutella hyacinthorum*, *Didymium Sowerei*, &c.; many fungi follow the decay of the bulb, others undoubtedly produce or greatly accelerate decay. No remedy is known, but we advise the purchase of the soundest and best bulbs. Good drainage and sufficient air are indispensable. All infected foliage and stems should be burnt.

DISEASE OF HOLLYHOCKS AND MALVACEOUS PLANTS.—In some parts of England, the cultivation of the Hollyhock had at one time quite ceased, owing to the attacks of a microscopic fungus named *Puccinia malvacearum*. In gardens and nurseries, where formerly Hollyhocks were one of the chief ornaments of the place, it was no longer possible to grow a single plant. The disease is not confined to the Hollyhock, but it attacks many malvaceous plants, notably the Mallows of our hedge-sides. We have seen plants of the white variety of the Musk Mallow (*Malva moschata*) totally destroyed by this parasite. The home of the Hollyhock fungus is Chili, whence the Potato fungus reached us. The Hollyhock fungus first attacked the malvaceous plants of Australia, and then reached England by the continent of Europe. Great fears have been entertained of this fungus attacking the Cotton plant, as the Cotton plant belongs to the same family as the Hollyhock. The best and cleanest seeds of the Hollyhock should be purchased.

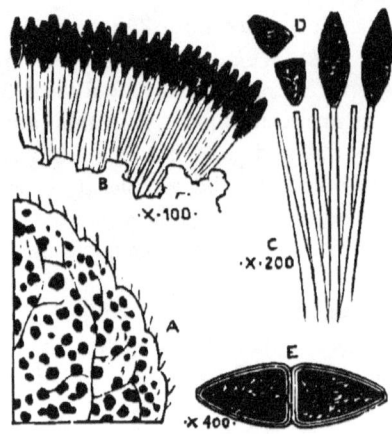

FUNGUS OF HOLLYHOCK DISEASE
Puccinia malvacearum

A fragment of a Hollyhock leaf is illustrated at A, dotted with the characteristic black pustules: these pustules cover the stems as well as the leaves. At B is shown the edge of a pustule enlarged one hundred diameters and seen in section; to show the whole of a pustule in section, from six inches to a foot of space would be required. Bursting through the skin of the plant may be seen a dense forest of threads, each thread bearing a spore with a joint across the centre. One pustule alone will produce thousands of these double spores. At C some of the threads and spores are still further enlarged to two hundred diameters, and at D one ripe spore is shown falling from the thread and breaking asunder—each piece is a reproductive body or spore. When mature, these minute blackish spores or seeds are carried in the air by millions. At E one of the compound spores is enlarged to four hundred diameters. As this disease is seated within the tissues of the plant, remedies are difficult of application, and in many cases all attempts at cure have failed. No doubt the fungus is nursed by malvaceous weeds. Infected Hollyhock plants and allied weeds should be destroyed by fire or by deep burying.

POPPY DISEASE.—Garden Poppies are often attacked by a fungus pest closely allied to the fungus of the Potato disease, and named *Peronospora arborescens*. It grows sometimes in abundance on the common Red Poppy of corn fields (*P. Rhœas*), and it badly attacks

P. somniferum and all its garden varieties. The fungus grows within the leaves, and emerges with a tree-like growth through the organs of transpiration on the under side of the leaves. Like the fungus of the Potato disease, it speedily sets up decomposition, and destroys the host plant.

At A is illustrated one of the stems of the Poppy *Peronospora* emerging from the leaf, engraved to the same scale as the Potato *Peronospora* — viz. enlarged seventy-five diameters to show the difference in size and habit. The fungus of the Poppy is very much more branched than that of the Potato, and every little branchlet carries a spore. To save confusion, a large number of spores are omitted from the branchlet in the illustration, and the branches growing from the stem both before and behind are for the same reason left out.

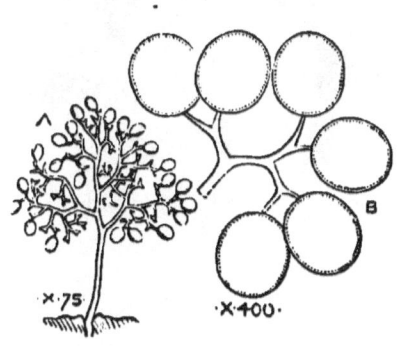

FUNGUS OF POPPY DISEASE
Peronospora arborescens

At B a tip of a single branch is shown further enlarged to four hundred diameters, or to the same scale of enlargement as the spore D on the Potato fungus illustration. The spores in the Poppy fungus are unusually large and numerous: an infected plant will throw off many millions of such spores. All the putrefactive spawn of this fungus is inside the host plant; cure, therefore, is difficult. This disease, like every other plant disease, is always at its worst in ill-kept places where red field Poppies are abundant. Field Poppies are often planted with unclean corn. As prevention is better than cure, all we can advise is, buy the best and cleanest garden and field seeds, cultivate in the best way, and look out for and burn, or deeply bury as soon as detected, all disease-stricken plants—whether wild or cultivated. When diseased plants of any sort are left to decay on the refuse heap, it is the most certain way of propagating a plant disease for the next year.

DISEASES OF VIOLETS.—Violets are subject to fungoid diseases, both in spring and autumn. The disease of autumn is caused by a brown *Puccinia* allied to the *P. graminis* of corn and the *P. malvacearum* of Hollyhocks and various malvaceous plants. The *Puccinia* of Violets has its yellowish or orange-coloured stage; it is then known as *Trichobasis* or *Uredo violarum*. In spring and early summer, Violets are often badly affected by a fungus named *Æcidium violæ*. This disease attacks leaves, stems, and sepals, and it is best examined on the leaves. In this position it is seen to consist of a considerable number of minute yellow pustules, each pustule less in size than a pin's head, and all congregated into one flat circular mass of about a quarter of an inch in diameter. This pest is very frequent on the Dog Violet, but it is perhaps equally common on the Sweet Violets of our gardens in early spring, and it not unfrequently spreads to other species of Viola. One of the most destructive pests of Violas is found in *Æcidium*

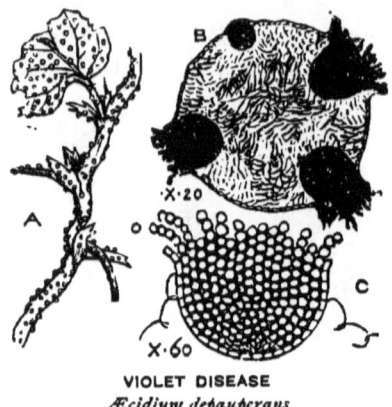

VIOLET DISEASE
Æcidium depauperans

depauperans, so called because its effect is first to starve and attenuate, and then to totally destroy plants of *Viola cornuta*. It is a close ally of *Æ. violæ*, but it differs in having its minute cups or pustules irregularly distributed all over the host plant instead of being congregated in circular patches, as in *Æ. violæ*. Our illustration shows, at A, a small portion of the stem of *Viola cornuta* attacked by *Æcidium depauperans*. The minute pustules are seen (natural size) distributed all over the stem, leaf-stalks, and ruined leaves; the effect of the fungus growth is to decompose the tissues of the plant. At B, a transverse section through the stem is illustrated and magnified twenty diameters. The section cuts through several of the abscess-like pustules, and it is seen how completely embedded they are in the flesh of the plant. At C, a pustule is seen in section, enlarged sixty diameters, to show more clearly the innumerable spores, or seeds, disposed in necklace-like fashion, which are destined to reproduce the pest in future seasons. Another disease of Violets in autumn is caused by a fungus named *Urocystis violæ*. This fungus causes gouty swellings to form on the stalks and principal veins. These swellings at length burst, exhibit black patches, and discharge sooty spores. The fungoid disease named *Phyllostica violæ* is frequently common on Violet leaves in June. In this the spots are whitish. No cure is known, and it is always well to burn or deeply bury all infected leaves or plants.

Index

	PAGE
Abutilon	211, 318, 328
Achillea Millefolium	372
Achimenes	279, 315
Aconite, Winter	309, 361
Æcidium depauperans	414
Agapanthus	279, 352
Agaricus campestris	73
Alcohol for vermin	401
Allium	280
— ascalonicum	117
— Cepa	81
— Porrum	63
— sativum	59
— Schœnoprasum	48
Alstrœmeria	280, 352
Althæa rosea	244
Alyssum	327, 349
Amaryllis	298, 352
American Blight	382
— Cress	50
Anbury	136, 396
Anemone	212, 280, 319, 347, 352, 358
Angelica	61
Anguillulæ	390
Annuals	205
— Half-hardy	209
— Hardy	209, 318, 327, 334, 348, 358
— Tender	210
Annual Stocks	264
Anthómyia brassicæ	385
— ceparum	87, 384
— trimaculata	385
Antirrhinum	212, 315, 339, 347
Aphis	380
— Bean	382
— fabæ	382
— Pea	381
Apium graveolens	42
April work among Flowers	334
— — in the Vegetable Garden	160

	PAGE
Aquilegia	213, 328, 343
Arsenic for vermin	401
Artichoke, Globe	4, 142, 154, 160, 176, 183
— Jerusalem	6, 154, 183
Asparagus	7, 142, 154, 160, 166, 172, 183
— officinalis	7
Asperula	327, 349
Aster	213, 328, 334, 349
Aubergines	161
August work among Flowers	348
— — in the Vegetable Garden	176
Auricula	217, 319, 329
Australian Oak	243
Autumn Broccoli	26
Autumn-sown Onion	86
Babiana	282, 352
Balsam	218, 329, 335, 339, 343
— Sultan's	245
Barbarea præcox	50
Bartonia	327
Basil	60
Bastard Trenching	101
Bean	14, 143, 149, 154, 167, 172, 183, 185
— Aphis	382
— Broad	14, 143, 149, 154, 167, 172, 183, 185
— Dwarf	17, 167, 174
— Kidney	17, 161, 167, 172, 174
— Runner	19, 167, 172, 174
— Weevil	386
Beet, Garden	20, 154, 162, 167, 182
— Spinach	121, 159, 165
Begonia, Fibrous-rooted	221
— tuberosa	219
— Tuberous-rooted	219, 283, 320, 329, 343, 347, 352
Bell Flower	225

INDEX

	PAGE
Bermuda Lily	299
Beta Cicla	121
— vulgaris	20
Biennials, Hardy	211, 318, 348
Biennial Stocks	266
Bird Pepper	35
Birdsfoot Trefoil	372
Black Bot	120
— Fly	380
Blacksmiths	395
Black Spot (Tomato)	407
Blight, American	382
Blue Fly	380
— Squill	305
Borage	60
Border, Warm	185
Borecole	23, 165
Brassica oleracea acephala	23
— — botrytis asparagoides	25
— — — cauliflora	39
— — bullata	34
— — — gemmifera	29
— — capitata	30
— — Caulo-rapa	62
— — costata	49
— Rapa	133
Broad Bean	14, 143, 149, 154, 167, 172, 183, 185
Broccoli	25, 149, 154, 162, 167, 172, 174, 177
Brompton Stock	266, 346, 351
Bruchus pisi	95, 386
Brussels Sprouts	29, 154, 162, 167, 177
Bug, Mealy	388
— Pea	386
— Potato	385
Bulbs, Flowering, Culture of	277
— in Store	364
Burnet	60
Cabbage	30, 143, 149, 155, 162, 167, 172, 174, 177, 179, 181
— Fly	385
— Lettuce	65
— Savoy	34, 152, 170
Cacalia	327
Calandrinia	327, 349
Calceolaria, Herbaceous	221, 329, 343, 347, 353
— rugosa	225
— Shrubby	225, 320
Calendula	327
— officinalis	248, 349

	PAGE
Campanula	225, 327, 329, 348
Canary Creeper	269
Candytuft	327, 349
Canna	226, 315, 344
Canterbury Bell	225
Cape Primrose	266
Capsicum	35, 150, 167, 172
— annuum	35
— baccatum	35
Cardoon	36, 162, 175, 177, 181
Carnation	226, 335, 350
Carrot	37, 155, 162, 168, 175, 181, 184
— Fly	383
— Moth	385
Carum Petroselinum	88
Castor-oil Plant	208, 261, 325, 337
Catchfly	263
Caterpillars	383
Cauliflower	39, 143, 150, 155, 163, 168, 172, 177, 179, 181, 184
Cayenne Pepper	35
Celeriac	46, 155, 181
Celery	42, 155, 163, 168, 172, 175, 177, 179, 181, 184, 185
— Fly	46, 384
Celosia cristata	231
— plumosa	227, 321
Centaurea	327, 349
Centranthus	327
Chards	5, 112, 175, 180
Cheiranthus Cheiri	271
Chemistry of Garden Crops	192
Chervil	60, 163
Chicory	47, 163, 181
Chili	35, 150
Chimney Campanula	225
Chionodoxa Luciliæ	284, 350
Chives	48, 156
Chrysanthemum	228, 321, 327, 349
Cichorium Endivia	57
— Intybus	47
Cineraria	229, 316, 339, 345, 350
— Disease	409
Cladosporium lycopersici	407
Clarkia	327, 349
Clay for destroying vermin	401
Cleaning old pots	312
Click-Beetle	395
Clover, Perennial White	372
Club	396
Cochlearia Armoracia	61
Cockscomb	231, 321
— Plumed	227
Coleus	231, 329, 340

INDEX

	PAGE
Coleworts	32, 175, 177, 179
Collards	32
Collinsia	327, 349
Columbine	213
Convolvulus minor	327
Coreopsis	327, 349
Corn Flag	240
— Indian	62, 169
— Salad	48, 150, 177
Cos Lettuce	65, 173, 178
Couve Tronchuda	49, 150
Crambe maritima	113
Crane's-bill	239
Cress	49, 143
— American	50
— Indian	269
— Land	50
— Water	50, 160
Crested Dogstail	370
Cricket Grounds from Seed	377
Crocus	284, 353, 358
— Disease	410
Crops, Garden, Chemistry of	192
— Rotation of	187
Croquet Lawns from Seed	365
Crowfoot	261
Crown Imperial	301, 353
Cucumber	50, 143, 156, 168, 173, 175, 177, 180
— Disease	390
Cucumis Melon	69
— sativus	50
Cucurbita	59
— Pepo ovifera	136
Culture of Flowering Bulbs	277
— of Flowers from Seeds	199
— of Vegetables	1
Curculio (Otiorhynchus) picipes	386
Cutting Flowers	236
Cyclamen	232, 285, 316, 335, 340, 348, 353, 358, 361
Cynara Cardunculus	36
— Scolymus	4
Cynosurus cristatus	370
Dactylium roseum	407
Dactylopius odonidum	388
Daddy Long Legs	385
Daffodils	303
Dahlia, Double	234, 321, 336, 340
— Single	234, 321, 336, 340
Dandelion	56, 169
Daucus Carota	37
Day Lily, Japanese	300

	PAGE
December work among Flowers	363
— — in the Vegetable Garden	185
Delphinium	237, 330
Depressaria cicutella	385
Dianthus	237, 322, 330, 345, 350
Dianthus Caryophyllus fl. pl.	226, 256
— plumarius	256
Digitalis	238
Dill	60
Disease, Cineraria	409
— Crocus	410
— Cucumber	390
— Gladiolus	410
— Hollyhock	411
— Lettuce	405
— Lily	410
— Narcissus	410
— Onion	405
— Parsnip	405
— Pea	406
— Poppy	412
— Potato	107, 403
— Senecio	409
— Tomato	407
— Violet	413
Dogstail, Crested	370
Dog's-tooth Violet	286, 353
Double Daffodil	303
— Dahlia	234, 321, 336, 340
Drainage of pots	313
Dwarf Bean	17, 167, 174
Earwigs	387
Easter Lily	299
Egg Plant	57, 161
Elater lineatus	395
— obscurus	395
— ruficaudis	395
Endive	57, 163, 173, 175, 178, 180, 182, 185
Eradication of Garden Vermin	400
Erysimum	327, 349
Erysiphe Martii	406
Eschscholtzia	327, 349
Eucharidium	327, 349
Eutoca	327
Evergreen Meadow Grass	371
Faba vulgaris	14
Feather Hyacinth	295, 359
February work among Flowers	318
— — in the Vegetable Garden	148

E E

INDEX

	PAGE
Fennel	60, 163
Ferraria	287, 361
Fescue, Hard	370
— Red	371
— Sheep's	370
Festuca duriuscula	370
— ovina tenuifolia	370
— rubra	371
Fibrous-rooted Begonia	221
Fingers and Toes	136, 396
Flowering Bulbs, Culture of	277
Flower of the West Wind	309
Flowers All the Year Round	310
— from Seeds, Culture of	199
Fly, Black	380
— Blue	380
— Cabbage	385
— Carrot	383
— Celery	384
— Green	380
— Onion	384
— Turnip	392
Forcing	142
Forget-me-not	250, 323, 348
Formation of Lawns from Seed	365
Foxglove	238
Fragaria	121
Frame Cucumbers	51
— Ground	149
Freesia	287, 350, 353
French Bean	17, 19
Fritillaria	288, 354
— imperialis	301
Fuchsia	239, 322
Fungus Pests of certain Flowers	409
— — of Garden Plants	403
Fusisporium Solani	403
Garden Beet	20, 154, 162, 167, 182
— Crops, Chemistry of	192
— Pea	90, 147, 150, 158, 165, 170, 174, 175, 178, 184
— Rubbish	174
— Vermin, Eradication of	400
Garlic	59, 150, 157, 175, 182
Geranium	239, 322, 345, 350
Gesnera zebrina discolor	240, 316
Gilia	327, 349
Gladiolus	240, 288, 323, 330, 336, 345, 358, 361
— Disease	410
Globe Artichoke	4, 142, 154, 160, 176, 183
Glory of the Snow	284

	PAGE
Gloxinia	241, 290, 316, 323, 330, 354
Godetia	327, 349
Golden-rayed Lily of Japan	299
Gourd	59, 169
Grape Hyacinth	295, 359
Green Fly	380
Grevillea robusta	243, 317
Groundsel	262
Gypsophila	327
Half-hardy Annuals	209
Haltica nemorum	393
Hard Fescue	370
Hardy Annuals	209, 318, 327, 334, 348, 358
— Biennials	211, 318, 348
— Perennials	211
Hawkweed	327
Helianthus	327
— annuus	125, 267
— tuberosus	6
Helichrysum	327
Hemerocallis Kwanso fl. pl.	300
Herbaceous Calceolaria	221, 329, 343, 347, 353
Herbs	60, 157, 163
Hibiscus	327
Hollyhock	244, 317, 331, 340, 345, 358
— Disease	411
Horse-radish	61, 145, 157, 184
Hot-bed	153, 156
Humus	198
Hyacinth	291, 354, 359
— Feather	295, 359
— Grape	295, 359
— Miniature	294, 359
— Musk	295, 359
— Roman	295, 350, 355, 359
Hyacinthus candicans	295, 361
Hyssop	163
Impatiens Balsamina	218
— Sultani	245, 331
Indian Corn	62, 169
— Cress	269
— Pink	237
— Shot	226
Intermediate Stock	266, 351
Introductory Remarks to Culture of Flowering Bulbs	277
— — — of Flowers from Seeds	199
— — — of Vegetables	1

	PAGE
Introductory Remarks to Flowers All the Year Round	310
—— Year's Work in Vegetable Garden	140
Iris	296, 355
Ixia	296, 356
Jacobea	262, 327
January work among Flowers	315
—— in the Vegetable Garden	141
Japan, Golden-rayed Lily of	299
— Pink	237
Japanese Day Lily	300
Jerusalem Artichoke	6, 154, 183
Jonquil	297, 356
July work among Flowers	347
—— in the Vegetable Garden	174
June work among Flowers	342
—— in the Vegetable Garden	171
Kale	23, 165
— Sea	113, 147, 152, 158, 184
Kaulfussia	327
Kidney Bean	17, 161, 167, 172, 174
Knol Kohl	62, 157
Kohl Rabi	62, 157
Lachenalia	297, 359
Lactuca sativa	65
Lamb's Lettuce	48
Land Cress	50
Larkspur	327, 349
Lathyrus odoratus	267
Lavatera	327
Lavender	60
Lawns from Seed	365
Leaf-mould	310
Lecanium hibernaculorum	389
Leek	63, 157, 163, 175
— Bulbs	64
Lepidium sativum	49
Leptosiphon	327, 349
Lettuce	65, 145, 150, 157, 163, 170, 173, 178, 180, 182
— Disease	405
— Lamb's	48
Leucojum æstivum	297, 359
Lilies	298, 361
Lilium auratum	299, 361
— Harrisii	299
— lancifolium	300, 362
Lily of Japan, Golden-rayed	299

	PAGE
Lily of Bermuda	299
— Disease	410
— Easter	299
— Japanese Day	300
Limnanthes	327, 349
Linaria	327
Linum	327
Lobelia	246, 323, 331, 336, 348
Lolium perenne Suttoni	371
Lotus corniculatus	372
Love-lies-bleeding	327
Lupine	327
Lycopersicum esculentum	126
Lygus Solani	385
Maize	62
Malope	327
March work among Flowers	326
—— in the Vegetable Garden	153
Marguerite	228, 321
Marigold	60, 247, 331, 336
— Pot	248
Marjoram	60
Marrow, Vegetable	136, 165, 171
Marvel of Peru	248, 331, 336
Mathiola	263, 327
May work among Flowers	339
—— in the Vegetable Garden	165
Meadow Grass, Evergreen	371
—— Rough-stalked	371
—— Smooth-stalked	371
Mealy Bug	388
Melon	69, 145, 158, 164, 170, 173
Mice	392
Mignonette	248, 327, 332, 337, 351
Milfoil	372
Mimulus	249, 323, 348
— moschatus	250
Miniature Hyacinth	294, 359
Mint	61
Mirabilis Jalapa	248
Monkey Flower	249
Montbretia	301
Mushroom	73, 173
Musk	250
— Hyacinth	295, 359
Mustard	81, 146, 150
Myosotis	250, 323, 345, 348
Narcissus	301, 356, 360
— Disease	410
Nasturtium	269, 327
— officinale	50
Nemophila	327, 349

INDEX

New Zealand Spinach 120, 159, 170
Nicotiana 268
Nigella . . . 327, 349
Nightshade 263
Nolana 327
November work among Flowers 361
—— —— in the Vegetable Garden 182

Oak, Australian . . . 243
October work among Flowers 358
—— —— in the Vegetable Garden 181
Œnothera 327
Onion . 81, 158, 164, 173, 178
— Disease 405
— Fly 384
— Grub 87
— Pickling . . . 86, 164
— Potato 87
— Salading 173
— Underground . . 87, 186
Ornithogalum arabicum . 303, 360
Ovularia elliptica . . . 410
Oxalis 304, 357

Pansy . . 251, 337, 345, 349
Papaver 257, 327
Paris Daisy . . . 228, 321
Parsley 88, 150, 164, 175, 180, 186
Parsnip . . 89, 150, 158, 182
— Disease 405
Pastinaca sativa . . . 89
Pea 90, 147, 150, 158, 165, 170,
174, 175, 178, 184
— Disease 406
— Siphon-Aphis . . . 381
— Sweet . . . 267, 327, 349
— Weevil . . . 95, 386
Peat for pot plants . . . 311
Pelargonium . . 252, 323, 351
Pentstemon . . . 252, 332
Pepper, Bird 35
— Cayenne 35
Perennial Phlox . . 256, 332
— Rye Grass 371
— White Clover . . . 372
Perennials, Hardy . . . 211
Perilla nankinensis . . . 208
Peronospora arborescens . . 412
— gangliformis . . . 405
— infestans 403
— nivea 405
— Schleideniana . . . 405
Perpetual Spinach . 121, 159, 165
Pests of Garden Plants . . 379
— Fungus, of certain Flowers 409

Pests, Fungus, of certain
Garden Plants . . . 403
Petunia . 253, 317, 324, 337, 340
Phacelia 327, 349
Phaseolus multiflorus . . 19
— vulgaris 17
Phlox Drummondii . 255, 324, 332
— Perennial . . . 256, 332
Phosphates 196
Phytomyza 95
Pickling Cucumber . . . 173
— Onion 86, 164
Picotee 256
Pink 237, 256
Pisum sativum . . . 90
Plasmodiophora brassicæ . 396
Plumed Cockscomb . . 227
Plusia 95
Poa nemoralis sempervirens . 371
— pratensis 371
— trivialis 371
Polianthes tuberosa . . 307
Polyanthus . . 257, 324, 348
— Narcissus . 301, 356, 360
Poppy . . . 257, 327, 332
— Disease 412
Portugal Cabbage . . 49, 150
Portulaca . . 258, 340, 345
Potash 196
Potato 96, 147, 151, 158, 175,
180, 182, 184
— Beetle 385
— Bug 385
— Disease . . . 107, 403
— Onion 87
Pot Marigold 248
Pots, Cleaning . . . 312
— sizes of 312
Potting Soil 310
Primrose . . . 258, 324, 346
— Cape 266
Primula Auricula . . . 217
— japonica 260
— obconica 260
— rosea 260
— sinensis . 259, 341, 346, 348
— variabilis 257
— vulgaris 258
Prince's Feather . . . 327
Psila rosæ 383
Puccinia malvacearum . . 411
Pumpkin . . . 59, 169
Purslane 258

Queen Stock 351

INDEX

	PAGE
Radish	109, 147, 151, 176, 186
Ranunculus	261, 304, 324, 362
Raphanus sativus	109
Rapid Flower Culture	203
Rats	392
Recreation Grounds from Seed	377
Red Cabbage	34, 162, 175
— Fescue	371
— Spider	388
Reseda odorata	248
Rheum hybridum	110
Rhubarb	110, 152, 182
Ricinus	208, 261, 325, 337
Ridge Cucumber	55, 168, 175
Roman Hyacinth	295, 350, 355, 359
Roots, Storing	182
Rotation of Crops	187
Rough-stalked Meadow Grass	371
Rubbish, Garden	174
Rumex scutatus	118
Runner Bean	19, 167, 172, 174
Rye Grass, Sutton's Perennial	371
Salsify	112, 165, 182
Salt	196
— for destroying vermin	401
Sanvitalia	327
Saponaria	327, 349
Savory	60
Savoy Cabbage	34, 152, 170
Scabious	349
Scale	389
Schizanthus	262, 333, 351
Schizoneura lanigera	382
Scilla	305, 351, 360
Scorzonera	113, 158
— hispanica	113
Sea Kale	113, 147, 152, 158, 184
Seed Sowing	141
Senecio	262, 333
— Disease	409
September work among Flowers	352
— — in the Vegetable Garden	179
Shallot	117, 152, 175, 182
Sheep's Fescue	370
Shrubby Calceolaria	225, 320
Silene	263, 327, 349, 351
Sinapis alba	81
— nigra	81
Single Daffodil	303
— Dahlia	234, 321, 336, 340
Siphonophora pisi	381
Sizes of pots	312

	PAGE
Slugs	391
Smooth-stalked Meadow Grass	371
Snapdragon	212
Snowdrop	305, 357
Snowflake, Summer	297
Soda	196
Soft Soap for destroying vermin	402
Soil for Pot Plants	310
Solanum	263, 325, 333, 346
— esculentum	57
— melongena ovigerum	57
— tuberosum	96
Sorrel	118, 158, 165, 180
Sparaxis	296, 357
Sparrows	96, 251, 285
Sphenogyne	327
Spider, Red	388
Spinach	119, 148, 152, 159, 165, 176, 180
— Beet	121, 159, 165
— Moth grub	176
— New Zealand	120, 159, 170
— Perpetual	121, 159, 165
Spinacia oleracea	119
Spring Broccoli	27
— Flowers from Seeds	273
Spring-Jack	395
Spring-sown Lettuce	67
— Onion	83
Sprouting Broccoli	29
Sprouts, Brussels	29, 154, 162, 167, 177
Squill, Blue	305
Star of Bethlehem	303
Sternbergia lutea	306, 362
Stock, Annual	264
— Biennial	266
— Brompton	266, 346, 351
— Intermediate	266, 351
— Queen	351
— Ten-week	264, 333, 337, 341
— Virginian	327, 349
Stored Bulbs	364
Storing Roots	182
Stork's-bill	252
Strawberry	121, 159, 178
Streptocarpus	266
Suckling, Yellow	372
Sulfosteatite coprique	132, 408
Sulphur	196
— for destroying vermin	402
Sultan's Balsam	245
Sultan, Sweet	327
Summer Broccoli	27
— Snowflake	297

INDEX

	PAGE
Sunflower	125, 267, 327, 338
Sweet Herbs	60, 157, 163
— Pea	267, 327, 349
— Sultan	327
Tagetes	247
Taraxacum officinale	56
Tarragon	60
Temperature of Greenhouses	313
Tender Annuals	210
Tennis Lawns from Seed	365
Ten-week Stock	264, 333, 337, 341
Tephritis onopordinis	384
Tetragonia expansa	120
Tetranychus telarius	388
Thrips	389
Thyme	60
Tigridia	287, 361
Tipula	385
Tobacco	268, 325, 342, 346
— for destroying vermin	402
Tomato	126, 148, 152, 159, 170, 178, 180
— Disease	407
Torenia	269
Tragopogon porrifolius	112
Traps for vermin	396, 400
Trefoil, Birdsfoot	372
Trichobasis senecionis	409
Trifolium minus	372
— repens perenne	372
Triteleia uniflora	306, 360
Tritonia	307, 362
Tropæolum	269, 327
— canariense	269
— majus	269
— tuberosum	307, 357
Tuberose	307, 360
Tuberous-rooted Begonia	219, 283, 320, 329, 343, 347, 352
Tulip	308, 357, 360, 362
Turban Ranunculus	304, 325
Turnip	133, 153, 160, 165, 171, 174, 176, 179, 182
— Beetle	393
— Fly	338, 392
— rooted Celery	46
Turpentine for destroying vermin	402
Underground Onion	87, 186
Uredo senecionis	409
Urocystis Gladioli	410

	PAGE
Valerian	327
Valerianella olitoria	48
Vallota purpurea	309, 326
Vegetable Garden, a Year's Work in	140
— — Rotation of Crops in	187
— Marrow	136, 165, 171
— Oyster	113, 165
Vegetables, Culture of	1
Ventilating Greenhouses and Frames	313
Venus's Looking-glass	327, 349
Verbena	270, 317, 326, 333, 342
Vermin, Garden, Eradication of	400
— Traps	396, 400
Vervain	270
Viola	271, 338, 349
— tricolor	251
Violet Diseases	413
— Dog's-tooth	286, 353
Virginian Stock	327, 349
Viscaria	327, 349
Wallflower	271, 342, 346, 360
Warm Border	185
Wasps	394
Water Cress	50, 160
Watering Pot Plants	312
Weevil, Bean	386
— Pea	95, 386
White Clover, Perennial	372
Whitlavia	327, 349
Wigandia	272, 326
Windflower, The	212, 280
Winter Aconite	309, 361
— Broccoli	27
— Cucumber	54
— Greens	160, 165, 176, 182
— Lettuce	68
— Spinach	180
Wireworm	39, 289, 335, 395
Woodlice	387
Xeranthemum	327, 349
Yarrow	372
Year's Work in the Vegetable Garden	140
Yellow Suckling	372
Zea Mays	62
Zephyranthes candida	309, 363
Zinnia	272, 334, 338, 342, 347

BOOK ON GRASSES—REVISED EDITION.

PERMANENT & TEMPORARY PASTURES.

BY MARTIN J. SUTTON.

DEDICATED BY SPECIAL PERMISSION TO

His Royal Highness the Prince of Wales.

Illustrated with 23 BEAUTIFUL PLATES OF GRASSES, CLOVERS, &c., PRINTED IN NATURAL COLOURS. The book also contains 46 ANALYSES OF GRASSES, CLOVERS, &c., prepared expressly for this work by Dr. J. AUGUSTUS VOELCKER.

Price 21s.

POPULAR EDITION, 5s., in which the Grasses and Clovers are illustrated by superior wood engravings instead of coloured plates.

From The Times, *February* 9, 1891.

'The high place which grass land management now occupies in connection with our agriculture makes the publication of a fourth and entirely revised edition of Mr. Martin J. Sutton's work on grasses and their management an event of more than ordinary importance. The first thing to strike the reader is the handsome character of the volume, more especially with regard to the 23 beautiful plates of grasses, clovers, and other forage plants, which are printed in natural colours. As one reads it, however, it soon becomes apparent that it is as complete and modern as it is handsome. The first part deals with the entire question of grass land and its management, and in this we have not only the cream of the best practice in different parts of the country, but the latest statistics and the results of the most modern experiments. The second part deals with the leading grasses, clovers, and forage plants, of which 23 are represented by coloured plates, and two analyses by Dr. J. A. Voelcker. Each is also described botanically and agriculturally, and illustrations are given of the seed, both natural size and enlarged. All interested in the land will be pleased to have such a practical and scientific guide to grass land culture.'

May be obtained through all Booksellers, from the Publishers,
SIMPKIN, MARSHALL, HAMILTON, KENT, & CO. LIMITED, LONDON:
or direct from SUTTON & SONS, *Reading.*

THE ART OF PREPARING VEGETABLES FOR THE TABLE.

BY SUTTON & SONS.

'Endless are the ways in which vegetables may be cooked and rendered wholesome, palatable, and attractive on the table, and the various directions given in the work before us are so simple that there can be no difficulty in following them. All the ordinary kitchen garden materials are dealt with in this little volume, and we trust it may do something to remove from us the reproach that while we have the best of vegetables in this country we are a people of one idea as to the cooking of them.'
— GARDENERS' CHRONICLE.

'The novel and original comments upon the cookery of all the principal varieties of vegetables for the table ought to make this handy little publication a favourite work of reference in every well-regulated kitchen.'—THE CATERER.

'Gives much practical advice on the cookery of vegetables, so much neglected by a large portion of humanity.'—THE VEGETARIAN MESSENGER.

Cloth gilt, 1s.

THROUGH ALL BOOKSELLERS, FROM THE PUBLISHERS,
SIMPKIN, MARSHALL, HAMILTON, KENT, & CO. LIMITED, LONDON;
or post-free from SUTTON & SONS, READING, for 12 stamps.

SUTTON'S AMATEUR'S GUIDE IN HORTICULTURE.

PUBLISHED ANNUALLY ON JANUARY 1st.

Containing Descriptive Lists of Vegetables and Flowers. Beautifully Illustrated with Coloured Plates and Woodcuts. Price 1s.

SUTTON'S BULB CATALOGUE.

PUBLISHED ANNUALLY IN AUGUST.

Containing Descriptive Lists of Hyacinths, Narcissus, Tulips, Lilies, and other Bulbous Roots, and beautifully Illustrated with Leading Flowers.

SUTTON'S FARMERS' YEAR-BOOK AND GRAZIERS' MANUAL.

PUBLISHED ANNUALLY IN FEBRUARY.

Containing Descriptions of Natural Grasses, Clovers, Turnips, Mangels, and other Farm Crops. With Cultural Notes.

READING:

SUTTON & SONS,

Seedsmen by Royal Warrants to Her Majesty the Queen
AND TO
His Royal Highness the Prince of Wales.

www.ingramcontent.com/pod-product-compliance
Lightning Source LLC
Chambersburg PA
CBHW051737300426
44115CB00007B/609